De Orbe

The eight Decades of Peter Martyr D'Anghiera

(Volume II)

Pietro Martire D'Anghiera,

Francis Augustus MacNutt

Alpha Editions

This edition published in 2020

ISBN : 9789354012402

Design and Setting By
Alpha Editions
email - alphaedis@gmail.com

The Eight Decades of
Peter Martyr D'Anghera

Translated from the Latin with Notes and Introduction

By

Author of " Bartholomew de Las Casas, His Life, His Apostolate, and His Writings,"
" Fernando Cortes and the Conquest of Mexico."   Editor and translator of
" The Letters of Cortes to Charles V."

In Two Volumes

Volume Two

New York and London
The Knickerbocker Press
1912

CONTENTS

ILLUSTRATIONS

The Fourth Decade

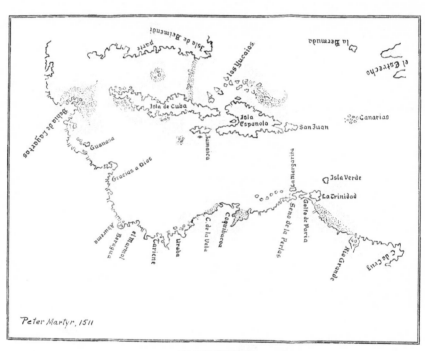

Peter Martyr, 1511

MAP OF THE WEST INDIES.

From the Map in the Edition of Peter Martyr's *Decades*, Published in Seville in 1511   Original in the Library of Henry C. Murphy, Esq.

INTRODUCTION

M OST HOLY FATHER, when the Augustinian
Ægidius di Viterbo,[1] one of the luminaries of the
Sacred College of Cardinals, left Spain after accomplishing his mission as legate *a latere*, he commanded
me, in the name of Your Holiness and in his own, to add to
my three decades already written all the marvels the ocean
has produced. These decades began in the year 1492, and
closed with the year 1516. I have delayed somewhat,
because many futile particulars, unworthy of remembrance, were recorded. Our Royal Council for Indian
Affairs daily received letters devoid of interest, written
by correspondents bereft of intelligence, from which I was
able to draw little material. The one boasted of having
discovered the finger of a hand, another a joint of that
finger; and they glorified themselves far more proudly
and vociferously for having found new countries and
accomplished great deeds, than did the true discoverers
of the entire continent. They resemble the ant, which
believes itself to be crushed beneath a heavy burden,
when it has taken one grain from an immense heap of
wheat sown by another, and dragged it to its underground
storehouse. I mean by a finger of the hand or a grain of
wheat, all the neighbouring isles which dot the sea about

[1] Egidio Antonini was sent to Spain on a mission in 1518 by Leo X.
He was a native of Viterbo, who became general of the Augustinians in
1507; was afterwards Patriarch of Constantinople, and was created Cardinal
in 1517. He was learned in Latin, Greek, Hebrew, and Chaldean; he died
in Rome in 1532.

Hispaniola, Cuba, and the land supposed to be a continent. For these countries are surrounded on all sides by innumerable islands, like hens with their chicks, swarming about them.

It is, nevertheless, necessary to reward each one according to his labour. We, therefore, place in the hands of Your Holiness the narrative of what we have learned about the lands of Yucatan, Cozumel, and the great country of Hacolucana, that your ears may thereby be delighted; of the last country it is not yet known whether it is an island or a part of the continent. I shall relate, avoiding irrelevancy, everything that appears to me worthy of remembrance; and I shall sum up the events that have happened upon the supposed continent, and terminate with Hispaniola.

BOOK I

TO

THE SOVEREIGN PONTIFF LEO X

FROM THE SAME PETER MARTYR D'ANGHERA OF MILAN

IN my first Decades, which the printing-press has distributed to the public, was a story of how some fugitives, landed in the neighbourhood of Darien, were astonished upon beholding our books. They related that they had formerly inhabited a country where the people, living in a state of society under organised laws, used similar things. They had palaces, magnificent temples built of stone, public squares, and streets properly laid out for commercial purposes. It is these countries that the Spaniards have discovered, and to the authors of these discoveries and the manner in which they were carried out, I beg Your Holiness to now graciously give attention; because all these countries should become, as soon as known, subject to your domination. I have thus far spoken but little of Cuba, which Diego Velasquez,[1] governor in the name of the Admiral Columbus, named

---

[1] Diego Velasquez was a native of Cuellar, and was born about 1465. He sailed with Columbus on his second voyage in 1493. He was deputed in 1509 by Diego Columbus to effect the conquest of Cuba, of which island he was later named Governor. The story of his bitter rivalry and struggle with Fernando Cortes is told by Peter Martyr in his pages which follow. Compare with other narratives: Las Casas in his *Historia General de las Indias;* Gomara, *Historia de las Indias;* Bernal Diaz, *Historia Verdadera;* MacNutt, *Fernando Cortes.*

Fernandina. This island lies to the west of Hispaniola, but far enough to the north to be divided by the Tropic of Cancer, while Hispaniola lies some degrees distant from both the tropic and the equator. Six fortified stations have been already established in Cuba, the first being placed under the patronage of Santiago,[1] protector of all the Spains. Native gold is found both in the mountains and in the rivers, and one of the occupations is mining.

In the same year[2] that I ceased the publication of the Decades, three of the oldest colonists of Cuba, Francisco Fernandez de Cordoba, Lopez Ochoa Cayzedo, and Cristobal Morantes, resolved to undertake the discovery of new lands. Fernando Iniguez, a Galician, receiver of revenues for the King of Spain, was to be captain of one of the ships. The Spaniards are of a restless character, and constantly seek to accomplish great undertakings. Their ships, of the kind called in Spain caravels, were fitted out at their own expense and sailed for the western extremity of Cuba, named Cape San Antonio. Altogether there were one hundred and ten soldiers on board, and the pilot was Anton Alaminos. This point of Cuba is well adapted for ships' repairs and renewing supplies of water and wood. Driven by a wind between the *Zephyr* and *Auster*, called by the Spaniards south-west, they discovered land the sixth day[3] after sailing. They had only covered a distance of sixty-six leagues in those six days, for they anchored at sunset, fearing to strike upon reefs in that unknown sea or to be lost in the depths. The country they discovered being apparently very large, they landed, and were amicably received by the natives. When they demanded by signs and gestures what was

---

[1] The other settlements made by Velasquez were Havana, Trinidad, Matanzas, Puerto del Principe, and San Salvador.

[2] 1517.

[3] Bernal Diaz describes the voyages as lasting twenty-one days; see *Historia Verdadera*, cap. vi.

the name of the country, the latter replied *Yucatan*, a word which means in their own language, "I do not understand you." The Spaniards imagined that this was the name of the country; and because of that unforeseen circumstance the country will always be called Yucatan. The name given by the Indians to this country is Eccampi. The Spaniards discovered a fortified town on the bank, of such importance that they named it Cairo, after the capital of Egypt. It possesses houses with towers, magnificent temples, regular streets, squares and market-places. The houses are built of stone or brick, held together with mortar and skilfully built. Access to the first courts and habitations is had by stairs of six or seven steps. The roofs are not made of tiles, but of thatch or bundles of grass.

Presents were mutually exchanged between the Spaniards and the natives, the barbarians giving beautifully worked buckles and necklaces, in exchange for which they received silk stuffs, woollen garments, glass beads, and copper bells. These gifts were graciously received because they came from strangers, but they attached no great value to them, because they make much more brilliant objects themselves out of certain stones. The natives wore clothing, not of wool, because they have no sheep, but made of a thousand different kinds of cotton dyed in divers colours. The women are covered from the waist to the heels, and they envelop their breasts in several veils, and take modest care that neither their legs nor their feet shall be visible. The natives visit the temples, to which paved streets lead, starting from the residence of the principal people of the community. They worship idols, and some of them, but not all, are circumcised. They have laws, and are extremely honest in trading, which they carry on without money. Crosses[1] have been

[1] Whether the existence of these and other crosses in Mexico and Central America is to be ascribed to some remote and passing Christian influence or not, has been much discussed with a wealth of argument for and against

seen amongst them; and when they were asked, through interpreters, the meaning of that emblem, some of them answered that a very beautiful man had once lived amongst them, who had left them this symbol as a remembrance of him; others said that a man more radiant than the sun had died upon that cross.

---

this theory. The celebrated cross of Palenque is now held by the best authorities to symbolise the four winds; as the symbol of Quetzalcoatl, god of the air and particularly associated with the rain-bringing winds, the cross was the emblem of fertility. Consult Icazbalceta, *Documentos para la Historia de Mejeco*, tom. i., pp. 306, 307; Torquemada, *Manarchia Indiana*, tom. iii., p. 134; Las Casas, *Hist. Apologetica*, p. 123; Mota Padilla, *Hist. de la Nueva Galicia*, p. 36; Zelia Nuttall, *Fundamental Principles of Old and New World Civilisations;* Beauvois, *Migrations d'Europe pendant le moyen âge.*

BOOK II

THE Spaniards remained some days in that country.
They noticed that the Indians began to tire of
their presence; for visitors who prolong their
stay are never agreeable. They, therefore, collected
their supplies, and pushed straight on westwards, following the coasts of the provinces called by the natives
Corus and Matam, and stopping nowhere, save for wood
and water. The barbarians along the coasts admired
the great size of the floating hulks, and both men and
women came from all directions with their children to
look at them. From on board their vessels the Spaniards
likewise beheld with astonishment the buildings, especially
the temples resembling fortresses, which stood near the
shore. They finally decided to anchor one hundred and
ten leagues farther on in a province called Campeche,
whose capital had as many as three thousand inhabitants.
The meeting was cordial on both sides, the barbarians
regarding with amazement the agility of the sailors,
the size of the vessels, their sails, tackle, and all the rest.
When they heard the thunder of the cannon and smelt
the smoke and sulphurous odour, they thought a thunder-
bolt had fallen from heaven. The cacique was pleased
to receive the Spaniards in his palace and to offer them
magnificent hospitality. They sat down to a sumptuous
repast, where they were served with peacocks, fat chickens,
wild birds from the mountains, woods, and swamps;
partridges, quails, doves, ducks, geese, and wild game

9

such as boar, deer, and hare; not to mention wolves, lions, tigers, and foxes.[1]

The natives conducted them with a royal escort to a large square just outside the village, where they showed them a square platform built of marble and approached by four steps. The floor was of hard bitumen in mosaic pattern; and upon this platform there stood the statue of a man surrounded by four quadrupeds of unknown species, resembling fierce dogs, in the attitude of tearing out the bowels of the marble man. Just near to the statue there was a serpent made of bitumen and small stones, forty-seven feet in length and as large round as an ox, which seemed to devour a lion made of marble. It was splashed with newly shed blood. In the immediate neighbourhood there were three beams set in the ground, and three others leaning obliquely upon stones. This is the place of punishment for criminals, as was proven by the Spaniards seeing marks of blood in many of the streets, broken arrows, and the bones of victims thrown into a neighbouring court. The houses of Campeche are built of lime and bitumen. The Spaniards gave the name of Lazarus to the cacique, because they landed there on the feast-day of that saint.

Pursuing their course to the west, the Spaniards landed fifteen leagues farther on, in the province of Aguanil, whose capital is Moscobo and the cacique Chiapoton;[2] a word pronounced with the accent on the last syllable. This cacique was ill-disposed towards the Spaniards and sought to draw them into an ambuscade when they were taking in a supply of fresh water. The latter were told there was a spring on the other side of the hill,

---

[1] The narration throughout may be profitably compared with that of Bernal Diaz in his *Historia Verdadera*. Mr. Maudslay's admirable English translation, published by the Hakluyt Society in 1910, renders this valuable old chronicle easily accessible.

[2] Champoton; the Indian names throughout the decades are mostly misspelled.

reached by narrow paths; but the natives had painted their faces and were armed with bows and arrows.[1] The Spaniards circumvented their plot, and refused to go any farther; but when they were scattered, and off their guard a thousand barbarians attacked them and overcame them. They fled towards the coast, but the ground being swampy, they sank into the mud, and twenty-two of them were killed with arrows. Almost all the others were wounded and the commander of the expedition, Francisco Fernandez, is said to have received thirty-three wounds.[2] Hardly anybody escaped unhurt, and had they gone as far as the hill they would have perished to the last man. The discouraged survivors returned to the island of Fernandina whence they had sailed, where they were received by their companions with tears and sighs both for the lost and the wounded.

[1] In other words, the natives being armed and in their war-paint, the Spaniards became suspicious.

[2] Bernal Diaz states that the commander received twelve arrow wounds: fifty-seven men were killed.

BOOK III

UPON receiving this news, the governor of Cuba,—or Fernandina,—Diego Velasquez, armed four caravels, manned by about three hundred men, and gave the command of this squadron to his nephew, Juan de Grijalva[1]; associated with him as lieutenants were Alfonso d'Avila, Francisco Montejo, and the commander Pedro de Alvarado. The pilot was the same Anton Alaminos, who had served the other fleet. The same route, but bending more toward the south, was taken. After sailing seventy leagues, a high tower was sighted from one of the ships, but no land; and taking that tower as an objective, they reached an island called Cozumel.[2] During three full leagues before landing, the land-breeze blowing from the island wafted perfumed airs to the ships. This island is forty-five leagues in circumference and is flat; its soil is fertile, and gold is found there but not in the natural state, for it is brought from elsewhere. There is plenty of honey, fruits, vegetables, birds, and quadrupeds; to sum up in a few words, these islanders have the same customs and laws as those of Yucatan; the same temples, streets,

---

[1] The expedition of Grijalva is described in the *Itinerario de l'Armata*, compiled by the chaplain of the fleet, Juan Diaz. The original of this chronicle is lost, but an Italian translation was published in Venice in 1552, and another in French was published by Ternaux-Compans, in the tenth volume of his *Voyages, Rélations et Mémoires*. The expedition sailed April 5, 1518.

[2] Sometimes written Acuzamil from Ah-Cuzamil, meaning "The Swallows." See Cogolludo, *Historia de Yucatan*, lib. iv., cap. vii.

occupations, and clothing both for men and women. Their clothing is not made of wool, but of spun cotton, such as the Italians call *bombasio* and the Spaniards *algodon*. The houses are built of brick or stone, roofed with thatch when there are no stones, but with stone flags when there are quarries in the neighbourhood. In most of the houses the door-jambs are made of marble, just as with us. The Spaniards noticed some ancient towers and the ruins of some fallen towers, which seemed of great antiquity. They mounted to the top of one of these towers, resembling a famous temple, by a staircase composed of twenty-four steps.[1] The natives admired the ships and the dexterity of the sailors. In the beginning they were reluctant to receive the Spaniards, but they soon did so with amiability. Conducted by one who was undoubtedly a priest, the Spaniards mounted a tower and unfurled a flag on its summit, taking possession in the name of the King of Castile. The name of Santa Cruz was given to the island, because they landed there the fifth day of the nones of May, on the Feast of the Holy Cross. Its true name is Cozumel, after the cacique Cozumel, who boasted that his ancestors were the first inhabitants of the island.

Inside the tower were chambers filled with marble statues, mingled with images of bears made of terracotta. The natives venerate these objects, giving vent to loud cries, always on a single note. They offer them sacrifices and incense and sweet perfumes, and honour them as Penates. Mass was celebrated in these chambers. The natives are circumcised.

[1] For a correct understanding of the aboriginal architecture of Yucatan, Mexico, and Central America, the following authorities should be consulted: Stevens and Catherwood, *Incidents of Travel in Central America; Chiapas and Yucatan;* Brasseur de Bourbourg, *Histoire des nations civilisées de l'Amérique Centrale;* Charnay's *Cités et ruines Américaines;* Maudslay, *Biologia Centrali Americana;* Bandelier, *An Archeological Tour;* Tozer, *A Comparative Story of the Mayas and Lacandones;* and the reports of Teobert Maler published in the Memoirs of the Peabody Museum of Harvard.

The cacique, who also wore a cotton costume, had the toes of one of his feet cut off; this was due to a ferocious shark which snapped them off at one bite while the cacique was swimming. This chieftain entertained the Spaniards with long and copious banquets.

At the end of three days the Spaniards left, sailing straight to the west. They perceived mountains in the distance; this was Yucatan, which had already been sighted, and is only five leagues distant from Cozumel. Following the south coast of Cozumel, very near the land believed to be a continent, they sailed round it, but could not continue because of the numerous reefs and shoals which protect it. The pilot Alaminos, therefore, conducted the fleet to the north side which was already known, returning to Campeche, governed by the cacique Lazarus, which they had visited the preceding year. They met with a good reception and were invited to enter the town. The natives later repented of their invitation, and at a stone's throw from Campeche they ordered the Spaniards to stop and go back. The latter asked permission to take water before leaving, and were shown some wells behind them, which they were given to understand they might use, but no others. The whole night was passed in the neighbourhood of these wells; about three thousand of the suspicious natives, carrying arms, camping not far distant. There was no sleep in either camp, for the natives feared an attack upon the town, while the Spaniards feared a sudden attack from them; while the piercing noise of their trumpets and drums kept everybody awake. When day dawned, the barbarians approached and called through interpreters, whose language, though not the same, is sufficiently similar, saying: "Behold this torch of incense which we will light and place between the two armies. If you do not make haste and retreat before the torch is burnt out, you will all perish. We do not want you as guests."

The torch either went out or burned out, and immediately the battle began. A Spaniard, whose shield insufficiently protected him against the arrows, was wounded, as were also many others. The Spaniards retreated towards their cannon, which they had left near the wells, and when they gained them, they fired a volley against the natives, who withdrew into their town. The Spaniards, whose courage was roused, wanted to pursue them; but Grijalva refused.

The Spaniards then proceeded to the remotest extremity of Yucatan and found that its length from east to west is two hundred leagues. They discovered a good harbour which they named Deseado, and from thence they visited other countries, landing in a neighbouring province of Yucatan, lying to the west. It is not known whether that is an island or not, but it is believed to be part of the continent. There is a gulf there, whose waters are thought to wash the coasts of both regions, though nothing is positively known. The natives call this country Coluacan, or Oloa. The Spaniards discovered a large river there, whose current carries the fresh, drinkable water two leagues out to sea; in honour of the captain they named it Rio de Grijalva. The natives lined both banks of the river, staring with surprise at the great bulk of the ships covered with sails. They numbered about six thousand men, all armed, with gilded shields, bows and arrows, large wooden swords, and lances with burnt points. It was their intention to resist any landing and to protect their coasts. All night both sides remained face to face.

We have elsewhere stated that canoes are barques dug out of tree-trunks. The Cuban interpreters and these natives understood one another with facility. The natives made offers of peace, which were accepted, and one of the canoes approached, the others remaining at rest. The commander of the canoe asked what the

Spaniards sought in a strange country; to which the latter replied they were looking for gold, not as a gift or to be obtained by violence, but by trading.   The canoe returned and reported the answer to the cacique, and the latter responded to the invitation and willingly came on board. Astonishing to relate, Most Holy Father, he ordered his valet to bring the entire furniture of a chamber, and to load the captain, Grijalva, with ornaments.   They began by giving him gilded shoes; afterwards leggings, and cuirasses, and all the parts of the iron and steel armour a cuirassier ordinarily wears when going into battle, only these were made of gold, beautifully worked; this done the cacique paid homage to Grijalva.   The latter gave him in exchange some silk, linen, and woollen clothing and some other articles of Spanish manufacture.

Off the coast of Yucatan and well on the way from the island of Cozumel, the Spaniards encountered a canoe filled with fishermen.   There were nine of them, and they fished with golden hooks.   They were not armed nor on their guard, so they were taken prisoners.   The cacique, who recognised one of them, promised Grijalva to send him the next day the weight of his prisoner in gold, but in spite of his companions, Grijalva refused and kept the prisoner.   After which he departed, to continue his discoveries.

BOOK IV

ABOUT a hundred leagues farther on, and always to the west, the Spaniards discovered a large gulf, in which lay three small islands, upon the largest of which they landed.

Alas! Most Holy Father, what a horrible crime! Alas, that men should be so cruel! Let not Your Beatitude be overcome with disgust! The natives sacrifice children and young girls to their gods. They are circumcised. Some of the idols they adore are made of marble, some of clay, and in the midst of them there is a lion, on whose head the blood of the victims is poured, afterwards trickling down into a marble basin. We shall describe the sacrificial ceremony. They tear out the heart and smear the warm blood upon the lips of their idols, allowing the remainder to run into the basin. They next burn the heart, without cutting it up, as well as the entrails, thinking that the gods love the smoke from these offerings. Amongst these idols one, representing a man with bent head looking into the basin of blood as though he delighted in the immolation of the victims, is noticeable. They eat the fleshy part of the arms, also the fat of the hips and calves, especially if the victim is an enemy captured in war. The Spaniards discovered a stream of dried blood, like those which flow from slaughter-houses. They seek their wretched victims for these sacrifices in the neighbouring islands. The Spaniards found a number of heads, headless and entire bodies still in their clothes.

In exploring the island one of our men found two half - buried alabaster vases, which were artistically decorated and filled with precious stones of various colours. One of these stones was sent to the governor, and was valued at two thousand castellanos of gold. The Spaniards named this island Isla de los Sacrificios.

A number of other islands lie off the coast of Coluacan, which are inhabited only by women,[1] who have no relations with men. Some people think they live as did the Amazons, but others who have studied the question more closely believe they are virgins dedicated to God, who take pleasure in solitude, just as those amongst us; or in ancient times, did the vestals or the priestesses of the *Bona Dea*. At certain epochs of the year, men cross to the islands, not to have intercourse with these religious women, but out of the spirit of piety to cultivate their fields and gardens, and thus assure their means of existence. The report is spread, however, that there are other islands likewise inhabited by women of bad morals, who from their earliest youth cut away the breast to enable them to draw their bows with greater facility. Men go to these islands to have relations with them, but they do not stop there. I think this story is a fable.

Our people landed on the coast of Coluacan, and quietly began trading operations. The cacique made them a present of a gold kettle, some bracelets and balls, as well as a number of jewels of different shapes. In exchange, the Spaniards presented him with some of their manufactures which pleased him. They would have stopped there and founded a colony, but Grijalva forbade it, which aroused their resentment against him.

Everywhere in Coluacan there are edifices ornamented with towers. There are fifteen large towns, one of which has as many as twenty thousand houses, not built near together, but separated by courts and gardens,

---

[1] This oft-repeated story is a fable, devoid of foundation.

and sometimes by large open spaces. There are, in these towns, courts of justice surrounded by walls, and also market-places. They also possess paved streets, ovens, furnaces, lime, and baked bricks. Their potters, carpenters, artisans and other workmen in the mechanical trades are capable. The cacique is called Tabasco, and the country Palmaria. The royal residence is called Potenchian, and numbers fifteen thousand houses. In receiving their new guests, with whom they desired to live peaceably, the Indians drew a little blood with a razor either from the tongue, the left hand, the arm, or some other part of the body; and this serves as a pledge of friendship, the operation being performed in the presence of the guest.

The priests are celibates and observe chastity. Nobody has sexual relations before marriage, and to act otherwise would be a crime which only death could expiate. The morals of the women are admirably pure. Every powerful chief may take as many concubines as he pleases after marriage. A married woman taken in adultery is sold by her husband, but the cacique has the right to ransom her. It is forbidden to any unmarried person to sit at the same table with a married person, to eat from the same dish, drink from the same cup, or in any way to comport himself as an equal. During the months of August and September they fast for thirty-five days, not only from meat such as chickens and game, which they like, but also from fish or any other animal food. During this period they subsist on fruits and vegetables.

The Spaniards passed some days amongst them, abundantly supplied with provisions. Upon leaving, they followed the same coast and visited a cacique to whom they gave the name of Ovando. As soon as this chief understood that the Spaniards wanted gold, he presented them with some bars of it melted. The captain having told him through his interpreters that he desired a large quantity, the next day the cacique brought a small golden statue of a man, also a golden fan and mask, beautifully worked and decorated with stones. He also distributed amongst them many beads for breast ornaments and others of divers kinds and variety adorned with precious stones. He invited them to magnificent banquets, served with great taste; and as the men were without protection from the weather, the cacique gave orders that cabins made of green branches should be quickly erected for them. He struck any of his slaves, who were slow about carrying the branches, with a sceptre which he carried in his hands. The slaves bowed their heads and submitted to the blows without complaint. When asked where he obtained so much gold, the cacique pointed with his finger to the neighbouring mountains and the streams flowing from them. The natives are so accustomed to swim in the rivers and lakes that they are as much at home in the water as on land. Whenever the humour takes them to collect gold, they dive into the river and bring up handfuls of sand, which they then sift from one hand to the other, taking out the gold. It is claimed that within a space of two hours they can fill a tube as long as your finger.

Much might be said of the perfumes and soft odours of these countries, which incline people to idleness and luxury, but it is better to pass these over in silence. Such things contribute more to effeminacy than to the encouragement of virtue. The commander refused a boy twelve years old, but accepted a young girl wearing beautiful ornaments; in spite of his companions he dismissed the boy. Among the precious stones given by this cacique, one worth two thousand castellanos of gold was noted. The Spaniards finally quit this country, laden with gold and precious stones.

The captain, Grijalva, sent one of the caravels to his uncle, the governor, to carry to Fernandina the news of the discovery and the treasure amassed. The other ships continued to follow the coast in a westerly direction, one of them, commanded by Francisco Montejo, keeping well in towards the shore, while the other two stood out more to sea. The natives were astonished at this novel spectacle, believing they were witnessing a miracle. Thirteen canoes approached the ship of Montejo, and conversation began through interpreters. After an exchange of amicable signs, the islanders invited the Spaniards to land, promising them a good reception if they would visit their cacique. Montejo responded that he could not accept the invitation, because his companions were too far distant; but he distributed some presents and sent them away well satisfied. The Spaniards afterwards sailed towards another populous town, the three caravels approaching the shore together. The natives, however, opposed their landing; armed with their shields, bows, quivers full of arrows, large wooden swords, and their lances with burnt points, they advanced, letting fly volleys of arrows. The Spaniards replied with cannon-shot, and the natives, amazed and frightened by the explosion, took flight. A little later they sought to renew negotiations. Provisions were getting short, and the Spaniards found their ships damaged by the long voyage; so Grijalva determined to return to Fernandina. He was well satisfied with the result of his discoveries and acquisitions, but his companions were extremely dissatisfied.[1]

[1] Diego Velasquez disapproved of the conduct of Grijalva, who fell into permanent disfavour with the petulant and avaricious governor. He afterwards joined Garay's luckless expedition to Panuco, and was finally killed during an Indian uprising at Villahermosa in Nicaragua.

BOOK V

WE must now digress a little, in order to describe a new expedition, after which we will return to the present subject. While equipping this squadron of four caravels, the same governor,[1] Diego Velasquez, had simultaneously armed a fifth, which was to be accompanied by one single brigantine, carrying provisions and forty-five soldiers. The Spaniards used force against the natives who inhabited the coast of the neighbouring continent; these people are circumcised and worship idols. During their voyage the Spaniards passed a number of small islands, remarkable for the fertility of their soil and the abundance of their crops. These islands are called Guanaxa, Guitilla, and Guanagua[2]; and in one of them they captured three hundred natives of both sexes, who had in no wise molested them. They named this island Santa Marina. Crowding their prisoners upon the caravel, they returned to Fernandina while the brigantine, with a crew of twenty-five sailors, was ordered to continue this man-hunt.

The caravel touched at a port called Carenas, distant about two hundred and forty leagues from the capital of Cuba, Santiago. It is known that the length of this island extends towards the west, and that it is divided in the middle by the Tropic of Cancer.

[1] *Progubernator:* Diego Velasquez was governor of Cuba, the title of viceroy being held by Diego Columbus.
[2] Islands lying in the Bahama channel.

22

Fortune took upon herself to avenge the prisoners. Some of their jailers having landed, and only a few remaining on board the caravel, the islanders seized this opportunity to recover their freedom. They obtained possession of the arms of the Spaniards, fell upon them, killing six and driving the others overboard. Once masters of the caravel, which they had learned to sail, the islanders returned to their country. They first landed on a neighbouring island where they burned the caravel, taking care to keep the arms, and regained their native land in their own barques. They took the Spaniards who had been left in charge of the brigantine by surprise. Upon the shore there grew a large tree, on the top of which they set up a cross, and upon the upper part of its trunk they wrote in Spanish letters *Vamos al Darien*. Darien is the river on whose banks stands the capital of what is supposed to be a continent, Santa Maria de la Antigua.

As soon as the news of the disaster reached him, the governor of Fernandina hastened to send shiploads of soldiers to rescue the abandoned Spaniards. The decision was wise but tardy, for the catastrophe was complete. They saw the cross and, following the coast, they read the letters carved on the tree-trunk; but not venturing to attack the fugitives, who were desperate and better armed than themselves, they retired, not, however, without capturing in a neighbouring island five hundred prisoners of both sexes, as easily as if they had been hares. The excuse offered for this iniquitous proceeding was that the natives were circumcised. Hardly had they landed at Fernandina than they themselves had to undergo the same trials, for the prisoners attacked one of the two caravels with fury and, despite their desperate resistance, killed a number of the Spanish soldiers. Others threw themselves overboard and swam to the other caravel, which was not far distant. A general attack upon the caravel in the possession of the natives was then made, and during four hours the result of the battle was uncertain. The barbarians, both men and women, fought with fury to regain their liberty, while the Spaniards were still more excited at the thought of losing their plunder. The latter finally conquered, because they handled their arms more skilfully. The defeated savages threw themselves into the sea, and though some of them were picked up by shallops, about a hundred were lost either in the fight or by drowning. Only very few Spaniards perished; and the prisoners were sent to Santiago or to the gold mines.[1]

The Spaniards next undertook an expedition to another of the neighbouring islands, which are more numerous thereabouts than the Symplegades[2] in the Ionian Sea, to which the vulgar give the general name of Archipelago. They got a bad reception, and all who landed were either killed or wounded. It is thought that this island is the one discovered by Juan Ponce, captain of a small fleet, and afterwards abandoned by him when he was repulsed by the natives. He named it Florida, because he discovered it on the Feast of the Resurrection, which is called Pasqua Florida. They claimed to have sighted twenty-six islands. Columbus had already navigated amongst them, for they are like daughters to Cuba or Hispaniola, and are the guardians of what is believed to be a continent, their rocks forming a breakwater against the ocean storms. In most of these islands the Spaniards

---

[1] We owe the description of this typical act of piracy and slave-hunting to Spanish sources; the same sad tale is repeated throughout the years of misrule that depopulated the islands and disgraced Spain.

[2] *Hæ sunt ibi frequentiores quam in nostro Ionio Symplegades, quarum congeriam archipælagus vulgus appellat.* This sad slip of Peter Martyr's pen must have provoked derisive mirth amongst the humanists of the Pontifical Court, whose critical ears his lapses from Ciceronian purity had already offended. The Symplegades lie far distant from the Ionian Sea, being found in the Euxine, opposite the entrance to the Thracian Bosphorus. Being but two in number, nobody, however vulgar, ever called them an archipelago.

found gold in the form of grains. The natives wear various kinds of necklaces and masks made of gilded wood or ingeniously wrought gold, for they are very clever artisans. Francisco Chieregato, nunzio of Your Holiness to the court of our Spanish sovereign, has taken back one of these masks so that you may see and examine the clever workmanship.

They make a razor in the following curious fashion: they use certain yellow stones,[1] transparent as crystal, and razors made of these stones cut as well as those of good steel. What is still more singular is that when the blade is dull with usage, they do not sharpen it on a wheel or a stone or with powder, but merely dip it in water. A great variety of elegant instruments and other objects is found amongst them, but it would take too long to enumerate them, and perhaps, Your Beatitude, absorbed as you are in grave affairs, would feel little interest in such a description.

I now return to my original subject, the islands of Cozumel, Yucatan, and Coluacan or Oloa; rich and truly Elysian lands, which have just been discovered, and from which I have somewhat wandered. The great importance of these regions is already fully understood.

---

[1] Obsidian or *iztli* as the Mexicans called it, was the stone used for making sacrificial knives, spear-points, maquahuitl blades, razors, and all sharp instruments for cutting; its colour however is usually black, sometimes grey, but I recall no yellow.

BOOK VI

THE Spaniards recently settled in Cuba obtained the governor's authorisation to fit out a fleet of ten caravels carrying five hundred soldiers, and three brigantines similar to lightly harnessed horses.[1] They intended to make use of these brigantines in shallow waters and along the coasts fringed with reefs. Seven war-horses were taken on board the fleet. Fernando Cortes, at that time a judge in Cuba, was appointed commander,[2] and with him were associated Alfonso Fernando Portocarrero, Francisco de Montejo, Alfonso d'Avila, Alvarado, commander of Badajoz, Juan Velasquez, and Diego de Ordaz. They sailed[3] from the same western point of Cuba favoured by the same wind that had already served Francisco Fernandez and Juan de Grijalva.

They arrived within sight of the Isla de los Sacrificios, which we have already mentioned, where a sudden and violent storm prevented their landing, and drove them out of their course to the island of Cozumel, off the eastern coast of Yucatan. There is only one port

---

[1] The simile does not seem apt. As is explained in the next sentence, the brigantines were for use in places where the larger vessels could not penetrate, and hence in this somewhat strained sense might be likened to light cavalry skirmishers.

[2] Consult Bernard Diaz, *Historia Verdadera;* English translation by Maudslay 1910; Prescott's *Conquest of Mexico;* MacNutt's, *Fernando Cortes* in Heroes of the Nations Series, vol. xix; Gomara, *Cronica de la Conquista;* Las Casas, *Hist. de las Indias,* tom. iii.

[3] February 18, 1519.

on this island and to this they gave the name of San Juan de Porta Latina. They counted six towns in this island, where the only drinking water is from pits or cisterns, for it is flat and there are no rivers. The island is forty-five leagues in circumference. The islanders, seized with terror, abandoned their towns and fled into the depths of the forests, and the Spaniards took possession of their empty houses and ate the supplies they contained. They found there a number of ornaments, tapestries, clothing, and beds of native cotton called hammocks. They even discovered, Most Holy Father, many books. We shall later speak of these, as well as of different other articles which have been brought to our new sovereign.

The Spaniards explored the entire island, keeping well together in order to avoid a surprise. They found few inhabitants and only one woman, through whom, by means of interpreters from Cuba and three natives of Yucatan who had been carried off during a preceding expedition, they invited the caciques who had fled, to return. These natives were servants of the woman who served as guide to the envoys, and they succeeded in bringing back the caciques. Peace was concluded and the islanders gladly resumed possession of their houses, and many of the pieces of furniture which had been taken, were restored to them. They are pagans and circumcised. They sacrifice boys and young girls to their zemes. The zemes are figures representing nocturnal goblins, to which they pay veneration.

The pilot Alaminos, Francisco Montejo, and Portocarrero, who were later sent with gifts to the King, have been questioned by me. I asked them whence the islanders obtained the boys and girls for their sacrifices, and they told me that it was in the neighbouring islands. They traded gold and other merchandise for them. In fact, nowhere throughout the length and breadth of this vast new country do the natives busy themselves about money, which is the cause of so much evil; and it is the same in the more recently discovered countries, among which are the islands Bia and Segesta. When there are no children they sacrifice dogs. They raise dogs for food, just as we do rabbits. These dogs never bark, and have the snout of a fox. Those destined for food are castrated, and only a limited number of males are preserved for propagating the species, just as do our shepherds with their flocks. The castrated dogs become very fat.

The Spaniards advised them to renounce human sacrifices, explaining their odious character. In reply, the barbarians asked to what law they should then conform. It was then proven to them without difficulty[1] that there is one God, creator of heaven and earth, giver of all good things, who is unique in his substance though triune in his Persons. They consented to the destruction of their zemes, and placed a picture of the Blessed Virgin painted by a Spaniard, in their temple. They swept and cleaned the temple, washed its floor, and accepted a cross, bearing the image of God made man, sacrificed for the good of the human race, to which they offered worship, and they placed upon the summit of the temple a large wooden cross. The natives told the Spaniards, through their interpreters, that there were seven Christians in the neighbouring province of Yucatan, who had been wrecked there during a storm. The distance separating this island from Yucatan being but five leagues, the commander Cortes sent two caravels with fifty men to rescue these prisoners. Three guides from Cozumel assisted them in their search, and the chief of the expedition was Diego de Ordaz. Cortes carefully explained

[1] The missionary zeal of Cortes was compelling and took little heed of any difficulties the natives may have experienced in understanding or accepting the doctrine he expounded. He repeatedly announced with evident conviction, that the Mexicans were eager to receive the faith.

to them the importance of their achievement, if they succeeded in bringing back one of these Spaniards; and he warmly encouraged them, for he hoped that these men would furnish him with necessary information concerning all that region.

The expedition started under favourable circumstances, and six days was the period fixed for awaiting their return. Two days in excess of that time passed, and still the messengers of Cozumel failed to appear; so it was conjectured that they had either been killed or captured. Ordaz therefore gave them up, and returned to Cortes at Cozumel. The latter was preparing to leave the island, having lost all hope of finding both the much desired Christians and the islanders of Cozumel who had been left behind, but a rough sea delayed him. This delay proved most fortunate, for a canoe, rowed by islanders and one of the Christian prisoners, was seen coming from the west coast of Yucatan. This man was called Geronimo de Aguilar; he had passed seven years of his life amongst the Yucatecans, and was a native of Encija in Andalusia. The joy with which they embraced may be imagined.

Aguilar recounted his misfortunes and the massacre of his companions, while the others attentively listened. I think it will not be out of place nor distasteful to Your Beatitude, to describe how this catastrophe happened. I have spoken in my first books of a certain nobleman, Valdivia, whom the colonists of Darien on the gulf of Uraba on what is supposed to be a continent, had sent to the Admiral Columbus, Viceroy of Hispaniola, and to the Royal Council charged with the affairs of the supposed continent. His mission was to give notice that the colonists suffered from destitution, and it proved an unfortunate one for him. When off the southern coast of Cuba, Jamaica, or Hispaniola this unfortunate man was overtaken by a tempest

in some sandy shallows, to which perilous shoals the
Spaniards have given the name of Las Viboras; a name
which is merited, for many ships have been lost there,
like lizards in the coils of a viper's tail.

The caravel was broken to pieces, and with great difficulty Valdivia and thirty of his companions succeeded in
embarking in the shallop, destitute of oars or sails. These
unfortunate creatures were buffeted about by the ocean currents. We have already told in our decades that there exists
in these waters a perpetual current flowing towards the
west. During thirteen days they drifted without knowing
whither, nor did they find any food. Seven of them died
of starvation, and furnsished food for the fishes. Finally
they fell into the hands of a cacique who massacred Valdivia and some of his companions, sacrificing them in
honour of his zemes, and afterwards eating them in company with his invited friends. These natives only eat
enemies or strangers whom they catch by chance, abstaining at all other times from human flesh. Geronimo
d'Aguilar and six of his companions were kept to be eaten
three days later; but during the night they escaped from
this cruel tyrant, breaking their bonds and taking refuge
with a neighbouring cacique, before whom they presented
themselves as suppliants. They were received, but as
slaves. [1]

[1] Valdivia, it will be remembered, was despatched by Balboa to carry
ten thousand pesos of gold to the royal treasurer of Hispaniola, Miguel
de Passamonte, and at the same time to solicit provisions, arms, and reinforcements for the colonists at Darien. Wrecked, as is here told, on the
reefs off the coast of Jamaica, the ultimate fate of the two survivors of
this luckless expedition was strange and not without a touch of romance.
One of them, Gonzales Guerrero was adopted by the Indians of Yucatan,
married a native woman, and became a captain of their warriors. He
tattooed his face, pierced his ears and nose, and became in all respects
one of them, even, so it was afterwards alleged, to the extent of taking
part in their ritual cannibalism. He was supposed to have led the native
troops in several engagements against the Spaniards, and when the letter
was brought from Cortes, he refused to abandon his family and adopted
people.

A very sad thing is told concerning the mother of
Aguilar. When informed of the fate of her son, she
suddenly became crazed by sorrow. She had vaguely
heard that her son had fallen into the hands of barbarians
who eat human flesh, and whenever she saw meat, either
boiled or fixed on spits, she made the house ring with
her cries, saying "This is the flesh of my son! Am I not
the most unhappy of mothers?"

When Aguilar received the letter from Cortes delivered to him by the messengers from Cozumel, he
informed the cacique, his master (who was called
Taximarus), of the message brought him by the islanders, furnishing many particulars concerning the
power of his sovereign and the qualities of those who
had just landed: their courage, their kindness towards
their friends, and their severity to those who rejected
or despised their wishes. Taximarus was frightened and
begged his slave to see that the Spaniards did not enter
his territory with hostile intent, for he wished on the
contrary to have them as his friends. Aguilar promised
to secure him peace and even, in case of necessity, assistance and protection against his enemies. The cacique
then decided to release Aguilar, and gave him as his
companions three of his servants.

Rejoicing at the deliverance and return of Aguilar, whose
services as interpreter would be most useful to him, Cortes
left Cozumel. It now remains for us to describe the country they next visited, and what there happened to them.

Geronimo de Aguilar of Encija was in deacon's orders. He likewise
came to enjoy some consideration and to exercise some influence among
his captors. This was largely owing to his ascetic mode of life, especially
his strict observance of his vow of chastity. Temptations were purposely
thrown in his way, but his resistance was never broken, and he rose in the
native estimation. His after life in Mexico was not a worthy sequel
to his heroic conduct in captivity. He rendered valuable services to Cortes,
and until Marina's gifts as an interpreter came into play, Aguilar was
indispensable.

BOOK VII

UNDER the direction of the pilot Alaminos, the
Spaniards reached the mouth of the river[1]
formerly visited by Grijalva. Sand-banks ob-
struct its entrance, similar to those alleged to exist at
the mouth of the Nile, when the etesian[2] winds are
blowing. It was, therefore, impossible to enter the river
with the brigantines, although higher up, the stream
was navigable for caravels. Cortes landed two hundred
soldiers, by means of the brigantines and the shallops of
the caravels. Aguilar made peaceful overtures to the
natives, who enquired what the Spaniards wanted.
Geronimo answered "Food." A large sandy square lay
in front of the town, and the natives made the Spaniards
understand that they should assemble there; after which
they departed. Next day they returned, bringing eight
of their chickens which resemble our peacocks, and are
of the same size and taste, but are dark coloured. They
also brought sufficient maize to feed ten hungry people.
At the same time they intimated to the Spaniards to
leave as quickly as possible; this, however, the latter
refused to do. A large multitude of men gathered round
them, repeatedly asking the intentions of those unknown
navigators. Through the intermediary of Aguilar, the
Spaniards answered that they wished peace and to trade
for food and also gold if any was to be had. The barba-

[1] The Tabasco River.

[2] *Etesiæ* being mild winds blowing from the north-west, about the
time of the summer solstice. Lucretius, x., 741.

rians answered that they wanted neither peace nor war, but that the strangers should leave unless they wished to be massacred to the last man. They then promised to bring provisions in the morning; but this was a falsehood, for three days passed during which the Spaniards remained camping on that shore and there passing the night, before the same small amount of food as formerly was brought them, with an intimation in the cacique's name to leave. The Spaniards answered that they wished to visit the town and required a larger supply of food. The barbarians refused and gathered about them muttering threats. The men being hungry and obliged to find food, Cortes landed his lieutenants with fifty men as reinforcements, who explored the country round about the town in different directions. The barbarians attacked and ill-treated one of these companies, but the others being near at hand came to their companions' assistance at the first sound of trouble. Meanwhile Cortes used the brigantines and shallops to land some cannon and had brought the rest of his men and sixteen horses on shore. In order to protect the coasts and to prevent the landing, the barbarians assembled, fully armed, letting fly their arrows and spears at the Spaniards, of whom they wounded about twenty who were taken off their guard. Cortes had the cannon fired at the enemy, who were frightened by the effect of the bullets and by the noise and flash. While they were still up to their knees in the water, the Spaniards pursued the disorderly natives and reached the town at the same time they did. The barbarians ran straight through the town and abandoned their houses.

It is reported that this town extends along the banks of the river. I hardly dare say what its length is. The pilot Alaminos mentions a league and a half. It contains twenty-five thousand houses. His companions reduce this number and diminish its grandeur, though they agree that it is large and spacious. The houses are separated

by gardens from one another, and are of stone covered
with plaster, built by architects of real talent.   The habit-
able parts of these houses are reached by staircases with
six or seven steps.   Nobody is allowed to rest his beams
or carpenter work upon the roof of his neighbour, and all
the houses are separated by an interval of at least three
feet.   The majority are covered with thatch made of
straw or marsh reeds.   Many are roofed with square, flat
stones.

The barbarians admit that there were forty thousand
of them engaged in the battle[1]; if they were defeated by
a handful of men it was because of the horses, a novel
feature of war with which they were not acquainted,
and the cannon.   Our horsemen had thrown themselves
upon the enemy's rear, dispersing their companies,
striking to the right and left, as shepherds do among
disorderly sheep. Astonished by this novelty, the
unfortunate creatures hesitated, and never again found
the opportunity of using their arms.   Thus they believed
in the fable told of the centaurs, that man and horse
were one animal.   The Spaniards remained in possession
of the town for twenty-two days, living luxuriously and
under shelter, while the barbarians were perishing of
hunger in the open country, not daring to attack them.
They chose the strongest part of the town for a citadel,
but never went to sleep without having first posted a
guard for the night; for they were on the alert, fearing an
attack of the natives and their cacique Tanosco.   This
town is called Potonchan, but in honour of the victory

---

[1] The battle of Ceutla was fought on March 25th.   Andres de Tapia
states that 48,000 Indians were in the engagement, but these figures are
based on no actual count and merely represent the idea of multitude.
In the *Cronica* of Gomara, as well as in Tapia's *Relacion*, the victory is
attributed to the intervention of St. James, the patron saint of Spain.
Bernal Diaz does not question the miraculous apparition but observes with
truly Christian humility that he was too miserable a sinner to be worthy
to behold it.

they won there, they named it Victoria. Astonishing things are told of the magnificence, the size and the beauty, of the country houses built by the natives round about, for their pleasure. They are constructed like ours, with courtyards shaded from the sun and with sumptuous apartments.

Thanks to the interpreters and the prisoners taken in the battle, the cacique and his principal officers were prevailed upon to return and sue for peace. Having consented to this step, all the people returned to their homes, and peace was made on condition that they renounced the horrible human sacrifices in honour of the dead, and the odious demons whose idols they adored, and henceforth lifted up their souls to the Lord Jesus, Father of heaven and earth, born of a virgin and crucified for the salvation of the human race. They destroyed their idols, and confessed themselves subjects of the King of Spain. They promised everything, and the Spaniards instructed them as much as was possible in so short a time, distributing presents amongst them, and afterwards dismissing them. These natives believe that the Spaniards are envoys from Heaven, since being so few they dared to give battle to so great a multitude. They presented the Spaniards with a few articles of gold and twenty female slaves.[1]

---

[1] Among these women was Marina of Painalla, an Aztec girl whose mother had some years previously sold her to some Indians of Xicalango in order to secure the girl's inheritance to a son by her second husband. Marina was taken to Tabasco and finally fell to the share of Portocarrero when the female booty was divided amongst the Spaniards. Knowing the language of the coast tribes which resembled that of Yucatan, she was able to communicate with Aguilar; Aztec was her mother tongue, and when the envoys from Montezuma appeared, it was speedily discovered that only through Marina could Cortes negotiate intelligibly with the Mexicans. Marina was thereupon promoted to the commander's tent, where she remained during the entire conquest, her importance daily increasing. She is described by Bernal Diaz as a woman of remarkable beauty and superior character. She betrayed her people and was faithful to the

Everything being thus settled, Cortes left to explore other countries along the same coast. They visited the gulf noted by Alaminos during the voyage of Grijalva, and named it the Bay of San Juan; *bay* in the Spanish being the same thing as *gulf*. A mile from the bank was a walled town, containing about five hundred houses, built upon a hill. The inhabitants offered hospitality and the half of their town, if the Spaniards cared to stay permanently. It is probable that they were frightened by what had happened to the inhabitants of Potonchan, the news of which had reached them, and they hoped to secure protection of such heroes against their neighbours, for they likewise are afflicted by that malady which never disappears, and is in some fashion inborn in humanity; like all men, they thirst for dominion. The Spaniards refused to stop there permanently but agreed to make a halt.[1] When they returned to the coast the people followed them and quickly built huts of green branches covered by improvised roofs against the rain. On that spot the Spaniards pitched their camp. To provide them with occupation Cortes commanded the pilot Alaminos and Francisco Montejo to explore the country towards the west, and meantime his weary men rested and those who had been wounded at Potonchan were cared for.

Fifty men embarked upon the two brigantines, the other soldiers remaining behind with the chief. Up to that time the gulf current had moderated, but hardly had the Spaniards advanced somewhat to the west, than they were seized, as it were, by a torrent rushing down from

---

Spaniards throughout. She bore Cortes one son, Martin, and a daughter; possibly other children. In 1524 she was married to a Spanish soldier Juan Xaramillo and in the year 1537 she was still living. Consult Alaman, *Disertaciones Historicas;* also MacNutt's *Letters of Cortes.* Appendix I. to Second Letter, vol. i.

[1] Cortes landed on Good Friday which fell that year on April 21st.

a mountain. The force of the waters was such that in a very short time they were carried fifty leagues away from their companions. They were next caught in a counter-current, and before them stretched a vast extent of sea, running contrary to the waves coming from the west; so that it seemed as though two great rivers were flowing in opposite directions and coming into conflict with one another. The current flowing from the south seemed to resist, as does the first owner of the soil resist enemies who seek to invade his property.

Along the horizon directly in front of them the Spaniards beheld the land, but neither to the right nor the left was anything visible. They drifted about in this terrible whirlpool, and were driven first in one direction and then in another by waves which threatened to engulf them. All hope was lost and doubt prevailed; finally they decided to sail back over the current that had brought them thither. They set all their sails and even used oars, but it was with the greatest difficulty they could master the current; and when they thought they had advanced two leagues, they found that in the course of one night they had been carried back four. With the help of God, they succeeded, but they had lost twenty-two days in the course of this little maritime expedition. Rejoining their companions they recounted what had happened, believing that they had found the extremity of the land of Coluacan, and of the sup-posed continent. They imagined the land sighted in the distance was a part of our continent or was joined to the southern part of the coast of Baccalaos, of which I have spoken at length in these Decades. This point is still doubtful, Most Holy Father; some day it will be explained. Meanwhile I report what has been related to me.

While Alaminos and Francisco de Montejo sought to discover these secrets, the king of that country, called

Muteczuma, sent one of his vassals called Quitalbitor[1] who commanded a fortified town of which we have spoken, bearing a number of valuable presents, some beautifully wrought in gold and silver with precious stones. It was decided to send them to our sovereign. The project was also formed, but without consulting Diego Velasquez, the governor of Cuba, of founding a colony. The opinions on this point were divided, some believing that they had not the right to proceed thus, while others,—and they were the majority,—seduced by the artifices of Cortes, held the contrary view. It is in this connection that many stories circulated about the disloyalty of Cortes,—a thing to be discussed at length later on. The decision reached was that no heed would be paid to the governor, and that the matter would be referred to a higher tribunal, that is to say, the King. The Spaniards applied to the cacique Quitalbitor for food. The site chosen for the colony was in the midst of a fertile tract twelve leagues distant from that place, and the commander Cortes, was elected governor.

Cortes likewise appointed officials for the colony about to be founded.[2] Portocarrero and Montejo, about whom enough has been already said above, were chosen to carry the gifts to our King, the Emperor, with the pilot Alaminos to accompany them. Four great leaders and two women, who, according to the national usage, were assigned for their service, accompanied them. These natives are of a brownish colour. Both sexes pierce the ears and wear

---

[1] The messengers of Montezuma were Teuthlili, governor of Cuetlaxtla, and Quitlalpitoc who had discharged a similar mission to Grijalva. Consult Las Casas, *Historia de las Indias*, tom. iii., p. 119; Torquemada, *Monarchia Indiana*, tom. iv., cap. xvii.; Orozco y Berra, *Conquista de Mexico*, tom. iv., p. 139; MacNutt, *Fernando Cortes*, cap. iii.

[2] Read in this connection the letter of the magistrates of Vera Cruz, included under the title of First Letter in the *Cartas de Relacion;* MacNutt, *Letters of Cortes;* Prescott's *Conquest of Mexico*, tom. i., cap. v.; Orozco y Berra, *Conquista de Mexico*, tom. iv.

golden pendants in them, and the men pierce the extremity of the under lip, down to the roots of the lower teeth. Just as we wear precious stones mounted in gold upon our fingers, so do they insert pieces of gold the size of a ring into their lips. This piece of gold is as large as a silver *Carolus*,[1] and thick as a finger. I cannot remember ever to have seen anything more hideous; but they think that nothing more elegant exists under the lunar circle. This example proves the blindness and the foolishness of the human race: it likewise proves how we deceive ourselves. The Ethiopian thinks that black is a more beautiful colour than white, while the white man thinks the opposite. A bald man thinks himself more handsome than a hairy one, and a man with a beard laughs at him who is without one. We are influenced by passions rather than guided by reason, and the human race accepts these foolish notions, each country following its own fancy. In deference to another's opinion, we prefer foolish things, while we reject solid and certain ones.

It is already known whence the natives obtain their gold; but the Spaniards were amazed to learn the whereabouts of their silver, which comes from lofty mountains. The summits of these mountains are covered with perpetual snow, and are only perceptible at certain periods of the year because of dense clouds and fogs. It appears therefore, that the plains and lower mountains produce gold, while silver is found in the rugged mountains and their colder valleys. So it is also with copper, of which war-hatchets and hoes for digging the ground are made, but neither iron nor steel. Let us now examine the gifts sent to the King, and we will begin with the books.[2]

[1] A Flemish coin of the period.

[2] A list of the various articles of value taken to Spain by Portocarrero and Montejo may be found in the first volume of *Letters of Cortes*, at the end of the first letter; also in Gomara, *Cronica*, pp. 321–323.

BOOK VIII

W E have already stated that these natives possess books. The messengers sent from the new country of Colhuacan brought a number of these books amongst other presents. The pages on which the natives write are made of the thin bark of trees, of the quality found in the first, outer layer.[1] It may be compared to those scales, found, not precisely in the willow or the elm, but rather in the edible palm-leaves, in which tough filaments cross one another in the upper layer, just as in nets the openings and narrow meshes alternate. These membranes are smeared with a tough bitumen, after which they are limbered and given the desired form; they are stretched out at will and when they are hardened, a kind of plaster or analogous substance is spread over them. I know Your Holiness has handled some of these tablets, on which sifted plaster similar to flour was sprinkled. One may write thereon whatever comes into one's mind, a sponge or a cloth sufficing to rub it out, after which the tablet may be again used. The natives also used fig leaves for making small books, which the stewards of important households take with them when they go to market. They write down their purchases with a little point, and afterwards erase them when they have been entered in their books. They do

[1] The fibrous leaves of the maguey were used for making writing tablets. See Humboldt's, *Vie des Cordillières*, p. 53; Prescott, Orozco y Berra, Clavigero, Bustamante, and other writers on ancient Mexican civilisation, describe the paper used and the manner of its preparation.

not fold the leaves into four but extend them to a length of
several cubits: they are square-shaped. The bitumen
which holds them together is so tough and flexible that,
when bound in a wooden cover, they appear to have been
put together by the hand of a skilled binder. When the
book is wide open, both pages covered with characters
are visible, and these first two pages conceal two others,
unless they are pulled out to their whole length; for although there is one single leaf, many such leaves are
fastened together. The characters are entirely different
from ours, and are in the forms of dice, dots, stars, lines,
and other similar signs, marked and traced as we do our
letters. They almost resemble the hieroglyphics of the
ancient Egyptians. Among the figures may be distinguished those of men and animals, especially those of
kings or great lords. Thus it is permissible to assume
that they report the deeds of each king's ancestors.
And do we not in our own times see engravers of general
histories or fabulous stories draw pictures of what is told
in the books, in order to entice those who see them to buy
the volume? The natives are also very clever in manu-
facturing wooden covers for the leaves of these books.
When these books are closed, they seem to differ in no
respect from our own. It is supposed that the natives
preserve in these books their laws, the ritual of their sacrifices and ceremonies, astronomical observations, and the
precepts of agriculture.[1]

[1] Unfortunately for American history there seems to have been no one
amongst the band of Cortes who perceived the importance of preserving
these records. Many of the first missionaries who followed in the wake of
the conquerors regarded the systematic destruction of everything calculated to perpetuate the heathen belief and practice they were bent upon
obliterating, as essential to their success. Posterity has deplored their in-
discriminating zeal. Just what loss history has suffered by the destruction of books and records decreed by the Bishops, Fray Juan Zumarraga
in Mexico and Fray Diego Landa in Yucatan, is problematical. It seems
certain that the Mexicans knew surprisingly little about the origin and
early history of their tribes; there was no one in Yucatan when the Spaniards

They begin the year with the setting of the Pleiades, and close it with the lunar months. To each month they give the name of a moon, so that in counting by months they count by moons. In their language the moon is called *Tona*. Days are counted by suns, so many suns being so many days. The sun in their language is called *Tonaticus*. Whether for some unknown reason or for no reason whatever, they divide the year into twenty months of twenty days each.[1]

The temples in which they assemble are vast, and are decorated with tapestries embroidered in gold, and furnishings decorated with precious stones. Each morning at sunrise, they burn perfumes in these temples and offer their prayers in the presence of the Creator. A most execrable crime of which all the inhabitants are guilty is the sacrifice of boys and girls as victims, in the manner I have above described. In sowing time and when the grain begins to bud, the people offer sacrifices to their idols, and if youths are not forthcoming as victims, slaves, who have been carefully fattened and are dressed in rich clothing, are chosen. All the victims destined for sacrifice are circumcised, and this operation is performed during twenty days of the year. When the destined victims pass through a town the inhabitants salute them, with great respect, as being destined soon

conquered that peninsula, able to decipher the hieroglyphics carved on the temples and monuments. While we cannot measure the blame due to the destroyers, we can and should recognise our debt to men like Sahagun, Torquemada, Motolinia, Acosta, and others, all members of religious orders, to whose painstaking labours we owe the preservation of such records of ancient Mexican civilisation as the world possesses. Within a few years after the conquest there was hardly any one who could decipher the native records or interpret the picture-writings; Ixtlilxochitl states that in his time there existed but two very old men able so to do.

[1] Brasseur de Bourbourg's, *Nations civilisées de l'Amérique*, tom. iii., explains the Mexican calendar. Clavigero, Prescott, and Mrs. Nuttall in her *Old and New World Civilisations* have lucidly treated this interesting subject.

to have a place in heaven. Another singular fashion they have for honouring their idols is to offer their own blood, which they draw from the tongue, lips, ears, breast, hips, or the legs. In doing this, they first use a sharp razor and, collecting the blood in their hands, they cast it heavenwards and sprinkle the floor of the temple. By so doing they hope to win the favour of the gods.

Twelve miles west of the new colony of Villarica stands a native town composed of five thousand houses. Its former name was Cempoal, and its present name is Nueva Sevilla. Five slaves whom the cacique was keeping to be sacrificed were liberated by the Spaniards, but the cacique begged them to return them to him, saying: "You will ruin me and all this kingdom if you rob me of those slaves who are destined for sacrifice. Our angered gods will send locusts to devour our harvests, hail to wreck them, drought to burn them, and torrential rain to swamp them, if we offer them no more sacrifices."

Fearing that the inhabitants of Cempoal might desert them, the Spaniards thought it better to assent to a lesser evil in the present than to risk a greater in the future, and convinced likewise that the time had not yet come for suppressing the ancient rites, they gave up the slaves, hoping that the priests would promise them eternal glory and undivided joy, as well as the society of the gods, when they were once delivered from the miseries of this life. The slaves, however, listened with chagrin to these promises, preferring liberty to immolation.

The bones of their enemies captured in war are cleaned of their flesh and tied in bundles, to be suspended at the feet of their idols as battle-trophies, and to them are attached the names and titles of the victors. Another custom, of which Your Holiness will learn with pleasure, is that boys one year old, and girls, are led with pious ceremonies to the temples where the priests take water from a small cup and sprinkle it upon their heads in the form of a cross, as though baptising them. Nothing is known as to the words they use, but the celebration of the rite may be seen and the words heard. Differing from the Jews and Mussulmans, the natives do not consider their temples profaned by the presence of strangers at their ceremonies. I have spoken enough concerning their temples, their religious rites, and their books; let us now examine the other gifts presented to the King.

BOOK IX

THE Spaniards have brought back two hand-mills,[1] one made of gold and the other of silver. They are massive and their circumference is about twenty-eight palms. The golden mill weighs 3800 castellanos, a castellano being a golden coin which is worth one-third more than a ducat. In the centre is the image of a man, a cubit high, resembling a king seated upon his throne, the figure being draped to the knees; it is like a zemes; that is to say it has the features we ascribe to nocturnal goblins. The bottom of the mill is decorated with branches, flowers, and leaves. The silver mill resembles the gold one, and their weight is almost identical; both mills are pure, without any alloy. Besides these, there are some shapeless grains of gold, not smelted, so as to show what the native gold is. They are the size of lentils or peas. There are two golden necklaces, one of which is composed of eight small chains set with thirty-two red stones, which however, are, not rubies, and one hundred and twenty-three green stones. The natives value these last as much as we do emeralds.[2] Twenty-seven golden bells surrounded by four figures set in jewels of wrought gold hang from the collar. From each of these bells hangs a golden pendant. The second collar is formed by four circles of little golden chains, ornamented with two hundred red stones and one

---

[1] These objects were far from being *mills* of any kind. Consult Bernal Diaz, *Hist. Verdad.*, i., 39.

[2] Chalchihuites, commonly mistaken by the Spaniards for emeralds.

45

hundred and seventy-two green stones; ten large precious stones set in gold, from which are suspended one hundred and fifty admirably wrought pendants, hang from this collar.   There are twelve pairs of leather buskins of different colours, decorated with gold and silver and precious stones of both the blue and green varieties. Little golden bells are attached to each of these buskins. There are tiaras and mitres, spangled with stones chiefly resembling sapphires.

I am at a loss to describe the aigrettes, the plumes, and the feather fans.   If ever artists of this kind of work have touched genius, then surely these natives are they. It is not so much the gold or the precious stones I admire, as the cleverness of the artist and the workmanship, which much exceed the value of the material and excite my amazement.   I have examined a thousand figures which it is impossible to describe.   In my opinion I have never seen anything, which for beauty could more delight the human eye.   Many of their brilliantly plumaged birds belong to unknown species.   Just as these natives would admire the tails of our peacocks and pheasants, if they could see them, so are we delighted on beholding the feathers of which they make their fans and head-dresses, giving to their work a note of a very special elegance. These feathers are of bluish tints, greens, yellows, whites, and even browns.

Gold enters into the composition of all their manufac-tured objects.   I have seen two helmets brought from there, both entirely covered with blue stones; one of these helmets edged with golden bells, and covered with scales of gold, each supporting two golden bells; the other helmet decorated with the same stones, and twenty-five little golden bells.   Upon its crest is a green bird, whose comb, feet, beak, and eyes are of gold.   Each little bell is attached to a golden ingot, and has a three-pointed fork terminating in plumes of various colours, and whose points are of precious stones attached by golden wires. There is also a large sceptre decorated with jewels, two golden rings, and an arm-band; deer-skin sandals, sewn with golden thread and having white soles; a mirror made of brilliant stone, of the same bluish colour, surrounded with white gold. Let us finally note a transparent stone shaped in the form of a sphinx, a lizard wound round with gold, two large shells, two golden ducks, and numerous other birds,—two made of gold; four fish and a staff of copper, not to mention the feathers which commonly serve as ornaments; small shields and bucklers, twenty-four breast cuirasses of gold, and five of silver. There is another shield made of leather, ornamented with various coloured feathers and having in its centre a disk of wrought gold representing a zemes. Four other blades of gold surround this in the form of a cross, on which are represented different animals, such as lions, tigers, and wolves; hides of animals stuffed with twigs and wooden splints, over which the skin of the beast is stretched, ornamented with copper bells.

What shall be said of the carefully tanned hides of other animals? There are also large cotton cloths dyed with black, white, and yellow checks, which proves they are acquainted with the game of checkers. One of these cloths is black on one side, and red and white on the other; another such cloth is dyed in different colours. It has in its centre a black wheel surrounded by rays, and is decorated with brilliant feathers. I must still mention two other white draperies, bed-covers, tapestries, mantles such as the natives wear, shirts, and different very light head-dresses. There is a number of objects to examine which are pleasing rather than precious, but as I fear the enumeration of these things may tire rather than divert Your Holiness, I pass them over in silence, as I likewise do the different incidents of the voyages,

the labours, the miseries, the dangers, the wonderful
achievements, and all the misfortunes which each of our
navigators has noted down in his log-book, and which have
later been brought to our knowledge in our Royal India
Council. Nevertheless, here are some particulars that
I have chosen amongst the rest, and for which I am
indebted to private correspondence.

The Spaniards who brought the gifts, and the captain,
Fernando Cortes, who had formed the project of establish-
ing a colony in those distant countries, were accused
before the Royal India Council of having acted contrary
to law and justice, in that they had not consulted the
governor of Cuba, who had commissioned them by virtue
of the powers he held from the King; and of having acted
contrary to their instructions, and of having referred to
the King without first offering their obedience to him.
Thus the governor, Diego Velasquez, described them
through his representatives, as fugitives, thieves, and
traitors. The accused alleged in reply that they had
displayed a spirit of obedience in referring to the superior
justice of the King; moreover, that they had fitted out
the fleet at their own expense, the governor of Cuba
having given them nothing more than would a merchant
selling his goods, and that, moreover, he had sold his
merchandise too dear. Velasquez asked the death
penalty for them, while they hoped on the contrary to be
rewarded for the fatigues and dangers they had undergone.
Both punishment and reward are postponed, until both
parties shall be heard. Such is the decision.

Let us now return to the colonists of Darien, along the
gulf of Uraba on the supposed continent. We have said
that the Darien is a river emptying into the gulf on the
west coast. The Spaniards founded a colony on the banks
of this river, after having expelled the cacique by force
of arms. In fulfilment of a vow made in the midst of
battle, they gave to this colony the name of Santa Maria

de la Antigua. We have related at the close of our Decades that the same year we stopped writing, twelve hundred soldiers had been sent to Darien under the command of Pedro Arias d'Avila; this was done in response to the solicitation of Vasco Nuñez Balboa, the first discoverer of the unknown South Sea, and the first chief of Darien. Scarcely had he landed at Darien, and assumed the most extensive powers, than Pedro Arias sent several captains in command of troops in various directions.

I shall recount what happened to them in a few words, for the story is not pleasing; in fact it is quite the contrary. From the moment when we suspended our report, there has been nothing done but killing and being killed, massacring and being massacred. Balboa had been long ago named Adelantado by the Catholic King, and he could not long endure the official superiority of Pedro Arias. They became enemies and threw everything into confusion. The bishop, Juan Quevedo, who is a Franciscan monk, sought to intervene. Although Pedro Arias promised to give his daughter in marriage to Balboa, the rival leaders could not come to an understanding. Their hostility became bitterer, and finally assumed such a character that Pedro Arias profited by the first excuse furnished him by Balboa, to cite the latter before the judges. He condemned him and five other leaders to be strangled. Pedro Arias accused Balboa and his companions of wishing to desert and proceed to the South Sea, where he had built a squadron of four brigantines for exploring the southern coasts of the land supposed to be a continent. Vasco Nuñez was believed to have spoken to his three hundred companions as follows: "My brave men, you have shared my labours and my dangers; I ask, do you wish to serve under another leader? Who can endure the insolence of this governor? Let us follow these shores which chance has revealed to us, and among the Elysian provinces of this vast land, let us choose one where we may live the remainder of our lives in freedom. Who would be able to find us, or if we were found, who could attack us?" These words were repeated to the governor. Pedro Arias recalled Vasco from the South Sea, and the latter, obeying, was put into irons. He denied the plot of which he was accused. Witnesses to prove the alleged crime were everywhere sought, and from the very first day, everything he said was turned to incriminate him. He was condemned to death and executed; and this was the outcome of the labours and dangers he had endured at the very moment when he believed himself to be on the eve of winning new titles to glory.[1]

Leaving his wife at Darien, Pedro Arias sailed with Vasco's little squadron to explore the new countries. We do not yet know if he has returned successful. Lopez Sosa, who was for a long time viceroy of the Canary Islands, has been already named to replace him as governor of Darien. The rage of Pedro Arias when he gets back may be imagined beforehand; he has accomplished no really glorious deed, and he is accused of having been too easy from the beginning and lacking in severity in punishing disorders. But we have said enough on this subject; let us return to some matters we have omitted.

[1] For full information concerning the trial and execution of Balboa, consult Gaffarel's *Vasco Nuñez de Balboa.*

BOOK X

I HAVE already spoken at length of the great and deep Dabaiba River which the Spaniards have named Rio Grande, and which flows into the sea at the head of the gulf of Uraba, by seven mouths similar to those of the Nile. According to the statements of the natives, the mountains round about it are rich in gold deposits. Vasco and other captains had organised parties for the exploration of this region and had embarked in boats of different sizes to ascend the river. For a distance of forty, fifty, and even eighty leagues they sailed without difficulty, but from thenceforward their fortune entirely changed. Oh, what a wonderful adventure! In fact, naked and unarmed savages attacked the clothed and armed Spaniards, and defeated them, killing the majority and wounding all the rest. These natives use poisoned arrows in fighting. The instant they see an uncovered part of an enemy's body, they pierce it with an infallible aim. They throw such volleys of javelins in the midst of the battle that the sun is obscured from the enemy's sight, as though by a cloud. They also have heavy swords of hard wood, which they use with courage in hand-to-hand engagements. Vasco himself was covered with wounds inflicted by them, and thus the river and region of Dabaiba were abandoned and left unexplored.

A few words more concerning Hispaniola, the metropolis of the other colonies. The Royal Government Council has been increased, five new judges having been sent to administer the different districts of the island. Although there are rich gold deposits, mining has been almost abandoned for want of miners; for the natives, on whose labour the work depended, have been reduced to a very small number. Pitiless wars destroyed many at the beginning, famine killed numerous others, especially during the year when they tore up their yucca, from which they make their caciques' bread, and refused to sow maize which serves for their own daily bread. The survivors have been attacked by the germs of hitherto unknown maladies, especially smallpox which, during the preceding year, 1518, raged among them like an epizoötic among cattle. Let us be strictly truthful, and add that the craze for gold was the cause of their destruction; for these people, who were accustomed, as soon as they had sown their fields, to play, dance, sing, and chase rabbits, were set mercilessly to work, cultivating the ground, extracting and sifting gold. The Royal Council has, therefore, unanimously decided to restore them their liberty, and henceforth they will only occupy themselves with agriculture, and will make efforts to repeople the country. Slaves bought in other countries will be put to the hard work of mines. Enough for the present concerning this fatal craving for gold.

It is wonderful to hear how everything grows in this island. Twenty-eight presses have just been set up, by which a large quantity of sugar is extracted. The sugar-canes in this island are larger and taller than anywhere else. They are as thick as a human arm, and are half again as tall as a man. The most extraordinary thing is that at Valencia in Spain, where large quantities of sugar have been gathered yearly for a long time, or in other sugar-cane producing countries, each root throws off five, six, or at most seven shoots, whereas in Hispaniola twenty or sometimes even thirty may be counted.

There are immense numbers of quadrupeds. Up to

the present time the deplorable craving for gold has diverted the people's attention from the soil, although cereals give such excellent results.   Any one who takes the trouble to sow grain on the hillsides or the mountain plateaus, especially if they have a northerly aspect, may sometimes harvest a hundred grains for one; but in the plains and fields where the soil is rich and damp, it is chiefly straw that grows.   Vines prosper under the same conditions.

I have already spoken in my preceding Decades of the cinnamon trees, which come from the islands near the supposed continent.   I need only add that, within the period of a few years they have become so abundant that we now buy a pound of cinnamon from the druggist instead of an ounce.   I have also said enough about the forests of dyewoods, and the other sources of wealth in this fortunate island, which nature has overwhelmed with benefits.   I have judged it proper to recall these details, because I hope the recollection of them will divert the mind of Your Holiness from the great affairs which burden it.   Moreover, it is a pleasure to repeat what it is a pleasure to hear.

Precious material should be clothed with precious habiliments.   This subject merits golden tissues and jewels but we are content to vest it in the modest cowl of a monk. The fault belongs exclusively to the Reverend Egidius di Viterbo, the venerable Cardinal of Your Apostolic Chair, who has ordered such a mediocre craftsman as I to melt the gold in my laboratory and therefrom to make jewels.

The Fifth Decade

ADRIANVS · VI · PAPA · TRAIECTENSIS ·
CREATO DEL · 1522 · ALIO · DI · GENARO

227

BOOK I

MOST HOLY FATHER and most gracious Sovereign: I have dedicated the Fourth Decade of my Indian history to the Sovereign Pontiff, Leo X., your most gracious brother and cousin.[1] We have enumerated in that work with great fidelity and absolute integrity the peoples, the islands, the unknown lands discovered in our time in the ocean up to the year 1522, from the Incarnation. Since that epoch other letters have arrived from Fernando Cortes, commander of the Imperial fleet, describing the countries he has brought under Spanish rule.[2] These letters contain new and extraordinary particulars, astonishing from every point of view. In this Fifth Decade of my commentaries I have reported these particulars with as much precision and

[1] Although dedicated to Adrian VI., this Decade is addressed to his successor, Clement VII., a natural and posthumous son of Giuliano de' Medici, who had been legitimised by his cousin, Leo X.

[2] The letters of Cortes to Charles V., known as *Cartas de la Relacion*, contain the earliest description of Mexican civilisation under Montezuma, when the country was first seen by Europeans. Including the letter of the magistrates of Vera Cruz, these letters number five. The following are the editions in different languages of the entire series: Enrique de Vedia in Ribadeneyra's *Biblioteca de Autores Classicas*, 1852; Pascual Gayangos, *Cartas de Hernan Cortes al Emperador Carlos V.*; Désiré Charnay, *Lettres de Fernan Cortes à Charles Quint*, 1896; Francis MacNutt, *Letters of Cortes to Charles V.*, 1908.

57

fidelity as I could, carefully observing the chronological order of events. I have dedicated this work to the Sovereign Pontiff Adrian, your predecessor, who died before receiving it. You have inherited his dignity, and you shall likewise inherit my labours, and receive henceforth all I shall write worthy to be preserved in history. It is therefore under your most gracious patronage that I place my work, and I desire that it should appear under such favourable auspices in order that all human beings may know how widely the Christian name has extended since you govern the Catholic world. I hope and desire that the most good and great God may recompense your piety and clemency by the unlimited extension of that name. May you continue as you have begun, to assure perpetual peace amongst Christian princes, especially the Emperor and the Most Christian Kings at variance with him, and to unfurl above heretics the standard of faith which brings salvation, and to transmit to posterity an eternal monument of your glory, which no age may ever forget.

Let us return to our subject. At the close of the preceding book we have mentioned the all-powerful King Muteczuma, who from his capital, Temistitan, situated in a salt lake, imposed laws upon a number of towns and vassal kings. Cortes had sent two Spaniards, Montejo and Portocarrero, to the Emperor Charles, resident at that time in the most celebrated town of Spain, Valladolid, to whom they bore gifts as remarkable for their value as for their beauty. I have enumerated them above. Pending the return of his envoys, Cortes, fearing that idleness would demoralise his soldiers, resolved to continue the expedition he had begun. After securing the large city called Potenchan, governed by the cacique Tabasco, as we have related in the preceding book of the Decades, and afterwards named Victoria in honour of the victory won over a multitude of barbarians,

Cortes sailed forty-eight leagues in a westerly direction
and founded a colony on the shore, one league distant
from another native city, Cempoal, in the neighbourhood
of the Rio Grijalva and half a league distant from a small
fortress crowning a lofty hill called Chianistam. He
named his colony Vera Cruz, since he had landed there in
the month of May, on the Feast of the Cross.[1] Cortes
next decided to learn something about the great King
Muteczuma, of whose power he had heard so much,
and of his capital, which was reported to him as being so
important. Upon learning his plans, the people of Cempoal, the neighbours and vassals of Muteczuma but likewise his mortal enemies, resolved to seek a conference
with the Spanish commander. Just as the Eduins and
the Sequanis came weeping to implore Cæsar to deliver
them from the horrid tyranny of Ariovistus King of the
Germans, so did the Cempoalans come to make complaint
of Muteczuma. Their complaints were all the more
serious, because, without mentioning the other heavy
tributes paid by them, they were also obliged to supply
slaves, or failing them their own children, to be sacrificed
to the gods of the emperor. We have already remarked,
and Your Beatitude is not ignorant of the fact, that in
these countries human sacrifices are offered; we will later
return to this subject at greater length.

The Cempoalans promised to give Cortes not only hostages as a guarantee for their loyalty, but also auxiliary
warriors to march against their tyrant. Their hope was
that, helped by such a powerful God, creator of heaven
and earth, such as the Spaniards described theirs to be,
and who had permitted them to destroy their former
idols, they would deliver their town from the bloody
tyranny which oppressed them; and if Cortes would

[1] The landing took place on April 21st, which was Good Friday, hence
the name Vera Cruz, referring to the ceremony of the adoration of the
Cross performed throughout Christendom on that day.

only have pity on their unmerited misfortunes and protect them against the ill-treatment they suffered, they might perhaps win for the entire province freedom, the source of so much good. Nor did they doubt about victory, for they believed that Cortes and his companions were sent from heaven, since they showed themselves gracious to the conquered and formidable to those who repulsed their friendship. They had beheld a small handful of men dare to withstand the warriors of Potenchan. On that day the Spaniards had put to flight forty thousand soldiers, as Your Holiness may perceive from the reports of eyewitnesses and by the letters sent by the chief officers; and they were not more than four hundred foot-soldiers with sixteen horses and a few cannon.

It seems opportune to say a few words on the type of people whose suspicious minds treat everything their judgment finds beyond their powers, as a fable. Such people will make gestures of incredulity when they learn that thousands of foes have been scattered by a handful of soldiers. Let us cite two examples, one taken from ancient and one from modern events, which may serve to cut short their pleasantries. Have they not read that Cæsar, with an inferior number of troops, conquered the Helvetians and afterwards Ariovistus, with his innumerable hordes of Germans? Do they not know that Xerxes, King of the Persians, is said to have invaded Greece with such a multitude of warriors that when his soldiers, after building their camp, prepared their food, they dried up a river from which they drank, and nevertheless that Themistocles, at the head of only twelve thousand men, so signally defeated them at Salamis that the emperor was barely able to escape with one sole boat? What most helped the Spaniards in our battles with these barbarians were two methods of fighting the latter had never seen or heard of, the mere sight of which put them to flight: in the first place the noise of the cannon, together with the flames and sulphurous odours they belched forth. They believed that our people commanded the thunder and lightning from heaven. In the second place they were almost as much frightened by the horses, for they thought that both man and horse formed but one animal, as is fabulously recounted of the centaurs. Moreover the Spaniards were not always victorious; for they even suffered losses. The barbarians exterminated some of their bands, whom they would not receive as guests; but let us resume the course of the story we abandoned.

When the Cempoalans had pronounced their speech it was translated by Geronimo d'Aguilar, the victim of the wreck, who had for seven years been the slave of a cacique, and of whom I spoke at length in a preceding book of my Decades. Cortes then left Vera Cruz leaving there as garrison one hundred and fifty soldiers, and taking with him fifteen horsemen, three hundred foot-soldiers, and four hundred Cempoalan allies. Before starting he ordered all the ships of the expedition to be sunk, giving as a reason that they were unseaworthy.[1] He himself declares that he adopted this measure to cut his men off from all hope of retreat, because he wished to found a permanent colony in that country. The majority of his soldiers do not appear to have shared these views. They feared they would meet the same fate that had overtaken many of their companions who had been massacred by the barbarians, for they were not numerous and would have to face an infinite number of warlike and well-armed enemies.

Furthermore, the greater part of them were friends and adherents of Diego Velasquez, vice-governor of the island

---

[1] Several versions of the destruction of the ships exist. That of Cortes will be found in the second of his letters to Charles V. Bernal Diaz in his *Historia Verdadera* gives a somewhat different account. Both Las Casas and Gomara wrote from hearsay, as did Peter Martyr himself. Consult Orozco y Berra, *Conquista de Mexico*, tom. iv., cap. viii.; Alaman, *Disertacione* ii.; Prescott's, *Conquest of Mexico*, tom. i., cap. viii.; MacNutt's *Fernando Cortes*, cap. iv.

of Fernandina or Cuba, and they wished at the conclusion of their expedition to resume service under their former master. Several of them tried to capture a brigantine and rejoin Velasquez. This happened just as Cortes was sending a ship to Spain loaded with gifts for the Emperor. These men wished to warn Velasquez of the secret departure of this ship, so that he might keep watch and seize it. Cortes had four of them arrested and sentenced for treason. The four were Juan Escudero, Iago Zermegno, Gonzales Umbria, and Alfonzo Peñates, the first three being sailors. Having cut off all possibility of return by the destruction of the fleet and this quadruple execution,[1] Cortes left on the sixteenth of August, 1519, for the great city built in a lake and called Temistitan, which is situated about a hundred leagues west of Vera Cruz. Three of the principal chiefs of Cempoal, called Truchios, Manexos, and Tamaius accompanied them.[2] The town of Cempoal and a neighbouring town called Zacacami supplied him with thirteen hundred men who carried the baggage. It is the custom of the country for men to act as beasts of burden. I must now report what happened to Cortes during the journey, for these interesting particulars must not be omitted.

Just as he was about to set out, Cortes was informed that a squadron under an unknown commander was sailing along the coast. He understood that it was under the command of Francisco de Garay, viceroy of the island of Jamaica, who had set out to found a new colony. Cortes sent him messengers, offering him the hospitality of his colony of Vera Cruz and, any assistance he might require. One of these days we may learn whether, in proceeding thus, he was sincere. Garay rejected his

---

[1] Two of the men, Escudero and Zermegno were hanged, Umbria's feet were cut off, and Pegnates got two hundred lashes; the chaplain, Juan Diaz was protected from punishment by his clerical character.

[2] The names of these chieftains were Teuch, Mamexi, and Tamalli.

proposals and even protested through the intermediary of a royal notary and witnesses. He demanded that the limits of his jurisdiction should be defined. Cortes refused. He likewise stripped the notary and the witnesses sent by Garay, taking from them their old uniforms and giving them new ones. Garay did not push the matter farther, but departed, intending to discover other countries along the same coast. The preceding year, with three caravels, he had left the island of Jamaica of which he was governor, and had explored the coasts of the country Juan Ponce had taken for an island and named Florida; I have spoken of this in my preceding Decades.

Garay had not been fortunate in his explorations, for he had twice been defeated by the natives, and a number of his companions had been killed. Juan Ponce, the first discoverer of Florida, had shared the same fate; repeatedly defeated by the natives, he suffered from so many wounds that he had hardly returned to Cuba to care for himself and his men, when he died.

After the death of Juan Ponce, Garay explored the same countries. He declared that Florida was not an island but was joined by a continuous coast line to the land of Temistitan. During his voyage he came to a river emptying into the ocean by an immense estuary, and he beheld from his ships numerous farms covered with cabins. Both banks of that river belonged to a cacique called Panuco, from whom the region likewise takes its name. It is said that he is a vassal of the great King Muteczuma, to whom he pays tribute. Garay failed to obtain authorisation to establish trading relations.

We know this from a painted map he brought back. This map represents a bow; starting from Temistitan the line is traced towards the north as far as the bend of the arch; then inclining slightly towards the south in such wise that if it were prolonged to the extreme point of the land north of the island of Fernandina, first explored by Juan Ponce, it would correspond to the string of the bow. Garay thinks these regions not worth exploring, for there is little gold there, and what there is, is of poor quality. He wished to establish a colony not far from the one founded by Cortes, under the name of Vera Cruz, but the latter opposed this. He even founded one on the site chosen by Garay, and called it Almeria, after the port of that name in the kingdom of Granada, captured from the Moors a few years ago after a brilliant engagement.

When affairs were in order, Cortes, after taking counsel, resumed his course. Four days' march from Cempoal he entered a province called Sincuchinalara.[1] There is only one fortified town in this country, and it is built upon the slope of a small mountain, both art and nature contributing to its defence. There is but one path by which it is reached, and this consists of two removable ladders, very difficult to climb. It is the residence of the cacique of that province, who is a vassal of Muteczuma. There are numerous villages and a number of farms in the valley, each group being composed of three or four hundred houses, all resembling country houses. Upon the approach of danger the nobles would take refuge with the cacique. The latter received the Spaniards kindly in his fortress, and extended generous hospitality, saying that he was authorised by Muteczuma to accord them this reception. Cortes informed him that he would report this to Muteczuma and would thank him, for in conformity with orders he had received, he proposed to visit the sovereign.

After leaving this cacique, Cortes approached a very lofty mountain, which marked the limits of the province. He says that he never saw a higher mountain in Spain, and those who returned from that country confirmed

[1] The name of the town and province was Xicochimilco, the former being identified with probability as the present town of Naulinco.

this report.[1] When his men crossed it, although it was
the month of August, they suffered extreme cold, in
consequence of the frozen snows and the perpetual ice.
On the other slope of the mountain lies a plain of which
the capital is Texunaco. The country is very fertile,
and there are villages and cultivated fields. All the
inhabitants are subject to Muteczuma. After leaving
this valley, the Spaniards marched two days through a
country which the absence of water rendered arid and
unhabited. The men suffered from cold and hunger.
These privations and a sudden thunderstorm, accompanied
by lightning, killed several of them. They next ascended
a less rugged mountain, upon whose summit stood a temple
consecrated to the idols. Before the doors of this temple
an enormous quantity of wood was piled up; for at certain
times of the year the inhabitants offer these piles of wood,
together with victims, to the gods thinking thereby to
appease their wrath.

The Spaniards commonly call mountain passes *puertas*,
so they gave to this pass the name of Puerta de la Leña.
Descending this mountain they found another fertile
and inhabited valley, whose cacique was called Cacatamino.[2]
His residence is built of stones, and is large, divided as
are our houses into courts and sleeping chambers. It
stands on the shady banks of a stream which flows
through the valley. Cacatamino received the Spaniards
cordially. When asked if he was a vassal of Muteczuma
he replied, "And who is not, since Muteczuma is master
of the universe?" Nevertheless when asked what he
thought of our sovereign, he admitted that he must be
still more powerful since Muteczuma himself obeyed him.
They asked if he had gold, and he said he had, but would

[1] The march was through the pass now called *Paso del Obispo.*

[2] The cacique's name was Olintetl; he was an enormously fat man who
shook like a jelly when he walked; the Spaniards promptly nicknamed him
the "trembler." The name of the valley was Caltanmic and that of its
principal town, Xocotla.

give it to no one without Muteczuma's authorisation. The Spaniards did not venture to use force, for they feared to awaken Muteczuma's apprehensions.

The neighbouring caciques, who heard of his arrival, came to visit Cortes, each bringing him a golden necklace of light weight and impure metal. One of these caciques lived four leagues up, and the other two leagues down the river. Both banks of this stream are bordered with houses, separated from one another by gardens and cultivated lands. The palace of the cacique who lived up the river, is less remarkable for its beauty and grandeur than for its strength. In front of the building stands a citadel which protects the forward bastions and the embattled walls, rendering them impregnable. The town (of which the name is not given[1]) contains between five and six thousand houses. This cacique, who is also a vassal of Muteczuma, received the Spaniards with great honour.

While enjoying the hospitality of this cacique, Cortes had sent envoys to the town of Tascalteca.[2] These envoys were commissioned to sound the feeling of the inhabitants, and learn if they wished him to visit them, for he had learned that the Tascaltecans were a warlike people, and the declared enemies of Muteczuma. He remained two days with this cacique, awaiting the return of his messengers. Muteczuma had never been able to conquer the Tascaltecans, for they would never recognise his jurisdiction or obey him. Their young men were taught to nourish a perpetual hatred of Muteczuma, and to such a point that for several years they went without salt or cotton for clothing, because they were surrounded by Muteczuma's vassals and could not elsewhere procure these articles of prime necessity.

[1] Evidently Yxtacamaxtitlan, where Cortes awaited the reply from the Tlaxcalan council.

[2] Meaning Tlascala or Tlaxcala, both spellings being admissible.

They prefer to live free and poor rather than submit to the jurisdiction of Muteczuma. Their city is inhabited by many nobles who have country properties and are the chiefs of the military republic of Tascalteca. These men want no master. If any one were seized with the desire to raise himself above the others, his fellow citizens would inflict upon him a more wretched punishment than that which the Helvetians imposed upon Orgetorix when he dreamed of becoming dictator, and counselled the chief of the Eduins and Sequanis to associate themselves with him. The Tascaltecans are just, and love justice, as the Spaniards afterwards learned. I shall later tell about this.

Cortes awaited the return of his messengers, but as none of them appeared, he left the residence of the cacique and marched during a week through the valley visiting its towns. It was then that the Cempoalans urged him to win the friendship of the republic of the Tascaltecans, for their friendship might afford valuable help against Muteczuma in case he should undertake any enterprise against him. Cortes therefore marched towards the Republic, and on the way he passed through another valley, across which stood a wall extending from one mountain range to the other. This wall was twenty feet broad and half again as high as a man. Throughout his entire length there was only one opening, ten paces wide, but built with numerous bends, in such wise that an enemy arriving suddenly, could not surprise the scattered defenders. This wall marked the frontier of Tascalteca, and it had been constructed to block the passage of Muteczuma's soldiers through this valley.

The natives of the last valleys who escorted and guided Cortes urged him not to cross the territory of the Tascaltecans, assuring them that the latter were traitors, who never kept their word. They detest all strangers and devour their guests, whenever they have any, as well as their enemies. They offered to lead him through countries

belonging uninterruptedly to Muteczuma, and where, by
that sovereign's orders, the Spaniards would find everything
they desired.   The Cempoalan chiefs Teuchios, Manexios,
Tamaios, and the chiefs of Zacatamina who commanded a
thousand warriors, agreed in advising Cortes in the contrary sense, warning him to place no faith in the subjects
of Muteczuma; if he allowed himself to be guided by them,
they would lead him into traps and through passes already
converted into ambuscades.   They advised him to be on
his guard against the perfidy of Muteczuma's subjects,
and proposed to lead him through the territory of the
Tascaltecans, which he would find open.

Cortes accepted the counsel of the chiefs of Cempoal and
Zacatamina and took the road through the territory of
Tascalteca.

Surrounded by his horsemen, he rode at the head
of the column.   To avoid the possibility of the main
body being surprised, he sent two scouts ahead to reconnoitre the country and to report anything that attracted
their attention.   The two horsemen, riding about two
leagues in advance, perceived from the summit of a lofty
hill some armed men concealed in the plain below.   This
plain belonged to the state of Tascalteca.   As soon as
they saw the horses, the Tascaltecans, frightened by their
unexpected and novel aspect, and convinced that the
men and the horses were one sole animal, took to flight
or at least feigned so to do.   The Spaniards made amicable
signs, calling back the fugitives by gestures, and movements
of their arms.   About fifteen of them stopped, but the
others were placed in ambush.   The two scouts then
urged their comrades to hurry.   A short time afterwards
about four thousand Tascaltecans emerged from their
hiding-places.   They were armed, and attacked the
Spaniards, killing the two horses with arrows in the
twinkling of an eye.   The foot-soldiers advanced to
attack the enemy who, surprised by the arrows and the

musketballs, beat a retreat. Many of them were killed
while the Spaniards, on the contrary, lost nobody neither
killed or wounded. The following day Cortes received
envoys, deputed to negotiate for peace. They brought
with them two of the messengers for whom he had so long
waited. The Tascaltecans asked pardon for the attack,
giving as an excuse that that day they had had with them
foreign soldiers whom they could not control, and that the
attack had taken place in defiance of orders and of their
rulers. They were also ready to pay the value of the
horses and all other damages. Cortes accepted the excuses,
and later moved forward a distance of three miles, establish-
ing his camp on the river bank; he set a night-watch, for
he distrusted the barbarians. At daybreak he went to
a neighbouring farm, where he found the last two of the
messengers he had sent to sound the opinions of the
natives. These messengers had been captured and bound,
but they had managed during the night to break their
bonds. It had been decided to sacrifice them, so they
said.

During this halt, a thousand warriors suddenly appeared,
yelling fiercely and throwing javelins and all sorts of
projectiles at the Spaniards from a distance. Cortes
tried to attract them by amicable means, but it was useless.
He told them through his interpretess to cease their
attack, but the more mildness he displayed, the more
their insolence increased. Finally they retreated, and
the Spaniards pursued, only to find themselves gradually
drawn into an ambuscade where, according to the account of Cortes, more than a hundred thousand warriors
were concealed. Executing a turning movement, the
barbarians surrounded them, and the fight which followed
lasted from morning till evening, and was undecisive.
The people of Cempoal, Zacatamina, Ixtacmastitan, and
the other allies of Cortes, displayed great bravery. In
the first place they were forced to do so, for they were

surrounded by Tascaltecans, with their retreat cut off; their only safety lay in despair, for had they been defeated their bodies would have furnished the banqueting tables of the Tascaltecans; the vanquished being devoured by the victors. The Tascaltecans' mouths had watered when they learned that strangers had invaded their territory, for they had confidence in their own superior numbers, and counted upon banquets. Their expectations were not realised.

Cortes possessed six field-pieces, as many fusiliers, about fifty arqueousiers, and thirteen horsemen; all these engines of war being unknown to the barbarians. He ended by putting a crowd of his enemies to flight. Nevertheless he was disturbed, and passed the whole night without sleep in a rustic chapel consecrated to idols. The next morning at daybreak, he crossed the plain with all his horsemen, a hundred foot-soldiers, and all the allies from Ixtacmastitan. That fortified place had opened its gates to him and had furnished him a contingent of three hundred soldiers against Muteczuma. He had in addition five hundred allies from Cempoal and neighbouring cities. Leaving the remainder of his force to guard the camp and the baggage, he proceeded with the cavalry to scour the plain, burnt five villages, and pillaged every place he entered; upon his return to camp he brought in five hundred prisoners.

At the first glimmer of dawn, the following morning an immense multitude, which seemed to cover the entire country, fell upon the Spanish camp; their number has been estimated at fifty thousand men. A furious battle was fought in the entrenchments, which, it is said, lasted for four hours, and during which our men were exposed to immense dangers. The barbarians drew off, having failed in their undertaking but covering their retreat. They were by no means timid sheep, for every one was as brave as a lion. As soon as the enemy retreated, Cortes marched against the traitors, who were already scattered in their villages. Like a tigress with young he ravaged, destroyed, captured, exterminated everything he encountered, and finally approached the town, estimated to consist of three thousand and more houses. It was put to fire and sword; after which the natives were seized with fright, and their chiefs sent messengers to Cortes, asking pardon for what had happened and promising for the future to obey his orders and to recognise the authority of the king of whom he was the representative.

As a gauge of their intentions they offered him presents which have an honorary value amongst them, such as aigrettes, plumes, and admirably made war harness. They likewise sent him provisions, bread and, as is their custom, a quantity of chickens. We have already repeatedly stated and Your Beatitude is aware, that in this country they fatten birds, which are larger than our peacocks, and as delicate in flavour, just as we do chickens.

BOOK II

A FTER listening to what the messengers said,
Cortes was not chary of his condemnation of
their masters, but nevertheless he declared himself ready to pardon their crimes and admit them to his
friendship, on condition that they should for the future
conduct themselves as faithful subjects of the King of
all the Spains.

The following day fifty nobles appeared before him
unarmed, and under pretext of settling the conditions
of their alliance, studied the approaches to the camp.
Cortes noticed their spying manner and the want of
frankness that characterised them. He suspected that
they had come to study the situation of the camp. Taking
one of these messengers aside, he had him questioned by
a confidential interpreter, urging him to confess the truth.
Flatteries and bribes prevailed, and the messenger revealed
the plot. He declared that Quesitangal,[1] the chief of
the province, was hidden with numerous soldiers, in an
ambuscade, intending to surprise the camp on the following night. Under pretext of treating for peace,
he had sent the messengers to spy out the best place to
attack, or the easiest approach to the huts of boughs
the Spaniards had built as a protection against the night

[1] Xicotencal the younger, son of one of the Regents of Tlaxcala bearing
the same name, was commander-in-chief of the forces of the Republic.
Cortes spelled his name, *Sintegal*, while Bernal de Diaz came nearer
to a correct spelling, writing the name *Xicotenga*.

72

air. Once inside the camp, the barbarians were to fire the cabins, and while our people were busy putting out the flames, they would attack and massacre them. Their chief had declared he would use stratagem and artifice, since, in spite of his men's courage in battle, they had suffered so cruelly.

Desiring to confirm this first information concerning the plot, Cortes took five other messengers aside, either threatening them with his anger or promising them his friendship. All agreed in confirming the statement of the first. Before the news of this investigation became known, Cortes ordered all the fifty messengers to be seized. He cut off the right hand of each, and sent them back to their masters with these instructions: "Tell your chief that it is unworthy of brave soldiers and upright citizens to stoop to such odious stratagems. As for you, vile messengers, who have presented yourselves here as envoys, being our enemies the while, you are punished for your crime, by losing your right hands and may return to those who chose you to perpetrate such villainy. Above all, tell them that we are ready to receive them at any hour. Let them attack us by night or by day, and they will learn the strength of the handful of men whom they seek to destroy." The messengers departed to report what they had seen, and to exhibit their mutilation.

At night a mass of barbarians, divided into two bodies, appeared. Evening was falling, and Cortes judged it wiser to fight while there was still light, as the barbarians would then be frightened by the strange and unaccustomed appearance of the horses as well as by the noise of the cannon. If, on the contrary, he waited till the night, he and his men would be exposed to a thousand dangers incident to a strange country, and would be ignorant of the lay of the land, on which they would have to manœuvre.

And thus it happened that the sight of the horses and

the noise of the cannon frightened the barbarians, who fled through the harvest fields, scattering and seeking to conceal themselves. The harvests were of maize, as we have often said. Cortes was thus left entirely free in his movements. Nevertheless, for several days he did not venture to leave his camp, for he had learned that a league distant from the camp there was a hostile city where an immense crowd assembled in response to a trumpet-call. He has written, and those who have returned from that country agree in stating, that this town of Tascalteca numbers twenty thousand houses. As soon as he was assured by his scouts that the inhabitants of that great city were off their guard and feared no attack, he entered it during the second watch of the night and surprised the inhabitants asleep. He first occupied the strongest part of the city. At daybreak the principal citizens appeared before him, begging him to spare them. They declared themselves willing to obey him, and promised to supply him with an abundance of provisions out of their stores.

After this victory Cortes returned to his camp, where he found his companions discontented with him. They complained that they had been led into a situation from whence they could not possibly escape, and they were unwilling to go any farther.[1] They feared they would be killed to the last man, since they were surrounded by so many ferocious warriors, or would perish of hunger and cold, in case they escaped the arrows of the barbarians. Moreover the result of wars was uncertain and victory did not always depend on the men. They therefore prayed and begged Cortes to return to the coast. If he

---

[1] Cortes reported in his letter to the Emperor that he overheard some of his rebellious followers quoting a proverb in which the sobriquet of Pedro Carbonero was applied to him. *Pierre le charbonnier savait bien où il était, mais il ignorait les moyens d'en sortir.* He suppressed the sedition with one of his characteristic appeals to their Catholic zeal, their Spanish pride, and their cupidity, mingling blandishments with threats and scorn.

were unwilling to do so, they declared they were ready to abandon him.

Now Cortes had resolved to push on to Temistitan, the most important town of all that region. Thinking it better to use prudence and flattery rather than violence to his men, he spoke to them as follows: "What is the matter, my comrades? Why do you have these fears? Is it not evident that God protects us, since we have been successful in every engagement? Do you think that the men whom you will encounter are better or more courageous than yourselves? Do you not understand that it depends upon you to extend indefinitely the Christian religion? Do you not realise that you are about acquiring for yourselves and your sovereign entire kingdoms? What remains to be done is very little, and if by chance (which I do not fear) you fall, what happier end could you have? Would it be possible to end more gloriously one's life? Remember, moreover, that you are Spaniards, and that Spaniards know no fear, and hold their life as nothing in the service of God or the achievement of glory. On the other hand, where shall we go? What shall we do on the coast, where we would languish in idleness? Take courage, my friends, and help me to conquer these nations and bring them under the law of Christ and the obedience of our sovereign. What fame will you bequeath to your posterity in consequence of these great deeds such as no living person has ever accomplished! Upon our return home we shall be honoured by our neighbours as Hercules never was in Greece when he returned from Spain, although the remembrance of those honours lives to our own day. Our achievements will have been greater, and their recompense in proportion. Rouse yourselves, therefore, and finish courageously what you have begun, never again doubting victory."

Cortes showed himself astute in this harangue. His captains stood by him, and he was likewise applauded by the crowd which, more changeable than the waves, always moves before the wind and lends ears and tongue to the last man who speaks.

As soon as this sedition was suppressed, Cortes received messengers from the chief commander of that region called Zentegal.[1] They came to seek pardon for the recent events and their hostility, saying: "Be not astonished that we have never desired a king and have never obeyed anybody, and that we so dearly love liberty, for we and our ancestors have endured great evils rather than accept the yoke of Muteczuma. For example, we have gone without cotton clothes and without salt to season our food, since we could not obtain them in face of Muteczuma's prohibition. Nevertheless, if you will admit us to your alliance, we promise to obey your commands." Cortes pardoned them and made an alliance with them. The messengers begged him to honour the town of Tascalteca, which lay six leagues distant from the camp, with his visit. For a long time he refused, but finally allowed himself to be moved by the entreaties of the lords, and consented. Before continuing the account of what happened in that town, we must interpose another occurrence.

Six messengers of Muteczuma, bearing magnificent presents, had visited Cortes. These gifts consisted of different necklaces and garments embroidered in gold, worth one thousand castellanos. In addition there were cotton dresses dyed in various colours. When they learned that Cortes intended to visit Muteczuma in his capital, they asked him in the emperor's name to abandon this project, because the city of Temistitan was built in the middle of a lake and, owing to its position, was destitute of everything. Unless it was provisioned from outside, there would not be enough for such a large number of people. The messengers averred that Muteczuma

[1] Another and incorrect spelling for Xicotencal.

was willing to send Cortes gold, silver, precious stones,
or whatever else he wanted, at whatever place he might
fix. Cortes answered: "I am quite unable to respond
to your wishes; for my sovereign's instructions order me
to visit your capital and your king, and to carefully
examine everything in order that I may report exactly
what I have observed." When this determination was
communicated to them, the messengers asked permission
from Cortes to send one of their number to deliver his
response to Muteczuma. The authorisation being granted,
one of them left the camp, returning on the sixth
day, and bringing from Muteczuma ten wrought vases
of equal weight and of admirable workmanship, fifteen
hundred costumes, a thousand times more valuable than
the first ones, carried on the backs of slaves, for they have
no beasts of burden. Upon hearing this, people of weak
imagination will doubtless be much astonished and think
my report is fabulous; for they have never heard anything
equal to it and will find that it passes their understanding;
but I shall give them satisfaction, when I come to speak
of the revenues of Muteczuma.

We have now long enough abandoned the Tascaltecans.
Let us describe their town and explain its characteristics.
We have already touched upon the fact that Tascalteca
is a republic, somewhat democratic, somewhat aristo-
cratic, as was the Roman government before it degenerated
into a despotic monarchy.[1] Great chieftains have their
place in it, but nobility is not tolerated. Cortes writes,
and those who have returned from those parts confirm
this opinion, that Tascalteca is much larger and more
populous than Granada, and that it is amply provided
with all the necessaries of life. The people eat maize-bread,
chickens, game, and fresh-water fish, but not sea-fish,
because it is too great a distance from the sea, being fifty

[1] Cortes compared the form of government with that of Venice, Genoa,
and Pisa.

leagues inland. There are also various vegetables. Inside the town walls, which are built of stone, are lofty fortified houses, also of stone, for the Tascaltecans are always on their guard, living as they do in a state of perpetual hostility towards their neighbours. They hold fairs and markets; they wear clothes and shoes. Golden necklaces set with jewels greatly please them, and they attach great importance to aigrettes and head-dresses of various coloured feathers which serve them as ornaments in time of war. Gold is everywhere used. Firewood, carried on men's backs, as well as beams for carpenter's work, planks, bricks, stones, and lime are for sale in their markets. Their architects and their potters are very clever, and none of our earthenware vases are modelled with more art than theirs. Herbalists sell medicinal plants. They make use of baths. It is known that they have a system of government and laws which they obey.

The entire province has a circumference of ninety leagues. The capital is Tascalteca, but there are other fortified places, fortresses, and towns, not to mention very fertile valleys and mountains. The population is numerous and very warlike, on account of the perpetual state of warfare with Muteczuma. One of the neighbouring provinces, Guazuzingo, has the same form of government as Tascalteca; that is to say, republican. In both these countries thieves are detested, and when they are captured they are carried bound to the public squares where they are beaten to death. They love justice.

Cortes remained twenty days at Tascalteca during which time the envoys of Muteczuma never left him. They made efforts to dissuade him from the Tascaltecan alliance, and counselled him not to confide in such faithless and perfidious people. The Tascaltecans on the other hand affirmed that Muteczuma's people were tyrants, and that if Cortes put his trust in them, they would lead him to his ruin. Although he did not reveal the fact, Cortes was pleased at this contradiction, which could only turn to his profit; and so he answered both parties with fair speeches.

The messengers of Muteczuma insisted that Cortes should leave the town of the Tascaltecans, and betake himself to another city hardly five leagues distant which was a dependeny of Muteczuma. This place was called Chiurutecal,[1] and they pretended that it would be simpler to conclude a treaty there with their sovereign. The Tascaltecans informed Cortes, on the contrary, that ambuscades had been prepared along the roads leading to that town, and also inside the walls. They declared that the road had been cut in various places, rendering it impracticable for the horses, and that other roads had been opened; inside the town some streets had been blocked and others had been fortified. Moreover the inhabitants had collected quantities of stones upon the terraces and small towers and windows overlooking the squares and streets, in order to crush the Spaniards with them as they marched below. As a proof of the hostile intention of the inhabitants towards Cortes and his men, the Tascaltecans called attention to the fact that none of them had come to visit Cortes, as the people of Guazuzingo had done, although the latter lived at a greater distance. This fact was true, and Cortes sent to Chiurutecal to complain of this insolent negligence. Upon receipt of his message an embassy was sent, but it was composed of common people of no consequence, who told him that they had not appeared before because the Spaniards were in a hostile country, but that

---

[1] Meaning Cholula, a sacred city under theocratic government, where stood the great pyramid dedicated to Quetzalcoatl. This remarkable construction of unknown antiquity and uncertain origin still stands, though so covered over with earth and shrubbery that its outlines are disfigured and its artificial character hardly distinguishable. Consult Sahagun, *Historia de Nueva España*, lib. i., cap. iii.; also Bandelier's *Archéological Tour*.

otherwise their intentions towards him were of the very best.

When Cortes was informed of the outrage they had put upon him in failing to send their principal citizens, he sent these vulgar messengers back with threats that if within three days the chiefs of Chiurutecal did not present themselves in person before him, he would go and find them; and that he would teach them what it would cost them to provoke his wrath by thus delaying to pay homage to the King of Spain, who was sovereign master of the whole country. They came and presented their excuses. Cortes received them, but on condition that they should keep their promises, and they bound themselves to execute any orders they might receive; they added: "If you will come to visit us, you will be convinced of the sincerity of our promises; at the same time you will see that the Tascaltecans have lied and that we are ready to pay whatever tribute you may fix." Cortes hesitated a long time, but finally decided to take the risk and accede to the wishes of Muteczuma's messengers by going to Chiurutecal.

Upon learning this decision, and seeing their counsels were useless, the Tascaltecans declared they would by no means permit Cortes to trust himself to the loyalty of Muteczuma's people, to the extent of giving them a free hand to injure him. They showed themselves grateful to one who had been so gracious to them, and who, after such hostilities, had made friends of them when he might have wreaked well-merited vengeance and destroyed them. They insisted on furnishing him with a Prætorian guard of one hundred thousand warriors, and it was in vain that Cortes forbade them. During the first day he camped, surrounded by this phalanx of about one hundred thousand men, on the bank of a river to which he came. At this place he selected a body-guard of two thousand from amongst the number, dismissing the others with the thanks they merited. The priests of Chiurutecal came some distance outside the city to meet the approaching Spaniards, preceded, according to their custom, by young men and girls singing and by musicians playing on drums and trumpets. Upon entering the city the Spaniards were comfortably lodged and food was provided, though scantily, and ill-served. It was suspected that some streets were barricaded and that stones had been collected on the terraces of the houses as the Tascaltecans had foretold.

Meanwhile new messengers had arrived from Muteczuma, who held secret conversations with the people of Chiurutecal but none with Cortes. When asked what communications these envoys had made to them, the inhabitants were unable to reply. The suspicions of Cortes were aroused, for he remembered the warnings of the Tascaltecans, and through the interpreter, Geronimo de Aguilar, who knew the languages of the countries where he had been a prisoner for a long time, he called a young man and questioned him. The result of this interrogatory was as follows: the young man said, that the inhabitants of Chiurutecal had sent all the old men, women, and children out of the city when the Spaniards approached, but he did not know what their intentions were. The treachery was finally discovered in the following manner: a woman of Chiurutecal had taken into her house a young girl of Cempoal,[1] who had followed her husband or lover. This woman spoke in the following terms to her guest: "My friend, come away with me." The other asked, "whither?" To which the first replied: "Out of the city and far from here." The Cempoalan asked for what motive? to which her hostess replied: "This night a large number of Muteczuma's soldiers will enter the town, and everybody found inside its walls will be massacred. I am sorry for you, and therefore reveal this plot. Lose no time, unless you wish to perish

[1] The "young girl" was Marina.

with the others, and cut short your tender years by a cruel death."

The young girl exposed this plot to Aguilar, and as soon as Cortes was informed, he felt convinced that it was true. He summoned the chiefs of the town to him, and armed all his people; after which he explained the situation to his officers, and ordered that, at a signal given by firing a musket, they should fall upon the authors of this treachery, whom he would have gathered in the court of his residence for a parley. The chiefs of Chiurutecal came, and as had been agreed were at once put into irons, after which Cortes mounted his horse and rode out. The gates of his palace were already surrounded by armed men. These were the citizens who were waiting for the soldiers, ready to attack them as they came out. Cortes fell upon them before their reinforcements could join them. The battle was long and fierce: according to Cortes it lasted five hours. These treacherous barbarians were finally overcome and Cortes returned to his residence, where he called before him the manacled chiefs and asked them the reason of their conduct. They replied that the envoys of Muteczuma had deceived them; and that what had occurred was contrary to their wishes. They asked him to pardon them promising to obey him and to be no longer subjects of Muteczuma. In this day's fight the allies from Cempoal and Tascalteca gave proof of their courage, for they loathed the tyranny of Muteczuma. Cortes pardoned the chiefs of Chiurutecal, merely ordering them to summon back the women and children and all the fugitives they had sent away. This was done and all the inhabitants returned to their homes, after which Cortes sought to reconcile the people of Tascalteca with those of Chiurutecal. He desired to unite in a solid friendship these peoples who, until that time, had been enemies devoured by a mutual and mortal hatred, instigated by Muteczuma.

This town of Chiurutecal stands in a fertile plain, and inside its walls are twenty thousand houses built of stone and lime, and as many more in the suburbs. It was formerly a republic, but Muteczuma had conquered it and reduced it to a state of vassalage. Chiurutecal and Tascalteca readily obeyed the Spaniards. The inhabitants of the first of these towns are richer and better dressed than their Tascaltecan neighbours. They irrigate a large part of the country by a system of trenches. The walls of the town are solidly built and furnished with towers. Cortes writes that from the summit of a lofty temple he counted four hundred of these towers and an even greater number in the highways of the city; the latter being attached to temples. There are tracts of land in that country admirably adapted for cattle raising, and it is the only place where such have been found; for everywhere else the population is so dense that there is hardly room in the country for the crops.

After these events Cortes summoned the messengers of Muteczuma before him and reproached them with their master's treachery. He observed that it was hardly worthy of a great prince, such as he imagined Muteczuma to be, to resort to trickery, and to set traps through the intermediary of others. Henceforth, he would no longer feel himself bound by the promises he had given, since Muteczuma had so perfidiously broken his word. The envoys, half dead from fear, declared that their master had no such thought and that he was ignorant of all that had happened. Time would prove the truth of their statements. Muteczuma had never broken his word, and it was the inhabitants of Chiurutecal who had themselves invented this imaginary treason, to save themselves from the anger of Cortes. The envoys asked permission at the same time to send one of their number to Muteczuma, to acquaint him with what had happened. Cortes accorded this permission, and the envoy returned after the interval of several days, bearing gifts worthy of a king: ten golden platters, and as is customary, fifteen hundred cotton garments. I have already said elsewhere, in order to satisfy some doubtful souls, that I would later explain how this king came to possess such a supply of clothing. The envoy likewise brought a large supply of provisions, especially wines, such as the king and the lords drink. The quality does not resemble the sort used by the people, for there exist different beverages, of which the commonest, drunk by the people, is made from maize, while the others of better quality, are made from certain beans which are likewise used in place of money. I will later on return to the nature of these beans.

Muteczuma declared to Cortes through his envoy and by new messengers whom he sent, that the people of Chiurutecal had lied in attributing those projects to him, and that they had only done this in self-defence. Moreover, time would show that he was a true friend and that it was not his custom to govern by means of stratagems. Nevertheless he asked Cortes for the second time to abandon his project of visiting him in his capital. He feared famine, for his capital was built in the midst of the waters and because of its position, produced nothing. The inhabitants procure what they require by trading with their neighbours, but if guests arrived, they would find themselves in want. Cortes declared that he could not accede to the emperor's wish, for his sovereign had given him instructions in a contrary sense.

As soon as the resolution of Cortes was made known to him, Monteczuma said that he was awaiting him and would take measures that nothing should be lacking. He even sent him some of his most important officials, to serve as his escorts. Cortes therefore set out towards the city of Temistitan, consumed with the desire to behold it.

Eight leagues distant the Spaniards discovered a mountain, which is covered with ashes during the summer. Both its peaks are bare. It is called Popocatepeque, which means "The Smoking Mountain"; *popoca* in their language means smoke, and *tepeque* mountain. From the summit of Popocatepeque a cloud of smoke constantly issues, mounting straight into the heavens, and the steam it sends out is as thick as a dark cloud. The cloud of smoke is as large in volume as a great house, and it rises through the air with such force that the strongest winds are impotent to turn its course. This phenomenon amazed Cortes, and he sent ten of his most courageous companions[1] with some Indian guides to investigate, as far as possible, this freak of nature. In obedience to his orders they ascended the mountain, as high as possible, but the layer of ashes was so thick they were unable to reach the summit. They mounted to such a height that the roaring of the flames issuing from it and the frightful noise of the smoke were audible, to say nothing of the constant quaking that shook the mountain as though it were about to fall to pieces. Two Spaniards who were more daring than the others resolved, in spite of the contrary advice of the natives, to attain the summit. They climbed until they reached the vast crater from which the smoke poured forth, and which they say is a league and a half in circumference. Frightened by the furious roaring of the flames, they retraced their steps, and it was lucky they did, for they escaped the heat of the flames which, during their ascent, had somewhat subsided; but after a moment, the fire regained its fury and, at the same time, numerous stones were hurled into the air. Had they not been fortunate enough to find a cavern in which they took refuge while this rain of

---

[1] Diego de Ordaz lead this party. In remembrance of his exploit, Charles V. later authorised him to display a smoking volcano in his armorial bearings.

stones, which the mountain pours forth at intervals, lasted, they would have been killed. The natives were so much astonished by this exploit that they crowded about them, offering them gifts as though they were demigods.

There is another matter, Most Holy Father, which I must not omit. The natives believe that kings, who have governed ill during their lives, are confined for a time in the midst of the flames of this mountain where they are purged of the stains of their crimes, and where they have only wicked demons for their companions.

At the conclusion of this excursion, Muteczuma's envoys led Cortes by the road the Tascaltecans had urged him not to take. Parts of this road were sufficiently difficult because of ditches and lagoons, spanned by such narrow bridges that an entire army might be destroyed, since the soldiers could not keep together while crossing them. Cortes branched off on another road, longer and more difficult, because it crossed rocky country.

The Spaniards marched through the lower parts of the valleys, overshadowed by the lofty, smoky mountains. Scarcely had they emerged from these valleys, and reached the summit of some lofty hills, than they beheld right before their feet an immense plain. This is the plain of Colua, where stands the great lake city of Temistitan.[1] Two lakes[2] lie in this plain, the one of salt water, in which the town is built, and which is reputed to be sixty leagues in circumference; and a fresh-water lake, of which I shall speak more fully later.

Muteczuma's envoys, who escorted our men, were asked why they had tried to lead our army in another

---

[1] Tenochtitlan was the ancient name of the Aztec capital: several derivations of the word have been proposed, the most generally accepted signifying "Cactus on a rock."

[2] The two principal lakes in the valley of Mexico were Texcoco and Chalco as here stated. In addition to these there were three others, Zumpango, Xaltocan, and Xochimilco.

direction. They answered that they were not ignorant of the fact that the other road was easier, but they had not advised taking it, because it led for a whole day through the territory of Guazuzingo, where provisions might possibly be scarce. It may here be observed that the two republics of Guazuzingo and Tascalteca were united by treaties and by the common hatred they bore to Muteczuma. Both states were poor, because, being surrounded by a formidable enemy, they had no trading relations with any other nation.

Reduced thus to subsist upon local products, the inhabitants live miserably, refusing however to accept the yoke of any other sovereign. It was because they hoped, by means of the help of Cortes to extend their boundaries, that they became his allies; and as a proof of their good faith they gave him some slaves and clothing, though of little value. In addition they furnished him most generously with one day's provisions.

It was already the end of the month of August, and the mountain passes were just left behind, when the Spaniards arrived at a country house where Muteczuma loved to pass the summer. This house was large enough to receive commodiously the entire army for the night. After the forces were numbered, Cortes found he had his three hundred Spaniards, and more than four thousand allies from Cempoal, Tascalteca, Guazuzingo, and Chiurutecal. But, as I have already explained, to avoid startling weak and narrow minds, his force lay less in the multitude of combatants than in his cannon and horses, which to the natives were unknown. Provisions were not wanting, for Muteczuma's stewards provided for the needs of our men, no matter what road they took. The Spaniards suffered nevertheless from cold in the high mountain regions and were obliged to light great fires.

On that day Cortes received a visit from Muteczuma's brother, accompanied by numerous lords. They brought him a present in Muteczuma's name, consisting of superb necklaces, valued at three thousand castellanos; begging him, at the same time, to withdraw and stop wherever else he pleased. Muteczuma likewise pledged himself to pay Cortes whatever tribute the latter might fix, on condition that he would give up his visit to a town built in the water where such a multitude would necessarily be exposed to hunger, since the country produced nothing of itself. He would never at any time or for any motive cease to consider himself the subject of the king in whose name Cortes was sent. To these repeated requests of Muteczuma, Cortes replied as suavely as possible, that he himself would be quite disposed to satisfy a wish expressed by such a great monarch, but the instructions of his own sovereign forbade his doing so. It should by no means be imagined that his presence would incommode anybody; for, on the contrary, it would be useful and profitable for all of them. If he persisted in his intention, it was because he had no choice; if his visit should later prove disagreeable to Muteczuma, he would withdraw as soon as he had signed a treaty and regulated affairs, which could be more intelligently and easily done in person than by the intermediary of messengers sent from one party to the other.

During these negotiations, according to the report of Cortes, the natives never ceased to prepare ambuscades, and during the night the forests on the mountain overlooking his residence had been filled with armed men. But he had taken precautions in such wise as to forestall their perfidy and stratagem.

Continuing his march towards the lake city, Cortes came to another town in the plain, numbering twenty thousand houses. It is called Amaquemeca,[1] and is the capital of the province of Chalco. Its cacique, who is a vassal of Muteczuma, extended the largest and most abundant

[1] Amecameca.

hospitality to our men during two days. He presented them with gold necklaces valued at three thousand castellanos, as one of his colleagues had already done, and with forty slaves. Four leagues farther on, Cortes reached the borders of another lake whose waters were fresh, or at least hardly brackish. A city built half on land and half in the water stands on its banks, and near by rises a lofty mountain. At this place Cortes encountered twelve lords, one of whom was carried on a litter on men's backs. He was only twenty-five years old, and when he descended from his litter the men of his escort hastened to clear the road of stones and to scatter straw before him, as he marched to salute Cortes. When he had saluted the general in Muteczuma's name, he begged the former not to suspect his sovereign of indifference or negligence in not having come personally to meet him; the reason being that he was ill. He himself had been sent to act as escort. The general answered with fair words and presented the lords with some small gifts. They returned delighted.[1]

Cortes followed close after them and came to another town composed of fifteen hundred houses and standing in a fresh-water lake. The only means of communication with the mainland was by boat.[2] These boats are dug out of a single tree-trunk and resemble the canoes used by the islanders; these little boats are called *ascales*. Advancing amidst the waters of the lake, Cortes observed a causeway, built a lance's length above the level of the water leading to another town of about two thousand people. He was received there with many honours, and the inhabitants invited him to stop for the night, but the nobles of his escort opposed this plan,

---

[1] This noble was Cacamatzin nephew of Montezuma. Both Cortes and Bernal Diaz describe the particulars of this meeting.

[2] This town was Cuitlahuac, now called Tlahua, to which the Spaniards gave the name of Venezuela—little Venice.

and conducted him the same evening to another and much larger town on the shores of the salt lake, called Iztapalapa. This town is governed by Muteczuma's brother, Tacatepla,[1] and lies four leagues distant from the former town. Three leagues distant from Iztapalapa, in another direction, stands the town of Coluacan, which gives its name to the province of Colua. Thus the Spaniards who had heard of that town gave the name to the entire country when they entered it. Iztapalapa numbers eight thousand houses, most of them important ones, and Coluacan has about as many. The cacique of Coluacan was at that time with Muteczuma's brother, and offered valuable presents to Cortes.

It is reported that the palace of the cacique of Iztapalapa is a very remarkable building, constructed of stones cemented together with mortar. The wood work is also very artistic and some of the beams are of royal dimensions. The interior apartments and sleeping chambers are hung with tapestries, beautiful beyond all praise. This royal residence likewise contains gardens filled with various trees, vegetables, fruits, and sweet-scented flowers; not to mention vast ponds swarming with different species of fish and covered with families of every sort of aquatic bird. There is a marble flight of stairs leading down to the bottom of these ponds. Marvellous tales are told of the arbours bordered by hedges, which protect the fruit orchards. These hedges are so disposed as to please in a thousand different ways, just as about the houses of the more cultivated of our cardinals and in many other places are found myrtle, rosemary, and box; everything pleases the eye. Cortes goes into minute details on this point, which weary; let us therefore omit them, and take the hero, Cortes, into the town of Temistitan and to the arms of Muteczuma, who was not, however, so anxious to embrace him.

[1] The ruler's name was in reality Cuitlahuatzin.

BOOK III

FROM Iztapalapa to Temistitan, the capital of the great King Muteczuma, the way leads over an artificial causeway built at immense cost, and standing at two lances' length above the level of the water. This causeway serves the purpose of a bridge, for Iztapalapa is built half on the water and half on land. On one side of the causeway stand two towns, partly built in the water, and on the other side stands one; the first town is called Messicalcango, the second Coluacan, which I have before mentioned, and the third Uvichilabusco.[1] It is said that the first of these towns has more than three thousand houses, the second six, and the third four. They are adorned with magnificent temples ornamented with towers and dedicated to their idols.

All the towns on the causeway are engaged in the manufacture of salt for the use of all the tribes of the empire; water from the salt lake is brought by means of canals onto a field, where it is condensed, the salt baked and afterwards shaped into cakes or loaves to be carried to the fairs or markets, where it is exchanged for foreign products. Only the subjects of Muteczuma are allowed to sell this salt, all who do not recognise his authority being deprived of it. For that reason the Tascaltecans and the people of Guazuzingo and many others ate their food without salt for, as we have said, they were enemies of Muteczuma.

[1] These three towns were Mexicalzingo, Coyohuacan, and Huichilobusco.

There are other causeways serving as bridges to unite
the land cities to those built in the lakes. These causeways join like so many streets. On the causeway which
starts from Iztapalapa there is a junction with another,
and at this meeting-place of the two causeways there
stands a fort, provided with two impregnable towers.[1]
From this point there is only one causeway, leading to
Temistitan.

At intervals along these causeways there are laid movable
wooden bridges, which are raised whenever there is a fear
of war. I think these breaks in the causeways have been
arranged to facilitate the collection of duties. For, is it
not for precisely the same motive that we see the gates of
towns closed during the night, even in time of peace?
Once the bridges are raised the waters flow through the
open passages. According to what is reported, the phenomenon of the ebb and flow may be observed; a thing
truly extraordinary, Holy Father, both in my own opinion
and in that of others who hold it to be impossible, since
they have never heard mention of similar novelties.

This lake city, or if you choose, the site of this salt lake,
is more than seventy leagues distant from the sea. Two
chains of lofty mountains and two great valleys separating
them lie between the sea and the lake, and nevertheless,
if the truth has been told, the lake is subject to the ebb and
flow precisely like the sea; but nobody has been able to
discover whether the sea enters or leaves this lake.
When the tide rises, the salt water pours into the fresh-
water lake, through a narrow passage between the two
hills, while at the ebb-tide the fresh water flows back into
the salt lake; but this fresh water never becomes too salt
to drink, nor does the salt water ever lose its savour. I
have given enough particulars concerning the lakes, causeways, bridges, and fortresses.

[1] The fortress of Xoloc, where Cortes, afterwards fixed his headquarters
during the siege of the city.

The Spaniards were delighted to behold what they had so long desired to see. The more cautious among the inhabitants of Temistitan did not share their sentiments, for they feared their guests would trouble their Elysian repose. The people felt differently, however, and thought there could be nothing more agreeable than to witness novelties, not preoccupying themselves about the future. For this reason a thousand men, dressed in gala costume, met Cortes two marches distant from the capital. Each one saluted him according to the national etiquette, which prescribes touching the ground with the right hand, and then, in token of submission, kissing the spot of earth touched by their hand.[1] All these noblemen belonged to the court, and behind them the much-desired sovereign approached. The causeway, as I have already said, is a league and a half long, and some aver it to be two leagues in length. It is so straight that it would be impossible to trace a straighter line on paper. Any one with good sight looking straight ahead of him could see, from the fort whence Cortes set out to meet Muteczuma, the entrance of the city. The king advanced in the middle of the causeway, the others in the procession walking on both sides and carefully keeping their distance. All were barefooted. Two princes sustained Muteczuma under his arms; the one was this brother, the cacique of Iztapalapa, and the other was one of the principal lords. This does not mean that Muteczuma required their support, but it is their custom to render this homage to their sovereigns, so that they should seem to be upheld by the great.

When Muteczuma approached, Cortes sprang from his horse and advanced towards the King to embrace him, but the great officials intervened, for amongst them it is con-

---

[1] The hand, not the earth it touched, was kissed; the salutation being very similar to the Oriental gesture indicative of carrying dust to the forehead.

sidered sacrilege to touch the sovereign. The people who marched on both sides formed ranks, and one by one, according to the order of precedence, they advanced to pay the usual homage to Cortes, after which they took their places, without there being the slightest confusion. After this exchange of warm salutations, Cortes advanced towards the king, and taking from his neck a collar of no value that he wore, he placed it upon the king's neck. As a matter of fact it was made of different coloured beads and partly of an alloy of gold and copper. This gift, however, pleased Muteczuma, who in return gave Cortes two necklaces of precious stones, from which hung suspended shells and crabs worked in gold.

All who had advanced to meet Cortes having been received, the entire company took the direction of the great city, of which it is only possible to speak with astonishment. They returned in the same order they had come; that is to say, the procession marched on both sides of that wonderful causeway of which the middle was reserved to Muteczuma and the Spaniards.

Most horrible to behold and lamentable to report! On both sides of the causeway there arose from the waters of the lake numerous magnificent towers which served as temples; here and there upon the summits of these towers victims were immolated, either bought slaves, or natives whose lives were offered for that purpose in lieu of taxes. It was so inexpressibly horrible that most of the men declare that as they marched by those towers they shivered.

They finally reached a large palace adorned with royal luxury, which was formerly the residence of Muteczuma's ancestors. Muteczuma led Cortes into a court and placed him upon a throne, after which he withdrew to another palace. He ordered an abundant and magnificent repast to be served to the men and commanded that each of them should receive the most lavish hospitality. Some hours after this banquet, Muteczuma returned to Cortes accompanied by his chamberlains and personal servants, bearing cotton dresses embroidered in gold and dyed with various colours.   It is incredible to relate, but we will explain later on why the fact is true; eye-witnesses declare there were six thousand costumes, and Cortes himself gives the same figure.   At the same time numerous presents of gold and silver articles were brought.

Near to Cortes another similarly decorated chair was placed, on which Muteczuma took his seat and, calling about him the great lords of his kingdom, he delivered the following address which was taken down by the interpreters who understood Geronimo de Aguilar: "O ye men, illustrious for your courage and your clemency to suppliants, I wish and hope that your arrival within our walls may be beneficial for all.   You are welcome in this country." Turning then towards the great lords he continued: "We have known from the traditions of our ancestors that we are strangers in this country.   At a time beyond the recollection of any living man, a great prince, mounted on a ship, brought our ancestors to this land.   It is not known whether he came voluntarily or was driven hither by a tempest.   Leaving his companions here he returned to his own country.   When he was about to depart, he wished to take with him those whom he had brought hither; but his men had built houses, had married native women by whom they had children, and were happy in prosperous and peaceful homes.   Our ancestors refused to return or to any longer obey his orders.   They had chosen amongst themselves a council and chiefs for the people, under whose authority they lived.   It is reported also that this prince left them with threatening words.   Up to this time no one has come to claim the rights of this first prince.

"Thus I beg and counsel you, O chiefs of my kingdom, to yield to the general of this powerful sovereign the same obedience as to myself, and to pay to him, as he shall demand, the tributes you owe to me."

Turning then to Cortes he added these words:

"From what I have just said, it appears that the sovereign who has sent you here descends from that prince; come then amongst us with all confidence; rest from your fatigues, which I know have been considerable since you have been in this country, and restore your exhausted strength. Everything we possess belongs to you. The obedience of the kingdoms subject to me is due to you, whoever you may be, sent hither for this purpose. All that has been told about me at Cempoal, at Tascalteca and at Guazuzingo you must consider as having been inspired by hostile sentiments. Acquaintance with facts will show that these peoples have lied, in giving imaginary descriptions of my palaces built of gold, of my flowers, of my furniture made of gold, and of myself as being a god rather than a man. My palaces are of stone, my flowers are natural plants, my furniture is covered with cotton stuff, as you may see for yourselves. It is true that I have in my treasury many golden ornaments. They are all yours to use as you wish, in the name of your powerful sovereign. As for my imaginary divinity and immortality, behold my arms and my legs and see if they are not flesh and bone. You see for yourself." Speaking thus and weeping, he uncovered his legs and arms.

When he had finished this speech, Cortes comforted him with gentle words, after which he withdrew. Whether his face expressed satisfaction or his heart felt gladness, let those who have enjoyed power and suffered its loss decide. Let those who, without a joyous heart, receive uninvited guests imposed on them by violence, express their opinion. It was, moreover, easy to observe in the expression on the faces of those great lords present, who had listened to this discourse with eyes bent upon the ground. With tearful eyes, breaking into sobs and sighs, they remained a long time silent and sorrowful after listening to the speech; after which they promised to obey Muteczuma's orders. Such a sudden and important resolution could not be taken without troubling men's minds. When the council broke up, each returned to his home; but this is enough concerning this subject.

Let us now describe the consequences of this interview, disastrous and deplorable for Muteczuma, his vassals, and officials, as I shall later show; excellent, however, for the spread of religion, for we confidently hope that those sanguinary sacrifices will be one day abolished, and that these people will embrace the doctrines of Christ.

The first six days passed tranquilly. Each succeeding day was marked by such lamentable catastrophes as no people or sovereign ever endured. In fact, hardly had six days passed when Cortes, either aided by chance or profiting by an occasion he had sought, announced that he had just received letters of the commander [1] of the citadel left for the protection of the colony of Vera Cruz, announcing that Coalcopoca,[2] cacique of the province where Cortes had founded a colony called Almiria, had just committed an abominable action which must not be left unavenged. Coalcopoca had sent messengers to inform Escalante that he had not thus far come to salute him or to make oath of obedience to the great King whose power Cortes described, because he would have to cross the territory of hostile people, whose attacks he feared. He therefore asked that some Spaniards should be sent to act as his escort on this journey; hoping that his enemies would not dare to attack him if so accompanied. The commander, trusting the messenger, sent four Spaniards to Coalcopoca to escort him through the hostile country; but hardly had these Spaniards arrived

---

[1] Juan de Escalante.   [2] Quauhpopoca.

within the cacique's jurisdiction, than they were attacked; two of them were killed by these brigands and the others only escaped, covered with wounds.

Convinced that this assassination had been accomplished by the command of Coalcopoca, the Spanish governor organised a punitive expedition against him, taking with him only two horsemen, some musketeers, cannon, and infantry, numbering in all fifty Spaniards; but he had called to his assistance the hostile neighbours of Coalcopoca. With this force he attacked the cacique's town, meeting with a desperate resistance; and during the assault seven Spaniards and a much larger number of the allies were slain. The town was finally captured and pillaged, many of its defenders being killed or taken prisoners. Coalcopoca fled and escaped pursuit.

Cortes promptly seized upon this pretext for dethroning the wretched Muteczuma. He feared that either some disaster might overtake him, or that Muteczuma might weary of the insolence of the Spaniards, which he was unable to check now that they were living in the midst of luxury. He likewise feared that his hosts might be driven desperate by the duration and inconvenience of his stay. He therefore paid a visit to Muteczuma, to whom he said: "It has been reported to me by letter that Coalcopoca, your vassal, has plotted this treason against the governor of Vera Cruz, not only with your knowledge, but in obedience to your orders. I do not believe this; but in order to dispel any suspicions from my sovereign's mind, to whose ears the news of this treachery has come, it is necessary that you should change your residence from your palace to the one in which I reside, in order that I may report that you are in my power. Nothing, however, will be changed in the government of your city or kingdom."

Muteczuma realised the rapid diminution of his authority; nevertheless he obeyed, and ordered the litter in which he would be carried to the palace of Cortes. When this extraordinary news spread, the people murmured and began to grow violent. Muteczuma immediately made a sign that they should lay down their arms and be silent. He persuaded every one that he was acting voluntarily. With tears in their eyes the great lords and his attendants accompanied their master.

Some days later Cortes asked Muteczuma to summon Coalcopoca and his associates in the conspiracy, and to have them punished, in order that his own innocence might be made clear to the Spanish sovereign. Again Muteczuma obeyed, and calling some of his accustomed officials, he confided his secret seal to them as a symbol of his supreme authority. He further instructed them that, in case the guilty men refused to come, they should appeal to the vassal states of the neighbourhood and bring them by force. The cacique Coalcopoca, one of his sons and fifteen lords came in response to this summons. At first they declared they had acted without Muteczuma's assent. Cortes ordered a gigantic pyre to be constructed in the main square, and there, in the presence of Muteczuma and all the inhabitants, Coalcopoca, his son and his other accomplices were burned alive as a punishment for their crime of high treason. As they were being led to execution, the condemned men confessed that they had only obeyed Muteczuma's orders.

Cortes, who only sought a pretext for taking possession of the empire of Muteczuma who was in his power, had him put in chains and overwhelmed him with threats and upbraidings. The unfortunate sovereign, bewildered by the sudden turn things had taken, and likewise overcome by fear, completely lost his courage. Nevertheless he was released, but after being accused of the crime which had been committed. Muteczuma declared that he had deserved punishment. He appeared as meek as a lamb, and seemed to obey severer behests than the rules of grammar dictated to little children, enduring everything with patience in order to prevent a rising of his subjects and their chieftains. Any burden imposed upon him seemed less heavy than a revolt of his people. It might be thought that he sought to imitate Diocletian, who preferred rather to take poison than again seize the reins of the empire he had abdicated.

Cortes afterwards spoke to Muteczuma as follows: "I hope you will keep your word and your oath of obedience, as well as the treaties you have signed with the powerful king of Spain. The better to enforce your royal will, you may return to your palace where you formerly lived in such regal pomp." Muteczuma refused, saying: "That can by no means be done, for I should be urged by my chiefs and tormented by their insistence. They are disposed to provoke an uprising. I see and I know they gnash their teeth, for they are vexed because I have received you and your companions and this crowd of allies who are our enemies. I shall be more tranquil and more secure in your midst, than were I exposed to the importunities of my people."

From time to time Muteczuma visited his pleasure houses which he had built at great cost, and which I shall describe at length. During some days he and Cortes lived under the same roof, Cortes in the character of guest, and Muteczuma in that of master of the house. This state of things lasted during the day time, but when evening fell Muteczuma, instead of returning to the ancient palace of his ancestors, went to the residence of Cortes. When descending from his litter he made many presents to his attendants and also to the Spaniards, and was pleased to sit with the Spaniards at table, calling them about him, talking and smilingly addressing amiable speeches to them.

About this time Cortes asked Muteczuma to show him the gold mines whence his ancestors had obtained their gold.   The sovereign answered that he would gladly do so, and ordered expert workmen to be summoned without delay.   These men were despatched in different directions, in company with Spaniards selected by Cortes to make reports on what they saw.

They first visited the gold mines of a province called Zuzulla.[1]   This mine is eighty leagues distant from the capital, Temistitan.   The Spaniards collected some gold in the beds of three rivers in those parts without difficulty, though they had brought with them no tools for sifting the sands.   The natives take no other trouble to obtain gold, content to gather it from the river bottoms, and to pick up the grains they find amongst the gravel.

The entire region between the capital and the gold-mines is, according to the Spaniards' report, full of splendid cities.   Other Spaniards were sent into a region called Tamaculappa, where the inhabitants are richer and better dressed than those of Zuzulla, for their country is more fertile.   Cortes sent still others to a province called Malinaltepec, sixty leagues distant from the royal lake, and nearer to the sea.   Gold was found there in a large river.   Others went to a mountainous country called Tenis, whose inhabitants are valiant warriors.   They fight with lances thirty cubits long.   The cacique of this country called Coatelimacco does not recognise Muteczuma's authority; he told the Spaniards they might cross his borders but that he would not permit the subjects of Muteczuma to do so.   Indeed Coatelimacco received the Spaniards amiably and treated them magnificently.   The land of Tenis is watered by eight streams, in two of which gold is found.   The cacique sent envoys to Cortes, offering his submission and that of his people.

Some Spaniards were sent into a province called Ta-

[1] Gonzalo de Umbria, Diego de Ordaz, and Pizarro went with Montezuma's people to the state of Oaxaca, but their expedition was without important results.

chintepec, where they discovered two streams containing gold and noticed that the country was adapted for the establishment of a colony. Once assured of the fertility of Tachintepec, Cortes asked Muteczuma, in the name of his powerful sovereign, for authorisation to build a residence there, where the Spaniards who went in search of gold might find shelter. The king consented, and ordered his architects to lose no time. His orders were executed with such diligence that in less than two months the residence, capable of sheltering any chief whatsoever and all his family, was finished. Absolutely nothing was wanting.

While the house was building, numerous measures of maize, from which they make bread, was sown, as vulgar parlance has it, in the twinkling of an eye; and at the same time beans and young vegetables, not to mention two thousand feet of those trees whose nuts are used for money, and which I shall later on describe. I am well aware that people of feeble imagination will accuse me of being fantastic when I speak of trees bearing money. In addition to this very commodious house, three others destined for servants were built. Large ponds of fresh water for breeding fish and different species of aquatic birds, especially ducks, were formed. Five hundred were taken there the very first day, for their feathers are used in the manufacture of different kinds of stuffs. Each year in the spring their plumes are plucked. Chickens, larger than our peacocks and of as delicate a flavour, were added; some were for eating and the others were for propagating the species, and altogether they numbered thirteen hundred. All the necessary tools for agriculture need not be mentioned.

Cortes writes that this rapidly constructed residence would be worth, if sold, more than eighty thousand castellanos, and he adds that not in the whole of Spain could such a beautiful domain be found. I relate what has been told me.

When asked later concerning a port large enough for our vessels, Muteczuma answered that he knew nothing of such things, for he had never interested himself in maritime affairs. He however showed Cortes a drawing of the coast where the latter might choose whatever place suited him, and at the same time he sent men of expert knowledge to inspect the positions.

The cacique of the province of Guazacalco, who was Muteczuma's enemy, was quite willing to receive the Spaniards but refused to receive Muteczuma's subjects. From the time he had heard of our power and warlike virtues, after the submission of the people of Potenchan he declared he wished to become our friend, and that the Spaniards were welcome. He indicated the mouth of a large river where the water is deep enough for the largest ships. He even took the initiative in proposing to found there a colony, and his subjects built six houses in the native style on the river bank. He promised more when the work should begin, and he invited the Spaniards to stop permanently in his territory, promising that if they consented, they should live in his capital. In token of the alliance he desired he offered gifts, though they were of little value, and sent messengers to Cortes tendering his submission.

Let us now return to Muteczuma's affairs. While Muteczuma was kept a prisoner, or to put it less roughly, while he was detained in dissembled captivity, Catamazin, ruler of the province of Hacoluacan, whose capital is Tezcuco, rebelled. This ruler, who was Muteczuma's subject and kinsman, declared he would no longer obey Cortes or Muteczuma, and proudly defied both. He is ruler of four cities which are subject to Muteczuma. His country is called Nahautecal, for *nahau* means four, and *tecal* means a ruler. Your Beatitude is well acquainted with the system in our European kingdoms, where certain princes, though obedient to the emperors in Germany and to the kings in

Spain and France, enjoy sovereign rights within their own jurisdiction.

Tezcuco, the capital of this province, numbers thirty thousand houses and is remarkable for its walls, its magnificent temples, and its buildings. The other cities number three or four thousand households, besides farms, villages, and hamlets, all of which, thanks to the fertility of the soil, are prosperous.

When messengers called upon Catamazin in the name of Cortes to lay down his arms, he arrogantly answered: "How then? Do you think we are so base as to bend our head before you foreigners?" At the same time he bitterly reproached the King, Muteczuma, for having so weakly accepted the Spanish dominion, adding that they might come whenever they liked, and they would learn who he was. Thus speaking, he brandished his weapons.

When these insults were reported to him, Cortes wished to attack Catamazin at once, but Muteczuma thought that the matter should be managed otherwise. He said that a massacre would take place if they attempted violence against Catamazin, because he was powerful and had courageous soldiers at his command. The victory would be doubtful, and even if it were won, it would cost dear. It was better, therefore, to have recourse to stratagem. "Leave this matter to me," he said, "and I will easily humble the pride of Catamazin."

He summoned the nobles in his pay, and explained to them that he wished to punish the insolence of his vassal. These chiefs enjoyed the intimacy of Muteczuma and of Catamazin. He ordered them to corrupt the personal servants of the latter and to capture him; if he refused to come, he authorised them even to kill him, if they thought it indispensable. The preparations were lengthy, and as the story would be a long one to tell, it will suffice for me to report the result. The chiefs cleverly executed the orders of their master. They approached at night-time in barques and seized Catamazin in his own palace, which stands on the borders of the salt lake, for he suspected nothing and had taken no precautions. They brought him to Temistitan where Muteczuma delivered him to Cortes, who threw him into irons and appointed his brother, Cacuscazin, who was devoted to Muteczuma, to rule in his place. This exchange was exacted by the inhabitants of the towns, who complained that they were ruled too severely by Catamazin; his own brother did not venture to live with him, because he feared his obstinate temperament and violent outbreaks.

Some days later Cortes urged Muteczuma to send messengers to the different princes who, after hearing his speech on the obedience they owed to the great king of the Spains, had returned to their several provinces. Each of these princes should be required to give a part of their property in favour of the great king of the Spains who had begun some important works, which were still unfinished, and was doubtful about the success of his undertaking. Muteczuma acquiesced in this demand and, choosing among his principal confidants those whom he knew best and who were best acquainted with the royal administration, he sent two or three to each of his great vassals. Cortes sent the same number of Spaniards to accompany them. Such terror prevailed amongst these princes, that at the mere name of Spain, not one ventured to protest or to express any other sentiment than that of obedience.

All these embassies penetrated the country in different directions, a distance of fifty, sixty, eighty, and even a hundred leagues. In response to their demands, gifts were offered. The quantity of gold was so great, that Cortes, after melting this metal into ingots, writes that the royal fifth reached thirty-four thousand castellanos. Now Your Beatitude is aware that the value of this coin is one and one-third ducats. Not to mention melted gold, the Spaniards brought back very valuable necklaces, of great weight and artistic workmanship; the workmanship indeed is more valuable than the material, for there are very industrious artisans among these peoples, especially for goldsmiths' work. Your Beatitude is well aware of this fact, since before your elevation to the pontifical throne you saw a number of these wrought objects in my possession.

Cortes also says that they brought him an extraordinary amount of precious stones. The royal fifth of the silver exceeded one hundred pounds at eight ounces, which the Spaniards call *marcs*. The most incredible particulars are reported concerning the furniture decorated with cotton stuffs, the tapestries, clothing, and decorated beds. Nevertheless they must be believed, since such a man as Cortes ventures to write them to the Emperor and to our Council for Indian Affairs. He also adds that he omits a great deal for fear of being wearisome, enumerating such marvels. Those who return from that country are unanimous in their reports

The gifts Cortes has received from Muteczuma are so marvellous, both for their intrinsic value and for their workmanship, that it is better not to describe them until we see them. In company with Your Beatitude, we have examined in the famous city of Valladolid the first ones sent over, and we have described them in our Fourth Decade. Cortes writes that within a few days he will send a number of presents, but that the first to reach us are much inferior in number, quality, and value.

Cortes took his ease, nor, in this succession of important events, did he know what next to do. Reflecting upon the power of Muteczuma the greatness of his empire, and the order and wealth of his administration, he declared that he did not know which way to turn or where to begin his report. He finally decided to begin by describing the

province where lie the two lakes, the immense city of
Temistitan, and many other towns.

This province is called Mexico. It is surrounded by
lofty mountains. As I have already said, it is in this
valley that the two lakes lie, one of which is fresh and
the other salt. It is said that this valley, which is seventy
leagues in circumference, is largely occupied by these
lakes. The city of Temistitan,[1] capital of the great
King Muteczuma, is built in the centre of the salt lake,
and is separated on all sides from the land by the distance
of a league, a league and half, or two leagues. Day and
night, barques come and go over the waters of the lake.
The town is entered by four stone bridges,[2] one at each

---

[1] The religion, laws, manners, and customs of the Mexicans prior to
the Conquest, as well as their architecture and the aspects of their cities,
have been carefully studied and variously described by a number of learned
authors. We owe the first description to Cortes, who, in his letters to
the young King Charles, recorded in a terse, soldierly style what he thought
would please his sovereign and at the same time vindicate his own ambi-
guous methods. Bernal, Diaz, Sahagun, Torquemada, Motolinia, Herrera,
Oviedo, Gomara—these were the earliest students of the strange civilisation revealed by the conquest of Cortes, whose works have come down to
us. Authors of the seventeenth and eighteenth centuries were Acosta,
Duran, Vetancourt, Clavigero, Lorenzana, and Solis. Besides these,
Spaniards all, save Clavigero who was an Italian, there were several native
Mexican writers, of whom Ixtlilxochitl, Tozozomoc, and Camargo are the
best known. Nineteenth century writers sifted and classified according
to modern methods of historical criticism the masses of material, often
confused and bewildering, of the earlier chroniclers. Alaman's *Disertaciones sobre la Historia de Mexico*, and Prescott's *Conquest of Mexico*
are two standard works in Spanish and English respectively, full of
interesting and trustworthy facts presented in the most fascinating literary
style. In our own times, Mexico has produced historians of the highest
order,—Orozco y Berra, Garcia Icazbalceta, and A. Chavero—whose
labours have enriched the historical literature of their country and won
for themselves imperishable fame. In addition to their works, the following may be profitably consulted: L. de Rosny, *Documents écrits de
l'antiquité Américaine*; Bastian, *Die Kulturländer der alten Americana*;
Bandelier, *Sources for Aboriginal History of Spanish-America*; Daniel
Brinton, *Essays of an Americanist*; Zelia Nuttall, *Old and New World
Civilisations*; A. Maudslay, *Biologia Centrali Americana*.

[2] Meaning the causeways.

of the four sides. They are for the most part continuous and solid, with here and there openings cut across them, like gateways. Across these openings wooden bridges are laid, in such wise that the ebb and flow of the waters are free, and these bridges may also be easily raised in case of danger. The bridges are two lance lengths in breadth. We have already described one of these bridges when speaking of the interview between Mutec-zuma and Cortes, and the others resemble it.

An aqueduct flows along one of these bridges bringing potable water for the use of the inhabitants of the town. Here and there stations are established for the royal tax-gatherers who, by means of little boats, carry water to sell throughout the town; for drinkable water in this country must be paid for. This aqueduct is divided into two channels, and when one of these channels becomes choked with weeds carried by the water, the second is opened until the first has been cleaned, in such wise that one is always clean, and the inhabitants may always drink pure water. It is said that this aqueduct is as large round as an ox.

What shall I say concerning the numerous bridges inside the town, by which neighbours communicate with one another? They are built of wood and are wide enough for ten men abreast to cross. It is claimed that they are innumerable, and this is credible, since the majority of the streets are canals. There are, however, land streets, such as may be seen in our famous republic of Venice. It seems there are also other towns similar to Venice on these lakes, built half on the land and half in the water.

Temistitan itself numbers sixty thousand houses and, if what is told is true, one must recognise that this is quite possible. The squares are very large, especially one of them which is surrounded by porticos. Upon this square, traders of all kinds bring together their merchandise. The rented shops, where everything needed for clothing, food, or civil and military ornaments is sold, are most convenient; sixty thousand buyers and sellers may be counted daily at this fair or market. By means of barques they bring the products of their countries to Temistitan, and return with what they do not have at home; just as our peasants come, mounted on little donkeys or other beasts of burden, or perhaps in carts, from their hamlets and farms into the neighbouring towns, bringing the products of their labour such as straw, wood, wine, grain, barley, chickens and, when evening falls, take back home what they need or desire.

There is another very convenient custom for the traders or strangers at Temistitan. There is not a square, nor a cross-roads, nor a junction of two or three streets, where a lodging house is not found, where boiled or roasted meats, birds or quadrupeds are ready at any hour of the day. They eat neither beeves nor goats nor sheep; the meats in general demand are little dogs, which they castrate and raise for food, deer, and wild boars. The people are skilful hunters, and the country produces hares, rabbits, pigeons, quails, partridges, and pheasants.

Their domestic animals are geese and ducks, and they also keep a number of peacocks, which we call hens, and which they rear as our housekeepers do their chickens. I have already somewhere said that these animals resemble our pea-hens in size and the colour of their plumage, but I have not described their habits. The females lay twenty or sometimes thirty eggs, so the number of the flock is always increasing. The cocks are constantly in rut, and consequently their flesh is always mediocre. They constantly preen themselves before their females, just as our peacocks do, and pass their days in spreading their tail in the shape of a wheel before the object of their affection. They prance before them just as do our peacocks, and from time to time at regular intervals, after taking four or more steps, they shiver like the

victims of a strong fever, when their teeth chatter from
cold. They display the different coloured feathers
about their necks, sometimes blue, sometimes green or
purplish, according to the movements of their body;
they remind one of a lover seeking to captivate his beloved.

I will cite a fact, observed by a certain priest, Benito
Martin, who has travelled a great deal of that country
and who reported it to me. In my opinion it is hardly
credible. This priest tells me that he had reared large
flocks of these peacocks, giving special attention to
breeding them. The cock has certain obstacles on his
feet which makes it difficult for him to approach the hen;
so much so that some one whom he knows, must hold the
hen in his hands. It is said that the hen is not afraid
to be thus held, and that the cock has likewise no fear.
As soon as he sees the hen he prefers is caught, he runs
to her while she is being held.[1] Such is his tale; his
companions say that this only happens rarely.

These peacocks lay a considerable quantity of eggs,
as do likewise the geese and ducks. They are eaten
either boiled or cooked in different fashions, or made into
pies. Fish abound both in the lakes and streams; there is
no sea-fish to be had, because the ocean is too far distant.
The tradesmen buy fish raw, boiled, or baked as they
choose.

Their fruits are cherries, plums, and apples of different
kinds, just as with us; but in addition there are many
unknown to us. To satisfy exacting appetites, all kinds
of birds of prey are sold, either living or so cleverly stuffed
with cotton, that whoever sees them might think them
alive. Each trade has its special streets. The herbalists
and those who deal in medicines for the body are highly

---

[1] *Marem, ait, impedimentis quibusdam cruraribus esse implicitum adeo
ut captare fœmina ad coitum vix queat nisi notus aliquis feminam manu
captam teneat, neque feminam, inquit, a captu abhorrere, neque marem accessu
deterreri. Ubi primum teneri amatam cernit adit illico, remque suam in
detenentis manibus peragit.*

considered. I omit mention of the numerous kinds of vegetables, radishes, cresses, onions, and other things. They collect honey from the wax in certain trees, the bees furnishing them as they do with us. We have said enough concerning the poultry, quadrupeds, fish, and other food-stuffs. It is still more interesting to learn with what money these articles are bought. Your Beatitude already knows, because I have elsewhere written about it.

BOOK IV

A S I have already said, it is the fruit of certain trees resembling almonds, that is used by the natives as currency. These fruits are doubly useful, as they serve as money, and from the beans a beverage is made. This bean is not really good to eat; it is rather bitter, although soft, something like a skinned almond. To make the beverage the beans are crushed, and a handful of the powder thus obtained is thrown into water and stirred for some time until it produces a truly royal drink.

O blessed money, which not only gives to the human race a useful and delightful drink, but also prevents its possessors from yielding to infernal avarice, for it cannot be piled up, or hoarded for a long time. There are several other beverages in this country; just as in the country of Your Beatitude the people drink both beer and cider, so are maize, fruits, and certain herbs mixed and cooked in large wooden vessels or jugs. The taverns where these drinks are sold stand near to restaurants.

Before leaving Spain, Your Beatitude was already acquainted with these hitherto unknown particulars concerning the money, but we did not yet know how the tree producing it was planted and cultivated. Now we have exact information. These trees are planted in but few situations, for they require a climate both warm and damp, and a relatively fertile soil. There are caciques who pay their taxes with nothing but the fruit of these trees. By their sale they acquire what they want,—animals, slaves, clothing, and whatever they use for ornament or other purposes.

The traders visit them and provide them with the different articles, taking away a quantity of those fruits, which they afterwards disperse throughout the other provinces, and thus the beans circulate so easily that all the neighbouring people profit by the advantages they offer. After all, precisely the same thing happens everywhere else in the world; spices, gold, silver, steel, iron, lead, and other metals, and the natural products of the earth enable us to buy foreign merchandise. The merchants who visit countries which do not produce these things, or which, because of human laziness, are reputed not to produce them, bring back what they suppose will be acceptable to the neighbouring peoples. In this wise various natural products are everywhere disseminated. Such is human life, and thus must we speak. But let us now explain the method employed in the culture of those trees. They are planted under the shade of a tree which protects them from the sun's rays or against the dangers of fog, just as a child is sheltered in the bosom of its nurse. As soon as the tree begins to grow expanding its roots and gaining strength from the good air and sunshine, the protecting tree is cut down and removed. We have said enough about the currency. If vulgar or limited minds refuse to believe these particulars, I would not have them forced to do so.

In the market-places of Temistitan, everything necessary, for the construction and decoration of houses is sold: beams, timbers, combustible woods, lime, plaster, bricks, and dressed stone. They likewise sell different kinds of earthenware vases; jugs, cups with handles, bowls, plates, platters, kettles, cooking-stoves, basins, cups, and all hand-made utensils. In this country there is neither steel nor iron, but there is plenty of gold, silver, tin, lead, and copper, and metal in every state, whether ore, or smelted, moulded, or manufactured into jewelry.[1]

The artists are very clever in imitating nature; for they reproduce whatever they see with great artistic skill. There does not exist a single bird, or figure, or form of quadruped, of which Muteczuma does not possess a reproduction so real and so lifelike that at a little distance it seems alive. Your Beatitude is not ignorant of this fact, for you saw and examined some specimens of this industry among the presents brought to Spain before you left for Rome.

There is another detail which should not be omitted. On one side of the great market-place there stands a court of justice, where ten or twelve chosen ancients continually sit, as judges, to decide all cases presented. They are assisted by servants like lictors armed with staves, who carry out their orders. Ediles are also in attendance there to regulate accounts and measures. It still remains to discover what weights they use, for we do not know this. There is something else meriting notice. I have said that there is a great abundance of everything in this town built in the midst of the lake, and yet the inhabitants use no beasts of burden, neither mules, asses, nor oxen to draw their wagons and carts. It will not be unreasonable to ask how they manage their carrying, especially the transport of such large beams and building-stones and similar materials. All these, let it be known, are carried on the backs of slaves. It will also be thought very extraordinary that, having no steel, or iron, they execute their work with such delicacy and elegance. Let me say that all these things are fashioned with stone tools.

[1] Consult Reynolds, *The Metal Art of Ancient Mexico* (1887); Blake, *The metals of the Aztecs* (1888); Ed. Seler's paper in the report of the Americanist Congress of 1890 at Paris, on Mexican jewelry and feather-work; also Zelia Nuttall's interesting study on the same subject, contained in the same report.

At the very beginning of the Maritime Prefect's discoveries or to give him his Spanish title, the Admiral, Christopher Columbus, I had in my hands a stone brought from that country, which the Admiral had himself presented to me. It was of emerald green colour, set and fastened in very hard wood. I myself have struck bars of iron with it as hard as I could, but although the iron bars showed visible marks, the stone remained intact. It is of such stones they make the tools required for the lapidaries', carpenters', goldsmiths', and jewelers' arts.

Fearing vicissitudes—the changing events—might affect the disposition of the natives, and that the inhabitants of Temistitan might, contrary to Muteczuma's will, revolt, either from weariness of the prolonged hospitality they showed the Spaniards, or that they might seize any excuse that offered for taking up arms, Cortes, seeing himself shut in by water on one side, and by easily removable bridges on the other, built on the salt lake four small galleys with two banks of oars of the type called brigantines. He hoped, in case of necessity, to use these brigantines for transporting a score of his men and their horses to land. As soon as the brigantines were finished he felt himself, thanks to them, in safety, and resolved to inspect the curiosities of the capital, which are certainly not negligible.

He first visited the temples in company with Muteczuma. Just as we have what is called a parish in each quarter, and dedicate churches to particular saints, so amongst the Mexicans there are temples dedicated to the particular idols of the quarter. May Your Beatitude listen to the details concerning the largest temple and the idols which there hold the first place. This temple,[1] is square, and on each side is a large door, to which

---

[1] The great temple was begun by Montezuma I., called Ilhuicanima and finished by his son and successor, Ahuitzotl, in 1486 when it was dedicated with wearisome and bloodthirsty rites in which countless lives were sacrificed. Consult Tezozomoc, *Historia de Mexico*, and Orozco y Berra, *Hist. Antigua de la Conquista*, tom. iii., cap. vii.

those four magnificent causeways, which unite the town
with the mainland like so many bridges, lead in straight
lines. The space occupied by the temple is large enough
for a town of five hundred inhabitants. It is surrounded
by lofty walls of stone, artistically built. Upon these
walls are numerous towers and the whole has the appearance of a strong fortress. Four of these towers are larger
and more spacious than the others, because in them are
courts and chambers for housing of the priests. The
first halls, where the priests who perform the sacrifices, live
are reached by marble stairs of fifty steps. The sons of
the principal chiefs of the state are kept there from the
age of seven, never leaving or going a step outside, before
reaching the marriageable age for which they are educated.
During this period they never cut their hair. They live
simply, abstaining on certain days of the year from flesh
meat, and disciplining their bodies by fasts, to keep them
in subjection to their reason. They are dressed in black.

According to Cortes, one of these towers is loftier than
the highest belfry of Seville.[1] He adds: "Nowhere
have I seen more beautiful or more important monuments,
built with more perfect art." I shall doubtless be asked
by inquisitive people whether Cortes has ever seen any
monuments outside Spain.[2]

Those who return from that country report the idols as
horrible beyond description. I make no mention of the
marble statue of Vuichilabuchichi,[3] the greatest of their

---

[1] Meaning the famous Giralda tower.

[2] As a matter of fact he had not. Born in the insignificant town of
Medellin, Cortes studied two years at Salamanca; he spent a year of
poverty and hardship at Valencia and may possibly have visited Seville,
Cordova, and other cities in his wanderings. He sailed at the age of nine-
teen for San Lucar de Barrameda, so his knowledge of great architectural
monuments, seen in Spain, was obviously limited.

[3] Meaning Huitzilopochtli, at whose side sat the page Huitziton; the
companion idol was that of Tezcatlipoca. The temple first visited by
Cortes was not the great teocalli, but the one standing in the Tlatelolco
market-place.

gods, always accompanied by three human statues, and
which is in no way inferior to the Colossus of Rhodes.
Whenever a devotee, moved by piety, desires to dedicate
a statue to any divinity, he busies himself in collecting a
quantity of all kinds of edible seeds, sufficient to compose
a statue of the size he desires. These seeds are then
ground to flour.

Oh, what frightful crime! O, what horrible barbarity!
When this flour is ground, children, young girls, and
slaves in the required number are murdered, and their
blood supplies the place of tepid water in mixing a paste.
While this paste is still damp and soft, though sufficiently
thick, the artist and the overseer of this odious work,
assisted by the infernal sacrificing priest, handles this
substance as the potter does his clay or the wax-modeller
his wax, and complete their labour without repugnance.
If I remember rightly I have elsewhere reported that the
victims are not sacrificed by cutting their throats, but
by opening their breasts above the heart; and that while
these unfortunates are still living and realise their unhappy
fate, their hearts are torn out and offered to the gods.
The lips of the idols are smeared with the blood that
flows from the heart, and the latter is burned, to appease,
as they think, the anger of the divinity: at least the
priests have taught the people this absurdity.

I will be asked, and with reason, what is done with the
members and flesh of the unhappy victims. O abominable and nauseous disgust! Just as the Jews under the
ancient law formerly ate the lambs they sacrificed, so do
these natives devour the human flesh, leaving only the
hands, feet, and entrails untouched. Let us note that,
according to their wants, they construct different figures
of gods, one to secure victory, another to obtain health, or
for some similar motive.

But let us return to the visit of Cortes in the great
temple. In the vast courts we have mentioned, there are

numerous huge statues of gods and also dark sanctuaries, only entered by narrow openings, entrance to which is the exclusive privilege of the priests. The great courts dedicated to the important gods are set aside as burial-places for princes, and the smaller and less important ones for the burial of nobles. Human sacrifices are celebrated each year according to the means of each family, just as amongst us poor people burn a small dip to the divinity, while the wealthy light a large candle; or many are content to burn incense, while others found churches. We believe the incense and wax suffice to procure us the favour of Christ and the saints, provided our offering is fervently made.

In the course of the visit of Cortes and Muteczuma to the temple, it happened that some of the former's companions entered the narrow dark sanctuaries, in spite of the opposition of the guardians. They perceived by the light of torches that the walls were stained red; and wishing to convince themselves they scratched the wall with their daggers. O horrors! not only were the walls sprinkled with the blood of human victims, but there were pools of blood two fingers deep on the floors. It was enough to nauseate the stomach! Where the wall had been scratched with their daggers, an intolerable odour exhaled from the decomposed blood covered with fresh blood.

In the midst of all these horrors there is one thing that will cause us rejoicing. Cortes ordered all the idols in the court to be overthrown,[1] after which he smashed them to pieces, and the pieces, after being reduced to

---

[1] Two separate visits of Cortes to two different temples are here combined into one. Subsequent authors, ignoring the description penned by the Conqueror himself in his second letter to Charles V., have repeated this error. The smashing of the idols in the great teocalli took place five months after the first visit to the Tlatelolco temple. Consult, *Letters of Cortes*, Second Letter to Charles V.; *Hist. Verdad.*, cap. viii.; Orozco y Berra, *Hist. Antiq.*, tom. iv., cap. v.

powder, were scattered over the steps of the temple. The only one he spared was the marble colossus, which was too large to be easily broken up. Muteczuma, profoundly disturbed, witnessed this scene. All the courtiers who accompanied the emperor were horrified, and broke forth into lamentations, saying: "Miserable and unfortunate creatures that we are: the gods are angry with us. They will take from us the products of the earth by which we live, and we shall die of hunger; every malady will overtake us, as happens to those towards whom the gods are ill-disposed. If our enemies attack us, we shall have no shelter; we shall be attacked by the people, who will rise in fury against us, when they hear of this sacrilege."

Cortes answered: "Is it possible to imagine anything more monstrous and more absurd? Do you then believe that these figures, made by the hands of your own servants, are gods? Are the works of your own hands superior to your dignity as men? O Muteczuma! Is this thing, made by the hands of your artisan, perhaps a vile slave, more honourable than your own majesty? What blindness or rather what mad credulity! Is it because of these senseless idols that you yearly sacrifice so many human victims? Do you then believe that these objects, which neither see nor hear, can think? There is but one God, who has created the heavens and the earth, and it is him you should adore. This God, from whom all good things proceed, abhors your sacrifices. Moreover, it has been expressly forbidden by our King who, according to what you yourself say, descends from him who brought your ancestors to this country, that whoever sacrifices man or woman shall perish by the sword."

When this decision of Cortes was communicated by interpreters to Muteczuma, the latter, pale with fear and quivering with excitement, said: "Bear in mind, Cortes, that the ceremonies we have observed and solemnised until now were taught us by our ancestors. If you now teach us that we are in profound error and displease your sovereign, we are glad to know it and we shall endeavour to convince the people. Perhaps our ancestors, left to themselves, found these rites observed by the aborigines of that time; as for ourselves, we have followed the traditions of our forefathers and their wives, and you need not be astonished that we have committed these grave faults, if indeed faults they be. Give your orders, and we shall do our best to carry them out."

Upon hearing these words, Cortes repeated that there was but one God, in three persons, one in his essence, who created the heavens and the earth, the sun and the moon, and all the stars scattered about the earth for its adornment. The killing of men is an odious act in his eyes, for he created from the same substance both slaves and all who have human shape, like myself or you, or these others who hear us. This God is born of the womb of a Virgin; coming into our midst he suffered for the salvation of the human race. Wise men, whose coming we await, will one day explain this more clearly to you and to your people. The emblem of this God and the sign of victory is the figure of the cross, as well as the image of the Virgin Mother bearing a child upon her breast. Speaking thus, Cortes, who transformed himself for the occasion, from a lawyer into a theologian, exhibited for the adoration of the bystanders a cross and an image of the Virgin.

In this way were the odious vestiges of idolatry destroyed, and Muteczuma ordered his servants to cleanse the courts of the temple in his presence, and to so cleanse the walls that there should not remain a trace of those blood-stains. But this is enough concerning the abominable religion of the people of Temistitan. Let us pass to the palaces of the lords and wealthy people.

Cortes declares that he has never seen a royal palace

or a princely establishment in Spain, that was not inferior to seventy palaces in this town. These buildings are constructed of stone and marble, and are decorated with every architectural device. Everywhere are variegated pavements, doors of jasper or white transparent marble surrounding the courts, or immense stone colonnades open to the sun.

He adds that all the marvels concerning this country should be believed. Numerous kingdoms are certainly subject to Muteczuma, and in the different provinces of these kingdoms there live numerous lords, similar to the dukes, counts, marquises, and other nobles, subject to our Emperor's authority. At certain periods of the year and in conformity with an ancient custom, all these nobles betake themselves to Muteczuma's court whether they like it or not. Each resolves to eclipse his fellows by the splendour of his establishment. I might well compare the sojourn in Muteczuma's court with that of the cardinals at Rome, but it is not precisely the same thing, for the cardinals build for nobody but themselves, and care not at all for their successors; whereas Muteczuma's vassals consider their remote posterity. They send their sons, especially the eldest, to Muteczuma's court for their education, and there is such a great number of these children that more than five hundred of them may daily be seen walking in the courts or on the terraces of the palace; and during this period until the hour of their retirement, their servants and dependents are so numerous that they fill three large interior courts and the squares in front of the palace gates. They are fed at Muteczuma's expense, and a table stands all day laid for every comer who has a right to call for drink from the cellarers. Nobody may see the emperor before he leaves his private apartments to dine or sup, or to go into the large court described by Cortes as being larger than any other in the world. When he takes his seat, three hundred youths dressed in palace uniform

enter, bearing various dishes placed upon heaters, to prevent the viands from cooling in winter time.   These youths
do not approach the table, for it is protected by a barrier,
behind which stands but one person, who takes the dishes
from the young lads, and presents them to the sovereign.

According to an ancient custom, Muteczuma then distributes food from these dishes to six highly respected
ancients, who stand at his right.   While he is eating
everybody is barefooted.   The floors are covered with
mats.   If Muteczuma chances to speak to any one, the
person addressed advances, bending his body and fixing his
eyes upon the earth, nor does he raise them until he has
again retired backwards.   It is forbidden either to turn
the back, or to look the king in the face.   These attendants and domestic servants, as well as the greatest
nobles, listen to his words with eyes cast down, and
faces turned either to the right or to the left.   Cortes
was therefore rebuked for having permitted his soldiers,
who were summoned by the sovereign, to look him in
the face,[1] but he answered: "It is not our custom:
and our King, who knows that he is mortal, but is nevertheless very powerful, does not consider himself entitled
to so much respect and adoration."   This reply met
with approval.

In Muteczuma's presence, no matter what attitude he
assumes, all this crowd of people keeps such profound
silence that they hardly seem to breathe.   At each repast,
whether dinner or supper, the sovereign washes twice,
drying himself with very white linen and never using the
same linen twice.   Everything used in his service is
never used a second time, and it is the same with his
clothing.   When he rises, he puts on the dress he will
wear until dinner; when he enters his private apartments

---

[1] Meaning that the Aztecs thought the Spanish soldiers wanting in
respect because they looked Cortes in the face when speaking with him.
It is thus that Cortes reports this detail in his letter to the Emperor.

he dresses a second time; when he comes out to supper he dresses a third time, and after supper he dresses a fourth. This last costume he wears till night. All these particulars concerning his changes of costume have been reported to me by Spaniards who have returned from that country, and they all agree as to this fact and say that the clothing once worn is piled away in the sovereign's treasure house, and never again used by him. I will later explain of what delicate fabrics these garments are made, and then there need be no further astonishment that I have so often mentioned the costumes offered as presents.

There will indeed be no grounds for our astonishment if we count the years and days during which Muteczuma has enjoyed the sweets of peace, and add thereto the number of times he has changed his clothes each day. No doubt my readers will demand, not unreasonably, why Muteczuma accumulates such a quantity of clothing; they should learn that this sovereign's custom is to present his attendants or his bravest soldiers going or returning from war with these garments, as a recompense or extra pay. Thus did Cæsar Augustus, the master of the world and more powerful than Muteczuma, give to those who distinguished themselves by some great deed only a miserable ration of bread and food, until Virgil made him understand that this stingy dole of bread served to prove that he was the son of a baker.

Though it is written that this pleasantry was not displeasing to Cæsar, yet is it likewise credible that he was ashamed at being thus understood; for he promised Virgil that henceforth his gifts should be worthy of a great king, rather than of a baker's son.

Muteczuma eats and drinks from terra-cotta vessels, though he has a great number of utensils of wrought gold and silver, and of precious stones. All the earthenware vessels he has once used, whether basins, plates, platters, jugs or others similar, are never again placed before him.

Let us now say a few words about the palaces and great country houses.

Each noble possesses, in addition to his town house, beautiful pleasure houses in the country, about which are laid out gardens, orchards, and parks in which all kinds of plants, roses, and fragrant flowers grow. Great skill is displayed in the care of these parks, and in planting hedges to enclose and protect them from invasion and pillage. In all these gardens there are ponds well stocked with quantities of various fish, and upon whose surface a multitude of aquatic birds lives. Since each noble possesses such houses, it is only proper that their supreme chief, Muteczuma, should surpass them. He has three great palaces in which he takes refuge from the heat of summer. In the first he has collected a large number of monstrosities, dwarfs, cripples, albinos, and people with one leg or two heads; and these have servants to attend them.

The second palace is stocked with birds of prey: vultures, eagles, and other varieties of carnivorous hawks and birds are kept there. Each bird has its own open cage, standing above a court and provided with two perches, one outside on which it may sun itself, and one inside on which it roosts. Each cage is separated from its neighbour by a strong barrier, and the interior court is covered with a sort of wooden lattice, so arranged that the birds may enjoy the open air, and fly about fearlessly in the quarters assigned to them. There are not only servants to attend to these birds, but there are numerous paid surgeons who know how to discover and cure the different diseases to which birds are subject.

Of the aquatic birds, those from the sea are kept in ponds of salt water, while those from fresh waters have such ponds prepared for them. At certain times of the year the water is drawn off and the tanks carefully cleaned before it is renewed. Each species of bird receives from its particular attendant the fish, plants, grain, and maize that it requires; and this food is supplied by Muteczuma's intendants and administrators.

Round about these ponds are built marble porticos whose pilasters are of marble, alabaster, and jasper. There are also terraces, from which Muteczuma may watch the birds playing or fighting, especially at feeding time. The third palace is a menagerie of lions, tigers, wolves, foxes, and other wild beasts, and there are likewise enclosures and rooms for the peacocks I have already mentioned, and which serve as food for these ferocious animals. Each of these palaces has apartments always in readiness, so that should the King fancy to pass the night there with his attendants, he may easily do so.

This is the report, as it has been made to us, and we repeat it. We likewise believe what has been written and said, first, because we suppose that nobody would venture to tamper with the truth, and also because we have learned that everything possible and not miraculous may happen. Moreover, many details have been omitted, for fear of wearying the attention of the Emperor and the court by lengthy reports.

While the Spaniards were occupied with these investigations, envoys accompanied by some of our men had been sent into some of the different provinces composing Muteczuma's empire. They were authorised in the sovereign's name to announce to the rulers that they were henceforth to render allegiance to the great King of Spain and his representatives.

From the eastern coast to the extreme limits of Yucatan extends a territory believed to be three times as large as Spain. Yucatan, the first land sighted coming from Cuba, is believed to be an island, but the fact is not yet proven. From the town of Potenchan, now called Victoria, the distance to Temistitan is more than one hundred leagues;

and between the town of Potenchan and Yucatan to the gulf called Figueras the distance is the same.

In the western part, about two hundred leagues from Temistitan, is a town called Cumatana. The cacique of this town, whose name is unknown, and all the intermediary tribes and the provinces between, as far as Potenchan, were vassals of Muteczuma, with the exception of some republics of which I have said enough. All these tribes are now our subjects.

Cortes had often urged Muteczuma to return to his former palace, but the emperor refused, saying: "We must not separate; for, I repeat, my great vassals place their own interests above our friendship, and they will insistently urge me to raise a revolt among the people and make war upon you. As long as we remain together, we shall be safer against their insolent ambition."

Muteczuma was glad to sometimes return to his former palace, but in the evening he was always carried back in his litter to the residence of Cortes. In coming or going, nobody looked him in the face, and such was the respect he inspired that no one felt worthy of a glance from him. This is an ancient superstition prevailing amongst the natives.

But what? But what? and a third time, but what? Fortune, like a tender nurse, smiles upon us; her wheel turns, and caresses are changed into blows. Cortes had entered the lake city on the eighth day of September, 1519; and had there passed the winter and the greater part of the spring of the following year till the month of May, in perfect tranquillity. At this time, Diego Velasquez, governor of Cuba (or Fernandina), fitted out a fleet against Cortes, because the latter, without consulting him and in spite of him, as I have above explained, had landed and founded colonies in that region.

A little later I shall speak of this fleet, but for the moment I shall keep to Cortes alone. While he thus spent his time with Muteczuma, awaiting impatiently the return of his envoys, Montejo and Portocarrero, whom he had sent to carry gifts to the Emperor, the natives along the coast notified him that vessels had been seen on the high sea. Assuming it to be the ship carrying his envoys, Cortes at first rejoiced; but his joy soon changed into sadness.

Just here I shall omit many particulars. The Jews and Greeks, whose activities occupied a much narrower theatre, would have padded their histories with details, had their citizens been the heroes; but we may well leave out a large number of the many events that have happened. In brief, it was the fleet, sent by Diego Velasquez, whose presence was reported. It was composed of eighteen ships, including caravels armed with rams, and brigantines with two banks of oars. This fleet carried eight hundred foot-soldiers, eighty horsemen, and seventeen cannon, of which we shall speak later.

Velasquez had appointed a young man named Panfilo de Narvaez commander; and to him Cortes at once sent envoys begging him to treat amicably, and not to spoil the promising beginning he had made. Panfilo replied that the Emperor's instructions warranted him in considering himself to be commander-in-chief of all that region, and he therefore enjoined Cortes to resign his command and to present himself unarmed before him, to give an account of his conduct, and to abide by whatever decision might be taken, either by himself or by Diego Velasquez, concerning him. Cortes answered that he would submit to letters patent from the Emperor, but he requested that they should be shown to the magistrate appointed by him to administer the colony of Vera Cruz. If, however, Narvaez had untruthfully asserted such letters to be in his possession, he had better quit the country where he intruded, taking particular care to commit no pillage in the territory he might occupy, for it was conducive to the King's interest (as he might easily understand) not to interfere with an undertaking so happily begun, by landing men. The barbarians who were already conquered and obedient to the Emperor, whose name they revered, would revolt as soon as they understood that the Spaniards[1] were at strife amongst themselves and acting for different ends.

[1] Meaning the partisans of Cortes and those of Narvaez.

BOOK V

THE representatives of the two rival parties conferred
at length, but reached no decision; Narvaez
refused to make any concessions. During this
time Muteczuma received from some of his subjects,
bark tablets, on which were depicted the Spanish vessels,
each with its cannon and horses, not to mention the eighty
musketeers and the one hundred and twenty archers
who had landed. This news also greatly disturbed Cortes,
and he was uncertain what course to follow. If he ignored
the landing, he risked seeing the authority of his declared
enemy increased; not only over the Spaniards, but also
amongst the barbarians. It was hard for him to abandon
such an undertaking, for he divined the approaching revolt
of the barbarians which in fact followed. He judged it
wiser to go himself to meet Narvaez, hoping the latter
would respect the authority he bore as a justice in Cuba,
where he was the superior of Narvaez and the newcomers.

Leaving a garrison[1] in the palace inhabited by Muteczuma, Cortes spoke to the latter in the following words:
"Muteczuma, my king, you have now the opportunity to
assure your future happiness. If your sovereign is convinced of your fidelity, in these circumstances, all future
events will be advantageous and agreeable for you. I am

---

[1] Cortes left Pedro de Alvarado in command, and in so doing committed
one of the gravest blunders of his life. Alvarado was quick tempered,
violent, and cruel, in short totally unsuited to exercise authority under
the actual conditions and in his commander's absence.

leaving to obtain information for myself, and in my absence
do you take care that nothing occurs here. I commit to
your care the Spaniards I leave in your service."

Muteczuma promised all that was asked of him, and
affirmed that he would treat the Spaniards as his kinsmen,
adding: "Go, and may good fortune go with you; and
let me know if these men have landed with hostile intent,
for I will give orders for them to be driven from my
territory."

Leaving the garrison in Temistitan, and having made
some presents to Muteczuma and his son, which pleased
them, Cortes set forth to meet Narvaez. The latter
was established at Cempoal, where he had induced the
inhabitants to declare against Cortes. He was resolved to stop at nothing on his march. Cortes approached, and waiving all other formalities, summoned
his *aguazil* (that is to say the sheriff, and in Latin *miles*[1]),
whom he sent on ahead with eighty foot-soldiers, ordering
him, in virtue of his judicial powers, to seize Narvaez.
He himself prepared to follow with his remaining one
hundred and seventy men. He therefore had two hundred
and fifty men against Narvaez, who, acting upon the
information of his spies, was well on his guard. He had
fortified himself in one of the lofty towers of the temple
of Cempoal, upon the steps of which he had placed eight
cannon.

Less fortunate than the Trojan Hector, he and his
eight hundred soldiers were surrounded, besieged, and
captured. We believe the soldiers did not venture to
resist Cortes, who had intimidated them when he was
justice in Cuba. We rather think their chiefs had been
bought by Cortes, when, under pretext of negotiating,
they left their swords in their scabbards. Many insinu-

---

[1] (*is est justitiæ executor, quem latinus militem appellat, ut Rarus venit
in cœnacula miles*). The last six words appear to be a quotation, but it
seems inapt and of obscure origin.

ations in this sense were levelled at Cortes, which I will later explain. However that may be, as Narvaez showed some resistance, he lost one of his eyes and, in company with the officers who still remained faithful to him, was taken prisoner.[1] These officers were a very small number.

Narvaez had been accompanied by the licenciate Ayllon, an eminent jurisconsult and one of the chief officials of Hispaniola. In the name of the government of Hispaniola, which possessed sovereign power in all this region, Ayllon had forbidden Velasquez to send his fleet against Cortes, lest he should thereby provoke a great disaster. He said that the quarrel should be settled by royal authority, and not by an appeal to arms. He overtook Narvaez, and, animated by the same intentions, he strove by every means to divert the authors of this project from their intentions. Not only did this Terentian Panfilo reject this advice, but he put the licenciate into irons and sent him back to Velasquez, the director of the expedition in Cuba. The licenciate's ability was so great that he not only won over the sailors to his view, but he likewise prevailed upon them to carry his own gaolers back to Hispaniola. Such are the surprises of fortune; but these are only the lesser facts of history. Let us now proceed to the narration of serious events.

All the men who had embarked under Narvaez recognised Cortes as their new leader, and the latter immediately sent ships to Vera Cruz to announce his success to the garrison, while he himself set out with the rest of the men for Temistitan. He despatched a mes-

[1] After his defeat, Narvaez was conducted before Cortes to whom he remarked with bitterness: "You have good reason to thank Fortune for giving you an easy victory and placing me in your power." To which Cortes cuttingly retorted: "The least important deed I have accomplished in this country, was to capture you." Consult, Bernal Diaz, cap. cxxii.; *Relacion de Andres de Tapia;* Oviedo, *Historia de las Indias;* lib. xxxiii., cap. xlvii.; MacNutt, *Fernando Cortes,* cap. ix.

senger in advance to announce the happy result to Muteczuma and the Spaniards. This messenger was found on
the road, covered with wounds and groaning. He said:
"All Temistitan is in revolt; the barbarians have risen
and burned the four brigantines [above mentioned]
and which would have secured the escape of our men.
The Spanish garrison is besieged, and reduced to the last
extremity, for it is closely surrounded by armed men,
and is in flames. All provisions are intercepted; everything would already be lost but for the intervention of
Muteczuma, to whom, however, his subjects begin to
refuse obedience."

As soon as he reached the shore of the salt lake Cortes
sent some men in a canoe dug out of a tree trunk to
reconnoitre. They were met by another canoe carrying
a messenger from Muteczuma, and a Spaniard from the
besieged garrison. These men explained the dangerous
situation to Cortes, and assured him that what had
happened was in spite of Muteczuma, but that there
was no time to be lost. If Cortes would but quickly
arrive, Muteczuma hoped the revolt would soon subside.
The General immediately embarked on a number of canoes
and betook himself to the assistance of the garrison and
the Emperor, who was terrified by this sedition. This
was the eighth day of the calends of July.

The wooden bridges which divided the stone causeways
at intervals were all raised, and the streets were barricaded. Cortes at first attributed these precautions to fear,
but in this he was entirely mistaken. The natives were
resolved to die rather than endure the presence of such
guests, who held their king prisoner under the pretext
of protecting him, and took possession of their town. The
maintenance of their hereditary enemies of Tascalteca,
Guazuzingo, and other tribes lodged among them, constituted a perpetual outrage; all these people were
consuming the provisions, difficult to obtain in a town

surrounded by water and deprived by nature of resources; they heaped insolence upon them and loaded them with taxes; anything of value they wanted, they obtained by violence or fraud; moreover they had destroyed the images of the gods and banished the sacred rites and ancient ceremonies of Mexico. For these reasons the lords of the city, acting together with the vassals enjoying the king's intimacy and whose sons were educated from their youth in his household, resolved in their fury to exterminate these foreigners, as farmers tear up weeds from their fields. In spite of Muteezuma's wish, even in spite of his opposition, they determined to besiege the palace, and to either kill the garrison or starve them out. Thus the Spaniards were reduced to the last extremity, when the arrival of Cortes revived some hope in their wavering minds at a time when everything appeared to be lost.

The Spaniards were entrenched in the palace as though it were a fortress, but one of the lofty towers of the temple, surrounded by a pine grove, overlooked the palace. From the top of this tower and from the pine grove,[1] the natives threw stones and other projectiles, which did much damage to the Spaniards. As soon as they learned of the arrival of Cortes with reinforcements for his men, their anger and the fierceness of the combat redoubled. Stones, javelins, arrows, and every sort of missile fell like a black rain, in such numbers that they obscured the sun. The air rang with the cries of the multitude of determined warriors.

Cortes ordered an officer with two hundred soldiers to effect a sortie against the warriors in the square. This force opened a way through the hostile ranks, but was speedily surrounded by an immense multitude and found itself unable to advance a step. It was with

[1] No mention of a pine grove is elsewhere found, nor does the typography of the city, as we know it from drawings, maps, and written descriptions admit the existence of anything corresponding to a "grove" near the palace of Axayacatl and the great teocalli.

difficulty the men regained the fortress, for they had to cut their way through, losing several of their men, while the officer was seriously wounded. Cortes issued forth on the other side, but without much effect; for as soon as the barbarians had let fly their stones and javelins, they took refuge in the little towers called by the Spaniards *azoteas,* which are numerous in the town. The battle was long and furious, and Cortes was finally obliged to retreat inside his walls, which he only succeeded with difficulty in doing. Many of his allies were killed by the stones and other projectiles.

As soon as he had regained his quarters, the barbarians began a siege. They attacked on every side simultaneously, seeking to destroy or storm the palace and bending their efforts against the doors, which they sought to burn. The defenders killed a number of the assailants, with their cannon, muskets, and arrows, but such was the hatred animating the survivors, that they trampled, when necessary, over the bodies of their comrades, and returned to the fight. It seems they fought from dawn till dark, and their fatigue was intolerable, for they were forced to remain under arms the entire day; the assailants, on the contrary, replaced their weary men every quarter of an hour with others, while the places of the killed and wounded were taken by fresh troops, who hurled themselves into the battle with the same enthusiasm as those who had retired, worn out by fighting; to such an extent had their hatred of the Spaniards unbalanced their judgment.

They incited and encouraged each other to drive these dangerous guests from among them; it was better for them all to perish than to sit down peaceably under this odious yoke; better to lose their souls and save their country's freedom. During the whole day the barbarians, like wolves raging round a village, kept up the fight. Towards evening the combat ceased, but during the night they emitted such yells that everybody in the neighbourhood was deafened.   Even inside the citadel the men could not hear thenselves speak for the fearful noise of their cries. When the barbarians drew off at the close of the first day, Cortes took stock of his wounded, and found that they numbered eighty.

On the morrow, the eighth day of the calends of July, the barbarians renewed the attack more fiercely than ever, and a determined fight began.   Cortes protected his front by thirteen field pieces, some musketeers, and archers; but though every shot brought down between ten and twelve of the assailants to the ground, scattering their legs and arms in the air, it is marvellous to relate, they did not flinch.   They closed up their ranks wherever the bullets had made an opening, just as Germans or Swiss might do.

Driven by the scarcity of provisions, Cortes resolved the following day to try his fortune in the open field. The Spaniards marched out from their quarters like raging lions goaded by hunger.   They fell upon the enemy, killing great numbers and capturing some houses in the neighbourhood of their quarters.   They also regained some of the wooden bridges across the streets, but when night fell, they returned just as hungry, and with Cortes and fifty of his companions wounded.

As their necessities increased and the need of food became daily more urgent, the Spaniards were forced to devise some means for still further punishing their enemies and forcing them to make peace.   Cortes had three engines of war constructed during the night.   They were built of wood in the shape of a small square house; in military engineering they are called turtles, and each one held twenty soldiers.   These machines were mounted on wheels and sent out, each filled with musketeers and archers.   They were followed by men carrying axes and picks, to destroy the houses and break down the barricades; but from the roofs of the little towers commanding each of the streets, such a quantity of stones and darts was rained down upon the turtles that their roofs were broken, and the men were forced to beat a hasty retreat into the citadel.

During this time the unhappy Muteczuma, who was always a prisoner, asked to be brought before the assailants, promising to do his best to raise the siege. By an unfortunate chance he was conducted to an open platform at a place where the combatants were most numerous. Such a shower of stones greeted the Spaniards that whoever showed his face was wounded; and it was there that the omnipotent sovereign, Muteczuma, perished. He was a man well endowed by nature, and of great prudence. His end was lamentable when we remember his greatness and prosperity; on the third day of the battle, a stone thrown by one of his own subjects, struck and killed him.[1]   Thus did this master of many kingdoms, so feared by nations, disappear. The Spaniards delivered his body to his subjects, that it might receive the honours of sepulture, but what they did with it is not known. For the moment the only thing they were allowed time to think about was how to save their lives.

[1] Such was the version of Montezuma's death sent to Spain by Cortes. It is flatly contradicted by the Mexican accounts of the event and has failed to convince unbiased investigators. Clavigero and Prescott are two notable exceptions, both these learned writers generously accepting the statement of Cortes as truthfully presenting all the facts. The views of different authorities are discussed in MacNutt's *Fernando Cortes*, cap. x. For full information concerning the last hours, death and burial of Montezuma, consult: Ixtlilxochitl, *Historia Chichimeca*, cap. lxxxviii.; Herrera, dec. ii., lib. x., cap. x.; Bernal Diaz, *Hist. Verdad.*, cap. cxxviii.; Clavigero, *Storia Antica del Messico*, tom. ii., p. 103; José Ramirez, *Bautismo de Motecuhzoma II.*; Torquemada, *Monarchia Indiana*, lib. iv., cap. lxx.; Orozco y Berra, *Conquista de Mexico*, tom. iv.

BOOK VI

THE following day Cortes summoned the chiefs of the city and the relatives of the sovereign, amongst whom was his brother, Astapalappa,[1] to the place where the fatal accident overtook Muteczuma, and made them the following speech: "I conjure and exhort you to choose peace rather than war. If you persist in your present dispositions, I shall raze to its foundations this illustrious and noble capital where you were born. I lament the misfortunes that have overtaken you, for I consider you my friends." They answered that his proposal was not acceptable. "We do not want your friendship, for we regard you as our declared enemy. The peace you offer us we reject, until the day when you restore freedom to our country by withdrawing your troops." Cortes again reminded them of the serious harm and catastrophes to which they were exposing themselves, but they answered: "We all prefer to die bravely rather than to submit to such an odious yoke. Prepare therefore to withdraw, and do not place your faith in empty words. Death would be welcomed by us, if we succeeded in saving ourselves and our children from slavery."

Cortes replied by reminding them of what those nations who had refused his alliance had suffered, and he promised them a complete amnesty for the past, but they answered:

[1] Meaning presumably, Cuitlahuatzin, ruler of Iztapalapan.

"Neither friendship nor amnesty. Moreover, we are confident that you will all perish to the last man, either by hunger or in battle. Consider how easy it will be, since we are a multitude of desperate men, desiring your death and indifferent to the loss of thousands of our own. We will be satisfied to give a thousand lives for one of yours This is our unanimous and final determination. Go back, therefore, whence you came, and decide while you and your people still have time. We beg and entreat you to leave us our freedom to live in conformity with the usages inherited from our forefathers."

Cortes and all his companions were at the point of starvation unless they succeeded in opening a way through the enemy's ranks, for the scarcity of provisions had reduced them to the last extremity. Necessity wrung from them the greatest proofs of courage. They suspected that, should they decide to leave as the Mexicans asked, they would be taken by surprise at the bridges, which had been raised; for nothing was simpler than to raise or lower these wooden bridges. Their mistrust was further increased by the knowledge that the chiefs of the city were aware of the considerable treasures they had collected, and were anxious to obtain possession of them. This was not at all astonishing, for, according to the admission of the Spaniards, Cortes then had in his possession a treasure of gold, silver, and precious stones collected in different provinces, representing a fortune of 750,000 ducats. He therefore decided to prepare for the struggle, and to test the fortune of war by night.

He ordered the turtles we have mentioned to be repaired, and made a sortie at daybreak, in order to destroy the little towers from which the natives did such injury to our men by their missiles. His intention was to capture them if he could. The turtles were mounted on inside wheels, by which they were manœuvred. The cannon followed protected by soldiers armed with shields and muskets, and they were escorted by three thousand allies from Tascalteca and Guazuzingo.

From the top of the first tower attacked, such a quantity of stones and dart was rained down upon the Spaniards that the cannon could not be brought into play. One man was killed and a number wounded, the remainder being forced to retreat sadly into their quarters. As much injury was sustained from the tower of the temple overlooking the quarters, it was determined to take it by assault. More than one hundred marble steps led to its summit, and the natives who defended it, rolled the Spaniards down these stairs. The result served still further to discourage the besieged and to render the assailants proud of their successes, and they redoubled their audacity and persistence in the siege.

In the midst of this extreme danger, with death staring them in the face, unless they succeeded in capturing that tower, which, by its dominant position, prevented the soldiers from even showing a finger, Cortes seized a shield and left the fortress, followed by the most courageous, likewise protected by their shields. They attacked the tower, resolved to capture it by assault, or perish in the attempt. Nobody was ignorant of the fact that his life was at stake; but fortune favoured the daring. The enemy defended the steps the Spaniards sought to mount, and a desperate combat ensued. Our men finally conquered and reached the object of their desires; they captured the tower and drove its defenders out.

When the idols had been overthrown from the high places of the tower, the Spaniards had placed there a statue of the Blessed Virgin; this statue the enemy had ejected. Cortes ordered that tower and three others near by to be burned, so that no more projectiles could be thrown into the citadel. The loss of this position somewhat damped the ardour of the barbarians. The following night the Spaniards made a sortie in a street

near to the citadel, setting fire to three hundred houses;
and another night they destroyed all the buildings surrounding the square.   In this wise, killing and destroying,
but not without sustaining many wounds, they fought
day and night in the streets and on the bridges.   The
fighting on both sides was desperate.

The chiefs of the city pretended to be afraid and sent
representatives to Cortes to treat for peace, saying they
were ready to submit if he would forgive the past; Cortes
answered, agreeing.   A priest of great authority was
at this time held prisoner in the fortress, and the natives
asked that he be freed, in order to act as intermediary.
The priest was at once released, and the credulous Cortes,
believing everything was finished, sat down to eat, when
there suddenly arrived numerous messengers announcing
that the bridges were held by armed soldiers.   Cortes
had filled in certain openings formerly spanned by wooden
bridges, in such wise that if the bridges were removed,
the horses could freely manœuvre on this solid ground.
He was now informed that the earth and other material
had been removed from these openings, and that the
bridges were once more impracticable, leaving the ditches
open; so that not only horses, but even foot-soldiers could
not pass.

He immediately left the table, and charged the enemy
with his horsemen, pursuing and killing them over a large
space around the citadel.   He was badly inspired, however,
to go so far, for when he sought to return from the battle,
he encountered solid ranks of assailants, some in barques
on the water, others on the right, on the left, and in front
of him, while those he had just defeated fell upon his rear
and renewed the combat with fury.   All the bridges were
occupied, and the tops of the little towers were filled with
barbarians busy throwing their projectiles.   Many of the
Spaniards were struck by arrows and stones, and Cortes
himself was seriously wounded on the head.   Few indeed

of his companions came off safe and sound, and those few
were so worn out they could not move an arm. Once inside the fortress there was not sufficient food to restore
their strength, for there only remained a few mouthfuls
of maize bread of detestable taste, and water to drink.
Wine or meat was not to be thought of.

The discouraged Spaniards exacted that Cortes should
lead them into battle on the morrow, since they had no
other choice than death by the sword of the barbarians
or by starvation. Cortes listened to the entreaties of
his men and, comprehending that everything was lost,
he determined to escape. He had some beams prepared for replacing the stone bridges which were lacking. Deciding to leave by night, he divided the treasure
of 700,000 ducats giving to the intendant, the royal
treasurer and other officials, the fifth belonging to the
sovereign, and charging them with the responsibility
of guarding it. The rest of the treasure he loaded on
horses. He took with him the sons and two daughters
of Muteczuma, as well as the principal chiefs who had
been captured in battle, as hostages. It was on their
account, and also because of the overthrow of the divine
idols, that this popular revolt had broken out.

His route having been planned, his aides chosen, and
all particulars regulated, he set out during the silence of
the night. But in the twinkling of an eye the rumour
that Cortes and his companions were escaping spread
through the city. Swarms of warriors quickly appeared,
making the heavens ring with their cries; stones and
javelins rained upon our unfortunate countrymen. The
first divisions succeeded in escaping, but those which
followed and the rear-guard suffered cruel losses. Many
accounts have been given of this battle, and Your Holiness
will learn in a few words what happened. The barbarians
killed many men and horses. They fought furiously, because the soldiers were taking with them the sons of the

sovereign and the principal chiefs of the city, not to mention the treasure. All the treasure and pieces of furniture
that the Spaniards carried away with them, except the
share in charge of the vanguard, became the plunder of the
enemy. Such was their fury in the battle, that they
indiscriminately killed the children of Muteczuma and
the lords of the city, as well as the numerous slaves who
accompanied them.

When the surviving horsemen strove to attack them,
the first barbarians encountered threw themselves quickly
into the water,—for, like crocodiles or seals, they swim as
easily as they walk on land,—after which they crept along
the causeway, emerged from the water, and renewed the
fight. In this wise, divided and scattered, the Spaniards
evacuated the lake region.

Those who succeeded in escaping the rout gathered on
a plain near a town called Tacuma.[1] Cortes made a
halt upon one of the hillocks on that plain, in order to
collect the remnants of his scattered army, for he dared
not trust himself amongst the people of Tacuma, whose
grumblings were audible and of whose plottings he was
aware. When he had assembled the remains of his
unfortunate men, he counted them and found that one
hundred and fifty Spaniards were killed and missing.
Some two thousand of the allies from Tascalteca, Guazuzingo, and neighbouring tribes were likewise missing,
and forty-two horses had been lost. None of Muteczuma's
sons nor the captive lords had been spared, and every
single slave had likewise been killed before their eyes.

The victorious inhabitants of Temistitan followed
persistently in pursuit as far as Tacuma. Round about
this town there extends a great plain, which was crowded
during the night with barbarians of the neighbourhood

[1] Tacuba, also called Tlacopan. The best description of the retreat
of the Sorrowful Night—*Noche Triste*—is that given by Cortes in his
letter to Charles V.; compare also with the account of Bernal Diaz.

whom the people of Temistitan had called to their assistance. They did not venture, however, to attack during the night, but waited for daybreak.

Informed by his scouts of their intentions, and having acquainted himself with the numbers massed against him, Cortes had recourse to a stratagem. He ordered fires lighted in different places to mislead the assailants into thinking he awaited their attack in the morning; meanwhile, at the second watch of the night, he ordered the standards to be raised and the retreat to begin as best it might. One of the allies from Tascalteca had fled. Cortes was very anxious, for he was ignorant of the direction he should take on his forced march; but a Tascaltecan chief, who had escaped and who remembered having formerly gone over this country, offered his services, so they set forth under his guidance. The severely wounded were either carried or attached to the tails of horses. Those who were unable to fight, but were still capable of standing, though wounded or ill, were sent on ahead.

The rear-guard, in which marched Cortes himself with his horsemen and the small number of soldiers who were not wounded, had hardly left the night encampment a mile behind, than day began to dawn, and a multitude of the enemy assembled, following close upon their rear rank. When they became too troublesome the horsemen turned and charged them, killing a great number, and afterwards rejoining the army. The natives pursued them, fighting incessantly, for a distance of two leagues. The enemy's persistence made it impossible to continue farther, and what most inconvenienced the Spaniards was that they had brought no supplies from Temistitan and were obliged to defend themselves against the people of the country. The inhabitants living near the road left their houses, uttering cries of alarm as do shepherds when they surprise a wolf near the fold, never ceasing until well assured that the ferocious beast is gone.

Amidst these dangers they finally reached Tascalteca, where they found themselves in a friendly country. In that second battle[1] fought when leaving Temistitan, the Mexicans had wounded four horses with arrows. One of these horses was eaten, and as Cortes relates, he and his companions devoured its flesh with avidity. During five days they had had nothing to sustain their miserable lives but some parched maize, and even of that there was not enough. I omit many particulars which would warrant me affirming that the legendary Hercules of Greece, with his twelve labours, never faced such sufferings, such dangers in battle, or such hunger without succumbing, much less any living man. Of all our contemporaries only Spaniards are capable of withstanding such trials. This Spanish race is formed by nature to support more easily than any other, hardships of every kind,—hunger, thirst, heat, cold, long watches, and open-air encampments, as necessity may demand.

On the sixth day after leaving Temistitan in what resembled a flight, Cortes arrived at a Tascaltecan town called Guazilipan,[2] which according to his report numbers four thousand houses. He approached cautiously, for he feared, as often happens in human affairs, that changed fortune might have altered the people's sentiments, and transformed them from friends into enemies; but they were faithful to their pledges. A distance of four leagues separates Guazilipan from Tascalteca.

When the news of the disastrous defeat that had overtaken him, as well as the account of the retreat into their territory reached them, the Tascaltecans sent two lords of the city to meet Cortes; one of them was a civil magistrate

---

[1] Referring to the battle of Otumba, a most decisive engagement in which the Spaniards, according to Cortes and Bernal Diaz, performed prodigies of valour and endurance, conquering finally by the visible intervention of the Saints.

[2] Hueyothlipan.

and the other a general. Other envoys arrived from Guazuzingo, the republic allied to Tascalteca. These people
lavished consolations upon our people, encouraging them,
promising them speedy vengeance, and offering all the resources they commanded to accomplish this result. They
said: "For the present rest from your fatigues and remember
your allies. The massacre of the Spaniards and of our
citizens who have perished with them shall be speedily
avenged. The people of Temistitan shall be punished;
this we promise you." Cortes was doubtful but this promise
encouraged him and he retired to Tascalteca in response
to the invitation of the envoys. He distributed amongst
the people of Guazuzingo gifts, which are always acceptable because of foreign make, and dismissed them full of
zeal.

The Spaniards were received with enthusiasm, and were
able to rest in their beds and to restore their forces with
food. When Cortes first went to visit Muteczuma, he
had left a small amount of gold and silver at Tascalteca;
this deposit he found untouched, and the alliance faithfully observed. But what did it profit? These valuables
represented the sum of 21,000 castellanos of gold, without
counting the precious stones; they were packed in boxes
and sent to Vera Cruz, escorted by five horsemen and forty-
five foot-soldiers. When these men entered the territory
of Colua, a vassal province of Temistitan, they were captured, sacrificed to the gods, and eaten, while the treasure
was divided among the people of Colua.

Cortes stopped twenty days at Tascalteca to care for
his wounded and to encourage his exhausted companions,
after which he sent a second convoy to Vera Cruz. This
convoy returned with the satisfactory news that all was
well. His companions wished him to lead them back to
that colony, thinking that once united they might more
successfully resist the snares and perfidy of the natives.
Cortes refused to retreat farther, because he had found

the Tascaltecans and people of Guazuzingo faithful to the alliance. He succeeded in persuading his companions that they were bound to wreak vengeance for the crimes committed at Temistitan.

Towards the calends of July in the year 1520, the army set out on its march. Near Tascalteca stands a large city called Tepeaca, whose inhabitants are mortal enemies of the Tascaltecans. The people of Tepeaca had surprised, sacrificed, and eaten twelve Spaniards who traversed their country and, therefore, Cortes marched against them supported by the powerful reinforcements of Tascalteca, Guazuzingo, and Chiurutecal. Scouts brought the news that the people of Tepeaca had received reinforcements from Temistitan. To be brief and to put the matter in a few words, they and their allies were defeated and the city surrendered unconditionally. Its inhabitants took an oath of obedience to Cortes and gave hostages for their good faith. Our engines of war, the cannon, the horses,—all things they had never seen nor even heard of,—quickly intimidated them; but what served Cortes best was the union of three tribes as his allies.

He chose a site in the province, where he founded a new colony and built a fortress which he named Segura de la Frontera. But he was quite decided not to trust the inhabitants, not only because it was foreseeable that they would obey orders from Temistitan and revolt, but also because Tepeaca interrupts the communications between Vera Cruz and the allies.

While these events were happening, Cortes received messengers from Vera Cruz, saying that the Panuco king had repulsed the troops which Garay had sent to found a colony on that great river. The leaders, who had been scattered and succeeded in escaping, landed at Vera Cruz, After the defeat at Tepeaca, of which the news spread throughout the neighbouring tribes, the natives were torn by conflicting sentiments.

A mountain town called Guaccachiulla secretly sent to treat with Cortes and to offer assistance against the inhabitants of the province of Colua who were allies of Temistitan, and of whom they had reason to complain because of various outrages and assaults; they had even carried off their women. Guaccachiulla is on this side of the mountains while their enemies of the province of Colua are on the other side. Cortes was informed that in the regions beyond the range an ambuscade of thirty thousand soldiers had learned that the Spaniards were advancing with the intention of entering the territory of Colua. Taking with him only two hundred foot-soldiers, thirteen horsemen, three thousand allies, and some cannon, Cortes marched against Guaccachiulla. The commanders of the ambuscade, who were sound asleep in the town, were either all killed or captured. The town of Guaccachiulla is surrounded by strong walls furnished with towers and is protected by the mountains. The soil is fertile; the town numbers about six thousand houses, built of stone and mortar, and two rivers water the plain in which it stands.

There is one other town, four leagues distant from Guaccachiulla, whose inhabitants proposed to surrender to Cortes, but their cacique fled with the Coluans and would not give his submission when invited to do so. Cortes appointed his brother in his place and promised the inhabitants that he would not revoke his decision.

Some days later Cortes marched by another road to a city called Izzuccan, also four leagues distant from Guaccachiulla. He learned that an army of Coluans was awaiting him on the road not far from the frontiers of that town. Their number was reported to be twenty thousand men, who felt certain of repulsing the invasion of their territory. Six thousand men defended the town from within, and the others were scattered in groups amongst the villages and hamlets. The women and all men incapable of fighting had been sent, together with their treasure, into the forests and mountains. Both its situation and its defences render Izzuccan a formidable place; but I weary myself by enumerating all these fortified towns. Let it suffice to say that this city was taken by assault, and that the greater part of its defenders, fearing to be captured, sprang from the walls and fled towards the neighbouring river. The town once captured, Cortes gave quarter to the inhabitants, but ordered them to bring back the fugitives with all their treasure. They quickly returned, each to his own home, and the town was repopulated.

Two messengers were sent to the cacique who had fled with the people of Temistitan and Colua, but he refused to come, preferring exile. This cacique had a bastard brother older than himself, and also a grandson ten years old, who was of the legitimate line. Cortes named the latter king, but appointed his great uncle as his tutor, associating also in the government three inhabitants of Guaccachiulla, who were noted for their fidelity and loyalty. These counsellors were to administer the country for their people, until the youth became of age and able to govern in person.

This town of Izzuccan numbers three thousand houses and about a hundred temples, consecrated to various gods. Human victims are sacrificed in these temples. Cortes counted them from a lofty place, and ordered every one of them, together with the statues in them, to be burned. He forbade the celebration of any such ceremonies, declaring that God, who made the heavens and the earth, detested homicide, and that the killing of man by man was repugnant both to the law of God and of Nature.

Izzuccan is dominated by a fortress and surrounded by hills which protect it against the winds, so the temperature is warm. Cotton grows there in abundance. The soil is well watered, and during the summer the irrigation canals keep the fields green. Fruits are numerous and vegetables are not wanting. There are many towns and hamlets.

With the occupation of Guaccachiulla and the fall of Izzucca, the news that Fortune once more showed herself a tender mother to the Spaniards spread through the country. At this turn of her wheel the natives abandoned the people of Temistitan, and hastened to come back to Cortes. Messengers arrived from every direction, offering submission, saying that the only reason they had not sooner ventured to render the homage due to the great sovereign power the Spaniards possessed, was because they feared the reprisals of the Coluans and the great lords of Temistitan; but seeing that, thanks to their protection, there was nothing more to fear from the tyranny of the neighbouring caciques, they came to offer their submission.

It is time to bring this overlong narrative to an end. Some prisoners informed Cortes that after Muteczuma's death, his brother, Hastapalappa, had been named king at Temistitan, but after a reign of four months had died of a smallpox and had been succeeded by his sister's son, Catamazin[1]; of Muteczuma's three sons, the first had been killed at the bridges, during the retreat; the second was mad, and the third paralysed. Quauhtemotzin employed all his resources in collecting weapons, especially very long lances, with which it was hoped to strike the horses from a distance, for an attack by the cavalry is what they most fear. The new sovereign expected that Cortes would take the offensive, for he understood that all the neighbouring country was falling away from him and asking help from the Spaniards against himself.

In this he was not mistaken, for Cortes had ordered thirteen of those boats having two banks of oars, which

---

[1] Quauhtemotzin: the proper name of this ruler will be henceforth used in the text.

are called brigantines, to be constructed, intending with them to ravage the country bordering the great salt lake. He hoped that when Temistitan was deprived of provisions and its water supply was cut off, the city would be reduced to the necessity of accepting the yoke of the King of Spain. Moreover, he sent four ships to Hispaniola to obtain horses, a sufficient number of musketeers, and a quantity of powder.

Cortes writes that this region, with its mountains, rivers, and valleys well grown with fruit trees, resembles Spain; and he therefore asks the Emperor to confirm the name, New Spain, which he has given to the part he has discovered. He likewise, at the close of his most important report, begs his Majesty to send a man eminent for his virtues and experience to visit and report upon the con-quered country. This letter[1] is dated the thirtieth day of October, 1520, and was written at the fortress he founded and named Segura de la Frontera.

[1] This is the Second Letter of Relation. It was first published by Cromberger in Seville in 1522.

BOOK VII

WHILE these writings lay ready in my cabinet awaiting the absent secretaries from whom distance and insecure roads separate me, behold the pregnant ocean produces a new, recently born progeny. I shall therefore conclude this work with two appendices exceeding in interest anything preceding it. In the beginning I shall speak of the journey round the world, the discovery of the spice islands, and the most extraordinary and almost incredible events. In the second place I will state by what means, by what stratagems, force of arms, and courage Fernando Cortes, assisted by the Tascaltecans and the people of Guazuzingo and other peoples hostile to Muteczuma, captured the great city of Temistitan, annihilated and almost destroyed it from top to bottom. This conquest notably increases the number of states subject to Your Holiness, and especially the extent of the kingdoms of Great Castile.

I shall begin with the journey round the world and the description of the spiceries; but I must go back somewhat in my narrative. It was, if you remember, while the Emperor was presiding over the Cortes of Catalonia at Barcelona, and Your Holiness directed the affairs of our Imperial Indian Council, that the Portuguese, Ferdinand Magellan, who had quit the Portuguese service, was commissioned to visit the Moluccan archipelago, where spices grow. Magellan had, in fact, passed seven years at Cochin, Cananor, at Calicut in the Chersonesus, otherwise called Malacca, and was therefore acquainted with the position of these islands. They are not very far distant from the sea of Chersonesus, that is to say Malacca, and other markets.

Our Council, over which Your Holiness presided, confided this mission accordingly to Magellan, who sailed from the ocean port of Barrameda, at the mouth of the Bethis, on the twentieth of September, 1519. He commanded five vessels, of which the flagship was called *Trinidad*, and the others *San Antonio*, *Victoria*, *Concepcion*, and *Santiago*. They were manned by a crew of two hundred and thirty-seven men. Of these ships only two ever returned to Spain, of which one, after abandoning the flagship, returned without accomplishing anything; the second reappeared laden with precious woods and spices, three years after its departure from Spain; that is, it arrived on the sixth of September, 1522, at the same port from which it started. Very few of the crew survived, and the Admiral himself had perished at Matam, one of the islands of the archipelago, killed by the islanders. We shall relate these things farther on.

There exists between the Castilians and the Portuguese an inveterate hatred, and Magellan sought under every pretext and on divers occasions to kill a number of Castilians who refused to obey him. At the proper time I shall relate this, but for the moment I confine myself to the description of the voyage.[1]

The fleet first touched at the Fortunate Isles and afterwards sighted the archipelago of the Gorgades, which their actual lord, the King of Portugal, calls the Cape Verde Islands. From this point, Magellan sailed directly to the right, leaving our continent behind, towards that

---

[1] An account of Magellan's voyage was kept by a Venetian, Antonio Pigafetta, who accompanied him. The original MSS. is preserved in the Ambrosian Library at Milan. Consult the English translation by James Alexander Robertson, *Magellan's Voyage around the World* (1906).

great promontory the Castilians have named Cape San
Augustin, and the Portuguese, somewhat later, Cape
Santa Maria. This promontory lies five degrees beyond
the equinoctial line. The journey was afterwards continued as far as the gulf where the captain, Solis, who
visited these waters with our fleet, was killed and eaten
by the natives, together with some of his companions
as we have related in a preceding decade. This gulf
has received the name of Bahia de Santa Maria, and is
otherwise called simply Bahia.

Magellan sent some men to ascend the river which flows
into the gulf. They took with them one of the ships and a
shallop. They saw three men of half-savage type, entirely
naked, whose stature exceeded the normal by two cubits.
One of these men showed confidence and got into the
shallop. Thinking that if they treated him well, he would
attract his companions to the fleet, the Spaniards gave
him food and drink, and dressed him; after which they
let him go; but he was never again seen, neither he nor
any of his people. Trees cut with European hatchets
were discovered, and a cross had been erected upon the
summit of another tree, but nowhere were any traces of
our compatriots found.

The river is immense. Marvellous things, like those
told of the Maragnon, in the northern part of Paria,
which I have already mentioned, are related of it. The
Spaniards ascended it for a distance of twenty leagues,
and even at that point its width between its banks was
seventeen leagues. Its mouth is vast, for many other
rivers swell its volume. The water of the ocean is fresh
for a great distance out to sea. When the Spaniards
left this gulf they found that several degrees farther on
towards the south, the coast line of the continent took a
marked bend towards the west, and they discovered
another large gulf to which they gave the name of San
Julian, and in which there was a very safe harbour.

The Admiral ordered the anchor to be lowered. At that time the sun rose towards the Spaniards and left those countries. The cold became very severe when the sun crossed the constellation of the Bull; just as happens amongst us when it passes through the constellation of the Scales. During the period of four months until summer approached, our men were kept by cold and storm in the huts and cabins they had built on the banks. For it was the calends of April when they entered that harbour which they did not leave until the ninth of the calends of September.

It was during this period that Magellan treated the captain, Juan Carthagena, so severely.[1] He was a friend of the Bishop of Burgos who had been assigned to Magellan, with the royal approval, as his associate, and named second in command of the expedition. Under pretext of a plot formed against his life, Magellan put him ashore in company with a priest, giving them only a little biscuit and a sword. He would gladly have punished their plot with death, but that he feared the resentment of the Spaniards against him and did not dare to assume the responsibility. This action has been represented in different lights; but the description of other events is in agreement. According to some, Magellan was within his rights in thus acting, while according to others he was not, and the severity he showed was merely the outcome of the ancient hatred existing between the Spaniards and the Portuguese.

During this stop the men were able to visit the native houses. These barbarians are savages without weapons and are clothed only with skins; they are nomads without fixed habitations and without laws. Their height is very great and they are called Patagonians. Magellan left the port of San Julian on the ninth of September, 1521,

---

[1] Referring to the revolt led by Mendoza, Quesada, and Carthagena, which Magellan only suppressed with difficulty. See Pifagetta, above mentioned.

the moment the sun appeared above the horizon. He sailed first in the direction of the antarctic pole, for a distance of fourteen degrees.

At this point we must turn back somewhat in our history. During his childhood, Magellan had vaguely heard discussed in Portugal the existence of a strait, whose entrance was difficult to find. He was therefore ignorant of what direction to take but chance served him where his knowledge failed.[1] There arose a tempest so terrible, that it caught up one of the ships and drove it upon the neighbouring rocks. The crew was saved, but the ship was broken to pieces by the waves.[2] Thus perished one of the five vessels of the fleet. A little farther on the ocean, in all its immensity, stretched away towards the left, while to the right towered snow-covered mountains. While searching a shelter, one of the ships of least draught was driven by the force of the waves very close to the shore. A narrow channel was discovered, into which the ship entered, coming presently upon a gulf four leagues broad and six long, according to Spanish measure. The ship returned announcing that the passage was found.

I omit many particulars; but in a general sense, the following is what should be known. It is said that at places, stones may be thrown from a sling onto the mountains forming the sides of this strait. The country is a desert and on both sides rise mountains overgrown with cedars. After passing through this first gulf another strait was discovered, somewhat larger, but still narrow, after which came a third and then a fourth beyond which another gulf opened: just as we observe on the maps of Europe that towards the Hellespont there are two channels leading to an inland sea, so in this strait there are three

---

[1] Martyr here does scant justice to Magellan, whose discovery of the Strait was due primarily to his intelligence and persevering explorations, chance playing no greater part than it does in all human undertakings.

[2] The *Santiago* was thus lost.

channels leading to much larger inland seas. All these straits are full of small islands. The Spaniards sailed these straits in constant fear of striking a reef, and everywhere they found very deep water.

Midway during this course, they dropped anchor in a square-shaped sea where they found nothing remarkable, but where one of the ships, called the *San Antonio*, remained behind. The other vessels expected it would follow, but it turned back and arrived [in Spain] some time ago, bringing the saddest accusations against Magellan. We believe that such disobedience will not remain unpunished.

There remained, therefore, only three vessels to continue the voyage. These ships had entered the strait on the twenty-first of October and came out on the fifth day of the calends of December, during which time the days had been very long and the nights very short. This is comprehensible, in view of the shape of the terrestrial sphere. After sailing through the strait, the Spaniards entered another vast ocean. It is the ocean on the opposite side of our continent, and communicates with the sea, which I have called the South Sea in my Decades, and which was first discovered by Vasco Nuñez, under the guidance of the son of the cacique of Comogra.

The Spaniards affirm that they sailed three months and twenty days on that immense ocean, and during that time they saw nothing but sky and salt water. Their sufferings, both from want of provisions and from the intense heat, were very great, and during many days they had nothing to eat but a handful of rice, without a scrap of other food; potable water was so scarce that they were obliged to use one-third sea water for cooking their rice, and when a man drank this water he had to shut his eyes and stop his nose, so green was its colour and so nasty its odour.

While sailing in a north-westerly direction on this immense sea, they crossed the equinoctial line, and im-

mediately afterwards discovered two barren islands.
These they named the Unfortunate Isles,[1] because they
were deserted and sterile. They next sailed amongst a
multitude of islands which they called the Archipelago,
because of their resemblance to the Cyclades of the
Ionian Sea. They landed on most of these islands, which
were separated from one another by narrow channels
and extended throughout a distance of five hundred
leagues. They named these islands Ladrones,[2] in pre-
ference to any native name, because the islanders, although peacefully inclined, stole everything they could put
their hands on. They resembled that race of thieves
called by the Italians *Zingari*,[3] and which falsely pretends
to be Egyptian. Amongst the other things the islanders
stole was a barque our people used for landing. Hardly
had they turned their backs when it disappeared, but the
natives were forced to bring it back after having lost
several of their men.

These islanders go naked, and are half savage. There
is a tree growing in their country which bears cocoanuts.
The largest of their islands is called Borneo,[4] and the
Spaniards unhesitatingly write that it is two hundred
and fifty-four leagues in circumference. There grows
in one part of that island a tree whose leaves, when
they fall, squirm on the ground like worms. I suppose
there must exist a vital breath between the two faces
of the leaf which swells and agitates it like a short-lived
breeze. Two religions are practised in this country,
Paganism and Mohammedanism, but they are in agreement with one another. The people raise herds of cattle
and buffaloes as well as goats. Chickens are found in

---

[1] These islands are supposed to have belonged to the Tahiti group, but
their precise identity is undetermined.

[2] Meaning thieves or robbers.

[3] *Zingari* being the Italian name for gypsies.

[4] Compare with Pigafetta. Peter Martyr departs from the correct
order of the voyage, as Borneo was not visited until after Magellan's death.

abundance, but not a single sheep, nor wheat nor barley nor wine; there is plenty of rice which takes the place of bread, many different dishes being composed from it. The King of Borneo exchanged presents with the Spaniards, sending his gifts to our people on two elephants; and the following day he sent them different dishes carried on the shoulders of thirty-two noblemen. The capital of this prince is composed of twenty-five thousand houses, but they are built of wood, except the royal palace which is of stone.

Borneo is surrounded by many small islands, among which two are notable, Zubo[1] and Matam, the latter taking its name from its chief city. Magellan won the friendship of the King of Zubo, for he presented him with gifts which, on account of their novelty and because nobody knew their use, were acceptable. He baptised the king and declared him the vassal of the emperor.

Leaving the ships at Zubo, Magellan crossed to the island of Matam, visible on the horizon at a distance of only four leagues. He used the shallops and the native boats dug out of tree trunks. His intention was to persuade the ruler of Matam, through his interpreters, to make his submission to the great King of Spain, and to the chief of Zubo; and to pay tribute to the former. The king answered that he was willing to obey the King of Spain, but not the chieftain of Zubo. Thereupon Magellan ordered a fortress composed of about fifty houses, near the royal residence, to be sacked and burnt. He afterwards returned to Zubo, bringing his booty, some foodstuffs which were needed there, as well as several pieces of furniture; but the inhabitants of Zubo, who were hostile to the islanders of Matam, stole the greater part from him.

Eight days later Magellan returned with the same force and without the ships; he wished to capture the capital itself of the island. It was unfortunate for him that he

[1] Zebu or Cebu, one of the Philippines.

landed at Matam, for not only did the king refuse to
obey him, but advanced at the head of his people fully
armed to meet him. Without mentioning native javelins
made of cane and burnt wood, his soldiers carried long
iron lances; for the merchants from Serica and China
trade with these islanders. Magellan was killed,[1] together
with seven of his companions, while twenty-two others
were wounded. Thus did this brave Portuguese, Magellan,
satisfy his craving for spices.[2]

The Spaniards who escaped the massacre returned to
Zubo, invited by the ruler of that island. Juan Serrano,
the chief pilot and commander of one of the ships, whom
I have mentioned in my first Decades, and the captain of
another vessel with ten of their companions, accepted
this invitation. Meanwhile about forty other sailors
wandered about the island. A band of assassins suddenly
attacked them while they were eating and massacred
them all, with the exception of the leaders, who were
stripped of their clothing. The islanders hoped the sailors
would land to rescue them, but the men on board the ships,
not daring to approach, abandoned their companions
and set sail.

I have asked those who returned to Spain, and especially
a young Genoese, Martin de Judicis,[3] who witnessed all
these events, what crime provoked the King of Zubo to
commit this vile action; the Spaniards think it was on
account of women, for the islanders are jealous.

In my opinion these islands are those concerning

---

[1] Magellan was killed on April 27, 1521.

[2] *Nulla certe apparet ratio avaritiæ incusandi immortalem virum qui
pelagus nulli antea pervium navigaturus suis se redilibus perpetuo abdicat in
favorem fratrum minimorum hispalensium de Triana. Amplioribus hic
celebrandus erat, præconiis qui pro Christo, pro Hispania, pro civilitate
decertans, mortem oppetiit, nullam non emeritus laudem.* Edition of J.
Torres Asensio, Madrid, 1892.

[3] The name of Martin Judibicus appears in the list of the crew of the
Concepcion (Navarrete, iv., p. 19).

which many authors have written, but in different senses; for according to some they should number a thousand, and according to others three thousand or still more; they lie not far from the Indian coast. Among the islands surrounding Borneo there is one on which are the towns of Butara and Calega, where the Spaniards were kindly received. From this island they discovered another which the inhabitants of Calega pointed out to them, saying there was so much gold in the sands of the sea that it was only necessary to sift them to obtain grains as large as a nut or a small fruit; as for lesser grains nobody even notices them. This statement was confirmed by the people of Butara. From this last island two new ones were perceptible on the horizon, on which are two famous towns, Vindanao towards the south, and Chipico towards the north.[1] The southern country produces cinnamon and the northern gold. The Spaniards obtained various articles in both places by trading. I have already said that traders from Serica and China and the provinces of India frequently visit these islands in search of gold, percious stones, and other objects, for which they exchange stuffs, clothing, ornaments, and weapons.

The greatly desired Moluccas[2] are in sight of these islands. They lie seventy-five leagues from the equator, and according to the men's account they are within ten degrees, though I admit I do not understand anything of their calculations. The ancient philosophers calculated a degree at sixty Roman miles, and each mile measured a thousand paces. The Spaniards measure a marine league at four miles, and a land league at three. If we admit the calculations of the Spanish sailors, there are fifteen leagues in a degree; and, contrary to the accepted opinion, they affirm that a degree is seventy leagues and a half.

[1] Mindanao or Maguidanao is the next largest island to Luzon of all the Philippine group. Chilpico is the bay of Chilpit.

[2] The Molucca group consists of some ten or more islands.

Let any one who can, undertand this; for myself, I give
it up.

Let us return to the Moluccas, where the Spaniards
finally landed. There are five principal islands situated
under or very near the equator. None of them are more
than six leagues in circumference and, by a caprice of
nature, each is dominated by a lofty mountain; cloves grow
there spontaneously. Five of the southern islands are shut
in by the large island of Gilolo, where cloves also grow, but
they are of a bitter savour and half wild as is the case with
the chestnut and ungrafted olive-trees. In all the other
small islands, on the contrary, the cloves are aromatic.

It is most delightful to learn whence the islanders think
these trees obtain their aromatic savour. They say that
three times each day, in the early morning, at noon,
and in the evening, a cloud arises in the sky and spreads
over the summit of the hills where the cloves grow;
while it lasts, the tops of the trees are invisible, but after
a little it disperses, and the cloves, which resemble laurels,
are impregnated from this cloud. They adduce as a
proof that the cloud never descends to the lower parts
of the island and the cloves transplanted to not thrive,
nor does their fruit possess a savour.

The lowlands of each of the Moluccas are set apart
for rice culture. In one of the islands where the Spaniards
landed, they were kindly received and honourably treated.
They had only two ships left, having destroyed the third
because, after the murder of the commander and that
sinister feast, the crew was unsufficient to man them.
Only the *Trinidad* and the *Victoria* were kept. These
islanders go almost naked, wearing only small aprons
made of bark in guise of waist-cloths. The king of the
island told the Spaniards that he gladly received them
as guests, because a few months earlier he had read in the
circle of the moon that strangers, bearing an absolute
resemblance to the Spaniards, would arrive by sea.

The Spaniards think these islands are five thousand leagues from Hayti, that is to say twenty thousand miles according to Italian measure; but I think they are mistaken. They report that the islanders are happy, though they know nothing of our bread, nor wine, nor butchers' meat, contenting themselves with rice, which they prepare in a thousand different styles. They also have another kind of bread in common use, which is made of the old marrow of palms which have fallen from age. It sometimes happens in the thick forests on the mountain slopes far from human habitation, that great trees are felled by the violent storms, or because the roots are deprived of the earth necessary for their nourishment, since as they grow older and increase in size their roots require more strength than the earth can furnish them. It therefore happens that numerous trees fall in the forest and rot where they lie in rows covered with moss. The palm-marrow the natives use for bread comes from this source They divide it into squares, grinding it into flour, which they dry, and then bake in the form of thick, square cakes. I wished to taste some of it, and nothing is sourer or of worse flavour. This bread must only be eaten by miserable creatures who possess no fields and hence cannot cultivate rice.

In certain mountain districts and villages I have seen mountaineers living upon scarcely less tasteless bread, almost black, made from grain called in Spanish *centeno*,[1] millet, or other still worse materials. Is it not the rule of inconstant fortune that while few are satisfied many hunger, and that the pleasures and the delicacies of the table are reserved for a small minority? Nevertheless, people live, for nature requires but little, and we may accustom ourselves to live on almost nothing.

The natives are chiefly occupied in raising goats and poultry. They grow canes, similar to those which produce

[1] Common rye.

sugar, not to mention the African apples, called by Italians pomegranates, and Median apples of all kinds, among which the Spaniards distinguished lemons, limes, oranges, and citrons. In mentioning the plants growing about the springs, why should I call watercresses *Nasturtium aquaticum* when they are usually and unaffectedly called *berros* in Spanish and *cresones* in Italian? What shall I say concerning the poisonous herb unknown to me which acts as an emetic, and which the Spaniards call *anapelo*?[1] If we question one who refuses to preserve any intellectual treasure except in the Latin, and ask whether it is permissible to use *anapellus* for the necessary word wanting in Latin, but which may be easily borrowed from a foreign tongue, he will turn up his nose disdainfully and gravely whisper that the plant had better be called strangle-wolf. It is, however, my opinion, with the favour and leave of such delicate wits, that the islands of Molucca abound with oranges, lemons, citrons, pomegranates, and pot-herbs. Not without reason have I mentioned cresses and aconite, for sometimes at the beginning of a repast we eat this herb served with oil and vinegar, and my friend Fernandez Roderigo, of whose good offices the Emperor sometimes makes use—thanks to the recommendation of Your Holiness—found that aconite produced in him the same symptoms as though he had swallowed hemlock, or some other poison. He fell, half dead, and had to be promptly treated with Mithridates' antidote, in spite of which he was half benumbed for several days. Is not the word *anapelo* as well-formed and pleasing a name as the roundabout term strangle-wolf, upon which captious critics insist?

The wine manufactured by the islanders is not made from grapes, since none grow in the Moluccas, but from different kinds of fruits. One sort is particularly employed. There grows, just as in our continent, a tree resembling

[1] Meaning aconite.

the palm but differing strangely by its fruit. Upon this tree a dozen or sometimes more, but never more than twenty, bunches are found; the fruits are formed in bunches just like grapes, but are covered with a bark. When stripped of its bark, each fruit resembles a little oblong lemon. The bark, which serves as its shell, is as hard as that of a turtle; these fruits are called cocoanuts. They are covered with several layers, more numerous than those surrounding edible palms, and are held together by interlaced strings. It requires as much labour to get them out of their covering as to skin the palm-trees. When opened, the cocoanuts are good to eat, and are filled with a delicious juice. The spongy material, two fingers' thick, sticks to the shell, and its white colour and softness cause it to resemble butter or grease; only it has a more delicate taste. When detached from the exterior shell, it is very good to eat. If left in the shell some days, it liquefies, and changes into an oil much preferable to olive-oil, and excellent for sick people. This is not the only service rendered by this tree. Its trunk is bored at the point where the leaves grow, at the top; drop by drop a potable liquor of excellent taste and very wholesome runs into receptacles prepared for the purpose.

The natives also engage in fishing, for their seas produce many varieties of fish. There is one which is a veritable monster. It is a little less than a cubit long, with a large belly, while its back is covered but with a very tough skin instead of scales. Its snout is like a pig's, and its forehead is armed with two bony horns; its back is divided, high, and bony.

The king, on whose territory the Spaniards had landed, imagined they had been brought to him by some supernatural means. He asked them what they wanted, and they answered "spices." He told them to take whatever they wanted and, calling his island subjects together, he ordered them to show the Spaniards all the clove-trees they possessed. In return, for proper payment, permission was given to them to carry the cloves away. When the cloves are ripe it is customary for the natives to collect them in piles in their houses, and await the arrival of traders; and they do the same with their other products. The cloves are then taken to the markets of Calicut, Cananor, Cochin, or Malacca, in great ships, called junks. The same thing happens with pepper, ginger, cinnamon, and all the other unnecessary delicacies which render man effeminate. The only spice growing in the Molucca Islands is cinnamon, though they are only a short distance from islands which produce other spices. The islanders have brought this fact to the notice of the Spaniards, and it was further confirmed by an act of piracy they committed.

As soon as they left the large island of Borneo and the surrounding islands, on one of which the admiral, Magellan, had been massacred, they encountered by chance on the way to the Moluccas one of those native vessels called junks. This ship was not armed, but was laden with merchandise, including all kinds of spices, besides cloves. The quantity was small but the quality excellent, for they had been recently gathered. These ships do not venture to undertake long voyages, for they are not sufficiently well built to stand tempests as ours do, nor are their crews sufficiently experienced to navigate, unless they have the wind astern. This junk was carrying a cargo of native products to a neighbouring island: rice, cocoanuts, geese, chickens, and numerous other foodstuffs; there was likewise some gold dust. The delight of the Spaniards at the unexpected finding of this treasure was at the expense of the innocent natives, who had not suspected their whereabouts. They promptly decided to load their two remaining vessels with cloves, and as they had not found a sufficient quantity on the island where they had landed, the King, their host, visited the neighbouring islands thereabouts.

Out of the five Moluccas, four are visible from one another, the fifth being somewhat out of range of human vision. The two vessels were, therefore, laden with freshly picked cloves, the Spaniards having even brought some branches with the fruit still hanging on them. It afforded great pleasure to all the courtiers to see these twigs and feel the fruit still growing on the wood. The odour of freshly gathered cloves is not very different from that of the cloves sold by apothecaries. They gave me many of these branches, and I distributed a number of them in different directions. I still have some which I hold in reserve until I learn whether Your Holiness possesses any.

We shall now describe the remainder of the voyage.

One of the two vessels, the *Trinidad*, was rotten throughout and so full of holes made by the worms called by the Italians *bissi* and by the Spaniards *broma*, that the water poured into the hold as through a sieve. They did not venture to send it on such a long voyage without first making repairs, so *La Trinidad* remained behind. We do not know whether she still exists or not. It follows that out of five ships only two have returned The *Victoria* arrived this same year in which I am writing, the *San Antonio* a year before, and of their crews very few men have survived.

It remains for me to describe the return voyage of the *Victoria*, for it came by another route to its point of departure. The voyage lasted three years less some days, and by a series of misfortunes all the commanders perished. But what is most strange, and what had never before been attempted since the beginning of the world, is that this ship followed the entire parallel and made the circuit of the globe.

If a Greek had accomplished this what would not the Greeks have written about his incredible feat! The ship of the Argonauts is seriously and not jocosely reputed to have been carried up to heaven; and yet, what did it accomplish? If we reflect a little, it left the town of Argos to go through the Euxine to Œtes and Medea; what its crew of heroes did,—Hercules, Theseus, and Jason,—nobody knows; nor is anybody able to state precisely what the famous golden fleece was. Children in the primary schools learn the distance that separates Greece from the Euxine; it is less that the finger nail of a giant.

Let us now try to explain how the Spaniards have completed the circuit of the globe, for the fact is difficult to believe. There is, however, one proof: let Your Holiness have a terrestrial sphere marked with the different continents brought. Starting from the Pillars of Hercules, otherwise called the Strait of Gibraltar, and bending to the left, the Fortunate Isles, vulgarly called the Canaries, will first be encountered. Continuing directly south between these islands and the African coast, several islands belonging to the Portuguese and called by them the Archipelago and Cape Verde Islands are found; these are the Medusean Gorgades of the Latins. Let us now give our closest attention, for it is just here that our astonishment awakens. To the left of these western islands the Portuguese passed the equatorial line, crossing the Tropic of Capricorn, and advanced to the extreme point of the Mountains of the Moon; this point is called by them the Cape of Good Hope. Between the equator and this cape some reckon twenty-four, others twenty-two degrees. After doubling this promontory they sailed to the east, passing the entrance to the Red Sea and the Persian Gulf, across the mouths of the Indus and Ganges to the Golden Chersonesus, to which they gave the name of Malacca. At this point one half of the terrestrial globe has been encircled, and, of the twenty-four hours which, according to the calculations of cosmographers, the sun takes to complete its circuit, twelve are gone. Let us now measure the remaining half; and for that purpose we must return to the Gorgades Islands. Leaving this archipelago on the left, our fleet of five ships took the opposite direction from that followed by the Portuguese ships. Out beyond the land we call our continent and whose extremity belongs to the Portuguese, advancing as we have already described more than fifty degrees towards the antarctic pole,—I do not give the precise figures, for the calculations differ somewhat,—the Spaniards sailing west, as the Portuguese had sailed east, arrived east of the Moluccas, which lie not far from the country where Ptolemy placed Gatigara and the great gulf, the gateway to China. What shall I say of the great gulf and Gatigara? The Spaniards claim they did not find them where Ptolemy placed them; but I do not insist on this point, for perhaps I shall speak later more fully concerning it.

Let us return to the tour of the world. We have here, therefore, another route leading to the Golden Chersonesus and just opposite to that discovered by the Portuguese. The *Victoria*, that Queen of Argonauts, returned by the first route, passing in view of the Golden Chersonesus and following the track of the Portuguese. When she arrived at the Cape Verde Islands she was destitute of everything. A boat, manned by thirteen men, was sent to ask the Portuguese for fresh water and provisions, offering to pay for them; but the officials who imagined their right eyes plucked out if any other than their own prince gets a little revenue out of spices, seized the barque and detained the crew. This was a violation of the treaty concluded when the world was divided by Pope Alexander VI. The royal officers of the Archipelago even sought to capture the ship, which would have been easy enough, had not the Spaniards, suspecting the arrest of their companions, raised anchor and fled, before the Portuguese could take them, leaving their thirteen companions in the hands of the enemy.

Out of sixty who had embarked at the Moluccas, there only remained thirty-one. Let us acknowledge that the King of Portugal later ordered the release of the thirteen prisoners.

My narrative would be indeed a long one, were I to describe the dangers they courted: the famine, the thirst, long watches, and extreme fatigue they suffered, pumping night and day the water that poured through great holes in the ship. It may suffice to recall that this ship was more full of holes than the best sieve, and these eighteen men more fatigued than the most exhausted horses. They claim to have sailed fourteen thousand leagues, from one point to another. The circumference of the globe, however, is less that eight thousand leagues; but they were ignorant of any more direct course or other track to those desired islands than that followed by the Portuguese.

It is planned to profit by an undertaking so well begun. What will finally be decided, what treaty may be signed with the Portuguese, who claim to have been seriously injured by this voyage, I shall later make known to you. The Portuguese affirm that the Moluccas lie within the limits assigned to them by the division made by Pope Alexander VI., between the kings of Castile and Portugal, and they point out that villages, districts, and farms carry their produce to the markets of the Moluccas, Calicut, and Cochin, and that everywhere peasants bring to the towns and fortresses, whatever they produce and cultivate. We claim, on the contrary, that the Moluccas were usurped by the Portuguese, since they lie outside the line drawn from pole to pole separating the east from the west. You understand, moreover, this question perfectly well, since it has been more than once discussed in your presence.

It only remains for me to mention a fact which will astonish my readers, especially those who suppose they have a perfect knowledge of celestial phenomena. When the *Victoria* reached the Cape Verde islands, the sailors believed the day to be Wednesday, whereas it was Thursday. They had consequently lost one day on their voyage, and during their three years' absence. I said: "Your priests must have deceived you, since they have forgotten this day in their ceremonies and the recitation of their office." They answered: "Of what are you thinking? Do you suppose that all of us, including wise and experienced men, could have made such a mistake? It often happens that an exact account is kept of the days and months, and moreover many of the men had office books and knew perfectly what had to be recited each day. There could be no mistake, especially about the office of the Blessed Virgin, at whose feet we prostrate ourselves each moment, imploring her assistance. Many passed their time reciting her office and that of the dead. You must, therefore, look elsewhere for an explanation, for it is certain that we have lost one day."

Some gave one reason and some another, but all agreed upon one point, they had lost a day. I added: "My friends, remember that the year following your departure, that is to say, the year 1520, was a bissextile year, and this fact may have led you into error." They affirmed that they had taken account of the twenty-nine days in the month of February in that year, which is usually shorter, and that they did not forget the bissextile of the calends of March of the same year. The eighteen men who returned from the expedition are mostly ignorant, but when questioned, one after another, they did not vary in their replies.

Much surprised by this agreement, I sought Gaspar Contarino,[1] ambassador of the illustrious republic of Venice at the court of the Emperor. He is a great sage

---

[1] A learned Venetian, afterwards created Cardinal by Paul II. He died in 1552.

in many subjects. We discussed in many ways this hitherto unobserved fact, and we decided that perhaps the cause was as follows. The Spanish fleet, leaving the Gorgades Islands, proceeded straight to the west, that is to say, it followed the sun, and each day was a little longer than the preceding, according to the distance covered. Consequently, when the tour of the world was finished,—which the sun makes in twenty-four hours from its rising to its setting,—the ship had gained an entire day; that is to say, one less than those who remain all that time in the same place. Had a Portuguese fleet, sailing towards the east, continued in the same direction, following the same route first discovered, it is positive that when it got back to the Gorgades it would have lost a little time each day, in making the circuit of the world; it would consequently have to count one day more. If on the same day a Spanish fleet and a Portuguese fleet left the Gorgades, each in the opposite direction, that is to say one towards the west and the other towards the east, and at the end of the same period and by different routes they arrived at the Gorgades, let us suppose on a Thursday, the Spaniards who would have gained an entire day would call it Wednesday, and the Portuguese, who would have lost a day would declare it to be Friday. Philosophers may discuss the matter with more profound arguments, but for the moment I give my opinion and nothing more.

I have said enough about the tour of the world, the spice islands, the lost day, and the newly discovered countries. I now return to the country of Temistitan and I will sum it up as succinctly as possible, for this heavy labour wearies me. Old age creeps on and Your Holiness has already almost seen me fall into its rapacious clutches. With rapid flight it seeks to push me into the destroying arms of its decrepit sister; and yet I would have wished to pass more slowly through the paths of this grove.[1]

---

[1] . . . . *ac si per hujus lucis semitas placidius esset deambulandum.*

BOOK VIII

I HAVE already described how the Spaniards, driven out of the lake city of Temistitan, recuperated from this great disaster, thanks to the assistance furnished them by the neighbouring tribes hostile to that town. Let us return directly to the outskirts of Temistitan, omitting intermediate events.

There is a city called Tazcuco,[1] composed of eight thousand houses, but whose extensive suburbs reach from the lake to within eighteen leagues of Tascalteca. It was there that Cortes established his camp, surrounded by an immense army. The inhabitants of that town did not venture to oppose him, for the example of their neighbours was instructive, and they feared to be pillaged. Cortes had left workmen at Tascalteca engaged in building more boats. While he was occupied in subduing the neighbourhood with his army, thirteen brigantines were building for him, as we have already indicated; but as soon as he was established at Tazcuco, he ordered the framework of the brigantines to be brought to that town. The people of Tascalteca and Guazuzingo willingly carried this material on their shoulders; so cordially do they detest the people of Temistitan that any effort promising the destruction of their enemies becomes for them a pleasure. Even the Romans, when their prosperity was at its height, would not have found this undertaking easy.

At Tazcuco a little stream empties into the lake, both

[1] More properly spelled Texcoco or Tezcoco.

banks of which are bordered by houses separated by gardens. While waiting for the framework of the brigantines to be finished and the oars and other furnishings collected, Cortes dug a canal three Italian miles long, from Tazcuco to the lake; its depth was equal to four men's height, and it was bordered by fortified dykes, between which the brigantines might float. Eight thousand native workmen, labouring incessantly for fifty days, were required to complete this undertaking and enable him to launch the brigantines on the lake. But before this double labour of construction was finished, he destroyed and burned most of the towns, both along the lake or inland, whose inhabitants had attacked him during his retreat. Thus the people of Temistitan no longer ventured to fight our soldiers in the open country.

When this astonishing operation was finished and the thirteen brigantines were launched on the lake, the people of Temistitan realised that the hour of their downfall was at hand. Necessity, however, stimulated their courage. No sooner did they learn that the brigantines were launched, than an immense multitude of barques filled with armed men approached them. After the victory the people related that these barques numbered five thousand.[1] As they approached the brigantines, they were scattered by discharges from the cannon placed on the prows or along the sides of the ships. They looked like light clouds driven before the tempest.

Thanks to the brigantines, the lake was cleared, and the city hard pressed. Within a few days Cortes cut off

[1] Cortes states in his Third Letter that the enemy's boats numbered five hundred, and his calculation is probably correct. Bernal Diaz says there were four thousand of them, but he spoke from hearsay, as he was not present during the naval engagement. It has long since been accepted that the figures given by most of the early writers should be taken as representing the idea of multitude rather than an actual count. In this instance, the surface of the lake swarmed with boats, full of warriors: their actual number is a matter of speculation.

the fresh-water aqueducts. It was Cristobal de Olid who broke the aqueducts, and to prevent provisions from reaching the city from any side, Cortes surrounded it with three armies. He first led the Tascaltecans in the direction of Astapalappa,[1] which they entirely destroyed, not only because it was more powerful than the others, but because it was the former residence of Muteczuma's brother, who at that time was king. Cortes was in command of this army which, according to his report, numbered more than sixty thousand men; for more allies flocked to him from all the provinces than he desired. Some were attracted by a hope of plunder, others by love of liberty.

The bridge I mentioned above, as leading directly from Astapalappa to Temistitan, was occupied by Cortes. After numerous engagements in which the enemy was always defeated, thanks to the bravery of our men, the vigour of our horses, the cannon firing, and most of all to the brigantines, the Spaniards captured the bridge near the castle, where we have already said Muteczuma first met the Spaniards.[2] We have described this castle flanked by two towers, and protecting two bridges which met beneath its walls. Cortes established his camp at this point, thus finding himself at the junction of two bridges. To guard the great bridge on the other side, Cortes established another camp under the command of Gonzales Sandoval, a knight bearing the legal office called by the Spaniards *alguazil*. The third army, stationed on the other side of the town, was commanded by Pedro de Alvarado. It is said that these three armies together numbered one hundred and twenty thousand men.

Thus surrounded by enemies, the unhappy city endured every kind of privation. The ambition of some of her children, whose thirst for power had brought about this catastrophe, gave her as much cause for lament as her enemies did for fear. The people would have accepted

---

[1] Istapalapan.　　　　　　　　[2] The small fortress Xoloc.

our rule easily enough, had it not been for the resistance
of Muteczuma's sister's son who had usurped the empire,
and the pride of the nobles. During seventy days
Temistitan was besieged on all sides, without rest or
mercy. When our men returned to camp in the evening,
after each battle, they left in the streets of the city five
hundred, a thousand, or even more dead bodies. The
greater the slaughter, the more abundant and joyous
was the banquet to which the people of Guazuzingo and
Tascalteca gave themselves up; for it is their custom to
bury their foes, who have fallen in battle, in their bellies;
nor did Cortes venture to forbid it. Only a few of our
men, on the other hand, perished. The majority of the
inhabitants of Temistitan were destroyed, either by
sword or by starvation.

When our men invaded the streets of the town fighting,
they found piles of dead who had succumbed to hunger
and thirst. At several places they destroyed palaces,
after expelling the defenders.

Once Cortes was surrounded on a bridge, and captured
by the enemy, but was rescued by one of his servants,
Francisco Olea, who with one blow of his sword cut off
both hands of the man who clutched his master, and was
himself killed after he had given his horse to Cortes.

Finally the Spaniards were informed of the place where
the king, his principal chiefs and followers were concealed;
and immediately Cortes attacked with his brigantines
and captured the flotilla of barques indicated by the spies,
which carried the king to a place of concealment in the
lagoon. Brought into the presence of Cortes, the king
touched the dagger which the latter wore, saying: "With
this iron you may and should kill me. I have done my
duty and it will be painful and odious for me to live longer."
Cortes reassured him, saying that he had behaved as
becomes a magnanimous sovereign. Nevertheless, he
conducted him to dry land, and had him carefully guarded.

When these battles had reduced the great city of
Temistitan, and after its inhabitants were almost entirely
wiped out, Cortes brought all these peoples under the
Emperor's rule.

Two men of the rank called by the Spanish *hidalgos*,[1]
who have played an important part in these events,
either in exploring the unknown provinces or in fighting,
visited me.   They are called Diego Ordaz and Benevides.
They tell me that Cortes chose a king[2] for Temistitan
out of the royal family, commanding him to reside in that
town, in order that the abandoned capital might be
rebuilt under the protection of a sovereign; otherwise
this important city would have been deserted.

Impatient of idleness, Cortes sent messengers to collect
information concerning new countries.   He gave orders
that the country beyond the lofty mountains outlined on
the southern horizon should be explored.   He was informed that beyond the south slope of that mountain
chain lay another sea, the same I have mentioned in my
preceding decades as having been discovered by Vasco
Nuñez when he left Darien.   There are six cities in that
region, the smallest of which is larger than our celebrated
city Valladolid.   Their names are Teph, Mechuacan,
Guaxaca, Fuesco, Tequentepech,[3] and the name of the
sixth is not given.   In a private letter attached to the
report on the affairs of Temistitan, it is stated that it
has been learned that the spice islands, which also produce gold and silver, lie not far distant from the coast.

The names of the cities situated in the lagoon or around
its banks are as follows: Saltucar, Tenavica, Temistitan,

---

[1] The word *hidalgo* is derived from *hijo de algo* and was used pretty much
as *gentleman* in English.   Elastic and subject to abuse, it has gradually
lost its original exact significance.

[2] Meaning the Aztec functionary called *Chihuacoatl*, or lieutenant of
the sovereign through whom authority was directly exercised.   Cortes
wisely revived this office with which the natives were familiar.

[3] Tepatitlan, Michoacan, Oaxaca, Tasco, and Tehuantepec.

Scapuzalco, Tamba, Chapultepech, the two Coluacans, Quichilobusco, Suchimilco, Quitagna, Astapalappa, Mesechiche, Coluacan, Tezuco. Benevides has just returned from those countries. Cortes gave him command of one of the two ships carrying the presents chosen by the general, and which are more precious and beautiful than those offered to His Imperial Majesty the year he left Spain for Belgium, and which Your Holiness has inspected. Their value is estimated at two hundred thousand ducats. The two ships carrying them have not yet arrived, as they stopped in the Cassiterides Islands, which the Portuguese, who own them, call the Azores. They were afraid of being captured by French pirates, as befell another ship which sailed from Hispaniola and Cuba last year, loaded with seventy-two thousand ducats of gold, six hundred pounds of valuable pearls, and two thousand *rubi* of sugar: a *rubus* is called in Spanish *arroba*, and weighs twenty-five pounds, at six ounces to the pound. Moreover each man of the crew had his own little treasure. Everything was seized by the pirates. An armed fleet has been sent to the Cassiterides to escort the two ships, but at this present writing they had not yet been brought in.

According to the report of Benevides, there are on board these ships three tigers, reared from infancy in stout wooden cages. Two of these animals are on board one ship, and the third is on another. It happened that the ship carrying the two was so shaken by a tempest that the bars of one of the cages were loosened, and one of the tigers escaped. Once free, this ferocious beast tore about the vessel as furiously as though it had never seen a man. It was night-time, and the tiger rushed hither and thither, knocking over seven men, tearing off the arm of one, the leg of another, and the shoulders of a third. Two men were killed, and with a leap the tiger seized another unfortunate, who sought to escape up the mast. He was half dead, but his companions came to his assistance and saved him. Armed with hatchets, swords, and every sort of weapon, the sailors assembled, and the tiger, covered with wounds, was forced to spring into the sea. Fearing that a similar accident might occur with the other tiger, it was killed in its cage; but Benevides believes that the third will arrive on the other ship.

There is a great number of tigers, lions, and other ferocious animals in the mountains of that region. When asked what they eat, Benevides replied deer, stags, hares, rabbits, and other gentle animals of the country. The captains in charge of these ships are two brave soldiers who distinguished themselves during the conquest, Alfonso de Avila and Antonio Quiñones; it is they who are bringing the royal fifth to the King; the share of Cortes being administered by Juan Ribera, who has acted as his secretary and companion from the beginning of the expedition.

Acting on the advice of our Royal India Council, the Emperor has confirmed Cortes in command of the country he has named New Spain, while Diego Velasquez has been removed from authority in Cuba, or much the same thing; for it has been shown that he overstepped his powers in sending soldiers against Cortes in spite of the prohibition of the council of Hispaniola.

It has been recently learned that fifteen French pirate craft have been seen crossing the ocean in the hope of surprising the Spanish ships as they did last year, but a storm has driven them onto the African coast and sunk the greater number.

BOOK IX

I HAVE now come to the last reports made by Cortes, his companions in arms, the royal magistrates, the treasurer, the intendant and distributor, called in Spanish the factor, either in writing or verbally on their return. I have omitted many details, fearing to be wearisome in rehearsing too many small facts. I must note different reports received from Darien in the correspondence of Pedro Arias, governor of the continent, and through the intermediary of his eldest son, Diego Arias, who has just returned to Europe; nor shall I forget several recent events in Hispaniola and Cuba Fernandina.

Five colonies have been founded on the supposed continent; the first, situated on the northern coast, is Santa Maria Antigua, also called Darien, because, as I have said in my first decades, it is built on the banks of the Darien River. Why the Spaniards settled in that place, why they gave it that name when it already bore the name of its cacique Zemaco, I have already sufficiently explained.

The second colony is called Acla, and is west of Darien. Forty leagues west of Acla, another settlement was founded on the coast, and called by Columbus, who first discovered that region, Nombre de Dios, after the harbour of this name. Panama and Natan on the South Sea coast are the most distant and have kept their native names.

The continent is very extensive, especially in the direction of the large Maragnon River, concerning which I have already sufficiently spoken in my first decades. When searching for the causes which collected such a volume of water in a single river bed, I included among other reasons that the extent of land from north to south was probably very great and that numerous streams took their rise there, forming later a single river and flowing into the northern ocean. It so happens, Most Holy Father, that I have not been a bad prophet. The continent extends south from the northern coasts, rendered famous by the Maragnon in the country whose sovereigns, I have said, are called *chacones*, to the strait situated fifty-four degrees beyond the equator. Others estimate only fifty-two degrees; I have discussed this point in my digression concerning the spice islands.

The rigorous winter held the fleet of five vessels weather-bound in the neighbourhood of that strait, during almost five months. I have already elsewhere said that this was during our summer season, when the sun recedes from them and approaches us. It is, therefore, unnecessary to marvel further at the prodigious size of the Maragnon.

How does it happen that this continent, so broad in some places, shrinks in others to narrow isthmuses? This happens especially in the colony of Nombre de Dios, where the distance from the South Sea to the port of Panama is only seventeen leagues. Mountains, over which no road leads and which are inaccessible because of their rocks and dense virgin forests, intervene. These desert regions are likewise haunted by leopards, lions, tigers, bears, every kind of monkey, and other monsters, concerning which extraordinary things are told. It appears the tigers are no more afraid of men than though they were little dogs. Once they fall upon an isolated traveller there is no escape; he is torn into a thousand bits and devoured. The tigers are especially formidable for they are more ferocious than lions. There are numerous very fertile valleys and mountain slopes in this country, which elsewhere would be well populated, but are here abandoned because of the ferocious animals.

Many amusing things might be told about the monkeys, but they are also dangerous in the mountains the governor, Pedro Arias, has crossed, and which he daily renders more accessible by breaking down the rocks and burning the dense forests. The leaders of the monkeys (for they march in troops and are not courageous when alone) call together a great multitude of different breeds when they see a band of white men approaching, and give vent to horrible cries, springing from tree to tree, following the men wherever they can and amusing them with a thousand gestures and grimaces, especially the longtailed monkeys. Sometimes they descend almost to the tree-trunks, but as soon as they see preparations made to attack them with bows or firearms, whose power they understand, they remount to the tops of the trees with the rapidity of the wind, uttering furious cries and gnashing their teeth. They are so quick that they are able to escape the arrows shot at them by seizing them on the wing, as though they were being offered to them; but they are unable to avoid the projectiles of firearms. It is consequently by means of these latter that many monkeys are killed, especially the little ones which are less careful.

Whenever they see one of their number stricken to the earth wounded and about to be captured by our men, they tremble and lament so loudly that the air is filled with their complaints. They make more noise than a thousand roaring lions or whining tigers. Here is a sufficiently curious detail. Each monkey, when he climbs a tree, takes as many stones as he can carry in his hands and mouth to throw from the top branches when the Spaniards stop to shoot at him with their bows or muskets. One day an archer aimed his arrow at an old female with a very long tail. The animal feigned not to see it, half closing her eye; but hardly had the arrow left the bow than she severely wounded him in the face with a stone, which broke his teeth. The unfortunate beast was punished for its cunning, for the moment the stone dropped the arrow killed her. She was eaten with great satisfaction, for did the men not eat toads or still worse, when driven by the pangs of hunger? But this is enough concerning four-footed animals; let us return to bipeds, for the native bipeds are of hardly more account than the quadrupeds.

On the frontier of the colony of Natan in the south, there is a powerful and magnanimous king called Uracco. As the governor, Pedro Arias, was never able to win his friendship, he therefore announced he would organise a campaign against him. Uracco, strong in his authority and power, replied haughtily to the envoys sent to discuss peace conditions with him. He disturbed the colonists of Natan by invading Christian territory. The native arms are different kinds of javelins, which they throw from a distance, and large wooden swords, hardened in the fire, with which they fight hand to hand. They also have bows and arrows, pointed with bone or wood.

The cocoa-tree, which I have above mentioned, grows luxuriantly in the country, especially along the south coast, which is washed by the sea throughout a great extent. It is alleged that on one of these beaches, two leagues in extent, which is alternately covered with water and dried up, cocoa-trees grow spontaneously. Some people believe that the germs of these trees were brought by the waves from unknown regions; doubtless those regions of India whence they take their origin. It is also said that they were carried to Cuba and Hispaniola, as I have already related was the case with cinnamon-trees, and thence from the islands to the continent, finally reaching these southern countries.

Another wonderful tree grows on the islands, which I

think is not found on the continent. Its leaves are used as
paper. It is not the same one I have mentioned in the
decades; on the contrary it differs greatly. I will describe
it when I speak of the islands. For the present let us
resume the history of the continent.

Leaving the colony of Panama on the South Sea with
ships built there, the Spaniards sailed so far westwards
that they believed themselves to be behind Yucatan.
The proof given by Gil Gonzales, captain of this fleet,
and his companions is, that they met natives dressed in
the same fashion, with pierced lips, wearing gold and
silver necklaces covered with precious stones, similar
to those I have described in my Fourth Decade addressed
to Pope Leo, when I spoke of the country of Yucatan
and the gifts sent from that country.

According to their account the ocean on their right hand
was so turbulent that they believed some undiscovered
strait must exist between the continent and Yucatan,
but they did not venture amidst such raging waters,
because their vessels were half rotten and very worm-
eaten; they have promised to return there when their
ships are repaired.

Gil Gonzales has told Pedro Arias,—and his statement
is confirmed by his companions,—that during this voyage
he found an immense expanse of black-coloured sea,
about one hundred leagues from the gulf of Panama,
in which swam fish, as large as dolphins, singing melodi-
ously, as is recounted of the Sirens. Like the Sirens also
their song lulled to sleep. At this point the narrow-
minded will marvel, saying the thing is impossible. I
will answer them in a few words. Do we not read that
in the Erythræan Gulf the water is red, and is it not this
tint which has given the gulf its name? Whence is this
colour? From the quality of the water, or the red sands
or the red rocks reflected in it? Has nature so little power
hat she may nor fashion black sands and black rocks,

to give their sombre tints to the water? I likewise am perfectly willing to believe that the singing fish are a fable, although it is reported by men worthy of credence. What has been said about Tritons having voices, may serve to excuse them. People have sometimes heard Tritons, and dead ones have even been found cast up by the tempest on the western coast of Spain. Does not the frog croak under water? Why, therefore, is it astonishing that other fish should have voices, which until now have never been heard? Let each one keep his own beliefs; as for myself, I believe in the omnipotence of nature.

Crocodiles are numerous in all the continental rivers. They are dangerous while in the water, but not so when on land, as is the case with those along the Nile. The Spaniards have found a dead one measuring forty-two feet in length, with jaws seven feet wide.

The son of Pedro Arias who has returned to Spain, says that a tree suitable for ship-building, has been found as its wood is impervious to the attacks of worms. He also says that when burnt in the kitchen, this wood takes fire very slowly being thoroughly saturated with moisture.

Let me now say a few words concerning the resources of this country. It contains many gold mines, but I wish that neither Pedro Arias nor any of those who seek gold to the everlasting hurt of the unfortunate natives knew anything of them. We have often agitated the question before Your Holiness and in our India Council it is now settled. The Indians are to be free, and may work in their own fields or at Christian trades. If any of them choose voluntarily to labour for wages, they may be employed as paid workmen. This is enough concerning the continent; let us add a few words about the islands.

Nothing is changed in Hispaniola. It is the council residing there which dictates laws to all the other colonies. The products of that island develop daily; there are great numbers of horses, pigs, and cattle, and the same holds

good for the other islands. A mare is impregnated
ten months after its birth, and hardly is one colt born
before she is ready to have another. The native bread
is made from yucca and maize, and satisfies the people.
Wines are imported into the archipelago from Andalusia,
and although vines exist in different places they grow so
rapidly that they expend their vitality in branches and
leaves rather than grapes. Moreover they die a few years
after planting. The same may be said of grain, which
grows as high as canes, and produces enormous spears,
but the kernel ordinarily disappears before maturity.
The amount of sugar increases every year.

Let us now describe the tree[1] growing in the two islands
which produces parchment. It closely resembles a palm,
and its leaves are so broad that any one of them carried
over a man's head protects him against the rain, as well
as though he covered his shoulders with a woollen mantle.
Here is an extraordinary fact; the leaves of this tree grow
close to the trunk, like those of the palm. If one of these
is pulled off by the root attaching it to the stalk,—a thing
easily accomplished by the help of a knife,—the interior
of the stem is found to contain a sort of white skin,
resembling that covering the albumen of an egg. De-
taching this skin, as might be done with that of a slaught-
ered lamb, it comes off whole like that of a lamb or goat.
This is then used as that of one of these animals would be
and seems to be quite as strong. These leaves are sold
in small pieces, as required for writing. This tree is
called *yagua*, and its fruit resembles that of the olive.
It fattens pigs but is less suited to men. I have elsewhere
described how another leaf, which does not resemble this
skin, is used for writing.

There is still another tree growing upon the summits
of the rocks, which does not flourish in rich soil. It is

[1] The American agave. The description that follows is not especially
lucid nor is it in the author's best style.

called *pythahaya*. Its fruit is tart, and tastes like the African pear called the pomegranate, while in size it is similar to an orange. It is red both inside and out. The mamei which I have already described in the decades, and whose fruit is not larger than a small lemon, also grows in the island; on the continent the fruit becomes larger. It contains only three stones, each the size of a nut, which are for the propagation of the species.

Something may be said about the pepper gathered in the islands and on the continent. I mentioned pepper as growing in the forests; but it is not pepper, though it has the same strength and the flavour, and is just as much esteemed. The natives call it *axi*. It grows taller than a poppy, and the grains are gathered from this bush just as from a juniper or pine, although they are not so large. There are two varieties of these grains, five in the row; one of which is half a finger in length, and its taste is sharper and more biting than that of pepper; the other is round and has no more taste than pepper. Its bark, skin, and kernel have a hot flavour, but not very sharp. The third grain does not sting the tongue but is aromatic. When it is used there is no need of Caucasian pepper. The sweet pepper is called *boniatum* and the hot pepper is called *carribe*, meaning sharp and strong; for this same reason the cannibals are called Caribs, because they are strong.

There is another tree in the island called *guchon*, whose sap penetrates the skin of any who touch it and is absorbed like a poison. Any one who is unfortunate enough to look fixedly at that tree becomes blind and swells up as though he had the dropsy. Let us notice two other trees whose leaves and wood are fatal when burnt. It is only necessary to carry a piece of this burning wood for the smoke to suffocate people. There is also another tree equally poisonous if the smoke from its leaves is inhaled.

An atrocious crime has been related to me by a priest
who has crossed the vast ocean six times from the continent to Cuba and Hispaniola—three times going and
three times coming. This person is called Benito Martin
and he is a man of some eloquence. It was he who first
brought to Barcelona the news of the discovery of Yucatan and the neighbouring countries. According to his
account, a certain Madroñez, of Albaciti in Murcia,
had assigned to him a cacique and his subjects as forced
labourers, according to the ancient custom permitting
the mines to be worked under the whip. He lived in a
place called Santiago, where a gold mine was soon found,
and the cacique and his miners rapidly accumulated for
their temporary master nine thousand castellanos of
gold. We decided from the outset in our Royal India
Council that all the natives should receive as recompense
when their work was finished some article of European
manufacture; such as a hat, jacket, shirt, mirror, or
something similar. The cacique hoped that his remuneration would be increased, because the amount had been
so rapidly accumulated, but Madroñez showed himself
more avaricious than he had expected. The cacique was
so angry that he assembled all his miners to the number
of ninety-five persons in his cabin, and spoke to them as
follows: "My friends and companions: why should we
wish longer to live in this atrocious slavery? We had
better betake ourselves to the eternal home of our ancestors, where we shall be beyond the reach of the intolerable
sufferings these ungrateful creatures, in whose power we
are, put upon us. Do you go ahead, and I will follow you."
While thus speaking he held prepared in his hands packets
of the odorous herbs whose smoke is fatal. Lighting
them he distributed to each man a portion, that he might
inhale. His orders were carried out. The cacique and
one of his relatives, a wise man, waited to be the last to
inhale the smoke. The floor of the room was already

covered with bodies, and the two survivors disputed as to which of them should be the first to die. The cacique insisted that his companion should die first, but the other declined, promising, however, to follow his master. Finally the cacique decided, but his companion who loved the sweetness of life, did not imitate his chief or his companions, and refused to die as they had. Leaving the room, he revealed what had happened to Spaniards.

At about the same time in the province of Principe, a still more odious action was committed. A justice, called Orlando, had in his power the daughter of a cacique who was pregnant by him, but whom he suspected of having a lover. Wishing to frighten but not to kill her, he had her bound to two sticks of wood, and fire brought; after which he ordered his servants to burn her. The atrocious action and the novelty of the punishment so terrified the girl, that she died. Upon hearing this, the cacique, her father, invaded the house of the justice with thirty men, and during the latter's absence, killed the wife he had married after this crime, her servants, and all the domestics to the last man; after which he and his friends shut themselves up in the house, to which they set fire. They were burned, together with the bodies of the magistrate's dead family and all his goods.

Another still more horrible story is told of a young girl who had been raped by a Spanish muleteer. She returned home and related what had happened telling her parents that in expiation of this crime she would kill herself. Refusing all consolation, she drank the juice of the yucca, which, when raw is a poison. In this case the poison was not sufficiently strong to kill her, so the next day she announced that she was going to bathe in the neighbouring river; it being a native custom to bathe twice a day. She therefore found a cruel means of avenging herself. She bent down to the level of her head a small tree growing on the bank, and sharpened the top branch to a point;

she then climbed a somewhat taller neighbouring tree
and forced the point into her womb, remaining pierced
like an animal, spitted for roasting before the kitchen fire.

Some days later another young girl also wished to put
an end to the miseries of her existence. Choosing as her
companion the servant of a priest, who was the same age
as herself, she persuaded the maid to follow her example
and join their ancestors in regions where they might live
peaceably. They attached their girdles to the branches
of a tree, making a slip knot which they passed round
their necks, and then let themselves drop. Their hopes
were realised. Many similar stories are told.

I wish to terminate this narrative by a story of a giant
who, similar to the formidable Atlas, will serve me as an
ending and confirm what I have told. Diego Ordaz,
whom I have before mentioned, explored several unknown
parts of that region and conquered a number of caciques,
amongst whom was one in whose country the fruits used
as money grow. He it was who taught the Spaniards
how to cultivate that tree, as I have already told. Ordaz
found in the sanctuary of a temple the hip-bone of a giant,
which was half worn away by age. A short time after
Your Holiness had left for Rome, the bone was brought
to Victoria by the licentiate Ayllon, one of the most
learned jurisconsults in the Senate of Hispaniola. For
some days I had that bone in my possession; it measured
five cubits in length, and its thickness is in proportion.
Some of the men sent by Cortes into the southern mountains afterwards discovered a country inhabited by these
giants; in proof of their discovery they have brought back
several ribs taken from bodies.

All the other events we have witnessed are known pre-
cisely and at first hand, to Your Holiness, thanks to the
Emperor's envoys. You will not, therefore, exact that
I should describe the misfortunes which wait upon the
Christian princes now occupied in driving out the Moham-

medans and in mutually rending one another for motives of religious hatred. Permit me, therefore, to wish good health to Your Holiness, at whose feet I prostrate myself, offering my most humble homage.

BOOK X

WHEN the Hydra's heads are cut off they revive, and so it is with me; for I have hardly disposed of one narrative than a number of others spring up. I believed I had closed the door on the affairs of Temistitan, but the arrival of a new messenger obliges me to reopen it. Juan Ribera, a trusted servant of Cortes, has arrived on board one of the two ships, laden with the presents from Mexico, which waited at the Azores. The other ship, fearing the French pirates, is waiting there until an escort arrives.

Without mentioning the royal fifth, that ship brings the treasure which is composed of a part of what Cortes amassed, at the cost of risks and dangers, and the share belonging to his principal lieutenants; they offer it all in homage to their king. Ribera has been instructed to present to the Emperor in his master's name the gifts he sends, while the others will be presented in the name of their colleagues by the officers who, as I have said, remained behind at the Azores. This man Ribera speaks the language of Temistitan, and nothing of importance has happened during this war, in which he has not taken part, for he never left his master's side. He was sent here some time after the departure of his companions, so he is able to give us an exact report of everything that has happened.

First of all, he has been questioned concerning the origin of Temistitan, the signification of this name, the

ruin and actual condition of the city, the resources of
Cortes, and many other points. He says that Temistitan
was built upon a rock standing in the midst of the salt
lake; just as is related of the most illustrious city of
Venice, built upon a hill on the coast of the Adriatic.
Temistitan served as a refuge against the attacks of
enemies, and its name is derived from three different
words: *tem* refers to anything that appears to be of a
divine origin, *nucil* is a fruit, and *titan* is anything standing
in the water; hence the derivation of Temistitan, namely,
"A divine fruit growing in the water." The first people
who landed upon that reef found there a tree laden with
exquisite and nourishing fruits, somewhat larger than our
apples, which supplied them with food in their time of
need.[1] In sign of gratitude their standard displays a
representation of this tree, which resembles a mulberry,
although its leaves are much greener.

The Tascaltecans bear upon their standards two clasped
hands, kneading a loaf; for they boast that their fields
produce more cereals than those of their neighbours,
and this is even the origin of their name; for *Tascal* in
their language signifies a loaf of bread, and *teca* means a
mistress. Tascalteca therefore means "Mistress of bread."
The inhabitants of that mountain called by our people
Vulcan—I mean the one that smokes—have the same
usage, and upon their standards is represented a smoking
mountain, which they call Popocatepech, because *Popoca*
means smoke, and *tepech*, a mountain. On the eastern
side, and separated from Popocatepech by a short distance,
rises another mountain covered the entire year with snow
Other mountains are also snow-covered because of their
height. Let us mention the mountain Cachutepech,

---

[1] The *nopal*, or Mexican fig, called in Spanish *tuna*. Needless to add
that Peter Martyr's description is entirely mistaken and that the variety
of cactus producing this fruit bears not the slightest resemblance to a
mulberry tree.

where rabbits flourish, for *cachu* means rabbit and Cachutepech, "The rabbit mountain." A temple of the gods
is called Teucale, from *Teu*, god, and *cale*, meaning house
or habitation. In this wise the natives designate everything by what it represents; we will later return more
carefully to this subject.

Ribera reports that the city has been ruined for the
most part by fire and sword, and that only a small number
of the principal inhabitants survive. As the fury of the
war did not spare a single town or village in the neighbourhood, Cortes ordered the ruins to be reconstructed;
especially the royal palaces and the residence of Muteczuma, which was so vast that, according to common report,
no one who entered could find his way about without a
guide, unless he had been born and brought up there.
It resembles the intricacies of the fabulous labyrinth of
Minos. Cortes has insisted that this palace should first
of all be repaired.

As for the pleasure houses, where, as we have said,
different species of quadrupeds and wild beasts and birds
were kept, they stood inside the town and amidst the waters,
and not on the mainland as some persons have stated. So it
was with the groves and the orchards. Ribera has described
the howls of the lions, tigers, bears, and wolves while they
were burning in the houses, and the deplorable catastrophe
which overtook the natives. Some day the pleasure houses
will be rebuilt. They were constructed of stone from the
foundations, finished with *creneaux*, like a fortress.

The people's dwelling houses were also built of stone,
but only halfway up, because of the inundations and the
streams of water flowing into the lake. The rest of the
house, above this solid foundation, was built of baked
or sundried brick, mixed with beams; they usually had
but one story. The dampness of the soil caused the people
to live but little on the ground floor. The roofs were not
of tiles, but made of a sort of bituminous earth, which

more easily absorbs the rays of the sun, but which, it is supposed, must wear out more quickly.

The heavy beams and pieces of timber used in constructing their houses are treated as follows: The slopes of the mountains are covered with lemon-trees. It is known that when the Romans renounced frugality to give themselves up to debauchery and pleasure, they used citron wood for their tables and beds, because this wood is always in fermentation, and free from worms and rot; moreover, its planks are of various colours. Pines were also found mixed with lemon-trees in the forests of those regions. By means of their copper hatchets and well sharpened axes, the natives cut down the trees, hewing them smoothly and cleaning away the chips, to facilitate their transport.

There is no lack of plants from which they make string, cords, and cables, as though from hemp. Boring a hole through one side of the beam, they pass a cable to which slaves are harnessed, as though they were oxen under the yoke. Instead of wheels, they place rounded tree-trunks on the road, whether going up or down hill. The carpenters oversee the work, but slaves do the heaviest part of it. All materials and whatever is required in daily life is carried in the same way, for they have neither oxen nor asses nor any animal as beasts of burden. Incredible stories are told of these pieces of wood; I would not venture to repeat them had not eye-witnesses, called before us in full council, testified that they had verified them. Such witnesses are numerous. One of these beams found at Tezcuco is one hundred and twenty feet long, and as thick round as a fat ox. It sustains almost the entire building. We are assured that this has been seen, and nobody doubts it. Does not this example furnish a high idea of their industry?

The cocoa coinage is always used, and it seems useless to make any change. For the defence of this immense

empire, Cortes disposes of a force consisting of forty
cannon, two hundred horsemen, and thirteen hundred
foot-soldiers, two hundred and fifty of the latter being
engaged in manœuvring the thirteen brigantines. These
boats ply the lake, night and day, under the direction of
a specially appointed lieutenant. The other soldiers are
engaged in exploring the countries yet unknown. They
have visited the mountains separating the plain of Temistitan from the countries to the south; the extent of which
from east to west is asserted by those who have visited
them to be very great, and their length five hundred
leagues. These countries are highly productive of foodstuffs, are well wooded, and have remarkable cities.

Juan Ribera brings pieces of gold in various shapes,
such as lentils or peas, found in the several rivers which
water the plain of Temistitan, as well as pearls from the
south coast. He represents them as spoils of war taken
from Muteczuma or from his voluptuous chieftains,
and from other enemies. Ribera was with me when
the reverend protonotary Caracciolo, legate of Your
Holiness, and the Venetian ambassador, Gaspar Contarini
and Tomaso Maino, nephew of the illustrious Jason
Maino, envoy of the Duke of Milan,[1] came to see me,
desiring to learn and behold something new. They
admired the quantity and the natural purity of the gold
(for it is so pure that it might be coined into ducats
without the least alloy), less than the number and shapes
of the receptacles, in which the different tribes had sent
their tribute. That these vessels are used to hold this
gold is proven by the fact that each vase or basket has
attached to it the name of the tributary country.
Each of these receptacles weighs eight, nine, or ten

[1] Marino Caracciolo was created Cardinal by Paul III., and died while
holding the governorship of Milan. Jasone Maino was a celebrated
jurisconsult, author of voluminous works which were collected and published
in nine volumes at Turin, 1576.

drachmas of gold. What has been shown us is the best proof of the amount each of the companions of Cortes received as his share; and indeed Ribera is the sole possessor of all he has exhibited to us.

The treasure destined for the Emperor is on board the vessel which has not yet arrived; but it is said that it amounts to 32,000 ducats of smelted gold in the form of bars. Were all the rings, jewels, shields, helmets, and other ornaments now smelted, the total would amount to 150,000 ducats. The report has spread, I know not how, that French pirates are on the watch for these ships[1]; may they come safely in!

Let us describe Ribera's share, which is but a feeble forecast of what will come later. He has shown us pearls as pure as those human luxury calls oriental pearls; many of them are larger than a large nut, but they are not translucent, for they are taken from the shells after the latter have been boiled. Nevertheless we have observed some that are translucent. This, however, is as nothing. The necklaces and rings are curious to see, for there is not a quadruped, bird, or a fish the native artists have seen, that they do not reproduce faithfully to nature. The exactitude of the reproduction commands our admiration. What shall be said of the little vases, earrings, chains, bracelets, all made of gold, of which the workmanship is superior to the material; and likewise of the crests, plumes, shields and helmets of open metal work, so delicately wrought they deceive the eye? We have been particularly delighted with two mirrors of exceptional beauty; the first was bordered with a circle of gold one palm in circumference, and set in green wood. The other was similar. Ribera states that there is stone

---

[1] The French pirates were successful in their attack on the Spanish ships: Quiñones de Leon was killed, Alonso d'Avila was captured and carried a prisoner to La Rochelle, while the entire treasure fell into the hands of the corsair, Jean Florin.

found in these countries, which makes excellent mirrors when polished; and we admit that none of our mirrors more faithfully reflect the human face.

We also admire the artistically made masks. The superstructure is of wood, covered over with stones, so artistically and perfectly joined together that it is impossible to detect their lines of junction, with the finger nail. They seem to the naked eye to be one single stone, of the kind used in making their mirrors. The ears of the mask are of gold, and from one temple to another extend two green lines of emeralds; two other saffron coloured lines start from the half opened mouth, in which bone teeth are visible; in each jaw two natural teeth protrude between the lips. These masks are placed upon the faces of the gods, whenever the sovereign is ill, not to be removed until he either recovers or dies.

Ribera next opened a capacious box containing a great number of garments. The people of that country only use three materials for their clothing; that is to say, cotton, birds' feathers, and rabbits' hair. They make the feathers and the hair into a pattern upon a foundation of cotton, working them with such ingenuity that we are unable to comprehend their methods of fabrication. The cotton presents no difficulty, for they spin and weave cotton just as we do linen, wool, or silk. The shape of these garments is laughable. They call them garments because they use them to cover their bodies, but they in no way, nearly or remotely, resemble ours. One is a square covering similar to the one which Your Holiness sometimes in my presence wore on your shoulders; it leaves the head free and protects the garments, so that neither hair nor anything else may fall upon them. They draw this cover round their necks, tying the two or the four corners near the throat. In this wise the body is covered down to the legs. Having seen these garments, I ceased to marvel that they had presented such a number to Cortes as I said: for they are of small value, and most of them occupy little space.

The natives also wear trousers decorated with bunches of various coloured feathers; from the knee down their legs are bare, though many of them wear shoes, made for the most part of feathers. They mix plumes with the woofs of cotton, and also skilfully employ rabbits' hair, of which they make their winter clothing and their bed covers. For the rest they are naked and leave one of their arms uncovered, except when it is very cold. All these people are bronze-coloured.

Although the earth sometimes suffers from the cold, it is never serious, for the country, according to report, extends from the nineteenth to the twenty-second degree towards the arctic pole. Nevertheless, upon the numerous maps Ribera has brought here, I have found the following indications. Mountain chains extend in the north at equal distances from one another and are separated by very fertile valleys. The north winds sweep with great violence down through their defiles upon the plain. For this reason the northern side of Temistitan is protected against the force of storms by large ramparts of beams, set in the earth and by great rocks. I have observed the same thing at Venice where an erection of this description has been built to prevent the waves of the Adriatic from destroying the houses; this shelter is called the *Lido*. Towards the south, on the contrary, high mountains rise near at hand, affording protection against the heat and the south winds. North winds are, however, not wanting, but they prevail in the higher of the atmospheric regions above where the south winds blow. This accounts for the existence near to the valley of mountains covered with eternal snows. Volcanoes likewise are visible.

One of the maps we have examined is thirty feet long and not quite so wide. It is painted on white cotton cloth. All the plains and the provinces, whether vassal or hostile to Muteczuma, are there represented, as well as the lofty mountains which completely surround the plain. The map also shows the southern coast ranges, whose inhabitants stated that off the coast lie the islands we have above described as producing an abundance of spices, gold, and precious stones.

I shall now, Most Holy Father, permit myself a digression. Upon hearing this part of the reports, most of us gave signs of dissent, asserting that such dubious matters needed better proof. As is frequently the case with statements made by barbarians, they require to be confirmed by facts. We must admit that my associates were not wrong, remembering as they did three instances in connection with our new continent in which the reality did not come up to the expectations. In my first decades I have spoken of this, with some reserve.

The first instance was that of the son of the cacique Comogre, who ruled over seven other caciques. He had reproached the Spaniards with attaching excessive importance to gold, and had promised them to satisfy their desires, if they would obtain sufficient reinforcements to enable them to penetrate the mountain districts he pointed out to them and described as being governed by warlike caciques prepared to defend their rights to the end. On the southern slope of these mountains the Spaniards discovered another sea, extending towards the antarctic pole, and the inhabitants of the region were very rich. Crossing the mountains they discovered the South Sea, but promptly perceived that the power of those kings was very much less than was commonly supposed.

The same thing happened in regard to the Dobaiba River, of which I have sufficiently spoken. Nevertheless it was those two reports which prompted the Catholic King to send Pedro Arias and twelve hundred soldiers

into that country, which was equivalent to sending them
to the shambles. I have already described above how
they almost all perished, and to no purpose whatsoever.

A third instance, similar to the foregoing, should
constrain our compatriots to be less credulous; long
experience has shown that the natives, hoping to rid their
country of the Spaniards, asked them what they wanted;
and no sooner did they learn that our people wanted gold
and provisions, than they indicated remote localities,
emphatically insisting that they would find a far greater
abundance in the territory of such and such a cacique,
whom they name, than where they were. When the
Spaniards visited such caciques, they found they had been
tricked.

It is, therefore, not without reason that everything told
about these distant regions is suspected of exaggeration.
Nevertheless, in thinking of this particular case, I have
felt that such a great man as Cortes must have had positive
and determined reasons for his statements. I sustained
my opinion in the presence of Mercurio de Gattinaria,[1]
Grand Chancellor, Fernando de Vega, Grand Commander,
the Seigneur de la Roche, the learned Belgian doctor,
who has the confidence of the Emperor, son of the
Grand Chancellor Philip, and of the High Treasurer, the
licenciate Vargas; the last-named has taken his seat in
the India Council after the departure of Your Holiness.
My argument was as follows: I would blush to cite this
fact as miraculous or as belonging to the phenomena
of nature. Let it be remembered that the Moluccas,
where spices grow, are partly situated under the equator.
Taken altogether, these islands occupy but an insignificant space in the universe, and the equatorial line circles
the entire globe. May not other islands, therefore, exist,

---

[1] The celebrated chancellor of Charles V. was born in 1465 and died
in 1580. He had served the Duke of Savoy, the Burgundian parliament,
and the Emperor Maximilian; he drafted the treaty of Cambrai.

as well as the Moluccas, equally favoured by climate and fructified by the sun's rays, so as to produce spices? And why may not such countries have remained unknown until the present time, if such was the will of Divine Providence? Do we not likewise know that there exist numerous parts of the ocean and the continent, unheard of until our time? The southern coasts of the empire of Temistitan are not more than twelve degrees from the equator, so there would be nothing astonishing were we now to discover what was heretofore unknown, and were these discoveries to augment the fortune of our Emperor who was the pupil of Your Holiness. I would repeat this to all who are resolved only to believe what they understand, and I would do this in the name of Your Holiness, who has not only wisely pondered the secrets of Nature, the universal mother, but has also studied divine science.

I am, moreover, swayed by another argument. Cortes has accomplished such great things that I cannot believe him to be so wanting in common sense as to undertake, blindly, at his own cost, such an important enterprise as the construction in the South Sea of four ships, fitted out for the discovery of those countries, did he not possess some certitude or at least some probability of success.[1]

But let us return to his trusted friend Ribera. He states that, according to the native reports, the mountains are inhabited by savages as hairy as bears, who dwell in caves and live on roots and game. After seeing the large map I have mentioned, we were shown a somewhat smaller one but which interested us just as much. It is a native painting representing the town of Temistitan, with its temples, bridges, and lakes.[2]

---

[1] A most sensible appreciation of the character of Fernando Cortes. While enemies fabricated and disseminated the wildest and most contradictory accusations against him, Peter Martyr's exceptional perspicacity weighed and judged the conqueror of Mexico with singular accuracy.

[2] The plan of ancient Mexico drawn by Montezuma's artists frequently reproduced, notably in the *Theatrum orbis terrarum* of Ortelius.

I afterwards summoned a young native slave whom Ribera had brought back with him as a servant, into our presence, where we were sitting on an open terrace. He had dressed himself in my room. In his right hand he carried a simple wooden sword, without the stones which ordinarily decorate this weapon, for the battle swords have their two edges hollowed out and filled with sharp stones fastened in with solid bitumen, so that these swords are almost as stout in battle as our own. The stone is that used for the razors, of which I have above spoken. In his other hand he carried a native shield, made of stout reeds covered with gold. The lower extremity of this shield is decorated with a feather fringe, a cubit long. The shield was lined with tiger skin, and the centre of the exterior had coloured feathers resembling our raw silk. Armed with his sword the slave advanced. He wore a robe of woven feathers, half blue and half red, and cotton trousers; a handkerchief was suspended between his hips and his leggins were fastened to his garments like a cuirass which is taken off without undoing the strings that fasten the leggins. He wore beautiful sandals. He then gave an exhibition of a battle; first hurling himself upon his enemies, then retreating; then he engaged another slave who served with him and was trained to these exercises. He seized him by the hair, as they do their enemies whom they capture with weapons in their hands, dragging them off to be sacrificed. After throwing the slave on the ground, he feigned to cut open his breast above the heart, with a knife. After tearing out the heart, he wrung from his hands the blood flowing from the wound, and then besprinkled the sword and shield. This is the treatment they show prisoners.

Rubbing two sticks together he lighted a new fire, in which he burnt the heart; for the sacrificial fire must never have served any other purpose, as they believe the smoke of this sacrifice pleases the tutelary gods of their

country. The rest of the body is cut into pieces, as
the gestures of the slave showed, but the belly and entrails
are untouched; no doubt for fear of corruption. The head
of the enemy sacrificed in this wise is stripped of its flesh
and set in gold, after which the victor keeps it as a trophy.
They are even accustomed to make as many little golden
heads with half-opened mouths as it is proven each has
killed or sacrificed enemies, and these they wear round
their neck. It is believed the members are eaten.

Ribera affirms that he knows the principal vassals of
Muteczuma were accustomed to live on human flesh, and
he also suspected that Muteczuma himself did. Nevertheless he always abstained in the presence of the Spaniards,
doubtless after they had given him to understand how
odious and displeasing it was to the Divinity to kill a
man, and much more so to eat him.

When this representation was finished, and while we
were questioning Ribera concerning the customs and the
greatness of these countries, the slave was taken into
another room, where he donned his gala costume. He
then appeared before us in another dress, holding in his
left hand a golden toy with a thousand different ornaments, and in his right hand a circle of bells, which he
shook, gaily raising and lowering his golden toy. He
accompanied himself by singing a native air, and danced
about the room where we were assembled to see him.
The most curious thing to see was his representation of
the salutations with which they honour their sovereigns
when offering gifts. They approach, and with trembling
voice and bowed head, never looking at the king and
humbly prostrated, they spoke more or less in the following
words: "King of Kings, master of the heavens and the
earth, we bring you in the name of our city (or our fortress)
this pledge of our obedience. Choose what suits you
best. Do you wish that we should construct a palace for
you, bringing stones, beams, and lumber, or do you prefer

that we should cultivate your properties? We are your slaves. We have been very badly treated by our neighbours, who are your enemies, for we defend your interests. But we have endured everything without grumbling, for we desire to become obedient and faithful. This is the cause of our misfortunes."

While we were still questioning Ribera the slave appeared a third time; he now played the part of a drunkard, and never was the rôle more faithfully sustained. When the Indians hope to obtain what they desire from the gods, they assemble to the number of two or three thousand, and intoxicate themselves with the juice of an herb; after which they rush naked through the streets, and squares of the town, clutching at the walls, to sustain themselves and asking their way home of those whom they meet. Some spit, others puke, and oftener still they fall to the ground. But this is enough concerning that slave.

Ribera had vaguely heard of a region amongst the northern mountains exclusively inhabited by women, but nothing could be less positive. What might argue in favour of the truth of this story is that the land is called Yguatlan; for *ygua* in their language means woman, and *lan* means master. Hence it is believed to be the country of women. While the slave was preparing his several representations, Ribera cited as proof of Muteczuma's power, the large number of interpreters and envoys from different provinces who resided permanently at court, to represent their master's interests. It is precisely the same as in Europe where counts, marquesses, and dukes, form the emperor's court.

Though they are frivolous things, it may not be out of place to say something of their games. It is known that they have chess-boards, from the representations of them seen on their draperies, but the most popular game amongst them, as amongst the people of our own islands, is a game of tennis. Their balls are made of the juice[1] of a vine that climbs over the trees, as hop vines clamber amongst the hedges. They cook the juice of these plants until it hardens in the fire, after which each one shapes the mass as he pleases, giving it the form he chooses. It is alleged that the roots of this herb when cooked give them their weight; at all events I do not understand how these heavy balls are so elastic that when they touch the ground, even though lightly thrown, they spring into the air with the most incredible leaps. The natives are most skilful players at this exercise, catching the ball on their shoulders, elbows, heads, rarely their hands, and sometimes their hips, if their opponents throw when their backs are turned. When playing tennis they strip, as do our wrestlers.

Instead of candles and torches, they burn pine resin, but do not use soot, grease, or oil. Neither do they make any use of wax, although they have both wax and honey, which they have only learned to use since our arrival. In the palaces of the king and the great lords, there are fires burning throughout the night. Servants appointed for the service take turns in feeding them by continually putting on wood, and in keeping the flame burning on a lofty copper candelabra. One of these candelabra stands in the vestibule of the palace, another in the first court which serves as a waiting-room for the courtiers, and the third is in the sovereign's sleeping chamber. Any one wishing to move about takes a torch in his hands, just as we do a candle. In the islands they use turtle fat for their candles, just as we use grease.

The common people restrict themselves to one wife, but the chiefs may keep as many concubines as they choose. Only the princes sleep in beds, the others upon masses of flowers thrown on the floor, or on cotton carpets, using cotton coverlets. Ribera has shown us a number of these covers.

---

[1] Meaning rubber, of which mention is here made for the first time.

The natives are acquainted with figures and measures, but not with weights. I have already often said that they have books, of which a number have been brought here.[1] Ribera states that these books are not written to be read, but are various collections of designs the jewellers keep to copy in making ornaments, or decorating coverlets and dresses. Spanish needlewomen, as well as all women who do fine embroidery of roses, flowers, and other pretty designs in silk on linen, keep such models on stuffs which serve to train the young apprentices. I hardly know what to believe, because of the great variety one observes in these books, but I think they must be books whose characters and designs have a meaning, for have I not seen on the obelisks in Rome characters which are considered letters, and do not we read that the Chaldeans formerly had a similar writing?

I remember to have written above that Muteczuma, at the suggestion of Cortes, had ordered his architects to build a palace near the sea, sixty leagues from the capital. Two hundred cocoa-trees and numerous measures of maize had been planted; ducks, geese, and domestic peacocks had been stocked there, and farm houses had been constructed near the residence. When the Spaniards were expelled from Temistitan, the barbarians massacred all our compatriots who had been left there, and carried off everything they found.

According to Ribera the following are the advantages

---

[1] Consult Zelia Nuttall's *Analysis of Mexican Inscriptions and Paintings;* Aubin's *Mémoire sur la peinture didactique et l'écriture figurative des anciens Méxicains.* Seler's article in the *Revue d'Ethographie,* 1889. Also the valuable work of Borunda published in Rome in 1898 by the munificence of the Duc de Loubat. Numerous partial or entire reproductions of such Mexican books as escaped the wholesale destruction that followed the Conquest exist; notably the Codices Borgianus, Tellerianus, and Mendoza. Also in Orozco y Berra's *Anales del Museo Nacional de Mexico;* Brasseur de Bourbourg's *Manuscrit Troane;* Raynaud's *Monuments pre-colombiens;* Chavero's, *Antiquidades Mexicanos,* and *Histoire de la Nation Méxicaine depuis le départ d'Aztlan.*

of the drinkable and the salt water of the lake. The fish
living in the salt water are smaller and have less flavour.
When the salt-water current runs into the fresh, the fish
of the former return to their native habitat as soon as
they taste the fresh water, and the fresh-water fish do
likewise when they taste the salt water. Ribera has
informed us that the ancient rites have been modified,
and how the natives conformed to the sudden changes
in their ceremonies. He enumerated the idols the conquerors had destroyed, and informs us that human
sacrifices are prohibited. The natives display a good
disposition, and seem persuaded that it is no longer
necessary to murder men to obtain heavenly favours.
Nevertheless Ribera does not believe that it is yet the
moment to change suddenly the hereditary practice.
It is a good result to have obtained that the people of
Tascalteca and Guazuzingo, as well as our other allies,
no longer publicly give themselves up to these butcheries
of human flesh; whether they abstain in secret or not, is
not so certain. It is hoped that, little by little, these
ancient ceremonies, will disappear. Priests, bells, and
sacred vestments are wanted, all of which will be sent,
and several thousand converts will kneel before the throne
of Your Holiness.

The Sixth Decade

BOOK I

BEFORE you returned to Rome, after concluding the useful and honourable mission in Spain confided to you by two Popes during the Spanish monarch's absence to assume the imperial crown offered him, you were aware, I think, that amongst the noble Spaniards engaged in exploring the southern coasts of the continent of the New World, Egidius Gonzales, commonly called Gil Gonzales, and the jurisconsult, Espinoza, licenciate, have distinguished themselves. In my Third Decade, composed at the invitation of Pope Leo X., I have already, in your presence, written much concerning Espinoza. After an interval of two years, we have now received a letter from Gil Gonzales, dated the eve of the nones of March, 1524, from Hispaniola, the capital of those regions.

Gil Gonzales reports that he landed at Hispaniola with 112,000 castellanos of gold, and returned to Panama, the other year on the fifteenth of July, 1523. We have a thick volume of his reports, in which he gives a detailed account of everything that happened to him during his long voyage. He writes with prolixity concerning the execution of the orders he had received from the Emperor, for he has suffered much and been exposed to dangers, even to painful extremities during this voyage.

Complaints and reproaches are not wanting in this report concerning Pedro Arias, the governor-general of the countries which we unite under the single denomination of Castilla del Oro. Gil Gonzales urgently requests to be delivered from dependence upon him. He bases his request upon the fact, amongst other things, that he is of more noble family, as though any difference exists between the meanest camp follower and the descendants of Hector, among the men kings choose to accomplish such great and glorious enterprises; especially in Spain, where it is thought to be a prerogative of nobles to live in idleness except in war-time and especially if it is a question of commanding, rather than administering.

On the ninth of May you wrote me a letter from Rome, which was delivered me by your faithful Gian Paolo Olivieri, in which you informed me that the Sovereign Pontiff, Clement, takes as much pleasure in reading of the happenings beyond seas as did his uncle Leo and his predecessor Adrian, who commanded me by their briefs to compile a narrative of these events for their benefit. I have made a choice amongst these reports, but it is not destined for His Holiness. If, however, the Sovereign Pontiff, following the example of his uncle Leo and his predecessor Adrian, commands me to write, I shall gladly obey; otherwise I shall refrain, for I do not wish to be accused by severe judges of excessive zeal. Following my custom, therefore, I shall omit useless details from this letter and sum up what appears to me to be worthy of notice. I shall not modify my determination, although you inform me at the beginning of your letter that, upon the advice of Juan de Granada, Bishop-elect of Vienna, all the letters addressed to our India Council and the Emperor by Fernando Cortes, conqueror of the immense regions of Yucatan and Temistitan, have been translated in Germany word for word from Spanish into Latin.[1] For you are not unaware that I have

---

[1] The first Latin translation of the *Letters of Cortes* was made by Pietro Savorgnani and published at Venice in 1523. The translation published in Germany was issued at Nuremberg in 1524, the Latin text being that of Savorgnani, in one volume dedicated to Clement VII.; this book contains

extracted from these letters and other reports whatever seemed to me worthy of notice.

Let us now come to our subject, and begin by enumerating the colonies already founded. For, once we know the ancient geography, we shall the more easily comprehend what countries have been explored by Gil Gonzales.

I have already spoken of the immensity of this country, which is three times as large as Europe, and of which the limits have not yet been found. In those of my decades, which have been printed and are in circulation in Europe, I have described it as the supposed continent. In speaking of the width of the Maragnon River, we have said that this continent was washed by two seas, one being our western ocean, along its northern coasts, and the other the south sea. These premises once laid down, His Holiness will learn that the Spaniards have founded six colonies along the coast of the new continent, three of which are on the northern seacoast: the first, on the banks of the river Darien in the gulf of Urabais Santa Maria Antigua; the second, twenty miles from Darien, is Acla; the third, in the territory of the cacique Careta, thirty-seven leagues from Acla, is called Nombre de Dios. There are likewise three along the southern seacoast. The first of these has kept its original native name of Panama, with a long *a*; twenty-one leagues from Panama is the second, called Nata; and the third, called Chiriqui, has been founded seventy-five leagues from Nata.

---

only the second and third letters, the fourth and fifth not having yet been written. This translation was reproduced in the work, *De Insulis Nuper Inventis* published in Cologne in 1532 and was afterwards included in Simon Grineo's *Novus Orbis* of which one edition was issued at Basle in 1555 and another at Amsterdam in 1616.

BOOK II

BETWEEN the colony of Nombre de Dios, situated on the north sea, and that of Panama on the south sea, extend mountains covered with virgin forests which are impassable because of great rocks towering to the very heavens. Aided by the governor, Pedro Arias, the colonists resolved to unite the two settlements by a road. The distance between the two seas is only seventeen leagues, or fifty miles. The size of the country is so great that, from the mouth of the river Maragnon which flows south to the ocean, it extends to the forty-fourth degree beyond the equator. I presume you have already read this particular in the Decade [1] I addressed to the late Pope Adrian, and which I sent to you for presentation to his successor, despite its being dedicated to another; for the Pope was dead before he received the dedication of the book. I spoke at length in that Decade of the spice islands, discovered by following this new route. This road across the isthmus was, therefore, laid out at the cost of the King and the colonists, nor was the expense small. Rocks had to be broken up, and wild beasts had to be driven from their lairs in the forests. This road will be passable for carriages. The intention is to facilitate the exploration of the mysteries of these two immense oceans; but the work is not yet completed.

Egidius Gonzales started from the island lying off the coast of Panama, which I called Rica in my First Decades,

[1] The Fifth Decade.

and which is now called the Isle of Pearls, because many
pearls have been found there. He set out on the twenty-
first of January in the year of our salvation 1523. His
fleet consisted of only four little vessels—few enough!
In obedience to the Emperor's orders and the instructions
of our India Council, he laid his course to the west. He
had been commanded to visit most carefully the heretofore unexplored western coasts, to discover whether
there exists between the known point of the continent
and the frontiers of Yucatan some strait dividing these
immense regions. I may say at once that the Spaniards
did not discover the strait. I omit many lengthy particulars and come rapidly to the results of the voyage.

Gonzales writes that for a distance of six hundred and
forty leagues—nearly two thousand miles—he was in
unknown country and discovered new kingdoms towards
the west. The voyage lasted about seventeen months.
At the end of this time, the ships being damaged and bored
full of holes by those little worms the Spaniards call
bromas, he was forced by the want of provisions to continue his journey by land. He plunged into the interior
a distance of two hundred and forty leagues, accompanied
by an escort of about one hundred men, for whom he
begged bread along the way from all the caciques. He
received presents on his march amounting to 112,000
pesos. A peso exceeds a drachma by one-quarter, as
you will have necessarily learned during the fourteen years
you have lived in Spain. Gonzales reports that more
than thirty-two thousand natives of both sexes have
willingly received the waters of baptism, thanks to the
converts who accompanied him. He continued his
journey so far that he encountered, in the country lying
behind Yucatan, the same costumes and language of
that province. The Emperor's share of the 112,000 pesos
brought to Spain by the treasurer Cerezeda, to whom
Gonzales had entrusted it, consisted partly of 17,000

pesos of gold, twelve or thirteen per cent. alloy, and partly
of 15,160 pesos.   He writes that the official assayers
affirm that each of the alloyed hatchets, used by the natives
to cut down trees, instead of iron or steel hatchets, is
worth a little more than half a golden ducat.

What amazes us is the discovery of a country where
the carpenters' and labourers' tools are all made of gold,
even though the quality of the metal be inferior.
He further says that he has sent 6086 pesos worth of
golden bells, which the natives are fond of ringing; but
according to the experts, these bells contain very little
gold.   Our people think the quantity of gold in the bell
metal is small, in order that sweeter or sharper tones
may be obtained, for we are not unaware that the purer
the gold, the deader sound it gives out.

Returning to the particulars of the expedition, Gonzales
says that the crossing of rivers and the frequent rains
induced divers maladies amongst his companions, pre-
venting them from making long marches.   The season
was winter, though, being near to the equator, they did
not suffer from cold.   Crossing in native barques dug
from single tree-trunks to an unknown island ten leagues
long and six wide, as his companions agree in declaring,
Gonzales was warmly received by the cacique.   The
chief's dwelling, built of wooden beams, stood upon a
lofty hill and was protected against rain by a thatch of
plants, in the form of a tent.   A large river, divided into
two branches, flows through that island not far from the
cacique's residence.

Gonzales says that when forced by the waters to stop
with the cacique, the river swelled to such an extent that it
inundated almost the entire island, and in the royal
residence the water was up to people's waists.   The force
of the current shook the foundations of the beams supporting the house, and only their united strength saved it
from collapse.   Openings, through which to escape, were

made with hatchets, and the people took refuge in the top branches of the trees. Gonzales, with his companions and his hosts, passed two days there until the waters subsided into their channels and the rain ceased.

The particulars of other incidents of the expedition are reported, but I suppose you now know enough, especially if you intend to relate these details to the great and most holy saint, Clement, who must always be very much occupied with the immensity of pontifical affairs and important matters. Let it suffice to say that the inundation had destroyed all the provisions and Gonzales was forced to continue westward overland, in search of food. He never lost sight of the coast, however, and finally reached a port already known to our men, and called by them Port St. Vincent. There he found his companions who had debarked, when he left them, to repair their ships and water barrels as had been agreed between them.

BOOK III

A FTER saluting his companions as the circumstances warranted, Gonzales quickly decided what each should do. He ordered four horses they had with them to be landed, and that the sailors should sail towards the west, but without hurrying. They should not use their sails at night because of the hidden reefs and sandy shoals, amongst which they would be obliged to make their way along the unknown coasts. He himself, with his four horses and a hundred foot-soldiers, continued his march by land and met a cacique called Nicoiano, who received him warmly and presented him with 14,000 pesos of gold. The Spaniards made the cacique understand that beyond the sun, which the natives worship as a god, there exists a creator of the heavens and the earth, who created the sun itself, the moon, and the other visible stars out of nothing, and guides them by his wisdom and recompenses men according to their merits. Nicoiano and all his family wished also to receive baptism, and a thousand persons in his district followed the example of their sovereign and were baptised.

Gonzales remained seventeen days with Nicoiano, and when he left, the cacique was so well instructed that he was able to speak to him in his tongue these words, which were understood by the interpreters of the neighbourhood: "Since I may no longer venerate these statues of the gods, my ancestors bequeathed to me, and may no longer ask anything of them, I offer them to you." Speaking thus, he

offered Egidius Gonzales six golden statues each a cubit
high, ancient monuments of the faith of his forefathers.

The cacique informed Gonzales that some fifty leagues
from his palace there existed another kingdom whose
cacique was called Nicoragua. When Gonzales had
advanced to within a day's march of the residence of
Nicoragua, he sent messengers ahead to deliver the same
communications the Spaniards are accustomed to make
to caciques before attacking them; namely, that they must
be converted to Christianity and recognise the authority
and jurisdiction of the great King of Spain, otherwise
war and hostilities will be declared against them. The
next day, four of Nicoragua's principal vassals came out
to meet them and announced in the name of their cacique
that they wished for baptism and peace. The Spaniards
repaired to the house of Nicoragua, and not only he, but
more than nine thousand of his subjects, received the
waters of holy baptism. Nicoragua presented Egidius Gonzales with 15,000 golden pesos, in the form of different
necklaces; in return Gonzales presented the king with a
silk jacket, a linen shirt, and a red hat. Two crosses were
set up in this territory: the first in the native temple
itself, and the second just outside the village.

Marching always towards the west, Gonzales next came
to a region six leagues farther on, where he found six
villages, each containing about two thousand houses.
While he was engaged in visiting the villages of that
region, the news of his arrival spread, and a cacique called
Diriangan, whose states lie farther to the west, came to
see him. Diriangan was escorted by twenty women
and five hundred men, preceded by ten standard bearers
and five trumpeters. When he approached Gonzales, who
awaited him seated on a throne arrayed in royal apparel,
the trumpets sounded a fanfare; after which the standards
were dipped. Each of the soldiers forming the escort
carried one or two of those domestic birds resembling

peacocks, which correspond among the natives to our chickens.

Here, with your permission, I will make a digression. It often happens that I repeat the same details and that I, who am a rude peasant, offer you, who are an Æsculapius, medicines with which you are acquainted; in fact, most of what I offer you is already known to you, for you have learned these facts in my Decades. I repeat them because I may assume that these Decades will fall into the hands of seekers after knowledge, who are not only ignorant of these details, but who may be unable to recur to your explanations. Thanks to you, such people will there learn what they desire to know. You who are born for the benefit of many should not reproach me.[1]

The cacique Diriangan had his servants bring more than two hundred golden hatchets, each weighing eighteen pesos or a little over. The interpreters whom Egidius had with him and who understood our language, asked the cacique why he had come; to which he answered: "I wish to enter into relations with this new race of men, whose visit to this country was reported. I am willing to grant them everything they desire." The interpreters replied: "Become Christians, all of you"; and they enumerated the different conditions usually imposed upon other caciques, adding that they must acknowledge themselves vassals of the great King of Spain. The cacique said: 'We accept the two propositions, and we promise to return within three days to fulfil them'; after which he departed.

[1] *Ne me igitur accuses tu, qui natus es ad multorum utilitatem.* An apt translation for the compliment does not readily suggest itself.

BOOK IV

A NUMBER of incidents worthy of narration occurred during the stay of the Spaniards with Nicoragua. In addition to what I have gathered from the letters of Egidius, these incidents have been described to me by the royal *quæstor*, commonly called treasurer, who shared largely in his labours, and whose name is Andreas Cerezeda. When he left, he consigned me his report in writing.

Our general, Egidius, and the cacique, Nicoragua, employed their idle hours in conversing with one another, through means of an interpreter whom Egidius had educated and who was born not far from Nicoragua's territory. This interpreter knew both languages sufficiently well. Nicoragua asked his guest what was thought in the kingdom of the powerful sovereign whose vassal he had become, of the cataclysm which, according to the ancient tradition of his forefathers, had swallowed up the entire earth with all its inhabitants and animals. "I believe the same," said Egidius. When asked whether he thought that another similar catastrophe was to be expected, he answered: "By no means; but just as men's crimes, and particularly their unnatural lusts, were once punished by this flood which destroyed all living creatures with but a few exceptions, so after a period of time unknown to men, fire will descend from heaven and reduce the universe to ashes." This statement astonished his listeners; and Nicoragua, turning to the interpreter, tremulously asked him whether this race of men whose wisdom they could not sufficiently admire, descended from heaven. The interpreter responded affirmatively, and the cacique continued naïvely inquiring whether they came straight down or after circling through the air. The interpreter who was born in the same country as Nicoragua, or near by, answered that he did not know. The cacique asked him to inquire of his master whether the earth would one day be shaken by a sudden convulsion; and to this Egidius replied that this was known only to the creator of heaven and earth and mankind.

The total destruction of the human race, the destination of souls liberated from their earthly prison, the time fixed for the conflict of destroying fires, the epoch when the sun, moon, and stars would cease to shine, the number, the distance, and the influences of the stars, and many other similar questions were proposed by the cacique. Egidius is a learned man, who delights in translating Latin works into the vulgar tongue, but his erudition was not equal to furnishing the cacique with any other than the following response: "The knowledge of these mysteries belongs to Divine providence."

The cacique likewise asked him questions relating to the winds, the cause of heat and cold, the difference between night and day, though this difference is hardly perceptible in those parts because of the vicinity of the equator. Almost all these questions Egidius answered as well as his knowledge permitted, and the replies to the others he referred to the Divine intelligence. Coming down to mundane matters, Nicoragua and his courtiers asked if it was permissible to drink, eat, love, play, sing, dance, and fight. The reply was as follows: "Eating, and drinking are necessary, but excess should be avoided, for everything in excess of our needs weakens the mind and diminishes the bodily strength; nothing else so develops vice, disputes, and hatred. It is likewise permissible to love, but only one single woman, to whom the man must be united in marriage bonds. To please God, the creator of all things, one must abstain from every kind of debauch. It is not forbidden either to sing, to take part in innocent games, or to dance."

As the natives asked nothing concerning ceremonies and human sacrifices, Gonzales himself introduced this subject, affirming that such sacrifice was highly displeasing to the Divinity. The most powerful King of Spain had further prescribed by law that whoever shall strike a man with his sword, shall in his turn be punished by the sword. The blood-sprinkled idols are images of deceiving demons who, because of their pride, were driven from heaven and precipitated into the infernal regions. They come forth at night, and appearing to innocent men they persuade them, by their maleficent arts, to do just the contrary of what they should. By listening to them souls are weaned from the love of their Creator, who seeks to win them to Himself by the exercise of charity and other virtues. Those who resist, instead of passing into the place of eternal delight which awaits them after the separation of the soul and the body, will be seized by those demons and, like them, will suffer eternal tortures and nameless torments.

BOOK V

IN the foregoing, or in words practically identical,
Egidius, like a preacher from his pulpit, answered
as best he could through his interpreter the questions
asked by Nicoragua. The latter accepted his teaching,
and at the same time inquired what he and his people
must do to render themselves acceptable to that God,
sole author of all things. According to the treasurer,
Cerezeda, Gonzales's response to the cacique's inquiry
was as follows: "Not by offering human victims nor
by shedding blood will you please the universal creator.
Only a heart inflamed with love for Him is acceptable
from you. The secrets of our souls are known to Him
and He only loves what proceeds from the soul. He does
not feast on flesh or blood, and nothing more excites His
ire than the destruction of men whom He has created to
praise and glorify Him. Such abominable sacrifices only
please His enemies and yours, the demons of hell, whose
images you venerate. They rejoice in all the crimes
because of which, when you quit this life, you will be
delivered into their power to your eternal ruin. Expel,
therefore, these foolish and dangerous idols from your
temples and homes. Embrace the cross, bathed by
Christ the God-man with His blood for the salvation of
the lost human race, and you will live happily and gain
for your souls an eternity of bliss. The Creator of the
universe also loves not war, for He prefers peace amongst
neighbours, since He has commanded us to love our

neighbours as ourselves. If you are attacked while living your peaceful existence, it is permissible to every one to resist injustice, and to defend himself and his people. It is forbidden to offend others by ambition and avarice, for nothing is more contrary to good morals and the Divine will."

During this discourse Nicoragua and his courtiers there present were as though suspended upon the words of Egidius, and listened with open mouths, approving all these propositions. They made a grimace, however, at what was said about war, asking what they should do with their javelins and golden helmets, their bows and arrows, their war ornaments and their standards, glorious emblems of bravery. "Shall we abandon them to the women? Shall we spin and weave like them, or cultivate the earth like peasants?" Egidius did not venture to reopen this subject, for he perceived they were greatly troubled, but when they questioned him about the adorable mystery of the cross and its purpose, he replied: "Ask with a pure and sincere heart whatever you will, fixing your eyes on the cross and piously remembering what Christ has suffered thereon, and you will obtain it if your prayer is just;—peace, victory over proud enemies, abundant harvests, mild temperature, health or other similar desires,—they will be granted."

I have already reported that Egidius had ordered two crosses to be set up, one in the temple, and the other on an artificial mound built of bricks. On the day when the cross was brought to be erected on the mount, according to Cerezeda's account, the procession was headed by the priests followed by Egidius and his men, and by the cacique and all his subjects. While the cross was being elevated, the trumpets sounded and the drums beat, and when it was fixed in the ground, Egidius was the first to mount the steps leading to its base. With uncovered head he bent the knee, prayed silently, and embracing the feet of

the crucifix, he kissed them. The cacique, followed by
all the others, did likewise; and thus were the natives initi-
ated in our ceremonies.

Replying to the question, concerning the distribution
of the days, Egidius told them that they should work
six successive days, that the seventh was for rest and
prayer; this seventh day was fixed for Sunday. He
thought it useless to confuse them by explaining the long
series of feast days.

I add only one particular which Egidius omitted
from his report, but which Cerezeda did not forget.
These natives are beardless and they regarded bearded
men with aversion and fear. It was for this reason that
Egidius, who had twenty-five beardless youths in his
troop, had beards made for them out of their own hair.
He wished to increase the number of bearded men in
his troop, so as to terrify the natives, if he were forced into
conflict with them; which as a matter of fact afterwards
happened. Cerezeda has also informed us that Egidius
wrote him that he had just sailed with two hundred and
fifty foot-soldiers and seventy horsemen enrolled at
Hispaniola. He embarked about the ides of March of
this year, 1524, seeking to discover the much desired
mystery of the strait. No news of this expedition has
thus far reached our Council. I will promptly transmit
to you whatever we receive.

It is time to close this narrative, and to describe the
revolting customs worthy of the Læstrygonians,[1] as well
as the houses and temples of these people. I will add
a few words about the site and construction of these
edifices. The dwellings of the caciques are a hundred
paces long and fifteen broad. Their façades are open,
and the rear wall is solid. The floors of these residences

[1] The earliest inhabitants of Sicily who were reputed to be giants and
cannibals. They destroyed the vessels of Ulysses and devoured his
companions.

are half a man's height above the ground, and in the
other houses they are on a level with the ground. These
houses are sustained by beams and roofed with thatch,
having only one roof and no ceilings, as is the case with
the temples. They are of considerable size, and are
built above small, dark, underground caverns in which the
noble familes bury their tutelary deities. The temples
are also used as arsenals, and in them are preserved in
time of peace their arms, bows, quivers, gilded cuirasses,
helmets, and large wooden swords, which they use in
hand-to-hand combats, missiles of all kinds, as well as
war ornaments; all these in addition to their standards
on which are represented their idols. They honour the
idols left them by their ancestors and which are their
special patrons, by offering them, each according to his
means, human victims, reciting before them prayers
composed by their priests for the occasion.

BOOK VI

THE main façade of the cacique's dwelling is protected by a large open square, according to the size and plan of the village. If the village contains numerous houses, there are also smaller squares, where the people of the neighbourhood may assemble for trading. The royal square is surrounded by the houses of the nobles, and in the centre stands a building where the jewelers live. In this country gold is used to make various kinds of necklaces, or is beaten into little plaques and ingots according to the owner's wish, for his commands are executed with sufficient ability.

Standing in the open and in front of the temples, numerous mounds have been built of rough brick cemented by a kind of bitumen; they resemble tribunes and are used for different purposes. They are reached by eight, sometimes twelve or fifteen steps, and the arrangement of the top differs according to the kind of mysteries thereon celebrated. On one of these mounds there is space for ten men and in the centre stands a block of marble as long and wide as a man's height. This sinister stone is the altar upon which human victims are immolated. When the day fixed for the sacrifice arrives the sacrificing priest mounts upon this stone, in the sight of the prince and all the people; the latter has taken his place upon another mound to witness the ceremony. Acting as a herald, the priest brandishes a stone knife in his hand, informing the people whether the victims to be sacrificed are war prisoners or domestic prisoners. The natives of all those regions possess excellent stones for making hatchets, swords, and razors, of which we procure any number we like, as the Cardinal Ascanio was well aware.

There exist among them two grades of human victims, namely, those taken in war and those fattened at home. Each cacique and each noble, according to his means, fattens in his own house from their childhood, men destined to be sacrificed. These unfortunate creatures are not ignorant of the fate awaiting them; they know why they are well fed and are not disturbed thereby, since from their earliest years they live in the conviction that upon leaving this life they will go straight to heaven. They enjoy absolute freedom of the villages, are received with honour by everybody, as though they were already heroes; everything they want, whether food or ornaments, is given to them, and the givers believe that the day on which they make such presents is a lucky one for themselves.

These different kinds of victims are immolated in different ways. All alike are stretched upon the sacrificial stone and their breasts are opened with a knife, in order to tear out the hearts, while the same ceremonies are observed in anointing the lips and beard of the idol with their blood. But in sacrificing victims captured from the enemy, the priest, acting as herald, walks three times round the victims extended on the stone, holding his knife in his hand, and chanting dismally; after which he opens the breast and cuts the victims in pieces. The hands and feet are given to the caciques, the hearts go to the priests, their wifes, and children,—for this is their share—the legs go to the nobles, and the remainder, chopped up into small bits, to the people. The heads are suspended as trophies to the branches of certain small trees, which are grown especially for that purpose a short distance from the scene of the sacrifice. Every cacique has special trees cultivated in a garden near his residence, each bearing the name of a hostile country, and to whose branches the heads of the sacrificed war prisoners are suspended. Do not our own generals in token of that egregious madness they call "victory," suspend helmets, standards, and other war trophies on the walls of churches?

Anybody present at such a banquet who failed to obtain a portion of the human victim, no matter how small, would feel convinced the year would be an unlucky one for him.

Domestic victims are sacrificed with the same ceremonies, but their bodies are treated differently. Each member of their bodies is honoured. The feet, hands, and entrails are deposited in a terra-cotta vase which is buried at the gates of the temple. The heart and other parts are burnt upon a great pyre near those trees which represent the enemy, and their ashes are scattered amidst those of the first victims of the campaign. While this ceremony is being performed, the priests who are present manifest their joy in melodious chants.

BOOK VII

AS soon as the people see the priests smearing
the blood on the lips of the idols, reciting the
usual formula, they offer their petitions and
prayers, asking fertility for their fields, abundant harvests,
healthful temperature, peace; or, if they are about to
go to war, victory. Each begs to be delivered from what
he fears, — cockchafers, grasshoppers, inundations,
droughts, ferocious beasts, and all calamities. There are
other methods of sacrifice. The cacique, the priests, and
nobles also shed their own blood, but in honour of only
one god. The image of this god is suspended on a lance
three cubits long, and is carried in the daytime with great
pomp by the appointed elders, who bring it out of the
temple where, during the rest of the year, it is jealously
guarded. It resembles infernal deities, such as are
painted upon walls to frighten people.[1] At the head of
the procession walk the priests, wearing bands round
their foreheads. The people follow, carrying multi-
coloured banners of woven cotton on which are embroidered figures of gods. The priests wear upon their
shoulders mantles of different stuffs, from which straps
a finger thick, and with indented edges, hang down as
far as their calves; pockets in which they carry their stone

[1] This expression occurs frequently in the author's text. It doubtless
refers to the realistic representations of hell and purgatory which were
commonly painted on the walls of cemeteries, cloisters, and certain chapels.
The practice was continued in the New World.

razors and packets of powder, made from dry herbs, are
fastened to their ends. The cacique and the principal
nobles, each in his proper place, accompany the priests,
after which follows the confused popular multitude.
Nobody is absent, for every man who can stand must
assist at this festival of superstition. When the procession reaches the appointed place, fragrant herbs are
first thrown on the ground, after which draperies are
spread, so that the idol shall not touch the earth. The
procession stops, but the priests continue supporting the
idol, in whose honour they chant their accustomed hymns.
Young men perform sacred dances, lead the singing, and
play different games, in which they display their agility
in throwing javelins and using their shields.

When the priests give a signal, each man takes a razor,
and cuts his tongue, turning his eyes towards the divinity;
some pierce the tongue, others cut it in such wise as to
cause a great flow of blood. Each man then rubs the
lips and beard of this odious idol, with his blood, as we
have said in our first description of sacrifices, after which
the powdered herbs are sprinkled on the fresh wounds.
Such is the virtue of this powder, that the wounds close
in a few hours so that no trace of them is ever again
visible. When the ceremony is finished, the priests
lower the idol somewhat and then, first the cacique,
after him the nobles, and finally the people address it.
They expose their anxieties or supplicate it to give ear
to their wishes and petitions, always speaking softly
with bent heads and in a tremor of respect; when this
priestly mummery is finished they go home.

While the Spaniards were witnessing these ceremonies,
a scout appeared, quickly followed by a second and then
by a number of others, who announced the arrival of
Diriangen and his armed subjects. The cacique came
intending not only to take back what he had given, but
also to exterminate the Spaniards. He hoped to vanquish

this handful of soldiers and capture their possessions, for these natives also love gold; not because they use it for money, but because they make necklaces and ornaments of it. Diriangen was followed by a numerous escort of armed men, and if he had surprised the Spaniards off their guard, he would have killed them to the last man. He sounded the attack and the fight was gallantly sustained till night.

BOOK VIII

MANY particulars follow which I omit for fear of wearying you, and of making you a bore to the Sovereign Pontiff and your friends. To sum up, the little band of Spaniards routed the large native army, and Egidius piously reports that God, who is the master of armies, assisted them in their terror and rescued them safe and sound from danger. Fortune having changed her face, the cacique Nicoiano who had been left behind, formed a similar plan to kill the Spaniards and rob them of the important sum of gold they had with them.

Egidius Gonzales, suspecting this treason, took his precautions against Nicoiano, closing up the ranks of his soldiers and prescribing the order of march. The sick and the gold were placed in the centre of the troop; he with his four horsemen and seventy archers and arquebusiers sustained the charge of his assailants and killed a great number of them. He never slept the whole night, but when the natives asked peace the following morning, he granted it.

Upon reaching Port St. Vincent, their starting-place, the Spaniards found their ships had returned. While the captain, Egidius, was exploring the interior of the country, the ships had reconnoitred about three hundred leagues of hitherto unknown coast extending westward. They had only put into port to repair the damages their ships had sustained during a voyage of several months.

Gonzales describes the neighbourhood of the region occupied by Nicoragua as follows: in the interior, just near the residence of the cacique, was found a fresh-water lake[1] so large that its end was not discovered. The waters of this lake are subject to tides, and it must therefore be considered a fresh-water sea. It has many islands. When asked whether its outlet was into the neighbouring sea, only three leagues distant, the natives answered that they knew of no outlet; and Gonzales says he does not know whether it flows into the South Sea, which is near by, or elsewhere. He thinks, nevertheless, that this body of water connects with the northern ocean and that the much-desired strait may be found there, in which opinion he is sustained by several pilots. If you wish to know my opinion on this subject, I would say that Gonzales thus excuses himself for not finding the strait, since both the potable quality of these lake waters and also the ignorance of the natives along its shores concerning its extent and outlet leave us in the same uncertainty as before. We are ignorant whether or no a strait, dividing those vast countries, exists.

[1] Lake Nicaragua; its superficial area measures 950 square kilometres. Its outlet is the San Juan River which flows into the Atlantic Ocean. There is a tradition amongst the Indians that there existed in ancient times another river flowing from the lake into the Pacific. Of the several islands dotting the lake's surface the most considerable is that formed by the volcano Zapatero and named Ceiba.

BOOK IX

LET me now pause. The foregoing narrative being completed, my secretary had his hat on ready to start, when Diego Arias, son of the governor Pedro Arias, came to see me bringing with him the licenciate, Espinosa, whom I have elsewhere mentioned. Espinosa alleges that he and the governor, Pedro Arias, had been injured by Egidius Gonzales, affirming that these regions had long since been discovered by them and the caciques pacified and maintained in their authority over their states. The decision of our Royal Council which will be confirmed by the Emperor, will be made known, through you, to people interested in this kind of news. Enough for the present concerning this subject.

I beg you to profit by the first opportunity to kiss the feet of our Most Holy Clement on my behalf. The Spaniards will have faith in the favour and merit of His Holiness as long as he has faith in yours. They find it quite proper that the great of this world should take you into their confidence, because they have long appreciated you. The character of princes may often be accurately judged by the choice they make of their ministers.

There is a third piece of quite fresh news which, since the courier has not actually left, I believe His Holiness will be glad to hear. In the decade dedicated to Pope Adrian, in which I described the Moluccas where spices grow, I alluded to the dispute between the Portuguese and the Castilians regarding the discovery of that archipelago. We are so confidently convinced that this archipelago lies within the limits assigned to us by Pope Alexander, that we have prepared a new expedition at considerable cost, in one of the ports of the Biscayan coast; six ships being completely fitted out at Bilbao. We have decided to despatch this fleet about the vernal equinox from a Galician port, Clunium, which you know. This port has been designated for the spice trade, because it is more accessible for the northern merchants, who can trade more easily in the market there established for Indian merchandise than in Seville or in Portugal, where they only arrive by roundabout journeys.

Realising that they would be ruined if this enterprise succeeded, the Portuguese have insisted that this injury should not be inflicted upon them without their pretensions having been studied, for they affirm that the Moluccas were first discovered and visited by their sailors and lie within the limits assigned to them, and not to the Emperor; that is to say, three hundred and seventy leagues beyond the Cape Verde Islands. Ptolemy calls this cape Risardinum, and we believe these islands correspond to the Gorgones. The Emperor, who esteems justice above profit, particularly in dealing with a king who is his cousin and who, if public rumour is to be credited, will soon become his brother-in-law,[1] has acceded to the Portuguese request, and has consented that their claims should be examined. The ships have, therefore, been held back, their equipment suspended, at which the officers and sailors chosen for the expedition are discontented.

It was decided to summon a council[2] of astronomers,

---

[1] Through the forthcoming marriage of Charles V. with the Infanta Isabella of Portugal, which took place in 1526.

[2] The proceedings of this council may be studied in Navarrete, tom. IV, pp. 270, 326, 332, 342.

cosmographers, navigators, and jurisconsults in the town
of Pax Augusta, — called in Spanish Badajoz, — since
it lies near the Portuguese and Castilian frontier. The
representatives assembled, and about the calends of
April the disputes and discussions began. The Portuguese, determined not to give way on a single point,
admitted none of the arguments advanced by our nego-
tiators. The Spaniards wished the line of three hundred
and seventy leagues to begin at the most easterly island
of the Gorgones, namely, the one called San Antonio;
and they say this island is situated within nine and a half
degrees of longitude of the known meridian of the Fortunate Isles. The Portuguese, on the other hand, insist
that the line should begin at the first of these islands
called Sel, which lies only five degrees of longitude from
the same meridian. The reasoning of the Spaniards is
as follows: Suppose an arbitrator were appointed to
decide between two neighbours in disagreement concerning the boundaries of their fields; granted that John has
long possessed a well-known field and that his neighbour
Francis should take possession of another field, a hundred
paces distant, it would undoubtedly follow, if the distance
were actually counted, starting from the spot where
John's property begins, that John would be obliged to
give up his land, for it would be entirely included in the
claim of Francis. It follows that the Cape Verde Islands,
which have hitherto always belonged to Portugal, must
either be surrendered or the Portuguese must accept the
distance reckoned from the most remote of these islands.
One or the other of these solutions must be accepted.

The discussion was long and no conclusion was reached.

Had the Portuguese accepted the decision of the
plenipotentiaries of Castile, they would have been com-
pelled to recognise that, not only the Moluccas and the
islands touching upon China, the great gulf, and the
promontory of Satyres and Gilolo, but also even Malacca

had all along been usurped by them. For the Castilians affirm that the authority of Ptolemy and other authors, in disagreement concerning the length of degrees, suffices to show the weak foundations of their adversary's claims. The Portuguese answer with arguments of the same character.

Let us note that our sailors who returned from the long voyage received from the ruler of those islands in whose kingdom they had loaded their ship, the *Victoria*, cloves, letters, and superb presents which constitute a striking proof of the vassalage he had sworn. As for the Portuguese they exhibit no treaty signed by any of those kings. Nevertheless, they say that the Portuguese name is known in those islands and that Portuguese subjects have been there. Our people admit this fact, but assert there was only a single man, who was a fugitive fleeing from judgment for his crimes, and that, moreover, no other proof of commercial relations can be produced. The decision our Emperor will make in our Royal Council is still uncertain. It is evident that it will be very hard for the Portuguese to see themselves excluded from known countries, while for the Spaniards it would not be agreeable to lose such an admirable opportunity for profit.[1] May God help us! Fare you well. Burgos, the fourteenth of July, 1524.

[1] Charles V. renounced his claims to the Moluccas in 1525, accepting an indemnity of 350,000 ducats.

BOOK X

NUMEROUS French pirates and soldiers of the King of France, with whom we are at war, have blocked all the ways both by sea and land. In such difficult times do we live! I, therefore, send you this letter in duplicate, since you wish to hear the news from the other world. Eighty representatives, all of them experienced men, were chosen to decide the dispute with the Portuguese, of which I have spoken. Each faculty had its representative; that is to say, there are six astronomers, six jurisconsults, six cosmographers, and six sailors. You know only a few of them, and His Holiness knows none. They have all returned and have reported to our Council, and they will soon report to the Emperor the results of that congress. The first to open the negotiation seem to have been Don Fernando Columbus, second son of Christopher Columbus, the first discoverer of the new country, who is a very learned man, and the licenciates Acuna and Emmanuel, the first being auditor of the Royal Council, and the second chancellor of Valladolid; associated with them was the licenciate Periso, of the chancery of Granada.

Nothing more was accomplished than I have above mentioned. The Emperor having appointed the last day of May the arbitrators chosen by Spain gave their decision on that date, on the bridge of Caya, which spans the river forming the boundary between Spain and Portugal. The Portuguese, who had everything to gain by postponing

the decision, were unable to retard it by a single day or
hour. The verdict defined that the Moluccas are situated,
according to ancient and contemporary opinion, more
than twenty degrees inside the limits assigned to Spain.
The same holds good of Malacca and Taprobane,[1] that is,
if the latter corresponds to the island which the Portuguese
call Zamatra.

The Portuguese went home much disconcerted and
grumbling over what had happened. They do not
intend to abandon any of their pretensions, and we
have heard that their young sovereign has sent out a
large fleet and that they whisper among themselves
that they will destroy our vessels if they find them in
those waters. On the eve of the calends of July, our
India Council decided that the Emperor should order
our fleet of six vessels to sail before the end of next August.
They will not be ordered to begin hostilities, but should
they be attacked by a superior Portuguese force, the
Emperor has at his disposition upon the continent a
ready means of vengeance, should treaties be violated at
sea. You are aware that Portugal is like a wedge in
Castile, and precisely that part of Portugal in which are
situated the most flourishing cities is as though blocked
by the remarkable city of Medina del Campo; by Salamanca, Avila, Segovia, Toro, the prosperous kingdom of
Toledo, and many other regions lying between the
Guadiana and the Douro. I have often remarked in my
preceding Decades that Portugal was formerly only a
county of Castile, bestowed by an easy-going king,
together with the royal title, upon one of his grandsons.
It has also been decided that a certain Estevan Gomez,
an expert navigator, shall seek for a new route, leading
to Cathay, between the Baccalaos and Florida, which
belongs to us. He will be given only one caravel,
and his only instructions will be to search whether

[1] Presumably Ceylon.

amongst the multitude of windings and the vast diversities of our ocean any passage can be found leading to the kingdom of him whom we commonly call the Grand Khan.

The Seventh Decade

BOOK I

TO THE VISCOUNT FRANCESCO MARIA SFORZA,
DUKE OF MILAN

THE beginning of my Decades *De Orbe Novo* was
presented to Your Excellency's uncle, the Vice-
chancellor Ascanio, formerly one of the most illustrious of the cardinals, whose merits were exceeded
by none. He had often asked and commanded me
to inform him of everything that happened in those far-
distant western lands. I appeal to the confirming testimony of a man gifted with all the virtues and experience,
Marino Caracciolo,[1] Prothonotary Apostolic, Bishop-elect
of Catania, and at present Ambassador of the Emperor
Charles at your court. He was secretary to your uncle
when the ocean first opened its gates which had been
closed since the beginning of the world. He it was who
received my Decades in his master's name and penned the
answers dictated to him by the Cardinal. When Ascanio
died, I relapsed into idleness, since no one any longer
urged me to work. King Frederick, before Fortune showed
herself his pitiless stepmother rather than his mother,
obtained a second edition of my book from me, through
the intermediary of his uncle the Cardinal of Aragon.
Later the Sovereign Pontiff, Leo X., and his successor

[1] Marino Caracciolo, born in 1469, was a trusted friend of Leo X., for
whom he undertook several important missions, notably the negotiations
with the Elector of Saxony for the surrender of Martin Luther. He later
entered the service of Charles V., by whom he was named governor of
Milan after the death of Francesco Maria. He was created Cardinal
by Paul III., and died in Milan, January 28, 1538. Consult Guicciardini,
i., xv., xvi., xvii.

Adrian VI., urged me by their briefs and letters to continue
my labours. They gathered the dispersed Decades into
one volume, and charged me to preserve the records of
such great deeds from oblivion. You, Most Illustrious
Prince,[1] who have been born later and have ascended the
throne of your forefathers, will only receive the narrative
of the latest events. Since your secretary, Camillo
Gillino, has interpreted your wishes to the Emperor,
I turn from other sovereigns to address my narrative
exclusively to Your Excellency, in whose principality I
was born.

Your Excellency has suffered many trials, and you have
often affirmed and vowed that the perusal of my Decades
would prove the most agreeable diversion. From the
moment when the ocean, thanks to Christopher Columbus,
generously disclosed its secrets, up to this present time,
the narrative of events had been collected into one volume
by Giacomo Pierio, Prothonotary Apostolic, Bishop-elect of
Catania, when he repaired to your court as the Emperor's
ambassador. This volume was destined for Pope Adrian.
Thanks to the printers a part of its contents had already
been previously circulated. Another part had been
copied by him from my manuscript. He is now at
Your Excellency's court. Ask him what has happened,
and if he does not give a faithful account, treat him as an
unworthy servant.

Now that we have hastily summed up what has preceded, let us review the recent marvels revealed by the
ocean. For our ocean is more prolific than the Albanian
sow, to which tradition assigned thirty pigs at a litter;
and more liberal than a generous prince. Does it not

[1] Francesco Maria Sforza, last duke of Milan, was the son of Lodovico
il Moro and was born in 1492. He obtained possession of the duchy
after the battle of Bicoque in 1522. His independence was more seeming
than real, Charles V. being, practically, his suzerain. He died in 1535
Consult Giovio, *Vita F. Mariæ Sforziæ ducis*, 1539; Ratti, *Memoria della
famiglia Sforza*.

each year disclose new lands, new nations, and vast wealth?

We have sufficiently described Hispaniola, queen of the islands, that vast region and residence of the Royal Council; also Jamaica and Cuba, under its new name of Fernandina, and the other truly Elysian islands stretching under the Tropic of Cancer to the equator. In these regions the natives enjoy days and nights of equal length during the entire year. Their summer is not oppressive, their winter not rigorous, while throughout the year trees bear their leaves and are simultaneously weighted with flowers and fruits; while vegetables—pumpkins, melons, cucumbers, and other garden products—are always ripe. In those regions also the beasts of burden and the cattle brought from Europe (since no quadrupeds live in those islands[1]) propagate in great numbers and sizes. We have likewise sufficiently described the supposed continent, whose length from east to west is twice that of all Europe, and is of equal extent from north to south, although it narrows in certain places to isthmuses. This continent reaches to the fifty-fifth degree towards the arctic pole, traversing both tropics, covering the equator and extending to the fifty-fourth degree towards the antarctic pole. While the inhabitants of the Orcades Islands enjoy summer, the natives of this continent shiver with cold and *vice versa*. Your Excellency will understand this by considering what I addressed to Pope Adrian in Rome. By studying a little parchment map[2] I gave to your representative, Tomaso Maino, when he left Spain, you will also find the exact positions of these countries and the dependent islands.

Let us now consider the most recent events. In the waters off the northern coasts of Cuba—otherwise called

---

[1] Obviously a slip of the author's pen, since he elsewhere enumerates the quadrupeds of the West Indian Islands.

[2] See Frontispiece.

Fernandina after King Ferdinand—lie so many islands, important or insignificant, that I scarcely believe what is told of them; although I am kept informed of all the discoveries. Within the twenty years that have elapsed since the Spaniards arrived there, they claim to have explored four hundred and six of these islands, and to have carried off forty thousand of their inhabitants of both sexes as slaves, to satisfy their unquenchable appetite for gold. We will tell this story later on. These islands are embraced under the general name of Lucayas, and the islanders are called Lucayans.

The trees which grow wild in most of these islands are very useful. Their leaves never fall off; when age robs them of some, the tree is not stripped, for new leaves bud forth and grow before the old ones perish. Nature has endowed them with two trees which, above all others, deserve mention and description. The first is called the *jaruma;* the name of the second is unknown to us. The jaruma resembles a fig-tree, at least as regards its leaves. It is taller than a poplar. It is not as hard as the other trees, but is more solid than a bamboo. One might describe it as a sambucus. Its fruit is half a cubit long, and soft like a fig, with strong flavour, and is excellent for healing wounds. Its leaves possess miraculous virtues; of which I quote a proof, offered by trustworthy persons. Two Spaniards quarrelled and fought; one of the two almost cutting off the arm of the other at the shoulder with his sword, so that it only hung to the body by the skin of the armpit and of the breast. An old woman of the island put the limb in its place, and without other remedy than the crushed leaves of this tree, which she applied to the wound, succeeded in a few days in restoring to the unfortunate man the use of his arm. Let those who seek knots in cane, ponder on this at their pleasure. For my part, I am resolved to believe that nature has even more extraordinary powers than this.

The bark of this tree is said to be smooth and polished, and as it is not tough, but filled with a kind of pith, it is easily peeled off. This affords me an opportunity of relating to Your Excellency an interesting story, although it is not to the credit of its hero.

The Lucayans, torn from their homes, became perfectly desperate. Some have died from exhaustion, refusing all food and hiding themselves in inaccessible valleys, deserted forests, and unknown mountain heights; while others have put an end to their unendurable lives. Those of more hopeful temperament clung to life, in the hope of one day regaining their freedom. The majority of those who were able to escape, betook themselves to the northern parts of Hispaniola, where they might breathe the air wafted from their native country; with extended arms and open mouths they seemed to drink in their native air, and when misery reduced them to exhaustion, they dropped dead upon the ground. One man who clung to life more than his comrades had been a carpenter in his own country, engaged in building houses, for though they have neither iron nor steel they have stone hatchets and other tools necessary for this trade. This man undertook an almost incredible task. Cutting a trunk of jaruma, he took all the pith from the inside. He then filled it with maize and pumpkins full of water, as supplies for his journey, and sealed up the ends of the tree. Throwing this trunk into the sea, he, and two of his relatives, a man and a woman, who knew how to swim, embarked upon it. Using oars they drove this tree-trunk towards their country. It was an amazing invention, but it brought no luck to those unfortunates, for two hundred miles from Hispaniola they met a vessel coming back from Chicora, a country concerning which I shall speak later. In spite of their despair, the Spaniards captured this prize; they brought the hollowed trunk back to Hispaniola as proof of this extraordinary undertaking, and consumed their poor provisions. The tree-trunk and the inventor of this barque were seen at Hispaniola by several trustworthy witnesses, who have spoken with me. This, however, is enough concerning the jaruma and this particular tree-trunk.

There exists another tree, closely resembling a pomegranate, than which it is no larger, though its foliage is thicker. No mention is made of its fruit, but extraordinary things are told about its bark which is peeled from the trunk, just as every year cork is cut for making sandals without killing the tree, which continues to produce sprouts. This seems to happen with the cinnamon-tree. For my part, I believe it to be true, for I have tasted some of its bark that was brought from Hispaniola. I even sent a fruit to your uncle, Ascanio Sforza, when Columbus, the first discoverer of those regions, returned from his voyage and acquainted me with many of the new products he had found. At the close of the second chapter of my First Decade you will find this tree mentioned. The bark tastes like cinnamon, has the spice of ginger, and the delicate odour of cloves.

In our ignorance we search in foreign parts for spices which we should not need did we but make use of those which grow spontaneously in our own islands. No doubt one day they will be appreciated. It is only the frantic craving for gold that goads the Spaniards on. Everything else, no matter how useful or valuable, is neglected and despised as of no consequence. Our pepper, of which I sent a specimen to Ascanio Sforza, grows abundantly everywhere in this country, just like mallows and nettles at home. The islanders crush it and spread it on their bread, which they soak in water before eating. There are five varieties, and it is hotter to the taste than the pepper of Malabar or the Caucasus. Five grains of ours are equivalent to twenty of Malabar or Caucasian pepper, and seasoned with these five grains the juices of meats acquire more flavour than with twenty of the other. But such is human stupidity that whatever is difficult to obtain is always thought to be better.

It is not only on account of its bark that the above mentioned tree deserves to be noticed. It exhales sweet and refreshing perfumes, distinguishable at a distance of several *stadia*. Its shade is dense, and it grows throughout the archipelago. In its branches such a multitude of doves nest that the natives of the large neighbouring islands of Bimini and of the Florida coasts cross the sea to capture these birds, carrying off boatloads of them. The forests are full of wild vines, which overgrow the trees, as I have said is the case in Hispaniola.

It is alleged that the women of the Lucayan islands are so beautiful that numerous inhabitants of the neighbouring countries, charmed with their beauty, abandon their homes, and for love of them settle in their country. It is also said that the islanders of the Lucayan archipelago have more civilised morals than those who live farther from the cultivated regions of Bimini and Florida. You will be pleased to learn the curious fashion of female dress. The men, as a matter of fact, are all naked except in war time and at festivals, when they dance and sing choruses. On these occasions they all adorn themselves by wearing clothes or head-dresses of various coloured plumes. As long as the women are not fully developed and before the age of puberty, they wear no clothes; afterwards they wear loin-cloths of silk nets, mixed with herbs. When the critical period arrives, the parents invite the neighbours to festivities in order to marry off their daughters.

Only the middle part of the body is covered as long as the women are marriageable; when they have lost their virginity they wear a kind of trousers covering their hips down to the knees, and made of stout plants or cotton, which grows wild in those countries. They make nets, which they sew, knot, and weave. Although they go

naked, these natives make stuffs to decorate their rooms
and the suspended beds called hammocks. They have
kings, whom they obey with such respect that if one of
them ordered a man to throw himself over a precipice for
no reason whatever save that he commanded, "I want
you to throw yourself down," the man would immediately
obey.   It is well, however, to know the limits of the
royal power. The kings occupy themselves in planting,
hunting, and fishing. Whatever is sown or planted or
fished, and whatever has to do with hunting, or is manufactured in any way whatsoever, is done in accordance
with the king's order. He distributes these tasks among
his people according to his pleasure. Harvests are stored
in royal granaries, to be divided during the remainder of
the year, and are distributed among the different families
according to their needs. The king there is like the queen
bee—a treasurer and distributor among his subjects.
These natives, therefore, enjoy a golden age, for they
know neither *meum* nor *tuum*, that germ of all discords.
When they are not busy with sowing or harvests, they
are playing tennis, dancing, hunting, or fishing. Judicial matters, trials, disputes among neighbours, are absolutely unknown. The king's will is held to be law and
this same custom prevails in all the islands. In all things
they are contented with little.

A kind of precious stone which the natives highly prize
is found in the waters; it is taken from red shells. They
wear it in their ears. Another much more valuable stone
is taken from large snails, whose flesh is good to eat.
In the head of each of these snails are deposited little
diaphanous red pebbles, as brilliant as fire. People who
have examined them declare their value to be equal to the
red stone vulgarly called the ruby. The natives call
the snail *cahobi* and the stone *cahobici*. Transparent
yellow and black stones are also found in the earth, and
of these they make necklaces and bracelets for adorning

their arms and necks and even their legs when they walk about naked. At least this was their custom when they lived in the archipelago. I shall now describe the archipelago and speak of the extermination of the inhabitants.

BOOK II

WE believe, or rather we suppose, that the Lucayas Islands were formerly joined to the large islands, and the natives themselves declare that there is such a tradition transmitted to them by their ancestors. Little by little, violent tempests submerged the lands, and separated them one from another by arms of the sea. The same is told by authors concerning the strait of Messina, lying between Italy and Sicily, which were formerly united. We know, indeed, that in many places the continent has increased in size and that it daily stretches out, pushing back the sea. Examples of this may be seen in the cities of Ravenna and Padua, which were near the sea, and are now far removed from it. On the other hand, the sea often encroaches on the continent. What we behold with our own eyes enables us to imagine what has happened elsewhere.

It is stated that these islands formerly abounded in various products, which constituted their riches; I say formerly, for they are now deserted, as I shall later show. The islands of this archipelago are from twelve to forty miles in circumference, none being larger. They resemble what has been told of the Strophades and the Symplegades[1] of the Mediterranean, which were assigned as a residence to the proscripts of Rome at Giaro, Seripho, and many others; the difference being that the Lucayas

---

[1] For the second time the author misplaces the Symplegades; the Strophades lie in the Ionian Sea.

were formerly very populous, while now they are deserted. The reason for this is that large numbers of the wretched islanders were transported to the gold-mines of Hispaniola and Fernandina, when the native inhabitants there were exterminated, exhausted by disease and famine, as well as by excessive labour. Twelve hundred thousand of them disappeared. I am ashamed to tell this story, but I must above all things be veracious. It is true that the Lucayans sometimes took vengeance on their oppressors by killing them, as I have explained at length in my first Decades.

Some Spaniards, anxious as hunters pursuing wild beasts through the mountains and swamps to capture the Indians of that archipelago, embarked on two ships built at the cost of seven of them. They sailed from Puerto de Plata situated on the north coast of Hispaniola, and laid their course towards the Lucayas. Three years have passed since then, and it is only now, in obedience to Camillo Gillino, who wishes me to acquaint Your Excellency with some still unknown particulars concerning these discoveries, that I speak of this expedition. These Spaniards visited all the Lucayas but without finding the plunder, for their neighbours had already explored the archipelago and systematically depopulated it. Not wishing to expose themselves to ridicule by returning to Hispaniola empty-handed, they continued their course towards the north. Many people said they lied when they declared they had purposely chosen that direction.

They were driven by a sudden tempest which lasted two days, to within sight of a lofty promontory which we will later describe. When they landed on this coast, the natives, amazed at the unexpected sight, regarded it as a miracle, for they had never seen ships. At first they rushed in crowds to the beach, eager to see; but when the Spaniards took to their shallops, the natives fled with the swiftness of the wind, leaving the coast

deserted. Our compatriots pursued them and some of
the more agile and swift-footed young men got ahead and
captured a man and a woman, whose flight had been
less rapid. They took them on board their ships and
after giving them clothing, released them. Touched by
this generosity, serried masses of natives again appeared
on the beach.

When their sovereign heard of this generosity, and
beheld for the first time these unknown and precious
garments,—for they only wear the skins of lions and other
wild beasts,—he sent fifty of his servants to the Spaniards,
carrying such provisions as they eat. When the Spaniards landed, he received them respectfully and cordially,
and when they exhibited a wish to visit the neighbourhood,
he provided them with guides and an escort. Wherever
they showed themselves, the natives, full of admiration,
advanced to meet them with presents, as though they
were divinities to be worshipped. What impressed them
most was the sight of the beards and the woollen and silk
clothing.

But what then! The Spaniards ended by violating this
hospitality. For when they had finished their exploration,
they enticed numerous natives by lies and tricks to visit
their ships, and when the vessels were quickly crowded
with men and women, they raised anchor, set sail, and
carried these despairing unfortunates into slavery. By
such means they sowed hatred and warfare throughout
that entire peaceful and friendly region, separating children
from their parents and wives from their husbands. Nor
is this all. Only one of the two ships returned, and of
the other there has been no news. As the vessel was old,
it is probable that she went down with all on board,
innocent and guilty. This spoliation occasioned the Royal
Council at Hispaniola much vexation, but it remained
unpunished. It was first thought to send the prisoners
back, but nothing was done, because the plan would have

been difficult to realise, and besides one of the ships was lost.

These details were furnished me by a virtuous priest, learned in law, called the bachelor Alvares de Castro. His learning and his virtues caused him to be named Dean of the Cathedral of Concepcion, in Hispaniola, and simultaneously vicar and inquisitor. Thus his testimony may be confidently accepted. In describing the island of Taprobane under the dominion of Claudius, Pliny affirms that the information he received from the ambassador Bachia and his three companions, who were sent to Rome by the sovereign of the island because of the great fame of the Romans, should be confidently accepted. I do likewise, and whenever I am uncertain of my facts I cite my authorities. It is from Castro's report and after several enquiries into this seizure that we have learned that the women brought from that region wear lions' skins and the men wear skins of all other wild beasts. He says these people are white and larger than the generality of men. When they were landed, some of them searched among the rubbish heaps along the town ditches for decaying bodies of dogs and asses with which to satisfy their hunger. Most of them died of misery, while those who survived were divided amongst the colonists of Hispaniola, who disposed of them as they pleased, either in their houses, the gold-mines, or their fields.

Let us return to the country of these unfortunates, from which we have somewhat wandered. I believe this country is near that of Baccalaos, discovered by Cabot in the service of England some twenty-six years ago, or to the land of Bacchalais, of which I have already written at length. I shall now indicate their astronomical position, their religious rites, their products, and their customs. These countries appear to be situated the same distance from the pole, and under the same parallel as

Vandalia in Spain, commonly called Andalusia. The exploration of the country occupied but a few days. It extends a great distance in the same direction as the land where the Spaniards anchored. The first districts visited are called Chicorana and Duhare. The natives of Chicorana have a well-browned skin, like our sun-burned peasants, and their hair is black. The men let their hair grow to the waist and the women wear theirs longer. Both sexes plait their hair and they are beardless; whether nature so created them or whether this is the result of some drug or whether they use a depilatory like the people of Temistitan, nobody can say. In any case they like to show a smooth skin.

I must cite another witness whose credit is not less among laymen than that of Dean Alvares amongst priests, namely the licenciate Lucas Vasquez Ayllon. He is a citizen of Toledo, member of the Royal Council of Hispaniola, and one of those at whose expense the two ships had been equipped. Commissioned by the Council of Hispaniola to appear before the Royal India Council, he urgently asked that he might be permitted to again visit that country and found a colony. He brought with him a native of Chicorana as his servant. This man had been baptised under the Christian name of Francisco united to the surname of his native country, Chicorana. While Ayllon was engaged on his business here, I some-times invited him and his servant Francisco Chicorana to my table. This Chicorana is not devoid of intelligence. He understands readily and has learned the Spanish tongue quite well. The letters of his companions which the licenciate Ayllon himself showed to me, and the curious information furnished me by Chicorana, will serve me for the remainder of my narrative. Each may accept or reject my account as he chooses. Envy is a plague natural to the human race always seeking to depreciate and to search for weeds in another's garden, even when it is perfectly clean. This pest afflicts the foolish or people devoid of literary culture, who live useless lives like cumberers of the earth.

Leaving the coast of Chicorana on one hand, the Spaniards landed in another country called Duhare. Ayllon says the natives are white men, and his testimony is confirmed by Francisco Chicorana. Their hair is brown and hangs to their heels. They are governed by a king of gigantic size, called Datha, whose wife is as large as himself. They have five children. In place of horses, the king is carried on the shoulders of strong young men, who run with him to the different places he wishes to visit. At this point, I must confess, that the different accounts cause me to hesitate. The Dean and Ayllon do not agree; for what one asserts concerning these young men acting as horses, the other denies. The Dean said: "I have never spoken to anybody who has seen these horses," to which Ayllon answered, "I have heard it told by many people," while Francisco Chicorana, although he was present, was unable to settle this dispute. Could I act as arbitrator, I would say that, according to the investigations I have made, these people were too barbarous and uncivilised to have horses. Another country near Duhare is called Xapida. Pearls are found there, and also a kind of stone resembling pearls which is much prized by the Indians.

In all these regions they visited, the Spaniards noticed herds of deer similar to our herds of cattle. These deer bring forth and nourish their young in the houses of the natives. During the daytime they wander freely through the woods in search of their food, and in the evening they come back to their little ones, who have been cared for, allowing themselves to be shut up in the courtyards and even to be milked, when they have suckled their fawns. The only milk the natives know is that of the does, from which they make cheese. They also keep a great variety of chickens, ducks, geese, and other similar fowls. They eat maize-bread, similar to that of the islanders, but they do not know the yucca root, from which cassabi, the food of the nobles, is made. The maize grains are very like our Genoese millet, and in size are as large as our peas. The natives cultivate another cereal called xathi. This is believed to be millet but it is not certain, for very few Castilians know millet, as it is nowhere grown in Castile. This country produces various kinds of potatoes, but of small varieties. Potatoes are edible roots, like our radishes, carrots, parsnips, and turnips. I have already given many particulars, in my first Decades, concerning these potatoes, yucca, and other foodstuffs.

The Spaniards speak of still other regions, Hatha, Xamunambe, and Tihe, all of which are believed to be governed by the same king.[1] In the last named the inhabitants wear a distinctive priestly costume, and they are regarded as priests and venerated as such by their neighbours. They cut their hair, leaving only two locks growing on their temples, which are bound under the chin. When the natives make war against their neighbours, according to the regrettable custom of mankind, these priests are invited by both sides to be present, not as actors but as witnesses of the conflict. When the battle is about to open, they circulate among the warriors who are seated or lying on the ground, and sprinkle them with the juice of certain herbs they have chewed with their teeth; just as our priests of the beginning of the Mass sprinkle the worshippers with a branch dipped in holy water. When this ceremony is finished, the opposing sides fall upon one another. While the battle rages, the priests are left in charge of the camp, and when it is finished they look after the wounded, making no distinction between friends and enemies, and busy themselves

[1] Probably the coasts of the Carolinas and Virginia.

in burying the dead.¹ The inhabitants of this country do not eat human flesh; the prisoners of war are enslaved by the victors.

The Spaniards have visited several regions of that vast country; they are called Arambe, Guacaia, Quohathe, Tazacca, and Tahor. The colour of the inhabitants is dark brown. None of them have any system of writing, but they preserve traditions of great antiquity in rhymes and chants. Dancing and physical exercises are held in honour, and they are passionately fond of ball games, in which they exhibit the greatest skill. The women know how to spin and sew. Although they are partially clothed with skins of wild beasts, they use cotton such as the Milanese call bombasio, and they make nets of the fibre of certain tough grasses just as hemp and flax are used for the same purposes in Europe.

There is another country called Inzignanin, whose inhabitants declare that, according to the tradition of their ancestors, there once arrived amongst them men with tails a metre long and as thick as a man's arm. This tail was not movable like those of the quadrupeds, but formed one mass as we see is the case with fish and crocodiles, and was as hard as a bone. When these men wished to sit down, they had consequently to have a seat with an open bottom; and if there was none, they had to dig a hole more than a cubit deep to hold their tails and allow them to rest. Their fingers were as long as they were broad, and their skin was rough, almost scaly. They ate nothing but raw fish, and when the fish gave out they all perished, leaving no descendants. These fables and other similar nonsense have been handed down to the natives by their parents. Let us now notice their rites and ceremonies.

¹ The regions here described would seem to correspond to the Virginia and Carolina coasts, but no confirmation of this humanitarian custom, worthy of a Red Cross Society, which Martyr attributes to the Indians of those parts, has fallen under the translator's notice.

BOOK III

THE natives have no temples, but use the dwellings of their sovereigns as such. As a proof of this, we have said that a gigantic sovereign called Datha ruled in the province of Duhare, whose palace was built of stone,[1] while all the other houses were built of lumber covered with thatch or grasses. In the courtyard of this palace, the Spaniards found two idols as large as a three-year-old child, one male and one female. These idols are both called Inamahari, and had their residence in the palace. Twice each year they are exhibited, the first time at the sowing season, when they are invoked to obtain a successful result for their labours. We will later speak of the harvest. Thanksgivings are offered to them if the crops are good; in the contrary case they are implored to show themselves more favourable the following year.

The idols are carried in procession amidst pomp, accompanied by the entire people. It will not be useless to describe this ceremony. On the eve of the festival the king has his bed made in the room where the idols stand, and sleeps in their presence. At daybreak the people assemble, and the king himself carries these idols, hugging them to his breast, to the top of his palace, where

---

[1] Vestiges of ancient stone buildings have been found in various parts of the territory now embraced within the area of the United States. Norton Horsford's several articles on such ruins are published in the *Bulletins of the Smithsonian Institute*.

he exhibits them to the people.   He and they are saluted
with respect and fear by the people, who fall upon their
knees or throw themselves on the ground with loud
shouts.   The king then descends and hangs the idols,
draped in artistically worked cotton stuffs, upon the
breasts of two venerable men, of authority.   They are,
moreover, adorned with feather mantles of various colours,
and are thus carried escorted with hymns and songs into
the country, while the girls and young men dance and
leap.   Any one who stopped in his house or absented
himself during the procession would be suspected of
heresy; and not only the absent, but likewise any who took
part in this ceremony carelessly and without observing
the ritual.   The men escort the idols during the day,
while during the night the women watch over them,
lavishing upon them demonstrations of joy and respect.
The next day they are carried back to the palace with the
same ceremonies with which they were taken out.   If the
sacrifice is accomplished with devotion and in conformity
with the ritual, the Indians believe they will obtain rich
crops, bodily health, peace, or if they are about to fight,
victory, from these idols.   Thick cakes, similar to those
the ancients made from flour, are offered to them.   The
natives are convinced that their prayers for harvests
will be heard, especially if the cakes are mixed with
tears.

Another feast is celebrated every year when a roughly
carved wooden statue is carried into the country and fixed
upon a high pole planted in the ground.   This first pole
is surrounded by other similar ones, upon which people
hang gifts for the gods, each one according to his means.
At nightfall the principal citizens divide these offerings
among themselves just as the priests do with the cakes and
other offerings given them by the women.   Whoever
offers the divinity the most valuable presents is the most
honoured.   Witnesses are present when the gifts are

offered, who announce after the ceremony what every one has given, just as notaries might do in Europe. Each one is thus stimulated by a spirit of rivalry to outdo his neighbour. From sunrise till evening the people dance round this statue, clapping their hands, and when nightfall has barely set in, the image and the pole on which it was fixed are carried away and thrown into the sea, if the country is on the coast, or into the river, if it is along a river's banks. Nothing more is seen of it, and each year a new statue is made.

The natives celebrate a third festival, during which, after exhuming a long-buried skeleton, they erect a black tent out in the country, leaving one end open so that the sky is visible; upon a blanket placed in the centre of the tent they then spread out the bones. Only women surround the tent, all of them weeping, and each of them offers such gifts as she can afford. The following day the bones are carried to the tomb, and are henceforth considered sacred. As soon as they are buried, or everything is ready for their burial, the chief priest addresses the surrounding people from the summit of a mound, upon which he fulfils the functions of orator. Ordinarily he pronounces a eulogy on the deceased, or on the immortality of the soul, or the future life. He says that souls originally came from the icy regions of the north, where perpetual snow prevails. They therefore expiate their sins under the master of that region who is called Mateczunga, but they return to the southern regions where another great sovereign, Quescuga, governs. Quescuga is lame and is of a sweet and generous disposition. He surrounds the newly arrived souls with numberless attentions, and with him they enjoy a thousand delights,—young girls sing and dance, parents are reunited to children, and everything one formerly loved is enjoyed. The old grow young and everybody is of the same age, occupied only in giving himself up to joy and pleasure.

Such are the verbal traditions handed down to them
from their ancestors. They are regarded as sacred and
considered authentic. Whoever dared to believe differently would be ostracised. These natives also believe
that we live under the vault of heaven; they do not
suspect the existence of the antipodes. They think the
sea has its gods, and believe quite as many foolish things
about them as Greece, the friend of lies, talked about
Nereids and other marine gods,—Glaucus, Phorcus, and
the rest of them.

When the priest has finished his speech, he inhales the
smoke of certain herbs, puffing it in and out, pretending to
thus purge and absolve the people from their sins. After
this ceremony the natives return home, convinced that the
inventions of this impostor not only soothe their spirits, but
contribute to the health of their bodies. Another fraud of
the priests is as follows: when the chief is at death's door
and about to give up his soul, they send away all witnesses,
and then surrounding his bed they perform some secret
jugglery which makes him appear to vomit sparks and
ashes. It looks like sparks jumping from a bright fire,
or those sulphured papers which people throw into the
air to amuse themselves. These sparks, rushing through
the air and quickly disappearing, look like those leaping
wild goats which people call shooting stars. The moment
the dying man expires, a cloud of these sparks shoots
up three cubits high, with a great noise and quickly
vanishes. They hail this flame as the dead man's soul,
bidding it a last farewell and accompanying its flight with
their wailings, tears, and funereal cries, absolutely
convinced that it has taken its flight to heaven. Lament-
ing and weeping they escort the body to the tomb.

Widows are forbidden to marry again if their husband
has died a natural death; but if he has been executed,
they may remarry. The natives like their women to be
chaste. They detest immodesty and are careful to put

aside suspicious women. The lords have the right to have two women, but the common people have only one. The men engage in mechanical occupations, especially carpenter work and tanning skins of wild beasts; while the women busy themselves with distaff, spindle, and needle.

Their year is divided into twelve moons. Justice is administered by magistrates, criminals and the guilty being severely punished, especially thieves. Their kings are of gigantic size, as we have already mentioned. All the provinces we have named pay them tributes and these tributes are paid in kind; for they are free from the pest of money, and trade is carried on by exchanging goods. They love games, especially tennis; they also like metal circles turned with movable rings, which they spin on a table, and they shoot arrows at a mark. They use torches and oil made from different fruits for illumination at night. They likewise have olive-trees. They invite one another to dinner. Their longevity is great and their old age is robust.

They easily cure fevers with the juice of plants, as they also do their wounds, unless the latter are mortal. They employ simples, of which they are acquainted with a great many. When any of them suffers from a bilious stomach, he drinks a draught composed of a common plant called Guihi, or eats the herb itself; after which he immediately vomits his bile and feels better. This is the only medicament they use, and they never consult doctors except experienced old women, or priests acquainted with the secret virtues of herbs. They have none of our delicacies, and as they have neither the perfumes of Araby nor fumigations nor foreign spices at their disposition, they content themselves with what their country produces and live happily in better health to a more robust old age. Various dishes and different foods are not required to satisfy their appetites, for they are contented with little.

It is quite laughable to hear how the people salute
the lords and how the king responds, especially to his
nobles. As a sign of respect, the one who salutes puts his
hands to his nostrils and gives a bellow like a bull, after
which he extends his hands towards the forehead and in
front of the face. The king does not bother to return
the salutes of his people, and responds to the nobles by
half bending his head towards the left shoulder without
saying anything.

I now come to a fact which will appear incredible
to Your Excellency. You already know that the ruler
of this region is a tyrant of gigantic size. How does it
happen that only he and his wife have attained this
extraordinary size? No one of their subjects has explained
this to me, but I have questioned the above mentioned
licenciate Ayllon, a serious and responsible man, who had
his information from those who had shared with him the
cost of the expedition. I likewise questioned the servant
Francisco, to whom the neighbours had spoken. Neither
nature nor birth has given these princes the advantage
of size as an hereditary gift; they have acquired it by
artifice. While they are still in their cradles and in charge
of their nurses, experts in the matter are called, who by
the application of certain herbs, soften their young bones.
During a period of several days they rub the limbs of the
child with these herbs, until the bones become as soft as
wax. They then rapidly bend them in such wise that
the infant is almost killed. Afterwards they feed the
nurse on foods of a special virtue. The child is wrapped
in warm covers, the nurse gives it her breast and revives
it with her milk, thus gifted with strengthening properties.
After some days of rest the lamentable task of stretching
the bones is begun anew. Such is the explanation given
by the servant Francisco Chicorana. The Dean of La
Concepcion, whom I have mentioned, received from the
Indians stolen on the vessel that was saved explanations

differing from those furnished to Ayllon and his associates. These explanations dealt with medicaments and other means used for increasing the size. There was no torturing of the bones, but a very stimulating diet composed of crushed herbs was used. This diet was given principally at the age of puberty, when it is nature's tendency to develop, and sustenance is converted into flesh and bones. Certainly it is an extraordinary fact, but we must remember what is told about these herbs, and if their hidden virtues could be learned, I would willingly believe in their efficacy. We understand that only the kings are allowed to use them, for if any one else dared to taste them, or to obtain the recipe of this diet, he would be guilty of treason, for he would appear to wish to equal the king. It is considered, after a fashion, that the king should not be the size of everybody else, for he should look down upon and dominate those who approach him. Such is the story told to me, and I repeat it for what it is worth. Your Excellency may believe it or not.

I have already sufficiently described the ceremonies and customs of these natives. Let us now turn our attention to the study of nature. Bread and meat have been considered; let us devote our attention to trees.

BOOK IV

THERE are in this country virgin forests of oak, pine, cypress, nut- and almond-trees, amongst the branches of which riot wild vines, whose white and black grapes are not used for wine-making, for the people manufacture their drinks from other fruits. There are likewise fig-trees and other kinds of spice-plants. The trees are improved by grafting, just as with us; though without cultivation they would continue in a wild state. The natives cultivate gardens in which grows an abundance of vegetables, and they take an interest in growing their orchards. They even have trees in their gardens. One of these trees is called the corito, of which the fruit resembles a small melon in size and flavour. Another called guacomine bears fruit a little larger than a quince of a delicate and remarkable odour, and which is very wholesome; they plant and cultivate many other trees and plants, of which I shall not speak further, lest by telling everything at one breath I become monotonous.

Thanks to us, the licenciate and royal counsellor, Ayllon, succeeded in obtaining what he wanted. His Imperial Majesty accepted our advice, and we have sent him back to New Spain, authorising him to build a fleet to carry him to those countries where he will found a colony. Associates will not fail him, for the entire Spanish nation is in fact so keen about novelties that people go eagerly anywhere they are called by a nod or a whistle, in the hope of bettering their condition, and are ready to sacrifice what they have for what they hope. All that has happened proves this. With what sentiments people so saddened by the robbery of their children and parents will receive them, time alone will show us. In this connection there is a fact I should not omit to mention. It has again to do with the islanders of the Lucayas, whom the colonists of Cuba and Hispaniola sought for the hard and forced labour of their gold-mines. As soon as the Spaniards understood the simple beliefs of the islanders regarding their souls, which, after expiating their sins must leave the cold mountains of the nortʰ, for the south, they sought to persuade them to quit their native soil of their own accord and allow themselves to be conducted to the southern islands of Cuba and Hispaniola. They succeeded in convincing them that they would thus reach the country where they would find their dead parents, their children, relatives, and friends, and where they would enjoy every delight in the embraces of their loved ones. As their priests had already filled them with those false beliefs, when the Spaniards persuaded them, they left their country to pursue this vain hope. As soon as they understood that they had been deceived, since they found neither their parents, nor any one they sought, and were, on the contrary, obliged to submit to severe fatigue and heavy labours to which they were unaccustomed, they were reduced to desperation. They either killed themselves or, resolving to die of hunger and exhaustion, resisted both reasoning and force to make them eat. I have already related this above.

Thus perished the unfortunate Lucayans, and there only remains to-day a very small number of them, either in the Spanish colonies or in the archipelago itself. Nevertheless I think that the sighs and groans of those wretched innocents have provoked the Divine wrath, and that many massacres and disorders among these peoples have been punished, the more so because the Spaniards pretended they laboured to propagate religion while influenced by cupidity and avarice. Some of them are dead, killed by the natives or pierced with poisoned arrows or drowned or stricken with different maladies. Such has been the fate of those first aggressors, all of whom followed other ways than those laid down in the royal instructions.

In fact I, who, in concert with my associates, have daily drawn up these instructions, can affirm that all the prescriptions were so clearly just and equitable that nothing more legitimate can be imagined. Several years ago it was decided that these recently discovered nations should receive kindly, gentle, and amicable treatment; that the caciques and their subjects should be distributed by the King's grace amongst the colonists, by whom they should be treated as tributaries or vassals, and not at all as slaves; that they should receive established rations of bread and meat to sustain them in their work; all the clothing they required and the ornaments they preferred should be distributed amongst them as the wage for their daily work in the mines. It was commanded to furnish them with sleeping shelter at night, and it was forbidden to wake them before dawn or make them work after sunset. At certain seasons of the year, they were to be exempt from labour in the mines, and should work at planting yucca roots or maize. On feast days they should rest. They should assist at Mass, and when the Holy Sacrifice was terminated, they might pass their time in their usual games and dances.[1]

All these instructions have been thought out by prudent and humane jurisconsults and sanctioned by religious

---

[1] Many of these laws were the outcome of the active campaign of Las Casas. Consult Navarrete, tom. ii., pp. 186, 189, 198, 201, 204, 227, 239, 274, 331, 460; MacNutt's *Bartholomew de Las Casas* (1909); *The New Laws of the Indies*, reprinted in facsimile by Henry Stevens and F. W. Lucas, London, 1893.

men. But what of that? When our compatriots reach
that remote world, so far away and so removed from us,
beyond the ocean whose courses imitate the changing
heavens, they find themselves distant from any judge.
Carried away by love of gold, they become ravenous
wolves instead of gentle lambs, and heedless of the royal
instructions. It is vain to rebuke them, to condemn
and punish many of them; the more diligently we seek
to cut off the Hydra's heads, the more numerously they
spring up. And thus is the proverb verified: *Quicquid
multis peccatur, inultum restat, inhæreo.*[1]

We plan to publish new regulations and to send out new
administrators to apply them. The future will show what
more we have to do. To say the truth, we hardly know
what decision to make. Should the Indians be declared
free, and we without any right to exact labour of them,
without their work being paid? Competent men are
divided on this point and we hesitate.

It is chiefly the monks of the Dominican order who by
their writings drive us to the adverse decision. They
maintain that it would be better and would offer better
security for both the bodily and spiritual good of the
Indians to assign them permanently and by hereditary
title to certain masters. If they are given temporary
places, those to whom they are assigned by the King's
pleasure and in the name of some one often absent will
treat them as mercenaries. Fearing to lose their services
at the end of a few years, they are careless despite the
instructions, the laws, and the material interests of those
unfortunates; to satisfy their avarice and that of their
masters they work them to death in the mines, taking no
account either of sex or age. They underfeed them,
and are heedless of their health while they suffer under
the excessive toil to which they are not accustomed.
On the other hand, one who knew he would leave these

[1] Collective sins go unpunished.

Indians to his heirs would not only seek to keep them in good health, as people do with what they own, but he would endeavour to increase their number by favouring marriages and births.

It may be shown by many examples that we should not consent to give them their liberty. In fact these barbarians have plotted the destruction of the Christians, whenever they could, and have carried out their plans; and although the thing has been often tried, liberty only conduces to their destruction. They only wander about, idle and ignorant, and return to their ancient rites and abominable ceremonies.

There is a third argument which proves those natives established on the continent undeserving of liberty. In a part of the continent called the province of Chiribichi, the Dominican friars constructed a church about a dozen years ago. At the cost of great efforts and privations they educated the sons of caciques and the principal chiefs, and when they grew up the friars sought by their exhortations, counsels, instructions, and kindness, to attract them to our religion. They met with such success that those children served as acolyths at the altars with a certain ability and grace, knowing perfectly the Spanish tongue. But hear what a horrible thing they did.

Hardly had they emerged from infancy and reached the age of puberty, than two of these young men, whose native ferocity the friars have banished to make way for the Christian faith and civilisation, preferred to escape. They took to their old skins like wolves, resuming the old filthy habits in which they were born, and after collecting a large body of their armed neighbours to whom they acted as guides, they attacked the convent in which they had been educated with paternal charity. When the convent was captured and destroyed, they massacred their teachers and fellow-students to the last man.

I have been severe in my censures of the Spaniards,

but whether their opinion that liberty should not be given to the natives be excusable or not, Your Excellency may perceive by reading one of the documents presented to our India Council by some monks who had escaped that catastrophe, for at the present time they are here seeking provisions for their companions.

We were assembled with our President when this document was laid before us. Our President is Garcias Loayza,[1] Bishop of Osma, who is learned in the Latin tongue and, to speak plainly, is the Emperor's confessor. He is a member of the Order of Friars Preachers, and his merits have secured him election to the rank of General of the Order at Rome. I transmit you this document in Spanish, which all Latins and Italians easily understand, because of the similarity of the languages; and I have done this so, that no one may accuse me of having changed the sense of the words or the intentions of the author in my translation. The friar is called Tomaso Ortiz. Let us hear him speaking verbally before the Council, and writing in the name of the friars.

Enumeration of the reasons why the Indians are unworthy of liberty.

"On the mainland they eat human flesh. They are more given to sodomy than any other nation. There is no justice among them. They go naked. They have no respect either for love or for virginity. They are stupid and silly. They have no respect for truth, save when it is to their advantage. They are unstable. They have no knowledge of what foresight means. They are ungrateful and changeable. They boast of intoxicating themselves with drinks they manufacture from certain herbs, fruits, and grains, similar to our beers and ciders. They are vain of

[1] Consult Tourow's *Hommes Illustres de l'Ordre de Saint Dominique.* Loayza, who was born at Talavera in 1479, was created Cardinal in 1530 and became later Archbishop of Seville. He died at Madrid in 1546.

the products they harvest and eat. They are brutal.
They delight in exaggerating their defects. There is no
obedience among them, or deference on the part of the
young for the old, nor of the son for the father. They
are incapable of learning. Punishments have no effect
upon them. Traitorous, cruel, and vindictive, they never
forgive. Most hostile to religion, idle, dishonest, abject,
and vile, in their judgments they keep no faith or law.
Husbands observe no fidelity towards their wives, nor
the wives towards their husbands. Liars, superstitious,
and cowardly as hares. They eat fleas, spiders, and
worms raw, whenever they find them. They exercise none
of the humane arts or industries. When taught the mysteries of our religion, they say that these things may suit
Castilians, but not them, and they do not wish to change
their customs. They are beardless, and if sometimes hairs
grow, they pull them out. They have no sympathy with
the sick, and if one of them is gravely ill, his friends
and neighbours carry him out into the mountains to die
there. Putting a little food and water beside his head
they go away. The older they get the worse they become. About the age of ten or twelve years, they seem
to have some civilisation, but later they become like real
brute beasts. I may therefore affirm that God has never
created a race more full of vice and composed without
the least mixture of kindness or culture. Now let people judge what may be the root of such evil customs.
We here speak of those whom we know by experience.
Especially the father, Pedro de Cordoba, who has sent
me these facts in writing, and I have discussed these
things and agreed on this point and others I suppress; the
Indians are more stupid than asses and refuse to improve
in anything."

In studying this and other similar documents, daily
laid before us and carefully discussed by us, we observe,
as we have said, that the oppressors have been punished

for their cruelties.   First of all, a large number of Spaniards have fallen victims to their rivalries for control.
I have related their adventures in my preceding Decades,
in speaking of the Pinzons, natives of the two Atlantic
ports of Palos and Moguer in Andalusia, who, while
exploring the vast coast of the continent and the
banks of the marvellous Maragnon River, fell before the
arrows of savage cannibals, were massacred, cut to bits,
and served up in different dishes.   The cannibals—likewise called Caribs—are in fact anthropophagi.   I have
described the catastrophe of Solis, whom a similar fate
overtook when exploring the other extremity of the
continent.   In consequence of this lamentable disaster,
the name of Solis has been given to the maritime Gulf
where Magellan stopped for a long time with his fleet.

Such was the fate of Alonzo Hojeda and of Juan de la
Cosa, who with a numerous band of soldiers explored
the provinces of Cumaná, Cuchiibachoa, Cauchieta,
and Uraba.   They perished miserably, as did likewise
Diego Nicuesa in command of about eight hundred
soldiers whom he lost and for whom he searched along
the coasts of Veragua and the western shores of the Gulf
of Uraba.   Juan Ponce, the first discoverer of Florida,
was likewise mortally wounded by naked barbarians
and returned to the island of Cuba to die.   Many other
leaders and soldiers fell before the onslaught of the
cannibals and furnished great banquets for them; for it
is proven that the Caribs frequently go several hundred
miles from their shores in their fleets of canoes, engaging
in regular man-hunts.   The canoes are barques dug out
of single tree-trunks; the Greeks called them *monoxylon*.
Sometimes they will carry as many as eighty rowers.
Finally I have mentioned Diego Velasquez, viceroy of
Cuba, also called Fernandina, who, from his enormous
riches, was reduced to poverty and has just died, and the
quarrel with his mortal enemy, Fernando Cortes.

Of all these captains, the only one who still survives,
is Cortes.[1] It is thought that he keeps a treasure of
3,000,000 pesos of gold in that great city of Temistitan
which he conquered and ravaged. The Spanish peso is
worth a quarter more than a ducat. Cortes is, in fact,
master of many cities and lords, possessing an abundance
of gold in their rivers and mountains. The richest silver
mines are also his; but there is a vulgar proverb which
may be applied to him, namely: *De nummis, fide, sensu,
multo minus in secessu reperiatur quam fama gerat.*[2]
Time will tell.

Juan Ribera, who knew the ambassador Tomas
Maino, and Gillino, and was from his youth a representative of Cortes at court and shared all his dangers, asserts
that his master is keeping back three thousand pesos
which he wishes to send to his sovereign; but having been
informed of the capture of several freighted ships by
French pirates, he does not venture to send it. Large
sums of gold, silver, sugar, and cinnamon-bark are stored
on the continent, in Hispaniola, Cuba, and Jamaica.
Stores of yellow and red wood, excellent for dyeing woollens,
which the Italians call verzino and the Spaniards brazil,
have been ready for a long time. Hispaniola is covered
with forests of these trees, as commonly as pine or oak
woods with us. We have debated in our India Council
what measures should be taken for the protection of the
ships; acting upon our decision and advice the Emperor
has decided and commanded that all freighted ships should
go to Hispaniola, the most important of our maritime possessions. From this island a strong fleet, consisting of all

---

[1] Cortes lived for twenty years after the demise of Peter Martyr, dying
in Spain in 1547. He fell into disfavour and the last years of his life were
embittered by disappointments, false accusations, and endless litigation
which seriously impaired his fortunes.

[2] Of money, faith, and sense much less is found in reality than is
reported.

the ships there collected, will start, prepared to defend themselves against the attacks of any pirates they encounter.   What will happen to this fleet, divine providence alone can tell.

It is alleged that Cortes has had two cannon[1] cast in gold, capable of firing wooden bullets the size of little tennis balls; but I believe he has only done this out of ostentation, for, according to my opinion, gold could not withstand the force of an explosion.   Perhaps this tale is an invention to injure him; for the exploits of this hero are constantly presented in a false light by the envious.

[1] There was but one such cannon or culverin and it was of silver.   It weighed twenty-three hundredweight: it was ornamented with a phenix underneath which was the following inscription:

Aquesta nació sin par,
Yo en serviros sin segundo;
Vos, sin igual en el mundo.

BOOK V

WHILE engaged in writing the preceding, I learned that four vessels coming from the Indies had reached the coast of Spain. We do not yet know what riches they contain. The Royal Council of Hispaniola has sent a report to the Emperor on the subject of a recent painful and lamentable incident which it is feared may have hurtful consequences. I have already spoken at length concerning Francisco de Garay, governor of Jamaica, in letters I addressed to Pope Adrian, and which were carried to Rome by Giacomo Pierio.

Francisco de Garay had already twice essayed to found a colony on the Panuco River, which gives its name to the country, the cacique, and all the neighbouring regions bounding on the vassal states of Temistitan. Both times he had been repulsed by the inhabitants, although they are almost naked. The preceding year he renewed his attempt, with eleven ships manned by more than five hundred soldiers and many horsemen. He had been granted royal letters patent authorising him to found the colony he desired on the banks of that river. The Panuco is a broad river, navigable for large ships, and serves as a port—all the regions dependent upon Temistitan being without ports and affording vessels very imperfect protection

Garay and his companions succeeded in landing, but they had suffered from violent storms at sea, and evil fortune drove them on the coast. He lost all his ships in landing, and found the banks of the river occupied by the soldiers of Cortes. A colony had already been founded there and magistrates named for the administration, with the consent of the cacique of Panuco. In fact, Cortes affirms that this country is under his government of Temistitan and that the Panuco River lies within the limits of New Spain; such being the name he has given to that region, and which the Emperor has confirmed. Garay went to meet his compatriots established at that point, and questioned them, showing them his royal letters patent assigning the banks of the Panuco River as the site of his colony.

He informed them that this was his only motive in coming there, saying: "I counsel you, therefore, to obey the King's orders and to submit; I beg you to recognise my authority and not that of Cortes, to accept the laws and regulations necessary to assure a good and tranquil administration, and to obey my orders."

All these words were useless, for hardly had the colonists heard these studied phrases than, without consultation and likewise without any hesitation, they replied: "Cortes is resolved to found a colony upon the territory belonging formerly to Temistitan and which lies within the limits of New Spain, as traced by the Emperor. We might very properly be accused of treason if we deserted him and listened to you." A second time Garay cited and exhibited the royal letters. He was told they were forgeries, that he had obtained them from the Emperor by abusing his ignorance, that they were granted owing to the partiality of the Bishop of Burgos, President of the Council for Indian Affairs, who was personally hostile to Cortes, owing to Diego Velasquez, viceroy of Cuba, being an old friend of his brother Fonseca, and an enemy of Cortes. I have already spoken sufficiently of their rivalries in the narrative dealing with these two

captains, and the story would fill a thick volume. The
colonists proving obdurate, Garay accused them of treason,
if they did not obey the King's orders. They answered
that they placed the letters on their heads, as is the
Spanish custom, and that they would accept them with
the respect due to royal letters; but as to executing their
provisions, they would consult either the King or the
Council for Indian affairs. When the Emperor-King
had heard both parties he would decide as best suited
his interests. Nevertheless the colonists thought the
King would have given very different orders had he suspected the extraordinary dangers this novelty might
provoke; as a matter of fact, if the barbarians who had
just been subjugated realised that any rivalry existed
among the Christians, they would take advantage of it
to shake off the yoke.

They finally decided amongst themselves to send envoys
to Cortes. They were named and departed. They
reported to Cortes what had happened. The latter
commissioned two of his captains to go and see Garay
and to persuade the latter to meet him at Temistitan,
that great lake capital of a powerful empire, which lies
about sixty leagues distant from Panuco. The captains
found Garay, and succeeded in persuading him to come.
He decided to set out, for he recognised his inferiority
to Cortes. The latter accepted his son as his son-in-law,
giving him one of his natural daughters to wife.[1] Meanwhile, whether at the instigation of Cortes or spontaneously is not known, the fact is that the natives took up
arms, attacked and massacred the troops of Garay. The
members of the council at Hispaniola who have written
private letters to their friends express no opinion on this
point. As a matter of fact, it is of little importance.

[1] Supposed to have been Catalina, but her identity is not altogether
clear. The two children were formally affianced, but the marriage never
took place.

Garay's seven hundred men were none the less defeated, two hundred and fifty being killed. It is alleged that Garay himself was amongst the victims. It is not yet known whether he was with Cortes or elsewhere when he died; whether he succumbed to fever, or whether the kindness and considerate foresight of Cortes delivered him from the vexations of human preoccupations, leaving the latter to enjoy the sweets of tyranny alone. In fact, we have no reports concerning these events, either from Cortes or from the magistrates of that region.

We only know by letters sent by the council of Hispaniola to the Emperor and our own council, that a certain Cristobal de Olid had landed at the western extremity of Cuba, opposite the coast of Yucatan. This man Olid, who is a lieutenant of Cortes, had under his orders three hundred soldiers and one hundred and fifty horsemen. His fleet was imposing. He sought other recruits in Cuba, and announced his intention of exploring the country extending between Yucatan and the continent (for it is not yet known whether Yucatan is an island) and to found a colony there. The councilors were informed by a notary in Cuba of this event, and at the same time they heard different versions of the death of Garay. It is true that the councilors also believe these reports to be false and that they have been spread by Olid, who wished to attract wandering Spaniards necessary for his expedition, once they had lost hope of joining Garay.

In another passage of their letter, the councilors announce that Egidius Gonzales is at a port of Hispaniola preparing to sail in the same direction. I have described the expedition of Gonzales in the South Sea, and the ambassador, Tomaso Maino, took with him a copy of this narrative which the Archbishop of Cosenza presented to the Sovereign Pontiff, Clement. As everything is ready for the departure, it is necessary to take precautions so as to understand the intentions of those who desire to

explore with the consent and under the instructions of the
Emperor. For this reason, on his return from the South
Sea, where he discovered a large fresh-water sea dotted
with islands, Egidius has decided to continue his researches
in the north, hoping that chance may lead him to the discovery of the much-desired strait. He has, therefore,
come to Hispaniola with his wealth, leaving his fleet in
the South Sea, for he wishes to build a new one before
sailing the northern ocean. He thinks that the mass of
waters flows through a navigable river, which must be
situated between Yucatan and the continent, just as the
Ticino flows from Lake Maggiore, the Mincio from Lake
of Garda, the Adda from the Lake of Como, and the
Rhone from Lake Leman, carrying their waters to the sea.

We are not ignorant that Pedrarius, governor of the
continent, having decided to occupy the same provinces,
has assembled a considerable company of foot-soldiers
and horsemen and is preparing to set out in the same
direction. The council of Hispaniola opposed the
departure of Egidius Gonzales, hoping to prevent a meeting and conflict between the three—Olid, Pedrarius, and
Egidius. Couriers were expressly sent to Pedrarius,
to Fernando Cortes, and to Olid, threatening them with
punishment for treason should they resort to violence
in case they encountered one another. Whoever acts
contrary to this order will be ignominiously deprived
of his office; our council has approved this decision of
the council of Hispaniola. I will keep you informed of
what happens.

The explorers are devoured by such a passion to discover this strait that they risk a thousand dangers;
for it is certain that he who does discover it—if it ever is
discovered—will obtain the imperial favour, not to
mention great authority. If indeed a passage between
the South and the North Sea is discovered, the route to
the islands producing spices and precious stones will be

very much shortened, and the dispute begun with Portugal, which I have mentioned in my first Decades, will be eliminated. We are inclined to share the opinion of Egidius, namely that a river flowing from the freshwater sea and emptying into the ocean on the north may be discovered; for it is known that no river carries the waters of that lake towards the southern ocean. If this prove to be a fact, a convenient channel between the two oceans will have been found, since the shores of the lake are only separated from the coast of the southern sea by a tongue of land no more than three leagues wide. According to Egidius, it is in that locality that a convenient road may be opened for carts and all kinds of vehicles and that the equinoctial circle will be more easily reached.

BOOK VI

BASING my belief upon serious arguments, I believe, Most Illustrious Prince, that not many years will pass without other islands being discovered, either under the equator on one side or the other of that line; just as the Moluccas and other islands described in my preceding works were discovered. For if it is a fact that the sun's rays, falling upon a favourable soil well disposed to receive the gifts of Heaven, impart their aromatic flavour to the trees in countries under the equator; and if, moreover, other neighbouring islands possess rich auriferous sands, who will venture to accuse bounteous nature of such forgetfulness as to affirm that in the small area occupied by the Moluccas (corresponding to the little finger of a giant when compared with the immensity of the whole globe) she has exhausted her forces, and that from her womb she could only put forth so small a child? I will explain the reasons I have myself evolved and presented to my colleagues of the India Council, and I have enclosed a copy to make my meaning clear. It seems to me that I have already submitted these reasons to Pope Adrian, but I do not remember clearly, for I am nearly seventy years old, and my memory has been dulled with age and cares; moreover, the repetition of these arguments does not usually displease, although they may already have been seen elsewhere, and in a measure outside their proper connection.

During ten years, I enjoyed Roman life under the

pontificates of Sixtus IV. and Innocent VIII., either in the city or in its environs. When news came of the wars against the Moors of Granada I betook myself to Spain, and upon leaving Rome I travelled through the rest of Italy, passing through the part of France lying south of the Alps and bathed by our sea. During the thirty-seven years I have lived in Spain, where the flattering promises and honourable reception and intimacy of Ferdinand and Isabella have kept me, I have travelled throughout the entire country. You may ask, Most Illustrious Prince, what good purpose these oratorical preliminaries thus dragged in are supposed to serve? In travelling throughout Spain I found in some places oak forests, in others pine forests, separated by mountains or by plains, by rivers or by swamps. After which I beheld vast tracts occupied with other kinds of trees, growing wild, and I finally observed forests of oaks and pines resembling the former; rivers, lakes and plains similar to the first mentioned. The character of the soil was alone responsible for this variety.

In the same way, Most Illustrious Prince, both on this and the other side of the equator, from the Tropic of Cancer to that of the Capricorn (that is to say, within the space which the majority of philosophers have wrongly considered to be consumed by the sun's rays, falling directly upon it, and therefore deserted) extend vast stretches of land and of sea; in fact, the greater part of the terrestrial sphere, embracing in its greatest length the entire universe, lies there. This equatorial circle is the largest of all terrestrial circles. Consequently, if within the small extent of land I have mentioned, the productive action of nature is such that within a small portion of the same region, and in another enjoying the same climate, the same products are found, who will doubt that in the case of spices, heavenly power has enabled other islands besides the Moluccas and neighbouring islands to grow

the same spices—for example, countries situated under
the equator and those which extend directly to the north
or to the south of that equatorial line?

One of my colleagues in the council shrugged his
shoulders. He wished to appear more wise by refuting
my arguments, saying: "If they exist, as you say,
either we or some other nation would know them." This
objection, proceeding from ignorance of the ancients,
especially of philosophy, and which only rests upon
defective experience, I have easily refuted, earning the
approbation of the Grand Chancellor who is such a devoted
friend of Your Excellency, and of my other associates.
I answered: "We need not be astonished that the
Moluccas and neighbouring islands are known, while
other countries are not. The Moluccas form in some wise
part of trans-Gangetic India, and may be compared to
suburbs of China, of the great Gulf of Cattigara, and other
well-known countries. They are not very distant from
the Persian Gulf and Arabia, mistakenly called Arabia
Felix. Little by little these foreigners have known them,
and from the date of Rome's luxury they have, so to say,
glided into our ken, not without serious consequences to
us; for characters soften, men become effeminate, virtue
weakens, and people are seduced by these voluptuous
odours, perfumes, and spices. As for the other unknown
islands, the reasons why they have not been heretofore
discovered may be easily demonstrated. They are
neighbours of these continents, which by the design of
Divine Providence have remained hidden until our epoch."
Reflecting thus that if these lands are like palaces of the
universe, is it astonishing that as long as the palaces
were undiscovered, these neighbouring islands corresponding to the courts and ante-chambers should have
remained unexplored? For we have only found the
palaces by discovering these immensities of space, so vast
that they exceed three times the extent of Europe. And

we only reckon from the extremity of the continent discovered in our times, and called Cape San Augustin, as far as the Panuco River, situated about sixty leagues distant from the great lake city of Temistitan. I have more fully demonstrated this. We may rest assured, therefore, that the other parts of the palace will be discovered.

Perhaps we are not far from the realisation of our desires. In fact, we hope that Sebastian Cabot, the discoverer of the country of Baccalaos, will return more quickly and under better auspices than the *Victory*, the only one out of five vessels to return to Spain with a cargo of cloves, after encircling the world. About the calends of September the India Council, in response to his solicitation authorised him to undertake the voyage of exploration. I have told this story in its proper place. Cabot had asked from the imperial treasury the equipment of a fleet of four ships, completely furnished and provided with cannon. He said he had found partners at Hispalis, —otherwise called Seville,—a great port whence ships sail for India. Animated by the hope of large profits, his partners had themselves proposed to furnish him with the sum of ten thousand ducats for the expenses of the fleet; and at the ides of September we sent Cabot back so that he might settle his business with these men, each of whom will have a proportionate part of the profit if, as it is hoped, the undertaking succeeds.

It remains for me, Most Illustrious Prince, to show by some reasonable arguments why I am right in saying that Cabot should come back more quickly than did the *Victory*, and why we believe that the expedition will be fortunate; otherwise you may accuse me of presumption for indulging in prophecy. Cabot should start next August, in 1525. His departure will not take place sooner, because he cannot provide what is required for such a great undertaking before that date, nor would the

season be propitious for sailing before that epoch. For
he must go towards the equator when our summer draws
to its close and the days diminish in length. He must,
in fact, not only cross the Tropic of Cancer and the equator,
but he must follow a direct line across the Tropic of
Capricorn to the fifty-fourth degree towards the antarctic
pole, where the Strait of Magellan opens. The opening of
this route cost dear, and caused the deaths of many people.
Cabot will not have to creep from coast to coast, nor
stop, nor double back on his track, as Magellan had to do,
who for three years endured cruel fatigues and bitter
calamities during his voyage. He lost four out of five
ships of his squadron and most of his companions, and
he himself perished. I have dilated on this point in the
description of the voyage around the world, which I
dedicated to Pope Adrian. Cabot will, therefore, take
less time on his voyage, since the regions he will traverse
and which were so long unknown, are now very well known.

I must, however, sum up the arguments which enable me
to hope that Cabot will start under better auspices and
end more happily. At the period when northern peoples
have the shortest days, Cabot will have the longest.
He will thus easily follow the coasts until after passing
the tortuous Strait of Magellan, near the constellation
of Argo. He will guide the prows of his ships to the right
behind the new continent, of which I have spoken so
fully in my first Decades addressed to your uncle, Ascanio,
and to the Popes Leo and Adrian. He will again cross
the Tropic of Capricorn and return to the equator. In
the course of this voyage he will discover numberless
islands scattered through the immensity of the ocean.

Learn now why we hope that Cabot will collect great
wealth. After losing many men, Magellan's vessels
sailed through the strait they sought, and passed by all
the islands they discovered right and left as well as those
they beheld in the distance, without stopping. Their one

desire was to reach the Moluccas towards which they continued their course. All other islands were passed by in their hurried voyage, although they landed on a number to take provisions of wood and water and to trade for necessaries of life; their stop was never long.

Magellan, nevertheless, profited as best he could by these stops to inform himself by means of signs and gestures concerning the products of each island he touched, and he thus learned that in many places the sands were mixed with gold. In others, valuable cinnamon-trees, resembling pomegranates, were pointed out to him. Fragments of this precious bark have been presented to me, as Maino and Gillino will witness. He also obtained considerable information concerning the large pearls and other precious stones. He intended to revisit and examine these islands another time; for the moment he thought only of the Moluccas. And while he revolved great thoughts in his mind, a cruel destiny made him the victim of nude and barbarous people. I have related this story in its proper place. If, therefore, during this rapid voyage never before accomplished by man, such valuable information was collected concerning the excellence of these islands, what may not be expected from the trading relations which will be gradually opened with the islanders? It is necessary to proceed gently, without violence, or the least outrage, and these peoples will yield to kindness and gifts.

The ten thousand ducats Cabot's partners must furnish him for this enterprise will be spent, first in furnishing him with supplies for two years, next for paying the wages of one hundred and fifty men of the crew, and the remainder for purchasing such merchandise as is known to please the islanders. They will willingly exchange their natural products, of which they think little, for our merchandise, which they do not know; in fact they do not use money,—the cause of so many

misfortunes,—and every nation regards as precious those
articles which are foreign to it. When these islands shall
have been visited and carefully examined, Cabot will
follow the south coast of the new continent, landing at
the new colonies of Panama and Nata, stations established
at the extremity of Castilla del Oro. Whoever may
be governor then will notify us of the success of the
enterprise.

The advisability of replacing most of the governors
is just now under consideration, especially those who have
not conquered the provinces they administer; for it is
feared that long enjoyment of power may make them
insolent. Different treatment is accorded to the governors
who have conquered the countries where they rule.

As soon as we learn of his fleet's departure, we will
pray God that Cabot may succeed and bring his undertaking to a happy termination. [1]

[1] Consult the work of Henry Harrisse on the Cabots.

BOOK VII

B EFORE Cabot sails, another fleet is to go to the Moluccas, to confirm Spain's ownership of the islands. The alliance of the King of Portugal will not prove useless in this connection. The Emperor has given him his posthumous sister, the Princess Katherine, seventeen years old, and the most beautiful and intelligent of young girls, to wife.[1] A report was falsely spread that the Emperor had agreed to make over to the King of Portugal as a dower, such an extensive and rich domain, and nevertheless the King complains of not being able to trade further with the Moluccas,[2] as though this were disastrous and fatal to his little kingdom, formerly simply an earldom dependent on Castile. But the Emperor, who is very astute, judges it necessary to protect his Castilian provinces from such injury, for they are the very sinews of all his power. I have said enough about the Lucayas, Chicora, and Duhare, the tropics, the equinox, and other similar things.

Let us go on to other and more interesting particulars reported to me by Gillino. I shall first speak of a very extraordinary phenomenon, and in this connection I shall first repeat what is related, afterwards the opinion of

[1] John IV. of Portugal married on February 5, 1525, the Infanta Doña Catarina, daughter of Philip the Fair and Doña Juana, later to become known as Juana la loca.

[2] Charles V. relinquished his claims to the Portuguese in 1529 in exchange for a sum of 350,000 ducats. Consult Argensola's *Conquista de las islas Molucas* (1609) also Forrest's *Voyage aux Moluques*, 1780.

the philosophers, and finally my own modest opinion. I treat whatever is difficult to understand in this wise.

In my first Decades, which have been printed and circulated, I have spoken of a fountain whose waters possess such an extraordinary hidden virtue that when old men bathe therein and drink thereof, they regain their youth. Following the example of Aristotle and our Pliny, I take upon myself to note down and record in my books what men of serious reputation have not feared to advance. Aristotle in his Natural History describes, in fact, not only the animals he has seen, but those mentioned to him by Alexander the Great, who sought them for him at great expense. In the same way Pliny amassed twenty-two thousand notes upon noteworthy facts, taking them from the verbal reports and the writings of other persons. As for myself, those whose testimony I cite in my work are the dean, whom I have mentioned, the jurisconsult, Ayllon, and the licenciate, Figueroa, sent to Hispaniola to preside over the council, examine the accounts, take the residence of the judges, recall the disorderly to right living, encourage those who behave well, recompense the good, and punish the wicked. These three, without mentioning absent ones whose letters I quote, and men who report verbally to me on their arrival or departure, agree. They have heard the fortifying virtues of this spring mentioned, and believed the reports made to them, but they have neither seen it nor tested its properties, for the natives of Florida have sharp nails and are energetic defenders of their rights. They do not wish to receive any guests, especially those who intend to suppress their liberty and occupy their native country. The Spaniards, arriving there in vessels from Hispaniola, or more directly from Cuba, have several times sought to conquer them and occupy their territory, but every time they have penetrated inland, they have been repulsed, beaten, and massacred by the natives who, although naked, fight with different kinds of weapons and poisoned arrows.

The dean has furnished me with proofs of what I say. He has a Lucayan servant, called Andreas, surnamed "The Bearded," because he was the only one of his people who had a beard. This servant says that when his father was broken by age, he left his native island near Florida, attracted by the report of the power of that spring and the hope of prolonging his life. He took the necessary provisions for the journey, just as do the Romans and Neapolitans when they go to the baths of Pozzuoli, hoping to regain their health. He set out for the desired spring, where he made a stay of some time, drinking, and following the treatment indicated by the bathers. He returned home strengthened and with his manhood renewed, for he married again and had sons. As a proof of this cure, Andreas summoned several of his compatriots, who affirmed that they knew this man, almost exhausted by age and decrepitude, and afterwards regenerated, strong, and robust.

I know that all the philosophers and doctors are sceptical of things like this. They think it impossible, when one has been ill, to regain his former strength; likewise any one who only believes what is well proven and established, should only ask them the reason of many things they sustain. Amongst other assertions and arguments of the philosophers and ancient sages, is it possible that nature—leaving aside of course all question of miracles—should possess the necessary force to make us younger? We need give no attention to Medea's doctoring of her father-in-law Æson, nor need we think of the charms of Circe, who changed the companions of Ulysses into beasts, and then restored them to their former shape; let us only consider the examples with which animals furnish us, and we may prove in regard to this extraordinary phenomenon—held by many to be

impossible—that equally trustworthy personages have
not spoken idly. What shall we say of the eagle, which
begins its life anew, or the snake which sheds its old skin,
leaving it in the brushwood or amongst the cracks and
crevices of the rocks, and recovers its second youth?
What of the deer, which after sucking in an aspic through
its nostrils, hides itself during bad weather inside enclosing
walls or hedges, remaining invisible until the force of the
poison has made his flesh as soft as if it had been cooked?
He then entirely changes his skin, and renews his flesh
and blood; at least, so history tells us. What shall we say
of ravens and crows, which stop drinking at the time of
the solstice, during the time of the dog-star, when nature
teaches them that at that time the waters of springs and
rivers issue from a polluted earth and are unwholesome?
There are other phenomena just as extraordinary, concerning which reputable writers have transmitted numerous legends to posterity. If, therefore, all these things
are true; if Nature, that astonishing creatrix, graciously
shows herself so munificent and powerful towards the
dumb animals, who know nothing of her superiority
and repay her with no gratitude, how should it be astonishing for her to create and nourish in her bounteous
breast similar phenomena in a superior order? We
observe that different effects are produced by the waters
flowing through the various regions of the earth, absorbing
tastes, colours, odours, and qualities, and even different
bulk; we likewise know that the roots of trees, their leaves,
flowers, and fruits cure different maladies.

But enough of digressions on this subject. Let each
one take or leave what he pleases, for I have composed
my writings as best I could, placing them under the
patronage of Your Excellency's name and they will soon
leave for Rome, where they are desired by high personages.
I should still like to mention other phenomena which are
not impossible of belief, though sufficiently extraordinary,

and which are hidden from Europeans and the inhabitants
of the known world. In the island of Fernandina or
Cuba there is a spring of pitch. We have seen a specimen
of this pitch, which was sent to the Emperor. It is
softer than the pitch produced by trees, but is serviceable for careening ships and other ordinary uses. The
strangeness of this fact caused me to hesitate somewhat,
but I cease to marvel because I find in another order the
proof of this phenomenon. Without speaking of the
salt found in the mountains, the mines, and the sea, do
we not see the same thing happening in all the kingdoms
of Castile where water flowing down the mountains is
caught in channels where the sun heats it, converting it
into thick salt? Who will be astonished, therefore, if
by the same design of nature the water of this spring,
being carried into little ditches or receptacles or spread
out on the plain, condenses and solidifies into pitch under
the action of the devouring sun?

There is another phenomenon I have passed over. In
the same island of Fernandina there is a mountain producing round stones, but so symmetrical that no workman
could make more regular ones. These stone balls are as
heavy as metal bullets and may be used by princes in
their battles. The licenciate Figueroa (whom I have
mentioned as a magistrate charged to ask the officials
of Hispaniola for an account of their administration)
has brought back several of these balls and presented
them to the Emperor. We have now examined them.
It is positive that projectiles serviceable for muskets,
as well as for cannon and culverins, come out of this
mountain. I use vulgar words, for no suitable expression
can be found in the ancient Latin, and it is permissible
to clothe new facts in new words. I trust those who do
not share this opinion will pardon me. The stone balls
brought back by Figueroa, which we have seen, are not
smaller than a nut, nor larger than a tennis-ball. Small

or large, both are natural creations. Wishing to learn if this stone substance was mixed with any metal, we have had one of these balls broken by a smith. Such is its quality of resistance that the hammer and anvil were almost shattered before the ball was cut into pieces. Some metal veins were found, but the quality of this metal is not yet discovered. These balls are preserved in the Emperor's treasury.

A number of sufficiently curious facts are before my mind, which I believe Your Excellency, as well as those of your courtiers who love reading, especially those who are idle, will be pleased to know.

BOOK VIII

IN my first Decades I spoke of a vast maritime cavern in the province of Guaccaiarima in Hispaniola, which extends a distance of several stadia into the heart of the lofty mountains along the west coast. The interior of this cavern is navigable. In its gloomy depths, where the sun's rays hardly penetrate save for a moment at sunset, is heard such a roaring from a waterfall that those who enter shiver with horror. The following is the ancient tradition believed by the islanders concerning this cavern, and the story is a pleasing one. They ascribe life to the island, believing that it breathes, eats, and digests. They compare it to a monstrous female beast. This cavern corresponds to the sex organs of the woman, and at the same time to the anal canal, through which she discharges her excrement and impurities. This is proven by the name the region takes from this cavern; *guacca* means region or neighbourhood, and *tarima* means behind, or a place where filth accumulates. Upon hearing this I recollected the story of the fabulous Demogorgon, breathing in the bowels of the earth and, according to the ancient belief, producing the ebb and flow of the sea. It is just as well, however, to mix a little truth with these legends.

I have often related in my first Decades, addressed to Ascanio and to the Popes Leo and Adrian, that Hispaniola abounded in all kinds of products and precious materials. Every day an increasing number of medicinal

substances is found. I have already sufficiently described
the tree whose branches, when cut in pieces and powdered,
serve to compound a drink which, taken hot, expels from
the bones and marrow the sad malady *bubas*. Pieces
of this wood have already been distributed throughout
Europe, and will serve to prove its efficacy. Numerous
other aromatic spices also grow in Hispaniola. They
are obtained both from plants and trees, and amongst
many gums may be noted that called by pharmacists
animæ album, a sovereign remedy against headache.
Certain other trees exude a kind of oily liquor, and a
learned Italian called Codrus, who obtained permission to
visit this country to study the secrets of nature (for no
stranger is allowed to go there), has persuaded the Spaniards that this liquor has the properties of balm. Let
us now consider the hunting fish.

This fish formerly vexed me somewhat. In my first
Decades,[1] addressed to Cardinal Ascanio, I stated amongst
other marvels, if I remember properly, that the natives
had a fish which was trained to hunt other fish just as we
use quadrupeds for hunting other quadrupeds, or birds
for hunting other birds. So are the natives accustomed
to catch fish by means of other fish. Many people, given
to detraction, ridiculed me at Rome in the time of Pope
Leo for citing this and other facts. It was only when
Giovanni Rufo di Forli, Archbishop of Cosenza, who was
informed of all I wrote, returned to Rome after fourteen
years' absence as legate of Popes Julius and Leo in Spain,
stopped the mouths of many mockers, and restored me my
reputation for veracity. In the beginning I also could
hardly believe the story, but I received my information
from trustworthy men whom I have elsewhere cited, and
later from many others.

Everybody has assured me that they have seen fishermen use this fish just as commonly as we chase hares

[1] In the third book of the First Decade.

with French dogs, or pursue the wild deer with Molossians. They say that this fish makes good eating. It is shaped like an eel, and is no larger. It attacks fish larger than itself, or turtles larger than a shield; it resembles a weasel seizing a pigeon or still larger animal by its throat, and never leaving go until it is dead. Fishermen tie this fish to the side of their barque, holding it with a slender cord. The fish lies at the bottom of the barque, for it must not be exposed to the bright sun, from which it shrinks.

The most extraordinary thing is that it has at the back of its head a sort of very tough pocket. As soon as the fisherman sees any fish swimming near the barque, he gives the signal for attack and lets go the little cord. Like a dog freed from its leash, the fish descends on its prey and, turning its head, throws the skin pouch over the neck of the victim, if it is a large fish. On the contrary, if it is a turtle, the fish attaches itself to the place where the turtle protrudes from its shell, and never lets go till the fisherman pulls it with the little cord to the side of the barque. If a large fish has been caught (and the fishermen do not trouble about the small ones), the fishermen fasten stout cords to it and pull it into the air, and at that moment the hunting-fish lets go of its prey. If, on the contrary, a turtle has been caught, the fishermen spring into the sea and raise the animal on their shoulders to within reach of their companions. When the prey is in the barque, the hunting-fish returns to its place and never moves, save when they give it a piece of the animal, just as one gives a bit of a quail to a falcon; or until they turn it loose after another fish. I have elsewhere spoken at length concerning the method of training it. The Spaniards call this fish *reverso*, meaning one who turns round, because it is when turning that it attacks and seizes the prey with its pocket-shaped skin.

Information concerning the island of Matanino, which I have said was inhabited by women resembling Amazons,

but concerning which I only repeated what was told me,
is still doubtful. Alfonzo Argoglio, secretary to the
Emperor in Castile, and intendant to the most illustrious
Margaret, the Emperor's aunt,[1] has visited these countries
and affirms that the story is authentic. The aforesaid
Dean has brought back various other particulars, which
it is well to know, and which have since been frequently
confirmed.

About seven hundred miles distant from Hispaniola,
and near to the continent, there lies an island called La
Margarita (The Pearl), because a great quantity of pearl
oysters have been found there. On the continent,
opposite, about thirty miles from Margarita, a gulf in
the form of a bow opens; it resembles a crescent of the
moon or a mule's shoe. The Spaniards call gulfs of this
form *anchons*. This gulf is about thirty miles around.
It is distinguished by two peculiarities, the first being
that all its shores washed by the tide or storms are covered
with a layer of salt; the tides are not very strong all
along the northern coasts of this province, but this does
not apply to those facing the south.

The second peculiarity is the immense quantity of
fish, pollards, and mullets, assembled in the water
in such masses that they impede the free passage
of ships in the gulf; and fishermen who fall in with
one of these schools are delayed. When the men cast
their nets they only have to push the school towards
the shore. They then divide into three groups; some,
springing into the sea knee-deep near the coast, catch
the fish in their hands and pass them to the others
in the barques. The latter gut the fish and pass them to

---

[1] Margaret of Austria, daughter of the Emperor Maximilian and Mary
of Burgundy, was Governor of the Low Countries and directed the education of the young prince Charles after the death of his father, Philip the
Fair. She was born in Brussels in 1480 and died at Malines on December
1, 1530.

the third group, who salt them with salt collected on the shore and prepared beforehand. They are then exposed to the sun or the sandy beach, and left there only one day, for the sun's rays are of great intensity, not only because the equator is not distant and the shore is surrounded with mountains which reflect the heat in all directions, but also because the sun strikes the sand and heats it more deeply than it would a rich and fertile soil.

When the fish are dried, they are loaded on board the ships and again covered with salt. Everybody may take as many fish and as much salt as he pleases. The natives supply an abundance of this sort of fish to all the neighbouring country, and even in Hispaniola, which is a nursing mother to the whole country, no other kind of fish are eaten. I have already described at length in my first Decades how pearls are born and grow, and the method of obtaining them.

Trustworthy men, who frequently visit me to discuss such business as they have to settle with our council, further relate that there exist in Hispaniola and its capital, Concepcion, two little streams both of which are fordable, save when swollen by unusual rains. One of these streams is called Bahi and the other Zate, such being the ancient local names. Because of their properties, of which I am going to speak, the stream formed by their union is called by the Spaniards, the River of Convalescence. Owing to the vast extent of sea to cross between the strait of Cadiz and the coast of Hispaniola,—in all a little less than five thousand miles,—during which nothing but sky and water are visible, the change of food, drink, and especially of air, usually produces different maladies amongst the new arrivals.

Hispaniola and Jamaica are, in fact, situated several degrees on the other side of the Tropic of Cancer, towards the equator. Cuba is actually on the line of the tropic, that is to say, they are all countries which philosophers, with few exceptions, have judged to be uninhabitable because of the sun's heat.

The sick who bathe in and drink the waters of the united streams, Bahi and Zate, are cured of their malady within fifteen days, whether they suffer from nervous or spinal troubles, consuming fevers, or inflammation of the lungs. But if the treatment is prolonged, they contract dysentery. Gold-seekers in the sands of these rivers (for in all the streams and every corner of the earth gold is found) do not venture to work their labourers in the afternoons, nor do they allow them to use these waters for bathing or drinking, although they are fresh and good, because they easily bring on dysentery among healthy people.

The same travellers relate that in the northern extremity of Guaccaiarima in Hispaniola, many little islands lie along the coast, which are believed formerly to have constituted one sole island. One of these isles, called Iabbaque, is remarkable for its fisheries. The penultimate syllable of this word is pronounced long. The channels between these islands are not deep, but from time to time deep places like vast abysses are visible. Such pools are filled, all the year round, with all kinds of fish, collected there as though in ponds. Just as the owner of a loft filled with grain may help himself, so anybody may easily fill his vessel with these fish.

Let me quote some amusing details concerning certain sea-birds larger than eagles or vultures. According to the descriptions given me, they appear to me to be pelicans. These birds have such enormous mouths that a soldier, who used his military cloak to protect himself against one that attacked him, saw the entire cloak disappear into the creature's throat, and when the bird was afterwards killed, he got it back intact; his companions witnessed this incident. This bird can swallow a five-pound fish or even a larger one at one gulp. It swims about seeking fish which it catches in the following manner. In the first place it does not dive as other sea-birds, such as geese, ducks, and divers do, but rises high into the air like birds of prey circling about and waiting until a fish, attracted by the noise, rises to the surface. Great flocks of these birds may be seen hovering about, and from time to time they drop with such force on their prey that they dive half an arm's length under the water. The fish, astonished by the noise of the wings, do not move, and so let themselves be caught.

It sometimes happens that two birds seize upon a fish. Nothing is more entertaining than to watch, either from on board ship or from the shore, the battle that follows between them, for neither bird relinquishes the prey which is finally torn in pieces, each one carrying off his share. Their beaks are half a palm long, and are more curved than those of any other birds of prey. They are, indeed, longer, and their wings more spreading than those of eagles or vultures. On the other hand, their bodies are so lean that they are scarcely larger than pigeons. Provident nature has given them strong wings to sustain the weight of their enormous beak, for they do not require them for such a meagre body. The Spaniards call these birds alcatraz.[1]

Many other birds, unknown to us, are found in this country. Most remarkable for the variety of their plumage and their forms are the parrots; some are as large or even larger than our cocks, while others are scarcely the size of a sparrow. Flocks of parrots are as numerous as are flocks of ravens, crows, or jays in Europe. The natives use them for food, just as we do pigeons and blackbirds, rearing them about their houses for their entertainment, for they take the place of our linnets and magpies. There is another of nature's gifts which I must not omit to mention.

[1] The *alcatraz* is a pelican, but the description would rather seem to fit the albatross.

BOOK IX

HISPANIOLA has a wealth of harbours, in one of which the colony of Savana has been founded, thus named because it stands in a *savana*, that is to say, in a swampy plain overgrown with grass very suitable for rearing cattle and horses; such is the name given in Spain to a place of this kind. The new colony is rightly proud of a stream which flows through it and which is so swollen by rains at certain seasons of the year, that the entire plain, although large, is covered; and were it not for the hills, which arrest them, the waters would flow uninterruptedly to the harbour. During the period of inundation, such an enormous quantity of eels is washed in, that when the waters subside, the eels, caught by stumps and thick reeds, growing in the swamp, remain scattered over the ground. As soon as the news spreads, such sailors as are on friendly terms with their neighbours load their ships with these fish; but if the eel-hunters do not appear after the flood, or come too soon and are obliged to leave again, the islanders, fearing that the mass of these eels may rot and corrupt the atmosphere, turn droves of pigs loose on the plain, and thus furnish them with ample provender.

The number of pigs in this island is considerable. They all descend from some which were brought here. By a dispensation of nature, all these quadrupeds have one and sometimes two litters in the year. Mares and cows have one colt or calf, and sometimes two, when ten months old; and I am assured that they live longer than in our climate. I cite a convincing example. Twenty-six years ago, the same Dean, whose testimony I have often invoked, took with him to Hispaniola a live cow, which calved each year, according to the report of neighbours. The Dean, who at this moment is in my house, boasts that thanks to that one cow and its descendants, he has formed a herd of more than eight hundred head of cattle. The same is told concerning birds. Hardly are they out of their nests and got their feathers than they begin to breed.

Our dean also deserves praise because, amongst the colonists of Concepcion, the city of his deanery, he was the first to cultivate cinnamon. From that time forth these trees, which are as large as the mulberry, have propagated with such rapidity in Hispaniola, Cuba, and Jamaica (the last being the island where the Emperor recently conferred upon me a rich benefice with the title of Abbot) that a pound of cinnamon will not cost more a few years hence than the apothecaries now ask for an ounce. Unfortunately there is nothing pleasant in human things without some bitterness; attracted by the sweet odour of these trees the ants attack them in such swarms that they consume everything sweet in their neighbourhood, and do great injury to the inhabitants. The stems of the cinnamon-trees are so long that they look like sword-scabbards. A curious thing is told in this connection: when the winds blow, and especially when the cinnamon is ripening, the canes strike against one another with such a noise that it sounds like a flock of thousands of geese and ducks fighting. According to the quality of the sap, whether still bitter or ripe, and according to the weight and grain of the pith in the canes, the sounds vary and are sweet to hear.

I must again speak at length concerning a tree which I would rather call a stalk, since it is not hard, but filled

with marrow, like an artichoke; and yet it nevertheless
grows to the height of a laurel-tree. I have already mentioned it briefly in my First Decade. The possessors of
such trees say they are plane-trees although they are
different in every respect.[1] In fact they bear no resemblance to plane-trees, for the latter is a strong tree with
broad branches, more leafy than other trees, lofty,
straight, and strong; probably Your Excellency has
already heard this. The tree I mention is deficient in
resistive quality. It bears fruits but few leaves, and is
frail, drooping, and with only one stalk and no branches.
It has few leaves which, at the top, are half an arm's length
and two spans in breadth, and at the bottom, quite similar
to the long pointed leaves of canes. When touched by
the cold of winter, these trees droop their heads, as
though by their own weight. Their life is so exuberant
that they wither and die after nine or ten months. They
grow rapidly, and when they are mature some bunches
are put forth from the stock which contain about thirty
fruits, and sometimes more. In the islands these fruits
attain the size of our garden cucumbers and on the continent they are still larger. When they are unripe, their
colour is green, and when they ripen, they become white.
The pulp is as soft as fresh butter, quite recalling the same
taste. At first it is not agreeable to eat, but becomes so
if habitually eaten. The Egyptians commonly say this
was the apple eaten by Adam, the first created of our race,
by which he caused the perdition of mankind.

The merchants who visit those countries for the profit
of dealing in effeminating spices, useless essences, perfumes
of Araby, and unnecessary jewels, call these fruits *musa*.
For my own part, I do not know what Latin name to
give to these trees and vegetables. I have consulted
several Latin authors, and have applied to those of our

[1] Plantains or bananas are meant. The description which follows is
extremely faulty.

contemporaries who are reputed to have the best knowledge of that language, but none of them has satisfied me. Pliny, indeed, mentions a certain fruit called *mixa;* a learned man has told me I should call this fruit mixa because there is only a slight difference between mixa and musa; but I do not share his point of view, since Pliny affirms that they made wine of mixa, whereas that would be impossible with musa. I have seen many of these fruits and have even eaten some of them at Alexandria, when on my mission to the Sultan in the name of our masters Ferdinand and Isabella. I am therefore far from believing that wine could be made from them.

I must now explain from what country this plant migrated, so to speak, to the region occupied by the Spanish colonists, and what are its drawbacks. It was originally brought from a part of Ethiopia called Guinea, where it grows wild, as in its native country. When planted, it develops so rapidly that people generally regret having cultivated it on their property. As soon as it is sown anywhere, it vitiates the soil for any other product, contrary to the lupins, which fertilise the earth by their growth. Spreading more rapidly than mountain ferns, it grows and thrusts out its roots, so that the field where it once takes root can never be freed from it, either by the plough or by the hoe. Each minute little root, as small as a hair which hides itself in the sod, perpetually thrusts forth a large number of shoots, that draw such nourishment from the mother stem that they exhaust all its strength, and quickly kill it. Moreover, the same thing happens to the sprouts themselves, which die as soon as they have produced their fruit; as though punished for their unkindness to their mother. This plant is moreover so fragile, that, although it is as thick as a man's thigh and as tall as a laurel-tree, the blow of a sword or stick breaks it to the ground, as though it were an artichoke.

In the territory of an aged sovereign in Hispaniola, called Moccorix, whose name the country bears, is found another tree, the size of a large mulberry, and which bears cotton on the ends of its branches. This cotton is just as useful as that obtained from plants sown every year. Another tree produces wool as in China, suitable for spinning and weaving, though it is not commonly employed, because sheep's wool is much superior. Moreover, until now, experienced weavers have been wanting, and industries will only gradually develop as the population increases.

I must not forget to recall how nature furnishes the natives of this region with cords and cables ready-made. There is a certain herb resembling verbena, that grows quickly round the roots of almost all the trees. It is called *bexuco*. Like the sweet pea it clambers more tightly than ivy round the trunk of the supporting tree, reaching the highest branches, and then falling down and spreading itself over the smaller ones, which it covers like a mantle or a parasol protecting them against the heat. To bind fagots, however large they be, to sustain heavy burdens or to fasten the beams and planks of a house, this bexuco is excellent. Whatever is tied together with bexuco is more solid than what is fastened by iron nails, and when the houses there are shaken by violent tempests, the bexuco bends but never breaks.

The natives call these furious winds, which formerly tore up great trees by the roots and destroyed houses, hurricanes. Houses joined together with nails fell to the ground, the nails being torn out; those fastened together with bexuco were shaken, but the knots held firm and they preserved their original stability. Hispaniola was formerly ravaged with these storms, which were called typhoons, when they believed infernal demons were seen to appear. This terrible curse, it appears, ceased since the sacrifice of the Eucharist has spread in the island; and the demons, which formerly loved to show themselves to the ancient inhabitants, have no longer been seen. For this reason the islanders make the zemes,—that is to say, idols,—they worship, of wood and cotton so tightly stuffed that they acquire the hardness of stone. They resemble the goblins our painters draw upon walls to frighten men and convert them from sin. Columbus, the first discoverer of the mysteries of the ocean, brought back a number of zemes, and I sent two of them, together with numerous other objects, to your uncle, the Cardinal Ascanio, in the days of his brilliant fortune. Any quantity of bexuco desired may be had, for any work; for it may be termed a rope without end. Enough has been said about bexuco.

Let us now consider another of nature's marvels. In Hispaniola and the other islands of the ocean, there are swampy districts well adapted for cattle raising. The colonies in the neighbourhood of these swampy places are infested by all kinds of gnats, produced by the damp heat; and these insects do not attack people only at night, as in other countries. This is the reason why the natives do not build lofty houses, and make their entrance doors only wide enough to barely admit a man, and without any windows at all. For the same reason they do without torches, for the gnats instinctively follow the light; nevertheless the insects get into the houses. While Nature has bestowed this pest on the islanders, she has at the same time supplied a remedy, just as we have the cat to rid us of the filthy nuisance of rats. The gnat chasers, which likewise serve other purposes, are called *cucurios* and are winged worms, inoffensive, a little smaller than butterflies, and resembling rather a scarabæus, since their wings are protected by a tough outer covering, into which they are drawn when the insect stops flying. These insects, like the fireflies we see shining at night or certain luminous worms found in hedgerows have been supplied by provident nature with four luminous points, two of which occupy the place of the eyes, and the other two are hidden inside the body under the shell,

and are only visible when they put out their little wings
like the scarabs, and begin to fly. Each cucurio thus
carries four lanterns, and it is pleasing to learn how people
protect themselves against the pestiferous gnats, which
sting every one and in some places are a trifle smaller
than bees.

As soon as one knows that these dangerous gnats have
invaded his house, or wishes to prevent them doing so,
cucurios are immediately procured by the following artifice; necessity, the mother of invention, has taught this
method. To catch cucurios one must go out at nightfall,
carrying a burning coal, mount upon a neighbouring hut
in sight of the cucurios, and then call in a loud voice,
" cucurios, cucurios!"

Simple people imagine that the cucurios are charmed
by this noise and answer the call. As a matter of fact
they quickly appear in masses. We believe they are
attracted by the light, as clouds of gnats also rush towards
it, just as the martins and swallows do, only to be devoured
by the cucurios. When a sufficient number of cucurios
have assembled, the hunter throws down the coal, and
the cucurios, following the direction of the fire, fall to
the earth, where it is as easy to catch them as for the
traveller to catch a scarabæus creeping along with its
wings under its shell. It is also alleged that curcurios
are not caught at all in this manner, but rather by knocking them to the ground with branches or broad strips of
linen, when they are flying; they lie there stupefied and
are caught. It is also said they are caught as birds are,
by throwing the linen cloth or the branches of leaves
over them. However this may be, as soon as the hunter
has got his supply of these cucurios, he takes them
home, and closely shutting his house, he lets them loose.
The cucurio immediately flies about the room seeking
the gnats. He acts as though he mounted guard over
the hammocks and the faces of the sleepers, which the

gnats attack, assuming the duty of ensuring them a night's rest.

This is not the only service the cucurio renders. Another sufficiently curious one is the following: each eye of this insect is a lamp for the benefit of its owner; and by the light emitted by these cucurios one can sew, spin, and even dance. May it not be imagined that the cucurios, charmed by the songs of the singers and their movements in the dance, also follow in their flight the rhythmical movements? In chasing the gnats, the cucurios are obliged to execute turnings and returnings in their flight.

By the light shed by this insect, as long as his hunger is not satisfied, it is possible to read or write. When the cucurio's hunger is appeased by the gnats he has caught and swallowed, his light grows dim; and when the natives perceive this, they open the door and let the insect regain his liberty and search for food elsewhere. As a joke, and to scare people who are afraid of spectres, the facetious sometimes rub their faces with a dead cucurio, and show themselves, with flaming countenances, to their neighbours at night, asking them where they are going. Our own young people in like manner, when they wish to joke, put on a mask with gaping mouth well furnished with teeth, and seek to scare children or womanish-hearted people who are easily frightened. The face smeared with the cucurios looks like a bright flame; but this luminous property quickly grows dim and goes out.

There is another extraordinary advantage derived from the cucurio; the natives, whom the Spaniards send on errands, prefer to go at night; attaching two cucurios to their toes, they walk as easily as though they carried as many lanterns as the cucurios have lights. They also carry others in their hands, which help them to catch utias. These utias are a sort of rabbit, a little larger than a rat, and before the arrival of the Spaniards, the natives knew of no other and ate no other quadruped. They also fish by means of cucurios, this being a sport of which they are passionately fond and which they follow from their cradles.

Both sexes are just as accustomed to swim as to walk, which is not astonishing when we consider the women's customs in childbirth. When a woman feels the hour of her delivery to be near, she goes into a neighbouring wood and seizing the branches of a tree with both hands, gives birth without the aid of a midwife. Taking the new-born child she carries it to the neighbouring stream, where she washes both herself and the child, rubbing it and dipping it into the water without its crying or making any noise; after which she takes it home and nourishes it. During the following days she frequently washes herself and the child, and these habits prevail everywhere. It is also alleged that in other countries the women go to a stream when about to be delivered and allow the new-born babes to fall into the stream.

While writing these particulars relating to the interesting cucurios, I received the unexpected visit, a little before noon, of Camillo Gillino and the Emperor's chamberlain, Giacomo Canizares. The former is my habitual guest, not only because he is Your Excellency's minister but because of his character which I esteem. At the beginning of these events Canizares left in company with some of the young courtiers of Ferdinand and Isabella, desirous of seeing new things. He was one of those who followed Columbus on his second voyage to the New World, with a fleet of seventeen ships. I have described this voyage in my Decade dedicated to Ascanio. On one occasion at dinner, Canizares told me a number of stories in the presence of Gillino; speaking of cucurios, he assured me that having debarked once upon a cannibal island and being obliged to wait in a dark night on the beach, he was the first to discover one of these cucurios, which came out of a neighbouring wood and shed such a light over their heads that everybody could see and recognise his neighbour; and he declared under oath that the light was sufficient for reading A most trustworthy Sevillian, called Fernandez de las Varas, one of the first colonists of Hispaniola, and the first to build a house of stone from its foundations up, states that he has read Latin letters by the light of a cucurio.

I must not omit what the same Varas told me concerning certain small, thin scorpions, which are of a green colour and most dangerous. He says that when these beasts see a traveller passing, they run rapidly up the trees growing along the roads. Suspending themselves by their tails to the branches, they suddenly drop upon the voyager, springing at his face and seeking to strike his eyes. They appear to be attracted by the brilliancy of the eye. Few people now allow themselves to be surprised, for much experience has taught them to be careful when passing in the neighbourhood of suspicious-looking trees. The eminent Las Varas relates that he was once surprised by one of these snakes which sprang upon him and would have bitten him had he not profited by the lesson of his native guide and, by his left hand stopped the animal in its descent. The scorpion's sting is said to be very severe.

It appears that one must also believe what has been told concerning those islands inhabited only by women, armed with bows, who resist every attempt to land on their shores. At certain periods of the year cannibals cross over to these islands to have intercourse with them. As soon as they are with child they avoid men. They send their male children away, but keep the girls. I have already spoken of this in my first Decades, but half I said was not believed. I have above mentioned that the secretary, Alfonzo Argoglio, agreed in his report with Canizares. He communicated to me an interesting particular which I have omitted, because I was speaking at length about the religious ceremonies of the islanders. No horseman's steed reaches the goal in one leap nor does one breath of wind carry ships across the entire ocean.

BOOK X

IN the time of their power the caciques summoned
their subjects at stated periods, by means of messengers and heralds to the celebration of religious
festivals. Adorned in native fashion and painted in
divers colours with vegetable dyes, as were formerly the
Agathyrses, all the men, especially the young ones, assembled. The women were naked and unpainted, except
those who had lost their virginity, who wore a sort of
girdle hanging from their waists. Both sexes weighted
their arms, hips, calves, and heels with snail shells, in place
of bells, which produced a pleasant sound when they
struck against one another. Upon their heads they wore
garlands of flowers and grasses, but the rest of their bodies
was naked. Loaded with these shells they struck the
ground with their feet, dancing, leaping, respectfully
saluting the cacique who, seated at his door, received the
newcomers while beating on a drum with a stick

When the moment for sacrificing to the zemes arrived
(meaning the idols similar to the goblins people paint) it
was necessary in order to render themselves more agreeable
to the divinity, to be purified; and to accomplish this
they thrust a stick, which each carries on feast days,
down their throats to the epiglottis or even to the uvula,
vomiting and vigorously cleansing the body. After
that, they entered the cacique's house, where they seated
themselves, cross-legged like tailors, in a circle before the
royal idol, like in a theatre, or better still, in the turnings

of a labyrinth. With bent heads and trembling, fearful mien, they gazed towards the zemes, beseeching it to accept the approaching sacrifice. Then in a low voice each offered his prayer to the divinity. The bovites stood near the zemes. They were the priests and doctors and presented a different aspect from the others present.

While these ceremonies were being performed in the vestibule of the drumming cacique, the women were busy in another room preparing cakes to be offered in sacrifice. In response to a signal given by the bovites, the women entered in procession, chanting the hymns called arreytos, and carrying the cakes in artistically woven baskets. They wore garlands of different flowers, and upon entering, they marched round the group of seated men. The latter sprang to their feet and together with the women exalted in their arreytos the power of their zemes, commemorating in song the great deeds of their cacique's ancestors. They afterwards gave thanks to the zemes for favours received, beseeching it to hear their prayers; and bending the knee they offered their gifts to the divinity. The bovites received the cakes, blessed and divided them into as many pieces as there were people present. Each one took home his portion without breaking it, and kept it the entire year as a sacred thing. According to the opinion of the bovites, any house not possessing a piece of this cake would be unfortunate and exposed to all the dangers of thunderbolts and tempests.

Here is a sufficiently ridiculous thing you should know. The natives invoke miracles from this divinity cut in wood or stuffed in cotton, after having offered it their sacrifices. In the simple, ancient times so did people address Apollo. Deceived by some devil concealed in the idol or by the bovites, the natives imagine that the zemes answer, and they accept the interpretation of the answer given by the bovites, shouting with joy and dancing gaily, after which they return to their houses. They spend the remainder of the day in the open air, amusing themselves and singing. If, however, no voice was heard, they were convinced the zemes were vexed with them, and with bowed heads they sadly departed interpreting this silence as indicative of great misfortunes. They expected maladies and other catastrophes, or, if war was imminent, they looked forward to certain defeat. Both men and women left their hair undressed, sighed, wept, stripped themselves of their ornaments, fasted and endured privations to the point of exhaustion, as long as they believed the sentiments of the zemes towards them remained unchanged.

Such is the story told by Giacomo Canizares and his companions. In my opinion, Most Illustrious Prince, you will think these barbarians are deceived by their bovites, that is to say, their priests and doctors, who have recourse to magic arts and I know not what tricks. They are, in fact, much inclined to believe in auguries, thanks to their ancestors to whom the infernal divinities often appeared at night and delivered oracles. I have touched on this subject in my first Decades. The natives of the new continent perform other ceremonies quite as foolish, but unworthy of mention.

The great river Dabaiba, similar to the Nile which empties by several mouths into the Egyptian sea, is larger than the Nile and flows into the gulf of Uraba in Castilla del Oro. I have elsewhere described the river population. I wish to bring to your notice some of their customs unknown to me at that time, and which have recently been brought to my knowledge by the colonists of Darien. Dabaiba is the name both of a river and of a divinity, and the sanctuary of the latter is about forty leagues distant from Darien. At certain periods of the year the caciques of even the most distant countries send slaves to be sacrificed at that sanctuary. Great popular meetings also are held from time to time. The slaves are strangled and then burnt before the idol, for it is thought the odour of these flames is agreeable to it, just as we believe that our saints like the light of wax and the smoke of incense.

According to very ancient tradition, angry divinities formerly dried up the rivers and springs, at which time the greater part of the natives perished of thirst and hunger. The survivors, abandoning the mountain regions, came down to the vicinity of the seacoast, where they dug pits along the beach to replace the springs. For this reason the caciques and those who have not lost remembrance of those hard times piously and respectfully maintain within their houses priests and walled sanctuaries; they wash and sweep the latter each day, taking care that neither humidity nor blotches nor even grass or the least dirt shall pollute them. When the cacique desires to implore the particular zemes either for sunshine or for rain, or any similar favour wanted for the neighbourhood, he and his priests ascend a platform in the house-chapel, from which none of them come down until the divinity invoked shall have granted their prayers. They redouble the fervency of their petitions, which they believe to be efficacious, and the severity of their fasting, entreating the idol to grant their desires and imploring it not to forget them.

When the Spaniards asked them to what divinity they addressed their prayers they responded that it is to the god who created the heavens, the sun and the moon, and all existing things; and from whom every good thing proceeds. They believe that Dabaiba, the divinity universally venerated in the country, is the mother of this creator.

While the cacique and his companions are engaged in prayer inside the temple, the people, believing themselves obliged to do penance, pass the time in a strict fast lasting four days, during which period they neither drink nor eat anything. To prevent these excessive privations from weakening the stomach, they only drink on the fifth day a beverage in which maize-meal has been dissolved, and little by little their strength comes back. But perhaps it may not be useless to know the manner of summoning people to the ceremonies and the instruments used.

Goaded by their love of gold, a numerous band of armed Spaniards went one day to explore the banks of the Dabaiba River. They cut to pieces a cacique they met on the road, and robbed him of about 14,000 gold pesos. This gold was in the form of artistically wrought articles, amongst which there were three trumpets, and as many bells. One of the bells weighed six hundred pesos while the others were less heavy. When asked for what these trumpets and bells were used, the natives replied that the notes of the trumpets delighted them on feast days and the tinkling of the bells summoned people to ceremonies. The tongue of the bell seemed to be made as are ours, but was so brilliant and so fragile that at first glance one would have thought, save for its length, that it was made of pearls or of the shells of pearl oysters. It was later discovered that it was made from fish-bones. Although beaten gold has a dull sound, the natives affirm that their bells give forth sweet, soft tones which charm the ear. The bell tongue only strikes the extremity of the bell, when moved; just as do ours.

Amongst this plunder there were thirteen hundred golden bells, and all have a pretty tone, just as in Europe. There were also golden pouches, in which the nobles carried their private parts, attaching them behind their backs with little cords. Their priests are obliged to abstain from luxury, and if any one of them were convicted of having violated the laws of chastity, he would be stoned or burned, for they believe that chastity pleases the Creator above everything else. While fasting or praying, their faces are washed and rubbed, but at all other times they paint their bodies. They raise their hands and eyes towards heaven. It is not only from lascivious women and all carnal acts they must abstain during this period, but even from their wives.

So simple are these natives that they have no name for the soul, nor do they realise its power. When asked what is this mysterious something, invisible and incomprehensible, which gives life to men and animals, they are amazed and stammer. They, however, affirm that there exists something after this terrestrial life. This something after our passage through this world has to do with eternal felicity if we live unpolluted, and have preserved from contamination the body confided to us. If, on the contrary, we have allowed ourselves to be carried away by some shameful passion or have committed acts of violence or fury, we shall suffer a thousand tortures in gloomy places under the centre of the earth. In speaking of this, the natives raise their hands and point to heaven, or they lower them and point to the interior of the earth.

The bodies of the dead are buried in tombs, and women follow the funerals of their husbands. A man may have as many wives as he chooses, but not among his near relatives, unless they are widows. The reason of this is a superstitious belief, sufficiently ridiculous in itself, but which has taken a firm hold upon them; for they pretend the patch visible upon the face of the moon, when it is full represents a man who is cast into that damp and freezing planet to suffer perpetual cold, in expiation of incest committed with his sister.

Above each tomb a small cavity is scooped out, in which every year a little maize and some of their usual drinks are deposited; for they believe these gifts will not be useless to the manes of their deceased relatives. A barbarous act in excess of anything one could imagine is the following. When a nursing mother dies, the living child is buried with her. Widows either remarry with the brother or the nearest relative of the husband, especially when they have children. The natives are easily deceived by their priests, and from this arise a thousand silly practices which they religiously preserve. Their life is passed in the country watered by the Dabaiba River.

I quote some other similar particulars which have been reported to me by trustworthy witnesses who have visited these southern countries. It is well to remember that these details have been omitted by Egidius Gonzales and his companions. Besides Egidius, a number of other captains have, as I have stated, frequently explored with their fleets these immense regions and tribes towards the south.

Not to mention many errors peculiar to them, there is one amongst the caciques of this country like unto which I have never read or heard anything. The king and the nobles alone are considered to have immortal souls. Other people possess souls which die with their bodies. An exception exists for indispensable servants of princes and those amongst them who, when their masters die, choose to be buried alive with them. In fact they are convinced that the souls of kings, once freed from their human bodies, enjoy perpetual delights, in evergreen gardens where they eat, drink, play, and dance with young women, or divert themselves as they did in their lifetime. This is the tradition handed down from their ancestors and for them is an article of faith. For this reason, numbers gladly cast themselves into the graves of their masters. If the prince's servants fail to fulfil this duty, their souls forfeit immortality and perish. We have already noted the same custom among the widows of caciques in other regions.

Each year the heirs of the cacique and the lords repeat the funeral ceremonies, according to ancient rites. The ceremony proceeds in the following order: The cacique or lord invites his subjects and neighbours to the tomb. Each one brings some of the usual wine but the organiser of the ceremony supplies all the food. Men and women, but especially the women, pass the whole of the first night watching, during which they give vent to mournful cries, deploring in funeral canticles the fate of the dead, especially if he has been killed by his enemies in war; for although they are content with so little in their life, the barbarians nourish eternal hatred amongst themselves.

They speak in offensive language of the life and morals of the victorious enemy, heaping furious insults upon him; they call him tyrant, cruel traitor, accusing him of having triumphed over their master and ravaging the country by fraud, and not by courage and virtue. Such indeed is the habit of these barbarians. Presently they bring a figure representing the enemy, and engage in mimic combat with it, wounding it and finally cutting it into bits, as a sterile sort of vengeance for their master. Then they give themselves up to eating and drinking, until drunkenness and nausea overtake them.

They have intoxicating herbs, from which they manufacture different drinks, as the Flemish make beer of barley and fruits, and the Galicians cider from apples. Afterwards they begin to dance and sing until they drop exhausted, exalting the virtues of their master, congratulating him on being good, generous, devoted to his people, self-sacrificing for the good of his subjects, free-handed in distributing seeds amongst them,—this being the chief duty of the cacique,—and finally upon being a brave soldier, and a skilful general in war. The lamentations are renewed and they begin again to deplore his death, crying, "He has robbed us of you, O illustrious Prince! Alas! the fatal day that has deprived us of such a great joy. Alas, unfortunate creatures that we are, to have lost such a father of the country!"

After many repetitions of these laments and others of the same sort, they turn to the reigning cacique and praise his merits, his courage, and his other virtues. They

surround him, leaping and dancing like the furies of the
carnival; regarding him with respect and adoring him,
declaring that they behold in him the present and future
remedy of past misfortunes, and the consolation for all
their troubles.[1] Like courtiers, they declare him to be
the most elegant of the elegant, the handsomest of the
handsome, the most generous of the generous; pious,
gracious; in a word, they overwhelm him with all sorts
of praises and compliments.

At daybreak they leave the house, bearing an image of
the dead to a boat which has been prepared; it is dug out
of a tree-trunk and capable of carrying sixty rowers. In
fact it is reported that very lofty trees grow in this country,
especially lemon-trees, which are plentiful and of which I
recently learned that they possess a quality I had before
ignored. The planks of the lemon-tree, in addition to
their already well-known properties, are incorruptible, for
they are bitter to the taste and are never attacked by the
pest of worms, which, wherever the sea is deep, bore the
hulls of ships more effectually than an auger. These worms
are called by the Spaniards bromas. This boat, which is
held to be that of the dead, is filled with drinks, herbs,
fruits, such as he loved during his lifetime; also with fish,
meat, and bread. The administrators of the cacique have
had it already prepared against the moment when the organiser of the ceremony shall come out of his house. The
guests raise the boat on their shoulders and carry it round
the house, bringing it to the place from which they started,
where they burn it together with all its contents. They
believe the smoke from this fire is agreeable to the dead
man's soul. While this is happening, the women, who
have drunk immoderately, let down their hair, strip
themselves naked, and foam at the mouth as they stagger
forward. Their legs tremble under them, and they cling
to the walls or fall, sprawling as do the Bacchantes; or

[1] In other words: *Le roi est mort, Vive le roi!*

they snatch javelins from their husbands' hands, clashing them together. They brandish lances and wave spears and arrows. In their wild march they shake the house, and finally, wearied out, they throw themselves stark naked on the ground and sleep the sleep of exhaustion.

Such ceremonies have been especially observed in an island of the South Sea called Cesucuo, which the Spaniards under the leadership of Espinosa visited.

There is another moral trait of theirs, which is not exactly chaste, but which I do wish to omit. When the young men give themselves up to these follies and games, singing their arreytos, they pierce the virile member with the bone of a fish called in Latin and Spanish *raie* and in Greek $\beta \iota \tau \iota s$; continuing to skip and jump while their blood flows on the floor. A powder which they use on the wound, and which was discovered by the bovites, who discharge the functions of doctor, surgeon, and priest, cures it in four days.

Sorcerers and soothsayers are highly esteemed and nothing is undertaken which they do not inaugurate, whether it is hunting, or fishing, seeking gold in the mines or pearls in the shells; the natives do not dare to move a foot unless the sorcerer, *torquerugua* as he is called, has first declared the moment to be propitious. There exists among them no forbidden degree of affinity and relationship, and fathers marry daughters, brothers their sisters; widows, even those who have no children, pass with the rest of the property to the heirs by right of succession. It is said that they are obscene and debased.

A singular custom prevails in our islands of Hispaniola, Cuba, and Jamaica, where a marriageable woman who has granted her favours and prostituted herself to the greatest number is reputed to be the most generous and honourable of all. The following story, amongst others, is a singular proof. Several Spaniards, in company with islanders from Jamaica, crossed to Hispaniola having with them a very beautiful woman, who had until then kept her virginity and remained chaste. The Spaniards agreed amongst themselves to accuse her of meanness, and they were so skilful and persistent that they transformed that young girl into an enraged woman, who determined to accept the embraces of any one who wanted her. She, who formerly resisted everyone, showed herself more than generous to all who solicited her favours. Throughout the archipelago there is no worse insult than to be called mean. It is just the contrary in many ways from the continent, where the women are chaste and the men so jealous that they strangle adulterous women.

I will terminate this part of my narrative dedicated to you, Most Illustrious Prince, with an extraordinary prodigy. What remains to tell, or what I may learn later, the Sovereign Pontiff has enjoined me, by a parchment just communicated to me, to dedicate to himself.

Near the source of the Dabaiba River lies a country called Camara, the last syllable pronounced long. The recollection is still preserved amongst its inhabitants of a frightful tempest mingled with whirlwinds, which suddenly broke from the east upon that country, tearing up all the trees by the roots and carrying off many houses, especially those built of wood. While the tempest raged two birds, almost similar to the harpies of the Strophades celebrated by the poets, were blown into the country. They had the face, chin, mouth, nose, teeth, eyes, eyebrows, and physiognomy of a virgin; one of these birds was so heavy that no tree was strong enough to support it. It is even alleged that when it rested on a rock to pass the night, the mark of its talons was distinguishable. It seized people in its claws, and carried them off to devour them on the summit of the mountains, as easily as hawks rob chickens. The other bird was not so large, and was doubtless the offspring of the first.

The Spaniards who went up that river a distance of four

hundred leagues into the interior in their boat, talked with many natives who witnessed the death of the larger of those birds.[1] They are trustworthy men, to whose testimony I have often had recourse: the jurisconsult, Coral, Osorio, and Espinosa. It will be interesting to learn how the people of Camara on the Dabaiba got rid of this terrible pest. As necessity is the mother of invention, so the people of Camara found the means of killing that bird, of which history should preserve the recollection. Cutting a huge piece of wood, they carved on one of its extremities the image of a man; after which they carried it to a place where this monstrous bird often passed when descending from the mountain in search of prey. Profiting by a clear night and the full moon, they dug a hole and set up the beam in such wise that only the human figure should be visible. Just near the ditch was a thick forest, in which they placed themselves, in ambuscade, armed with bows and javelins. At dawn the frightful monster appeared, descending upon its prey. It swooped upon the statue, seizing it and plunging its claws so deeply into the wood that it could no longer fly away; upon which the barbarians ran from their hiding-place and dealt it so many blows that it was more full of holes than a sieve. It finally fell dead. They bound it with cords and suspended it upon long lances, transporting it throughout the whole neighbourhood in order to allay the general terror and to make known the fact that the roads, which no one had ventured to use because of that bird, were now free.

Those who had killed the monster were regarded as gods, were honoured by the people and loaded with gifts. The same thing happens in many countries, when the neighbours who have feared the presence of a lion, bear, or wolf, make presents to him who kills the wild beast. It is alleged

---

[1] The largest known bird of prey is the condor. A gigantic bird of that species may have committed depredations that served as the basis of the fantastic story repeated by Peter Martyr.

that the feet of this animal were larger than the thigh of a man, but were shorter, as is the case with the claws of other birds of prey. Once the mother bird was dead, the other one never again appeared.

May Your Excellency enjoy health and a tranquil life in the principality of your ancestors.

The Eighth Decade

.

CLEMENS . VII . PA . FLORENTINVS .
R . Z . CREATO DEL 1523 . AI 19 . DI NOVEMBRE . 22

BOOK I

TO THE SOVEREIGN PONTIFF, CLEMENT VII. FROM PETER
MARTYR D'ANGHERA OF MILAN, APOSTOLIC PRO-
THONOTARY AND ROYAL COUNSELLOR

M OST Holy Father: I have received a parchment
addressed to me by Your Holiness, sealed, according to pontifical custom, with the Ring of
the Fisherman. It is divided into two parts; the first
being a eulogy of my history of the New World, which I
dedicated to your predecessors; and the second, an im-
perative order not to allow succeeding events to be lost in
oblivion. Such is my desire to obey you, that I cannot
deny that on this point I deserve commendation; but my
inadequacy as a writer is so great that I must solicit in-
dulgence rather than praise. The vastness of the subject
I am treating requires Ciceronian inspiration, as I have
in my preceding narrative often declared. Since I do not
possess silks and brocades, I have been content with humble
draperies to clothe my gracious Nereids, by which I mean
those isles of the ocean, brilliant as pearls, and hidden
since the beginning of the world from mankind.

Before the orders of Your Holiness were delivered to me,
I had addressed the greater part of my narrative, first to
Pope Adrian—and with that you are acquainted—and
next to the Viscount Francesco Sforza, ruler of my native
country. This was when fate had delivered him from the
grasp of the most Christian king, and his envoys at the
court of the Emperor imposed this task upon me. Now
that I am to give my labours to Your Holiness, it appears
to be indispensable to add to the work a copy of what I

have heretofore written, although that narrative is dedicated to another than yourself. Is it not thus that in the Church, bishops and cardinals precede the Sovereign Pontiff? So then, let the Decade dedicated to a duke open the series. All that follows concerning different events, all that has to do with incidents in the lives of captains, with quadrupeds, birds, insects, trees, herbs, ceremonies, manners, and superstitions of the natives, and especially with the situation of New Spain and the fleets upon the high seas, Your Holiness will learn; for no mortal may neglect your invitation with impunity.

I shall first describe what happened to Francesco de Garay, governor of Jamaica, recently renamed Santiago, and where, by the Emperor's grace, I hold the title of Abbot. I shall explain how Garay planned, in spite of the wishes of Cortes, to found a colony on the banks of the Panuco River, and there perished. I shall next mention the place where Egidius Gonzales touched, while seeking towards the north the famous strait, of which the discovery is so desired; and Cristobal Olid, of whom I have already said something, in the preceding Decade addressed to the Duke Sforza. I shall not forget Pedro Arias, governor of the mainland, also engaged in looking for the same strait. Next in order will follow the licenciate Marcel Villalobos, member of the India Council at Hispaniola, and his intimate friend Diego Garcia who has recently returned bringing us important news from Cortes, governor of New Spain.

Many other persons will pass before your eyes, among them the Dominican friar Tomaso Ortiz, a man of great probity who has lived for a long time in the country of Chiribichi. Nor shall we omit Diego Alvarez Orsorio, a man of illustrious birth, priest and canon of the cathedral of Darien, who, under the orders of Espinosa, has personally visited the immense regions of the South Sea, at the cost of a thousand dangers and hardships, spending

many years there exploring the country of the Dabaiba.
I take my narrative from the detailed reports of those
captains and their colleagues, all of them trustworthy
men, or in their absence, from their own depositions made
when they came here on business; and I compose this
narrative in obedience to the orders of three popes and
other princes.

I shall begin by the life and deplorable death of Garay.
In my preceding Decades addressed to Pope Adrian,
predecessor of Your Holiness, I said that a secret hatred
sprung up between Garay and Fernando Cortes, conqueror
of New Spain and many other provinces; for Garay was
reputed to want to colonise the Panuco country, bordering
upon the states under the jurisdiction of Cortes. I have
already said that this same Garay had twice been disas-
trously defeated by the savage population, along the
Panuco River; and twice Fernando Cortes had received him
in his flight, helping him to repair his misfortune, when
he was reduced to the direst necessity. This is shown
by the letters of Cortes and by my own writings, which
circulate throughout the Christian world.

Four vessels have just arrived from the Indies, and from
letters written by the companions of his labours and
sufferings, and from the verbal reports of people who have
come by these vessels, we know about Garay's misfortunes.
On the eighteenth day of the calends of June, he left
Jamaica—now called Santiago—of which he had long
time been governor. He was authorised by the Emperor
to settle on the banks of the Panuco River,[1] a stream
already well known, and to there found the colony of
which he dreamed. His fleet consisted of eleven vessels,
six of between one hundred and twenty and one hundred
and fifty tons burthen, two of the type called in Spain
caravels, and also two brigantines. His force consisted

---

[1] The Panuco River empties into the Gulf of Mexico near the present town
of Tampico.

of one hundred and forty-four horsemen, three hundred foot-soldiers armed with bows, two hundred musketeers, and two hundred men armed with swords and shields. He first directed his course towards Cuba, otherwise called Fernandina. Cuba is divided in two by the Tropic of Cancer, and Jamaica lies in the zone most people wrongly call the torrid zone. Cuba is about twice the length of Italy. Garay landed at a place called Cape Corrientes at the western extremity of the island, where there are many ports, to obtain fresh water, wood, and forage for his horses. He passed several days there. This point of the island is but a short distance from the dependencies of New Spain, governed in the Emperor's name by Fernando Cortes.

When he learned that Cortes had established a colony on the banks of the Panuco, Garay assembled his captains and consulted them as to what action he should take. Some were of opinion that it would be better to seek a new country, since there were plenty of others, than to come into conflict with the good luck of Cortes. Others thought the enterprise should not be abandoned, especially as they were sustained by the Emperor's authority, authorising Garay to give his name to the future colony. The will of the latter party prevailed, Garay being pleased by their pernicious opinion. Understanding the disposition of his lieutenants, he made a pretence of founding a state, and divided amongst them the offices, the better to attach them to himself by the honours he offered them. He therefore named as the chief of this colony Alfonso Mendoza, nephew of Don Alfonso Pecheco, formerly Grand Equerry. He associated with him Ferdinando Figueroa, of a distinguished family in Saragossa, and to them he added two Spaniards from Cuba. He named as judges Gonzales Ovaglio, a noble of Salamanca, related to the Duke of Alva; Villagrano, a former member of the royal household, and Iago de Cifuentes, a man of the people, but endowed with prudence and ability. He chose amongst his soldiers men for the offices of alguazils as they are called in Spain, who are sheriffs and inspectors of weights and measures. He exacted from them an oath to sustain him against Cortes, in case it should be necessary to use force.

Deluded as they were, and failing utterly to realise either the success, the good luck, and the craftiness of Cortes, they set sail. They were ignorant likewise of the misfortunes awaiting them from which, however, fate supplied them a means of escape. They were over-taken by a southern tempest, which deceived the pilots and landed them near a river which they took for the Panuco, though it was smaller. They were in fact seventy leagues distant and too far north, the violent gale having driven them to a part of Florida already long since discovered. The twenty-fifth of June,—on which day Spain celebrates the feast of her special patron, Santiago,—the Spaniards entered the mouth of the river, and cast anchor. As they found palm-trees upon the banks, they called it Rio de las Palmas.

Gonzales de Ocampo, brother-in-law of Garay, was sent with one of the brigantines capable of penetrating amongst the shoals, to explore. He went a distance of fifteen leagues up the river, using three days in this expedition. Going still farther up, he discovered a number of other streams flowing into the river, but as his mind was set upon the Panuco, he falsely asserted that the country was uncultivated, sterile, and desert. It has since become known that it is populous, agreeable, and rich in productions of every kind. This lying report was believed, however, and it was decided to depart for Panuco. As the horses were weak from starvation, they were brought on shore with the majority of the foot-soldiers. The sailors were ordered never to lose sight of the coast— as though they could command the waves! Garay himself set out overland towards the Panuco, marching in good order to avoid a surprise by some sudden attack of the natives.

The first three days no traces of cultivation were seen. The country was desert, for it was swampy and muddy. Another navigable river, flowing between high mountains, was encountered, which they consequently called Montalto. Some of the men crossed swimming, others on rafts. After overcoming this obstacle with great labour and fatigue, a large town was seen in the distance. The ranks were at once closed up and the company advanced in military fashion, the musketeers and other soldiers armed with long-range weapons forming the vanguard. Upon their approach, the natives abandoned their houses and fled. These houses were filled with provisions, so Garay was able to feed his soldiers and horses, already worn out with the fatigue of the march. Out of what remained, they took a supply of provisions with them.

BOOK II

THE savages fill their storehouses with all sorts of food, namely a particular kind of bread they call maize-bread, which resembles Milanese bread; and fruits having a bitter-sweet taste, and giving forth an odour unknown to us. These fruits, which are as large as an orange or a quince, are efficacious against dysentery, producing the same effect as do our sorbes and cornel-berries. The natives call them *guaianas*.[1] After crossing the river Montalto, the Spaniards continued their march across uncultivated countries, until they came to a large lake which empties its waters by a broad, unfordable river into the neighbouring sea. They made their way towards the opposite shore of the lake, some thirty leagues distant from the river's mouth, seeking for fords by which to cross, for they had been informed that many streams emptied into the lake lower down; but they only succeeded in crossing with great difficulty and risk of grave dangers, swimming half the time. Before them extended a broad plain, and in the distance they beheld a large village. As the inhabitants were not frightened and did not fly before them, as those of the first village had done, Garay halted his men and set up his standard; after which he sent ahead interpreters, whom he had obtained the preceding year in that neighbourhood and who already spoke Spanish. The people of the village agreed to peace and accepted the alliance he offered them. They

[1] Evidently a mis-spelling of guaiavas, called in English guava.

furnished his men with an abundance of maize-bread, chickens, and fruits.

Continuing their march, the Spaniards came to a third village, and as the news that they abstained from pillage had spread, they were received without hesitation and furnished with provisions; but not enough for their needs. In consequence, a revolt broke out in this place because Garay would not permit the village to be sacked. Farther on the Spaniards crossed a third river, and in so doing they lost eight of their horses, which were carried away by the force of the current. Beyond this river they found themselves in vast swamps infested with poisonous gnats, and overgrown with various creepers and stubborn plants, which gathered about their legs and retarded their march. In my Decade addressed to the Duke Sforza I have spoken of the impediments created by these vines. Struggling through water, up to the men's waists and the horses' bellies, the Spaniards, half exhausted, finally emerged from these swamps into an admirably fertile country, where there were many villages.

Garay forbade the use of violence towards any of the natives. One of his servants, who escaped from the barbarous massacre we shall describe farther on, wrote a long letter to Pedro Espinosa, Garay's paymaster and at the present time guardian of his children's interests at the Emperor's court. This letter, written in Latin, is full of harrowing details, but the following are the facetious terms in which he alludes to the difficulties of the march: "We arrived in a land of misery, where no order prevails, but where eternal fatigue and all calamities habitually dwell; in a land where thirst, odious mosquitoes, stinking bugs, cruel bats, arrows, stinging flies, strangling creepers, and engulfing slime have worn us cruelly."

It was the Spaniards' misfortune to reach the neighbourhood of the Panuco River. Garay halted to await the fleet, for he found no food. Cortes was

suspected of having captured the supplies, in order to
force them either to retreat for want of provisions for
themselves and their horses, or to starve. They had to
await the fleet to obtain provisions. Garay's men scattered among the native towns and villages, and even he
began to suspect the ill-will of Cortes towards himself.
He therefore sent ahead his brother-in-law, Gonzales
Ocampo, to inform himself concerning the attitude of the
colonists established by Cortes. Whether Gonzales was
won over or deceived I do not know, but he came back
saying that there was nothing to fear and that everybody
was willing to obey Garay. The latter accepted as true the
report brought by his brother-in-law and those who had accompanied him. Driven by adverse destiny he approached
the Panuco; but at this point we must digress in order
to more fully understand the events which are to follow.

There stands upon the banks of this great Panuco River
not far from its mouth, an important town bearing the
same name as the stream. According to common report,
this town contained fourteen thousand houses, [1] built of
stone, many royal palaces, and magnificent temples.
This town had refused obedience to Cortes, who destroyed
it from top to bottom, afterwards burning it and refusing
thereafter to allow any other to be built upon its site.
He treated another town which stands some twenty-five
miles higher up the river in the same manner; this place
was larger than the first, for it is reported that it numbered
twenty thousand houses. Because it refused obedience
Cortes razed it to the ground and burnt it. The name of
this town was Chillia. [2] Some three miles distant from

---

[1] While Panuco is proven by the comparatively extensive ruins still
existing to have been a place of considerable importance, this statement is
certainly open to doubt. A town of fourteen thousand houses would have
a population of some seventy thousand people.

[2] Cortes describes the Panuco campaign in his Fourth Letter. He calls
this town Chila. Between the lake of Chila and the sea-coast, he founded
the town of San Estevan del Puerto.

its ruins Cortes founded on a small hill which dominated a beautiful plain a colony which he called Sant-Esteven.

The Panuco is navigable for freight-boats a distance of several miles. It was the inhabitants of this province who had twice put Garay to flight, an episode I have related above at length. The natives could not resist Cortes, before whom all obstacles are broken. It appears that this region is extremely fertile, and is adapted not only for crops and other vegetable products, but abounds likewise in deer, hare, rabbits, wild-boars, and many other wild animals, as well as aquatic and forest birds. Lofty mountains, covered in places with snow, rise along the horizon. It is alleged that beyond these mountains there are civilised towns and important fortified places, situated in an immense plain, separated from the maritime provinces by the mountains.

But for the jealousy of the Spaniards, who can never agree amongst themselves in their keen dispute about honours, all these countries would already be conquered. How each is the declared enemy of his companions in this dusty squabble of ambition, which blinds them; how nobody can endure to be commanded by the others, I have already sufficiently explained in my preceding Decades when I spoke of the quarrels between Diego Velasquez, viceroy of Fernandina, and Fernando Cortes; and again between Fernando Cortes and Panfilo Narvaez or Grijalva, who gave his name to a river in the province of Yucatan; again of Cristobal Olid's defection from Cortes and the rivalry between Pedro Arias, governor of the mainland, and Egidius Gonzales, and finally of that general conflict of contradictory interests in searching for the strait giving communication between the south and north oceans. To say the truth, all the leaders in that country who exercise any authority in the King's name are open rivals, as I have already noted.

I shall later give some particulars concerning these internal dissensions.

I now return to Garay, from whom I had strayed. He was not slow to note the ravages the country had suffered, and he perceived his brother-in-law had deceived him in regard to the colonists of Sant-Esteven, for he found no friendship among them. Partisans of Cortes alleged that the latter's officials had carried all the provisions away from the native villages in order that their rivals might be driven by hunger to withdraw or, at least, to scatter through the country in search of food, the expected ships having been delayed by storms.

There is in that country a large town of about fifteen thousand houses, called Naciapala. An officer of Garay called Alvarado, who went there with about forty horsemen to collect forage, was surprised by the people of Cortes, who accused him of trespassing on land he did not legitimately own, and brought him in chains to their town of Sant-Esteven. The unfortunate Garay, taken between Charybdis and Scylla, was therefore obliged to await his fleet.

Finally the sailors reached the mouths of the Panuco; out of the eleven ships three, or other people say four, had been lost. Two of the commanders of Cortes, Diego Ocampo, the judge, and Diego Vallejo, the military commander, went on board the flag-ship and captured the sailors without much difficulty, easily enrolling the remainder under the standard of Cortes. The ships sailed up the river to the colony of Sant-Esteven.

While these things were happening, Garay was informed that the country along the Rio de las Palmas, contrary to the false report of his brother-in-law, Diego Ocampo, was fertile and in many places was even richer than the Panuco region. Intimidated by the good fortune of Cortes, Garay would have transferred his colony to that region had he not been deceived by the persistent opposition of his brother-in-law. Unhappily situated as he was, he failed to perceive what decision he should take, nor did he suspect that the more he insisted upon his claim to the province the Emperor had granted him by letters patent, the more serious did his position become.

Acting on the advice of Diego Ocampo, he sent messengers to Cortes; one of them, called Pedro Cano, was an old friend of Garay, and the other, Juan Ochoa, was a former officer under Cortes, reputed to be well acquainted with the country. Both these men were won over by Cortes; at least, so the partisans of Garay complain. Pedro Cano returned, Ochoa remained with Cortes, whom it had been arranged Garay should come to meet. I have already mentioned this fact when the Council of Hispaniola, acting upon a rumour which circulated, transmitted this news to the Emperor and to our India Council.

The unfortunate Garay seemed to have a presentiment of his downfall, but he feigned pleasure at setting out and, although he had been forced to move, he concealed his sentiments and accepted the invitation of Cortes, who had really delivered it in the form of a command. Accompanied by Diego Ocampo, he started to meet Cortes, who at that time lived in the immense lake city of Temistitan called Mexico, and which is the capital of numerous kingdoms. His reception was cordial; whether it was sincere is another question, to be answered only by Him who reads the hearts of men.

When the news of Garay's disgrace and his departure spread, the barbarians attacked the soldiers quartered in their houses, and surprised stragglers throughout the country. They massacred about two hundred and fifty, or, according to some reports, even more. They regaled themselves with copious banquets, for they are anthropophagi.

Upon hearing the news of this massacre, Cortes sent

the most famous of his lieutenants, Sandoval, to exact
vengeance; he gave him forty horsemen and the necessary
number of foot-soldiers.   It appears that Sandoval cut
a large number of the barbarians to pieces, for they did
not dare to raise a finger against either Cortes or his
lieutenants, the very mention of whose names struck
terror into them.   Sandoval afterwards sent sixty caciques
(for each village is governed by a cacique) to Cortes;
and the commander ordered that each of these caciques
should bring with him his heir.   This order was carried
out, and all the caciques were then burnt on an immense
pyre, their heirs witnessing the execution.[1]   Cortes
afterwards summoned them before him, and asked if
they had taken note of the sentence executed upon their
relatives; then adopting a severe mien, he added that he
hoped this example would suffice, and that they would
not henceforth incur suspicion of disobedience.   Having
thus terrified them, he sent each one back to his own
territory, with the obligation to pay a tribute.   Some
people report this incident as I have given it; others with
some changes. We are aware that rumours vary according
to the neighbourhood, and all the more so in the case of
the other world.

Cortes ordered one of his domestics, a certain Alfonso
Villanova, formerly in the service of Garay but dismissed
from his house for having debauched one of his maids,
to give Garay hospitality and treat him with honour.
The better to accentuate his friendly sentiments, he gave
one of his natural daughters in marriage to a legitimate son of Garay.   On Christmas eve, Cortes and Garay

---

[1] In describing this holocaust in his Fourth Letter to the Emperor,
Cortes wrote: "Four hundred chiefs and notable persons, besides others
of lower class, all of whom—I speak of the chiefs—were burned."   The
precise number burned is consequently uncertain.   Herrera reduces the
number to thirty.   In one particular Peter Martyr is wrong: the chiefs
were not sent to Cortes, nor was he present at their execution, which was
carried out by Gonzalo de Sandoval.

went together to assist at the singing of matins,[1] according
to usage. At the close of the ceremony, they returned
home at daybreak, where they found an excellent breakfast awaiting them. Upon leaving the church, Garay
had complained that he had caught cold; nevertheless
he ate a little with his companions at table, but retired
to bed as soon as he returned to the house where he was
being entertained. His ailment increased, and after
three or four days he yielded his soul to his Creator.

I have already said that there are not wanting people
who ask whether in his case the duties of charity were
not exaggerated in liberating from the cares of this life
a man who had suffered so much, or whether it was desired
to prove the truth of the adage, *regnum non capit duos*,
or of the other *nulla fides regni sociis*.[2] It is alleged
that he died from a stitch in the side, or a pleurisy as
the doctors call it. Be that as it may, Garay who was
the best of the governors in the New World, died; whether
for this reason, or for another, matters little. The fact
remains that his sons, relatives, and friends were rich,
and that they have been reduced to poverty. He himself
might have lived tranquilly for a long time, had he been
content with his governorship of Jamaica, that Elysian
isle which has just been renamed Santiago. There he enjoyed unquestioned authority and the people's affection;
but ambition drove him to his ruin.

He might have known that Cortes would ill endure his
proximity. Had he only taken care to avoid that flaming
fire, he might have established himself at Rio de las Palmas,
whither favourable winds had driven him; or better still,
he might have profited by the opportunity to reach some

---

[1] *Ecce Christi natalis noctem ad ma tutinos cantus audiendos de more
nostro* . . . meaning the midnight mass celebrated on Christmas eve,
rather than the office of matins.

[2] *Nulla fides regni sociis, omnisque potestas impatiens consortis erit.* The
line is from Lucan's *Pharsalia*, i., 92.

other of the rivers of Florida, still farther distant, one of which is called Santo Spirito. It is there that all the great rivers of that region flow together, after having traversed fertile and populous countries. But his fate was foreordained and his destiny is accomplished.

Since I have just mentioned the Elysian island of Jamaica, where Garay governed for so many years, and since I am united to that charming nymph, it is only proper that I should describe her graces and charms. I give the following examples.

BOOK III

THAT remote and hidden part of the world where the Creator of everything placed the first man, after forming him from the slime of the earth, is called by the sages of the mosaic law and of the New Testament the Terrestrial Paradise, because during the entire year there exists no difference between day and night; summer does not burn nor is winter severe; the air is salubrious, the springs clear, the rivers limpid. With all these blessings our beneficent mother nature has adorned my spouse.[1]

Besides the various fruit-trees we have introduced there, Jamaica produces other trees peculiar to it, and which constantly enjoy perpetual spring and autumn. They put forth flowers and leaves simultaneously, while bearing both green and ripe fruits at the same time. In that island the earth is covered with grass, and the fields blossom with flowers. Nowhere does there exist a country enjoying a more agreeable climate. Thus Jamaica, my spouse, is more favoured than any other region. The length of the island, from east to west, is between sixty and seventy leagues, and its greatest width is thirty leagues.

Astonishing things are told of the vegetable products sown and gathered by man. I have already spoken at

---

[1] Histories of Jamaica have been published by Edward Long in 1774; by Harvin and Brevin in 1807, and by Gardner in 1873. Peter Martyr describes the beauties of his island spouse from hearsay, for he never visited Jamaica.

346

length concerning these in my first Decades, for I gave
practically the same particulars about Hispaniola. I
hope, however, that the repetition of the greater part
of these details will not prove repugnant, especially to
the Sovereign Pontiffs, under whose authority these new
lands develop, day by day. The taste of good things is at
all times agreeable, and it may be that precisely these
passages of my decades were never brought to the
knowledge of Your Holiness.

Bread, without which all other foods are valueless,
exists in two kinds, one being made from grain, and the
other from roots. There are three yearly harvests of
grain. Wheat does not exist. A measure similar to a
hemina[1] of the grain they call maize sometimes contains
more than two hundred grains. A kind of bread made from
roots is the most appreciated; it is made from the dried
and ground root of the yucca. Cakes called cazabi are
made of it, and may be kept for two years without spoiling.
There is a very singular secret of nature in the usage of
this yucca root. In order to squeeze out the juice, the
natives pile this root into boxes which are pressed with
heavy weights. The raw juice when first pressed out is
more poisonous than aconite, and produces instant death,
but when it is cooked it is harmless, and has a better
taste than milk.

Many other different kinds of roots are found in Jamaica,
to which the general name of potatoes is given. I have
elsewhere described eight species of these potatoes, distinguishable by their blossoms, leaves, and sprouts. They
are as good boiled as roasted, and even raw they have not
a bad taste. They resemble turnips, radishes, parsnips,
and carrots, but differ in their taste and substance. While
writing these lines I have before me a certain quantity
of these potatoes, which I received as a present. I would
willingly share them with Your Holiness did distance

[1] Both a liquid and a surface measure.

not forbid. The ambassador of Your Holiness at the Emperor's court has eaten a share. This ambassador, who is Archbishop of Cosenza, is not an ordinary man, in the judgment of all good Spaniards. After fourteen years passed at this court, he thoroughly knows the history of the New World and, if Your Holiness desires, may some day relate it to you. Great princes are inclined to prolong their repasts with entertainments of this character.

I have already spoken much concerning the character of the skies, the trees, and the fruits, the harvests, bread, and roots. But what about the gardens? I have often spoken of the vegetables, melons, cucumbers, and pumpkins to be had at all seasons.

My affection for Jamaica is certainly sincere, but perhaps exaggerated, and I have added too much fringe to the draperies of my spouse. Let us, therefore, bid her farewell, and return to those whom we have left behind.

Just recently a brave soldier, called Cristobal Perez Hernan has been to see us; he had been in Jamaica a long time as an officer of justice under Garay, being one of those agents called by the Spanish, alguazils. He had always accompanied Garay and was present at his death. According to him, all that is told concerning the misfortunes of Garay and his soldiers is true. Sent back by Pedro Cano after the massacre, he brought letters from Cortes to Espinosa, representative of the latter's and his sons' interests at the Emperor's court. At the close of these letters, Cortes counselled and exhorted Espinosa to give up Europe, leave his occupation, and return to that happy country. One would have thought he was enjoining him to leave desert sands to betake himself to the most fortunate of lands. He repeatedly insisted on the point that if Espinosa would follow his advice, he would quickly become rich.

The alguazil Hernan gives other information worth noticing. The waters of the Panuco and the Rio de

las Palmas are about equal in volume at their mouths.
Sailors find fresh water nine miles out at sea opposite
the mouths of each of those rivers. A third and narrower
stream, named by the Spaniards Santo Spirito, is nearer
to Florida. It traverses rich and populous regions.
The alguazil was asked whether it was chance, or a storm,
or the execution of a well-thought-out plan that directed
Garay's fleet to the Rio de las Palmas. He answered
that it was the favourable south winds, and also the ocean
currents that had driven them thither; meaning no doubt
that same impetuous current I have already mentioned
elsewhere, and which flows towards the west following
the movement of the heavens. The alguazil—to call
him by his Spanish name—moreover affirms that the
pilots who laid the course were deceived by various things
and mistook the Rio de las Palmas for the Panuco, until
they found themselves within the estuary and unable to
recognise the banks. He added that Garay was sufficiently advised to stop at that place and found a colony there.
His companions were opposed to this, preferring to occupy
the banks of the Panuco River, which had already been
explored, and the fertile and known districts. Garay had
the gloomiest forebodings, and it was very much against
his will that he acquiesced in the decision of his associates,
when they reminded him that the Panuco region had
been conceded to him by the Emperor and should henceforth and forever be called *Garayana*. When the Spaniards
had dropped anchor at the mouth of the Rio de las Palmas,
and were awaiting the return of Garay's brother-in-law,
who had ascended the river, most of them examined the
neighbourhood of the stream. They studied the nature
of the soil, and took many new observations, though
none of them very important. One of them, however,
I will here record.

In a neighbouring field the alguazil Hernan found a
quadruped grazing. This animal was no larger than a

cat, and had the snout of a fox, its colour being silvered, and half its body covered with scales; it was fitted out like an equerry who arms his horse when about to go into battle. This animal moves very little, and if he sees a man in the distance, he curls himself up like a porcupine or a turtle. This one was captured and brought on shipboard, where it lived with the other domestic animals; but when the troubles began and the provisions gave out, the abandoned creature died.

This alguazil acquits Cortes of the suspicion of having poisoned Garay, though he is very depressed, for he shared all the latter's troubles. According to him, Garay died of what the doctors call a pleurisy. While the captain and his dejected companions were wandering through the region that separates the great Panuco River from the Rio de las Palmas, they enquired of the natives what existed beyond the lofty mountains which bounded the horizon, and from which both their country and the ocean were simultaneously visible. They answered that beyond those mountains existed vast plains and great cities ruled by warlike caciques.

While we were at Mantua Carpentana, commonly called Madrid, the alguazil stated by way of comparison that those great kingdoms are separated from the maritime provinces just as the provinces of Madrid and Calatrava are separated by a mountain range from the countries of Valladolid and Burgos, where, as you know, there are beautiful cities and important fortresses, such as Segovia, Medina del Campo, Avila, Salamanca, and many others. The alguazil also knows Italy, and said that the Apennines divided Milan from Tuscany in the same manner.

When asked how Cortes dressed, what etiquette was used in his presence, by what title he wished to be saluted, what gifts he exacted, what treasures he is believed to have amassed, and whether he had seen that engine of war, the golden culverin, about which so much has been said, Hernan replied as follows: "Cortes usually dresses in black silk; his attitude is not proud, except that he likes to be surrounded by a large number of servants,—I mean intendants, stewards, secretaries, valets, ushers, chaplains, treasurers, and all such as usually accompany a great sovereign.

"Wherever he goes, he takes with him four caciques on horseback. The magistrates of the town and soldiers armed with maces to exercise justice precede him. As he passes by, every one prostrates himself, according to an old custom. He accepts salutations affably, and prefers the title of Adelantado to that of Governor, both dignities having been conferred upon him by the Emperor. The suspicion that Cortes did not pay homage to the Emperor, commonly entertained by our courtiers, is declared by this alguazil to be baseless; neither he nor anybody else has ever observed the smallest sign of treason in him. On the contrary, he has prepared and sent to the Emperor three caravels loaded with gold and silver, on one of which is the famous cannon or culverin, which the alguazil carefully examined, and which is of sufficient calibre to receive an orange, but the alguazil does not believe that it is all gold, as report has stated."

BOOK IV

THERE is one amusing thing I will relate. In conformity with a ridiculous and simple usage, whenever the Spaniards traverse a country the native barbarians come out of their villages to meet them, bringing as many chickens as there are strangers; and these chickens are not smaller than our peacocks. If there are horsemen the natives, believing the horses eat meat, give as many chickens as there are animals. But Your Holiness should hear what clever artisans these barbarians, subdued for the Emperor by Cortes, are. Whatever they see they reproduce in painting, in metal work, or sculpture, so that it appears that they are in this respect in no degree inferior to the ancient Corinthians, who were able to reproduce nature in marble, ivory, or in any other material.

According to the alguazil's account, Cortes has in his possession great treasures, though less than report assigns to him; for he maintains at his own cost numerous captains and soldiers, usually more than a thousand horsemen and four thousand foot-soldiers. He sometimes uses these troops to maintain his authority over the recently conquered people, sometimes to explore new countries. He has even built vessels on that South Sea, in order to sail towards the equator, which is only twelve degrees distant from the shore where he has founded his settlement. He hopes to visit the islands near the equator or below it and to find much gold and silver there, and new kinds of spices. He had already attempted this, but, embarrassed by his competitors, Diego Velasquez, viceroy of Cuba, Panfilo Narvaez, and finally Garay, he was supposed to have renounced his intention.

One example will serve to illustrate how tribute is everywhere collected. In the course of our narratives relative to Temistitan, addressed by us to the Sovereign Pontiff Leo X., uncle of Your Holiness, and to his successor Adrian, we have related how the omnipotent monarch Muteczuma was sovereign over numerous and different princes, who were themselves masters of great cities. Cortes has conquered them for the most part, because they refused to obey him, but he has installed in their office and kingdoms their sons, brothers, or other relatives of inferior birth, so that the people, seeing themselves governed by the representatives of the ancient dynasties, endure more easily the yoke.

Of these cities, the one nearest to the salt lake is called Tezcuco. It numbers about twenty thousand houses and is whiter than a swan, for all its houses are washed with white bitumen. They are so brilliant that any one, beholding them from a distance, might, unless forewarned, think he saw little hills covered with snow. Tezcuco is built in the form of a square, being three miles long and about the same breadth. Cortes designated a very young man, descended from the family of ancient rulers, as chief. Otumba is another town, a trifle smaller than Tezcuco. Cortes also placed there a mild, obedient chief, who was his godson, and had been baptised under the name of Fernando Cortes. The territory of this town is extensive, fertile, and traversed by rivers, whose sands gleam with gold. To escape a visit from the Spaniards, which cannot be made without disturbance, each of the caciques pays Cortes each year, according to agreement, sixty thousand gold pesos. We have stated that the value of the peso is equal to a ducat and a fourth. In addition they supply products of the earth, maize, chickens, and wild animals which abound in the neighbouring mountains.

All the native leaders received the same treatment, that is to say, each one pays tribute according to his resources. Cortes allows most of the provinces to enjoy real liberty, without a king, and with their old customs maintained. The only exception he makes is the odious custom of human sacrifices, concerning which he had lively disputes with Muteczuma. Even these free provinces pay a certain tribute to Cortes; one called Guaxaca has rich gold deposits. It is seventy leagues distant from the royal city of the lakes. Locpoteca is another province, where the conditions are the same. Most of the other provinces pay their tributes in gold. Cortes has also reserved certain gold mines for the royal fisc, which he has worked by prisoners of war. When he sets them at liberty, they occupy themselves in agriculture or in industrial arts.

I cite one peculiar fact worthy of notice. The province of Guacinalgo[1] is governed by a king bearing the same name. This prince, accompanied only by his mother, came to salute Cortes; but his hands were not empty. Slaves carried on their shoulders thirty thousand pieces of gold, which he presented to Cortes. You will learn, not without pleasure, how he paid his homage. He approached almost naked, although he possesses plenty of valuable clothing. But we understand that it is their custom for an inferior who approaches a powerful personage, to present himself poorly dressed, with bowed head, bending the knee and stammering when he speaks; this is in token of humility.

It will not be useless to hear what happy money they use; for they have money which I call *happy*, because they obtain it by merely scratching the earth, and because neither the envy of the avaricious nor the terrors of war cause it to return to its subterranean hiding-place, as

[1] Meaning Guachinango, situated 165 kilometres north of Mexico.

happens with gold or silver.   This money is produced by
a tree.   I have already described it at length elsewhere,
explaining how it is sown and transplanted, how it is
reared in the protecting shade of another large tree, until
it is full grown and may support the heat of summer and
the violence of tempests.   This tree bears a fruit similar
to a small almond.   When fresh it has a bitter taste
and is not edible, but from it is made the drink of the
noble and rich classes.   When dried these fruits are ground
into flour.   At the breakfast or dinner hour the servants
fill wine or water vessels, or cups having handles, with
water, adding a proportionate quantity of this flour.
They pour the mixture from one vessel to another, shak-
ing it by raising their arms as high as they can without
letting it fall like rain on a roof; this operation is repeated
till the liquid froths, and the more frothy the beverage
is, the better it is considered to be.   When the mixture
has been thus shaken for about an hour, it is left to stand
a little, so that the heavier grains may settle to the bottom
of the cup or wine-vessel.   This drink is sweet and not
very intoxicating.   Nevertheless those who drink it
immoderately begin to feel confused in the head, as
though by the fumes of our wines.

The natives call the fruit and the tree by the same name,
cocoa, just as we call the nut or the tree, *almond*.   The
Spaniards compare the drink with curds, because it
serves both as a food and a drink.   These trees and coins
only grow in certain regions, nor will they grow in every
soil when they are sown and transplanted.   The same
happens with our own fruits.   Lemons, citrons, and shad-
docks—vulgarly so called—and other similar fruits
only grow and prosper in very few places.   The caciques
and each of the rich provinces they govern pay their
tributes to Cortes, and it is with cocoa that he pays his
mens' wages, furnishing them with drinks, and with which
he buys whatever he needs.   It has been noticed that the

countries suitable for this precious product are not fertile in cereals. Merchants, therefore, visit them and carry on their trade by means of exchange. They bring maize, or cotton for making clothing and also made garments, in exchange of which the people give them cocoa. This is enough concerning this money. If I return to these particulars, Most Holy Father, it is that those who may study this book dedicated to you, and who may not be acquainted with the Decades addressed to Popes Leo and Adrian, may be informed concerning these things.

Some caciques who possess silver mines in their countries pay their tribute in silver. Cortes has furniture made of silver, and wrought vases artistically worked, both in gold and in silver. Your Holiness may now form some opinion about Cortes. It is alleged that he was much affected when the French pirates, some three years ago, carried off the great treasures he sent to the Emperor. Amongst the lost objects we noted the marvellous ornaments the natives offered their gods in the temples when sacrificing human victims. What shall I say of the gems and precious stones? There was especially an emerald of pyramidal form, almost as large at the base as a man's right hand. As was told us in the Royal Council and repeated to the Emperor, nothing of the kind had ever been seen. It is alleged that the French admiral redeemed it from him[1] who captured it for a large sum of money.

The unfortunate captain of the captured vessel, Alfonso de Avila, was inhumanly treated; he is a young man of noble birth, but not rich. They keep him shut in a dark prison, solely because this precious gem and the other treasures had been confided to him. They think they may exact twenty thousand ducats for his ransom. People who know the value of jewels say that this emerald is beyond all price, so transparent, brilliant, and admirably pure is it.

---

[1] The admiral was Philippe de Brion-Chabot. The pirate was John Florin or Fleury.

Our cereals grow when planted in the country of Temistitan, for it is cold there, because of the distance from
the sea and the neighbourhood of high mountains, although
the country is situated in the torrid zone eighteen degrees
from the equator.   The ears and kernels grow to larger
size than in Europe.   As there are three kinds of maize,
the white, the yellow, and the red; the natives prefer maize
to wheaten flour.   They find it also more wholesome.
Wild vines grow spontaneously in the forests, producing
large and palatable crops, but no time has yet been found
to make wine.   It is reported that Cortes has planted
vineyards; what will result we shall know in time.

BOOK V

IN addition to the above mentioned alguazil, who
furnished us with such ample information upon which
to form our opinion, there has just recently arrived
from New Spain, conquered by Cortes, a citizen of San
Lucar de Barrameda, called Diego Garcia. According
to his account, he left the port of Vera Cruz about the
calends of April in the year 1524, just when Garay died.
He also acquits Cortes of any suspicion of poisoning, and
says Garay died indeed of the pleurisy. Garcia furthermore states that Cortes has never displayed any symptoms of disobedience towards the Emperor, as some
envious people have whispered. On the contrary, we know
from Garcia and from others that his attitude towards the
Emperor is a most humble one. He is striving at the
present time to restore the ruins of the great lake-city,
due to the war; the aqueducts, which were broken to
assist in conquering the obstinacy of the besieged, have
been restored; the destroyed bridges and many ruined
houses have been rebuilt, and, little by little, the city is
taking on its former appearance. The markets and fairs
have not been suspended; boats come and go as actively
as before, and the multitude of traders appears to be just
as great as during the reign of Muteczuma.

Cortes has appointed a man [1] of the blood royal to
protect the interests of the natives and to administer
justice; but his functions are not very extensive. When

[1] Referring again to the Chihuacoatl before mentioned.

358

this man is in the society of Spaniards or with Cortes, he wears a Spanish dress presented to him by the latter; but when he is with his own people he resumes the national costume to which he is accustomed.

The Prætorian guard which protects the person of Cortes, and is ready to suppress any disorder that may occur, is composed of five hundred horsemen and four thousand foot-soldiers. A number of captains have moreover been sent with their companies to accomplish several missions on land and sea; amongst others, Cristobal Olid, whose acts and deeds I will elsewhere recount.

It will be well, and also interesting, to learn what a captain called Alvarado has done in a certain matter. We have somewhere said that between Yucatan, on the frontier of New Spain, thus named by Cortes, with the Emperor's consent, and the immense territories of the new continent, there exists a vast gulf which may possibly have an exit towards the southern extremity of that country. It is in this gulf that Egidius Gonzales de Avila thinks the mouth of a great river may be found, through which flow the waters of the immense freshwater lake, of which I have spoken at length in my book which the Archbishop of Cosenza has presented to Your Holiness, and also in the Decade preceding it, dedicated to the Duke Sforza. The extremity of that gulf has been known for a long time under the name of the gulf of Figueras.

According to the report of numerous natives, a larger city than Temistitan stands on the western side of this gulf, but more than four hundred leagues in the interior. The sovereign of this country is master of a great kingdom. Cortes commissioned Alvarado to go in search of this town, giving him five hundred men—horsemen and foot-soldiers. Alvarado set out straight towards the east, preceded only by two of his own men who knew the languages of the country. He discovered numerous regions, sometimes mountains or plains, sometimes marshes, but in general they were sterile.

I omit the particulars of this march, for I will not risk wearying Your Holiness with minute details; so at one bound I come to what is worth hearing. Passing from one kingdom to another conducted by their native guides, Alvarado's messengers returned to their commander who followed them at a distance of several leagues, and reported to him what they had discovered. The mere announcement that the Spaniards were coming produced calm[1] everywhere. None of the caciques dared to draw a sword against them, and everywhere they passed, the storehouses of provisions were opened to them. People crowded about to admire them, and especially the horses and weapons stupefied the natives, for all of them are nearly naked. They assisted our men by furnishing provisions and slaves to act as beasts of burden and carry their baggage. They make slaves of war prisoners as do all nations—not to mention kings—mad with cupidity or ambition.

Alvarado halted on the very frontier of the country ruled by that great king, and waited there, fully armed and in good order. He did not wish to trespass on his territory, so as not to appear to offer any offence, for there exists no greater outrage in the estimation of the caciques of that region than to cross their frontiers without their permission. In such cases it only remains to take vengeance for the insult; hence rivalries, disputes, and wars.

It was still about a hundred leagues farther on to the residence of that sovereign. Alvarado sent messengers and interpreters, obtained in the neighbouring countries, in advance. They approached the king, saluted him, and were amicably received by him, for the news of the Spaniards' arrival had reached his ears. He first asked

[1] The *calm* that reigned in Poland.

whether these men were sent by the great Malinge,[1] whom they believe to be sent down from heaven, and whom they call the invincible and all-powerful hero. The messengers answered him affirmatively. He further enquired whether they came by sea or land, and if by sea in what pirogues,—that is to say ships as large as the room of the palace in which they then were. Like all the natives they have only fishing boats, dug out of tree-trunks.

The king then declared that he knew about our vessels the preceding year. The ships of Egidius Gonzales, which sailed the seas lying behind Yucatan, had indeed been seen by the subjects of that cacique, whose country lay along the coast. The ships being under full sail, the natives believed them to be sea monsters, horrible and astonishing beasts newly created, and they thus informed their sovereign. The king asked one of the two messengers if he could draw a picture of a ship, and one of them, called Trevigno, promised to do so. This man who had been a woodworker and a skilful pilot set to work in a large room of the palace to paint a ship; for the dwellings of the king and the lords possess halls built of stone and plaster, as I have already said in speaking of Temistitan. Trevigno, therefore, painted a large freight-ship, such as the Genovese call carraca, with six masts and as many decks.

Appalled by this mass, the cacique fell into a long reverie. He next enquired how these vessels fought, and was told

---

[1] Meaning Malinche or more correctly Malintzin, the name by which Cortes was universally known amongst the Indians. The sobriquet derives singularly enough, from Marina, the Christian name given to the Aztec woman who accompanied Cortes throughout the conquest. The Aztecs did not pronounce the letter *r* but, after the fashion of the Chinese, substituted for it *l*, making of Marina, Malina. *Tzin* was the Aztec title of honour, meaning chief or commander, and Cortes was hence named by the natives Malintzin; this in turn was corrupted by the Spaniards into Malinche.

that each of them was sufficiently strong to easily triumph over thousands of men, a statement he was unwilling to believe, and which he held to be impossible; the more so as he saw that none of the Spaniards were above the ordinary height and possessed neither a more robust appearance nor stronger limbs than other men.

He was next told that our people had ferocious beasts in their service, swifter than the wind, and which helped them to fight. The cacique then asked that one of the messengers should draw him a horse as well as he could. Trevigno's companion did this, taking care to give the horse a terrifying aspect, and to make it larger than the brass horses of Phidias or Praxiteles, which stand on the Esquiline Hill, belonging to Your Holiness. Upon the animal's back, covered with harness, he placed a horseman. Struck with admiration, the cacique next asked whether they would undertake to conquer a hostile neighbour of his who ravaged his frontier, promising them an army of fifty thousand allies, in case they would do so. Alvarado's envoys next told him that the Spaniards by themselves were no stronger and no better than other men, but when in line of battle with their horses and their engines of war, they feared no other army. They promised to return to the general who had sent them, and who was awaiting them not far from the frontier of the kingdom. The cacique having asked them what report they would make, they answered that in their opinion the general would come to the cacique's assistance, and would easily conquer his enemies, their capital, and everything they possessed. The cacique answered: "If you carry out your promise, I and my subjects will henceforth obey this great and invincible hero." As a pledge of his future vassalage, he showed himself so well disposed towards the envoys that he gave them as an escort back to Alvarado, five thousand slaves laden with cocoa money used in the country, provisions, and also twenty thousand pesos of gold wrought into different kinds of ornaments.

The return of his envoys afforded Alvarado great joy, and he at once returned to Cortes to report to him what had happened, offering him the cacique's presents, which were shared according to the rule adopted.[1] One of Alvarado's two messengers had no confidence in the liberality of the generals towards him, and during the march he stole several pesos of gold. His companion exhorted him not to dishonour himself by breaking his word, saying that it was better to leave things to the generosity of Cortes and Alvarado. Seeing the other's obstinacy, his companion said no more, dissembling until they came to Cortes when he accused the thief. The guilty man was publicly whipped as an example, and was condemned to never again show his face in New Spain.

These events happened towards the end of the year 1523. Some days later, when the convalescents had recovered their health and the dead had been replaced by new-comers, Alvarado received orders from Cortes to depart. He set out amidst the sound of drums and trumpets.

This last messenger, Diego Garcia, formerly servant to one of the counsellors of Hispaniola, the jurisconsult, Marcel de Villalobos, had been sent by his former master to our council. He has obtained what he was commissioned to ask, namely that Villalobos might be permitted to found a colony, at his own cost and build a fortress in the island of Margarita. This island of Margarita lies opposite the Boca de la Sierpe near the mainland. Many pearls are found there, from which fact it derives its name of Margarita. If Villalobos carries out his intention he will be permanent governor of the colony, and according

---

[1] After deducting the royal fifth, one fifth of the remainder belonged to Cortes, the rest being divided equally amongst the others. *Documentos Ineditos*, tom. xxvi., pp. 5-16; tom. xxvii., p. 37; Bernal Diaz, cap. cv.

to custom will transmit his powers to his heirs, reserving, however, the supreme rights of the Castilian crown. To close the history of New Spain, it only remains for me to report one sole fact.

BOOK VI

SINCE the French pirate, Florin, captured the fleet carrying the valuable presents sent to the Emperor by Cortes and his companions in the conquest, the latter has sent no other letter either to the Emperor or to our Council, so great was his chagrin and so overcome was he by sorrow at this important loss. Nevertheless quite a number of other Spaniards have come at different times from those countries, and this has given rise to the suspicion that he meditated rebellion. It appears to me, however, that he gives proofs of the contrary and seeks to extend his conquests, not for himself, but for his Majesty. Should Your Holiness ever be puzzled to know whether Garay's misfortunes should be attributed to Cortes, whether he was responsible for the other's death, and how he should be punished, if that death was his doing, may Your Holiness suspend judgment as I myself have done.

In my opinion, an enquiry into so serious an affair should be concealed. One cannot put a bridle upon such a formidable elephant by similar means. Kindness and gentle treatment are better calculated to heal such a wound than severity, which might irritate it. Time, the eternal judge of all things will do this work. Nevertheless I believe that one day or another Cortes will be taken in the same net in which he first caught Diego Velasquez, governor of Cuba, who originally sent him to that country where he revolted against him; afterwards Panfilo Narvaez, and more recently Garay, that is, if the rumours about him are true. I have already explained this matter.

Perhaps the hour is not so far distant when this debt must be paid. In fact, we have just learned from Cuba and Jamaica and with fuller details from Hispaniola, where news focuses as in a common centre, that Cristobal Olid, sent by Cortes to seek the much-desired strait, had rebelled, and was acting on his own authority, after having violated his general's orders. Such is the report concerning the beginning of this business.

We also read in other letters that Egidius Gonzales de Avila, of whom I have lengthily spoken above, has landed on the shore known for a long time as the gulf of Figueras, where he is seeking to discover an outlet of that fresh-water lake he had found. Now Olid has just landed on that same coast, not more that twenty leagues from Egidius Gonzales. It is reported that upon hearing the news of Olid's arrival, Egidius sent him messengers, bearing letters in which he proposed peace and an alliance. It is further said that Cortes, upon hearing of Olid's rebellion, sent soldiers against him, with orders to capture him and bring him back in chains, or even to kill him.

People who know Olid affirm that he is a brave soldier and an able captain. He has from the beginning contributed largely to the success of the campaign but, as commonly happens, he had aroused the fears of Cortes and the latter, under pretext of favouring him, sent him away. He was advised so to do by his friends, who counselled him to place no further confidence in a man to whom he had used injurious language.

On the other hand, we know that Pedrarius, governor of the mainland, has assembled a large army and is marching to the same place. Thus we fear that the rivalries of these captains will result in general ruin, the more so since neither the Emperor nor we of the Royal Council, know what to decide; unless it be to increase by frequent decrees the power of the council of Hispaniola. In this wise, that council, invested with supreme authority and using courteous treatment, admonitions, and threats as they may be needed, may forestall any catastrophe, prevent dissensions, and bring about harmony. The disobedient would risk being accused of treason, and would be punished. Moreover, the other Spanish gentlemen, who command troops, would not share their views if they disobeyed the King's orders.

In our opinion it is not with armies that these discords are to be settled. Should we suspect treasonable dispositions in any of these captains, a little ink and parchment would suffice to reduce to powder any one who attempted to resist our decisions. In the heart of all Spaniards lives a great quality,—the desire for honour and praise; they wish to be thought loyal to their King. From one hour to another we expect ships from the New World. Should any hidden ill develop and come to a head, we will summon the surgeon to cure it.

Other particulars which deserve mention here have been communicated to me by the friar Tomaso Ortiz and his companions, Dominicans, who are trustworthy men. They have lived six years at a place on the continent called Chiribichi, near the Boca de la Sierpe, in the province of Paria; places we have often mentioned in our preceding Decades and the books dedicated to the Duke Sforza, where I related that the barbarians had destroyed a convent and massacred the monks. This friar, Tomaso Ortiz, who is at present here, wishes that twelve Dominican monks should be sent under his leadership to New Spain, to sow the seeds of our religion amongst the barabarous nations.

Thanks to the information furnished me by these friars, I have been able, if I remember correctly, to write on this subject to divers princes. They report that the natives are called cannibals or Caribs, and that they eat human flesh. The country of the Caribs extends over a vast area, and is larger than Europe. The natives have fleets of boats dug out of tree-trunks, and organise man-hunts through numbers of the islands, just as in other countries people hunt deer and wild boars in the forests. In all the languages of that region the word *carib* means *stronger than others*, and hence the origin of the name Caribs. No native of those islands pronounces that name without a feeling of terror. The Caribs also derive their name from the district of Caribana, east of the gulf of Uraba, where the barbarians, scattered over vast tracts have, at different times, exterminated whole parties of Spaniards.

These people go almost entirely naked, or sometimes conceal their genital organs in a little golden gourd;[1] when at home, idle, they wear no clothes; but in time of war they put on different ornaments. They are very agile, and shoot their poisoned arrows with unfailing precision; they are more rapid than the wind in their movements. They are beardless, and if any hair grows they pull out the single hairs, one by one, with little pincers; they cut their hair up to half the height of their ears. They pierce their ears and nose, and, out of vanity, the richer ones wear ornaments of gold in them, while the young people use different kinds of snail shells. Those who possess gold also like to wear crowns made of this metal. Between the ages of ten to twelve years, when puberty declares itself, they chew, all day long, leaves of trees, as thick as a nut, taking no other food nor drink. With this substance they blacken their teeth, until they are the colour of a dead coal. They contempt-uously call the Spaniards women and children because the latter like to have white teeth; or likewise wild animals because they let their hair and beard grow. Their teeth

---

[1] . . . . *funiculo præputium alibi colligunt, neque nisi coitus aut mictus causa solvunt.*

last a lifetime and they are ignorant of the aches which
sometimes oblige us to have our molars removed. Their
teeth never decay. The leaves I mentioned are larger
than myrtle leaves, as soft as those of the turpentine
tree, and they feel to the touch like wool or cotton.

The natives of Chiribichi cultivate nothing but this
tree, which they call *hay*, since with its leaves they
procure whatever they want. They dig ditches and
canals across the regularly laid out plantations of these
trees, by which means they water what they have sown.
Each proprietor encloses his field with a cotton cord,
breast high; and it is reputed a sacrilege for any one to
enter his neighbour's field heedless of that cord. They
are convinced that the trespasser will shortly perish.

It is well to explain how they prevent the powder
made from these leaves from spoiling. Before powdering
the dried leaves they bury them in the forests on the
mountains where, owing to the dampness of the earth,
snails live. They throw the shells of these animals, mixed
with a special kind of wood, into a hole prepared for the
purpose, and light a fierce fire which makes lime, which
they mix with the powder. That lime is so strong that whoever tastes it for the first time burns and hardens his lips,
as happens to labourers whose hands become callous
with constant use; or as would happen to us if we were to
rub our lips with quicklime. The natives preserve the
powder so made in boxes and baskets artistically made
from marsh reeds, keeping it until the arrival of traders
who visit them to trade for it, as is done at fairs and
markets. These traders bring them maize, slaves,
necklaces, made of the gold they call guanin, taking in
exchange this powder, which is used in all the neighbouring
countries for keeping the mouth clean. The inhabitants
of Chiribichi spit out the old leaves from time to time and
take new ones.

There are in this valley other trees remarkable for

their products. A milky juice runs out when they are tapped; when left to stand this juice coagulates like resin, and is transparent like gum, giving forth a delightful odour when it is burnt.

Another tree produces a similar juice which, however, is a fatal poison, into which arrows are dipped. Other trees produce glue, which they use for catching birds and for divers other purposes. The *guarcirima* resembles our mulberry-trees. but its fruit, when ripe, is harder than European mulberries. If first dipped in water, a juice, efficacious against throat trouble and hoarseness, is extracted from it. When the branches of this tree are dried, they produce sparks, as would a flint when struck. Large lemon-trees also grow in this valley. It is said that clothing put in lemon-wood boxes acquires an agreeable smell and is preserved from moths, but bread placed in them becomes bitterer than gall and uneatable. As we have said, ships built of lemon-wood are never attacked by worms.

Another tree produces cotton. It is larger than a mulberry, but dies at the end of ten years. In our preceding book, dedicated to the Duke Sforza, we have noted that a similar thing had been observed in Hispaniola, and many other regions of the New World. The Dominican Fathers claim that this cotton is more valuable than the kind yearly sown in Europe. It is not higher than the stalks of flax and grows pretty much everywhere, but is cultivated with success in Spain, especially in the plain of Andalusia.

Let us not forget another valuable product of the valley of Chiribichi. The Dominicans believe that the cinnamon-trees, which are unknown to the Indians, grow in unexplored parts of this country; at least they have thus far not been utilised, for the only condiment the natives know is that species of pepper of which I have spoken at length, and which they call *axi*. This fruit is so peculiar to this country that it is found in as great quantity as nettles or mallows with us.   As a proof the monks say that a tree, carried away by a flood was thrown on the bank near where their convent stood.   They dragged it up the bank and chopped it into pieces, for use in the kitchen.   Each chunk exhaled sweet odours.   They tasted the bark and found it strong of cinnamon, in spite of the fact that the trunk was half rotten from lying a long time in the water, buffeted by the current.

Time, which is a judge of everything, will furnish us an explanation of this mystery and many others still hidden from us.   We read that the supreme creator took six days to form and order all existing things.   We certainly cannot grasp so many secrets in a moment.

The waters of that river dissolve and purge the bladder and kidneys of gravel, but they affect the sight.   There is also a fountain producing an abundance of the unextinguishable fire, vulgarly called alchemists' fire, and which I think in Italy is commonly called Greek fire.[1]

[1] This last passage has been thought to refer, possibly, to a petroleum well.   No other interpretation equally plausible suggests itself.

BOOK VII

THERE is a fact worthy of notice proving that this valley produces aromatic plants which act as aphrodisiacs. At sunrise and in clear weather the valley is filled with extraordinary vapours, dispersed over the earth by the morning breeze. Whoever inhales these vapours too deeply, suffers from headache and heaviness such as many herbs in Spain produce, especially basil and musk, which should not be too deeply inhaled, though their scent at a distance is sweet. When it rains or when the sky is cloudy, these vapours scatter.

Another tree growing along the river banks produces a fruit which excites the flow of urine, making it as red as blood. Still another produces excellent plums, similar to those the Spaniards call *monacales*. Upon the same banks there grows a tree whose fruits are sure poison, and yet they are sweet. When the fruits fall into the water and are eaten by the fish, people who afterwards eat those fish are attacked by divers strange maladies. The friar Tomaso Ortiz declares that he has tasted, but not eaten these fruits; their taste is bitter-sweet. He was afterwards slightly indisposed. The antidote to this poison is to swallow oil. Even the shade of this fruit-tree affects the head and hurts the eyes. Dogs, cats, and other animals which eat of it die.

Other trees of different kinds grow in this soil; one of them produces a sap which resembles fresh curds, and is eatable. Another exudes a sort of gum, not inferior to rose honey. Even odoriferous plants grow wild in this country; here and there basil is found. Beets grow as high as a man, and clover is taller than parsley.

The vegetables and garden plants brought over by the monks all flourish; for example, melons, gourds, cucumbers, carrots, radishes, and parsnips. There are also deadly poisonous plants, among others a triangular swamp plant with sharp points like the teeth of a scythe. A prick from this plant provokes cries of pain. I must not forget to mention the sea-weed which, when torn up by the force of the wind, delays and even stops vessels.

A great variety of quadrupeds and birds peculiar to the region have been noted in Chiribichi. Let us begin by the less useful and more dangerous ones. In my first and following books I have often spoken of certain four-footed reptiles of ferocious aspect. These are called sometimes *iguanas* and sometimes *ivanas*. The flesh of this animal is good to eat, and one need not scruple when it is a question of a dainty dish. Its eggs, laid and hatched like those of a crocodile or a turtle, are nutritious and savoury. The Dominican monks, who lived for seven years in that region, were much molested by iguanas. As soon as their convent was built, as I have stated, they were nightly surrounded by a multitude of these animals, like so many enemies. They had to leave their beds, not to defend themselves against the beasts, but to drive them away from the fruit, especially the melons, which they had sown and cultivated, and for which the iguanas greedily searched.

The natives of the valley hunt the iguanas, but to eat them. Sometimes they kill them with arrows, and sometimes they capture them alive. In the latter case they merely grasp the animal by the neck, for although its aspect is frightful, especially when it opens its mouth and seems about to bite, it nevertheless remains motionless like a hissing goose and does not attempt to defend itself.

These creatures are so prolific that it is impossible to exterminate them. They emerge from grottos and sea-caverns where they have grown, and go in troops at night in search of food. They also eat the sea-drift left on the shore by the ebb of the tide.

Another cunning and ferocious animal is found in this country. It is the size of a French dog and is very rarely seen. When twilight falls, it leaves its hiding-place in the woods and comes into the town, where it prowls about houses, wailing loudly. Those who are ignorant of the animal's subtlety would believe a child was being beaten, and many inexperienced people were deceived into incautiously going to the place where the imaginary child was weeping. The wild beast, lying in wait, then springs upon the unfortunate creature, and in the twinkling of an eye tears him to bits. In the course of time necessity, which goads dull minds, will reveal a means of protection against this dangerous animal. Night travellers carry a burning torch, which they swing as they walk. Upon seeing this, the animal flies as rapidly as does a timid man before a madman's sword. This beast is never seen during the daytime.

The natives are also pestered by crocodiles, especially in remote and swampy places. These animals catch and eat children, but do not venture to attack grown persons. The monks have eaten crocodile meat, and found it similar to the fresh meat of an ass, but of insipid taste. The meat of the Nile crocodiles is the same, as I had occasion to write in my book about my embassy to Cairo, dedicated to King Ferdinand and Queen Isabella. The female crocodile exhales an odour similar to that of voluptuous musk.

Wild cats live in this country, and, when they are little their mother carries them, gliding amongst the trees. When the mother is killed with arrows the little ones are captured and kept for amusement as we do long-tailed monkeys and apes, though the monks report that they are very different. Sometimes these animals are caught in nets spread near springs. The natives relate that beyond the mountains to which they point, there live savage beasts whose faces, feet, and hands resemble the human form;[1] sometimes these animals stand up and walk with their heads erect. People who have heard these accounts think they must be bears; but none have been seen in the forests of that region.

There is another ferocious animal larger than an ass, which is the declared enemy of dogs, which it catches and carries off whenever it finds them, as does the wolf or lion with sheep. The monks have lost three of their watch-dogs in this wise, carried off from the vestibule of the convent. This beast's feet are unlike those of any other animal; it looks like a French shoe, large in front, round, undivided, and with pointed spurs. This animal is black, covered with hair, and is afraid of men; the natives call it *cappa*. Leopards and lions are also found in this country, but of such a gentle nature that they are not dangerous, without mentioning great numbers of deer, which the native hunters kill with arrows.

Another animal, larger than a French dog, has been noted; it is called *aranata* and has a man's face, a thick beard, and a grave and respectable expression. Its hands, face, and feet are those of a man; it lives on fruits and climbs among the trees, like a cat or a monkey. Such animals go in troops, and frequently quarrel amongst themselves to such an extent that the first monks, who settled in that region, thought they were demons, enraged at their arrival, who sought to frighten them by their cries. The aranata is very quick and avoids arrows shot at it by seizing them with its hand, and throwing them back at the bowman. It appears to me that it belongs

[1] Doubtless some animal of the larger species of monkey—possibly a gorilla.

to the race of monkeys or apes, but the monks declare the contrary.

There is also another very strange and lean animal, which instead of dung, throws forth snakes. The monks kept one of these animals, and my statement is based on their observation. When asked what became of these snakes, they answered that they went into the neighbouring forest and lived only a short time. The animal itself stinks as badly as a decaying corpse in need of burial. Disgusted by this stench the monks killed the beast. It had a head like a fox, and its hair resembled a wolf's.

It is known that worms frequently appear in children's stomachs, and that old people do not escape this infirmity. These worms which are discharged living are called *lombrices*. Who therefore shall prevent us believing that something similar may not be elsewhere repeated, especially when such respectable men affirm the fact?

There is another animal which, by a curious instinct, lives by feeding on ants, as does our magpie. It has a pointed snout a cubit long, and in place of a mouth it has an elongated opening through which it thrusts forth a very long tongue, which it introduces into the ant-hills concealed under the trees. By movements of its tongue it attracts the ants, and as soon as it feels it to be full of these insects, it draws the tongue in, swallowing the ants as food.

The animal covered with scales which I have frequently mentioned also lives in this country. Wild boars, hedgehogs, porcupines, and divers sorts of weasels are not wanting. Pelicans of numerous varieties and in excessive numbers are also found there. I have spoken at length of these birds in one of my books dedicated to the Duke Sforza. The bats, like the mosquitoes, attack sleepers during the night. The bats fasten upon any part of the human body which remains uncovered, biting quickly and sucking the blood.

There is an amusing story Your Holiness may read,

growing out of a bat's bite. A servant of the monks who suffered from a pleurisy was at death's door, and needed to be quickly bled. Two or three times the surgeon tried to open a vein with his razor, but could not draw a drop of blood. He was therefore abandoned as one who had but a few hours to live; and the monks, after bidding him a last farewell, made preparations for his burial. Meanwhile a bat dropped on the abandoned unfortunate, opened a vein in one of his feet which was uncovered, and only after gorging himself with blood did he quit, leaving the vein open. When the monks returned at daybreak, instead of dead, as they expected, they found the man fresh and lively and almost out of danger; he convalesced rapidly and resumed his former occupation. The bat had acted as doctor, and merited thanks. The bite of these creatures kills dogs, cats, and chickens. The natives call them *rere;* I give things the names they use, which are not many.

There are crows, not black, with hooked aquiline beaks, rapacious and slow of flight, as we commonly see in the case of the *avitade* in Spain, which is larger than a goose. At sunset they exhale fragrant perfumes, but at mid-day, or when the air is heavy, they have no odour. Large quantities of partridges, chickens, and doves are found in this country, as are likewise sparrows smaller than our wrens. Marvellous things are told of their industry in building their nests to protect themselves against birds of prey and other animals.

The neighbouring district to Chiribichi is called Atata, and is remarkable for its salt ponds, as we have already said. While the Spaniards were exploring their banks, those who were looking towards the sea while their companions were playing games or resting, beheld an unrecognisable object floating on the waves. It seemed to be a human head covered with hair and a thick beard, and with arms moving. As long as they watched it without

speaking, the monster moved quietly as though admiring
the ship, but when the sailors shouted to draw their
comrades' attention, the noise frightened the creature,
which dived, but not without exposing that part of its
body concealed under water. It ended in a fish's tail,
and its lashings stirred up the hitherto tranquil waters.
I believe it was a Triton, one of those named by the
fables of old, the trumpeters of Neptune.

Near to Cubagua—an island lying near the island of
Margarita celebrated for its pearl fisheries—it appears
that another monster of the same kind has been seen.
Is it not alleged that in our own Cantabrian Sea at certain
periods of the year, something like virgins' voices singing,
is heard? These are thought to be the cries of such animals
in the breeding season.

There are many other unknown species of fish in these
regions, of which two are especially useful. The first is
roasted and preserved, just as we salt meat or fish for
later consumption. The second is boiled, skinned, and
made into balls, after which it is traded for other merchandise with other tribes who do not possess this commodity.
There are two different methods of catching fish; if it
is a question of a general haul at a place where it is known
fish are plentiful, a number of young men assemble in a
circle, and silently move round the school of fish, as
hunters sometimes do hares; then throwing themselves
into the water as though they were dancing, they dex-
terously move sticks carried in their right hands, while
with the left they drive the fish, little by little, as though
they were animals in a park, towards the sands of the
shore, throwing basketfuls of their catch on the beach.

I am not astonished at this, for I noticed the same
kind of fishing on the Nile, when I went up that river on
my journey to the Sultan, twenty-four years ago. As
the ships carrying me, my companions, and the Sultan's
courtiers sent to meet me, had been forced to stop not

far from the bank to obtain fresh provisions, and as it was not prudent to go on shore because of the nomad Arabs, one of the natives advised me to throw a bit of bread in the water. A multitude of fish instantly assembled, exhibiting so little fear that they were caught in baskets. They swam in schools towards the bit of bread, like famished monsters throwing themselves upon something dipped in honey. Although whole basketfuls were taken, one might have gone on fishing for ever. When the people along the river were asked how it came about that these little fish were so numerous, we understood that they never ate them, because they were dangerous. They urged me not to touch one with my hand, showing me a red point on their back with which the fish stings a fisherman, just as bees do with their sting. The people of Chiribichi however encounter no such obstacle, for the fish are not dangerous.

The other kind of fishing is surer and more sportsmanlike; burning torches are brought at night amongst the boats which start at once for the place in which experience teaches they will find great schools of fish. The flaming torches are then waved upon the boats, the light attracting the fish in great numbers. As many as one likes are speared, after which they are sorted and dried at a slow fire. They are packed in baskets to await the arrival of traders, who buy them. Enough concerning marine subjects.

What shall we say concerning the multitude of insects and reptiles peculiar to this country? The salamanders of Chiribichi are as large as a man's hand, and their bite is fatal. They croak at night like clucking hens in breeding time. Scorpions, with stings in their tails, are everywhere; and the natives use these stings to point their arrows. The spiders are of various colours and are twice as large as ours; these insects and their webs are interesting to study. Their webs are so strong that any bird smaller than a sparrow, caught therein, cannot break loose. The monks have reported that it was with great difficulty they got rid of these webs.

The natives eat spiders, frogs, worms, and even fleas, without repugnance; and nevertheless their stomachs are so delicate that the mere sight of anything distasteful to them brings on a fit of vomiting. There are four different kinds of pestiferous gnats. To protect themselves against these, people bury themselves in the sand, covering their faces with leaves so as to breathe; the smaller the gnats, the more merciless they are.

Three species of bees have been noted, two of which, similar to ours, deposit their honey in combs. The bees of the third sort are smaller and black, and make their honey in the woods, without mixing it with wax. The natives like to eat little bees, raw, fried, or sometimes boiled. There are two species of wasps, one harmless, in the houses, and a dangerous kind in the forests.

Enormous serpents live on certain sea beaches. While sailors happen to be asleep, these serpents glide up the sides of the ship and, in the twinkling of an eye, kill, rend, and devour the unfortunate sleepers, as do vultures when they seize upon dead bodies.

At certain periods of the year the young growth of the trees is damaged by cockchafers, locusts, and grasshoppers. Unless great care is taken, a kind of weevil attacks the maize, while it is being dried and stored in the barns. It eats the grain and leaves the shell, as sometimes happens to our beans and wheat. As I have already said in my book addressed to Sforza, the natives like to use lanterns as a protection against gnats, and also for lighting purposes at night.

It is alleged that at certain periods of the year, the sea-coasts appear to be stained with blood. When questioned on this subject old people say they think large numbers of fish have their new-laid eggs swept away by the waters which thus acquire this blood-red colour; but they do not affirm this as a fact. On this point and many others, those who care to look for marrow on the outside of a bone may either believe my story or gnash their teeth, out of jealousy. I have already spoken sufficiently concerning quadrupeds, birds, insects, trees, herbs, essences, and other similar things. Let us now draw our bow upon the life and customs of mankind.

BOOK VIII

THE natives of Chiribichi[1] are very superstitious. They love games, music, and noise. At dawn and twilight they play various musical instruments, and sing amongst themselves; sometimes they pass eight days together making music, singing, chanting in chorus, drinking, and eating until they are completely worn out. Their songs are melancholy.

They love to wear jewels and crowns on their heads, and they decorate their necks and legs with sea-shells and snail-shells in place of bells. Some of them wear head-dresses of various coloured feathers. Others hang certain golden balls, which they call guanines, on their breasts, and they all paint themselves with vegetable colours. The people who seem to us the ugliest, appear to them to be the most attractive.

They assemble, and sometimes forming in a circle, a crescent, or sometimes like a wedge, and again in a circle alternately clasping and loosening each other's hands, they turn round and round, jumping and dancing, and always accompanying themselves with songs. They move to and fro, their faces assuming different expressions; some with closed lips are silent, others shout with wide-open mouths. The monks report that they have seen

---

[1] For information concerning the Indians of Venezuela and neighbouring regions, consult Oviedo y Barios, *Historia de la Conquista y Poblacio de Venezuela* (1723); Cassani, *Historia del nuevo reino de Granada* (1741); Bellin. *Description Géographique de la Guyane* (1763).

them continuing these futile and exhausting exercises for more than six hours without the least rest.

When people are invited by heralds' proclamation to the residence of an important cacique, the latter's servants clean and sweep the roads, clearing them of all grass, pebbles, thorns, straw, and other rubbish. When necessary they even widen the road. As soon as they are within a stone's throw from the cacique's house, the guests halt and form in orderly ranks in the open country, striking their war javelins and arrows against one another, singing and dancing incessantly. Presently they intone a measure in a low, quavering voice, and begin to advance. As they approach, they raise their voices, giving greater intensity to their song, which is always some such refrain as this: "The day is fair; fair is the day; the day is fair."

In each village there is a leader who sets the measure of the dance or song; and so harmoniously are the people trained, that although they are numerous, one would believe he heard one sole voice and saw a single movement. One of the cacique's servants precedes the procession walking backwards as far as the dwelling. As they enter the house, the chanting ceases while some of the people pretend to fish and others to hunt; one of them then steps forward and delivers a eulogy of the cacique and his ancestors, in the form of a speech. Another of them imitates the gestures of a buffoon, rolling his eyes and staring about. Afterwards they sit cross-legged on the ground in silence. Then they begin to eat to the point of nausea and drink till they are drunk.

The more intemperate a man is, the stronger is he reputed to be. The women, however, drink more moderately, for they have to look after their husbands prone on the ground from drunkenness. These orgies last so long that a woman is charged to take care and look after each man. The women also bring the stores of food and drink to the place appointed for the meeting. They serve drink to the men in the following manner: They begin by presenting a man who is sitting with a cup from which they have drunk. The man rises and the cup passes from one to another until each one of the assembly has drunk in turn. The monks report that they have seen one of these natives so swollen with drink that he looked like a pregnant woman.

They are not slow at quarrelling, complaining, and recalling old injuries. Hence duels, provocations, single combats, budding hatreds, and the revival of ancient feuds follow. As soon as they are able to get up and go home, they begin singing again and in a minor key, the women more melancholy than the men.

They practise magic, as we shall later explain, and are instructed therein by masters. They affirm that they have relations with demons and speak with them, especially when their minds are intoxicated. It is for this reason that, without mentioning fermented liquors, they make use of the fumes of an intoxicating herb which renders them completely insensible. They also drink the juices of certain herbs, which act as emetics, thus permitting them to prolong their gluttony and drunkenness. Young girls are present at these banquets. They wrap the calves of their legs and thighs with skeins of yarn, binding them so tightly that they swell. They actually imagine that this stupid practice renders them more beautiful in the eyes of their lovers. The rest of their bodies is naked, though married women wear short cotton trousers.

These natives have different kinds of military musical instruments, with which they sometimes rouse themselves to mirth, sometimes to sadness, sometimes to fury. They are made of large sea-shells across which strings are stretched, or else they are flutes made of stags' bones, or from river rushes. They also make little drums, decorated with different kinds of paintings, either out of gourds or from a piece of hard wood thicker than a man's arm.

Almost every night they shout from the tops of the highest houses in the village, like public criers, and from the neighbouring village the answer quickly comes back. When asked why they so exerted themselves, they answered that it is to prevent their enemies from surprising them by a sudden descent, for internal wars are incessant amongst them.

Their languages are difficult to understand, for their words are too abbreviated, after the manner of poetic licence which permits using *deum* for *deorum*. They bathe every day, before sunrise if it is warm, after sunrise if it is cold. To beautify themselves they rub their bodies with a sort of slimy ointment, upon which they stick birds' feathers. This is the punishment meeted out in Spain to wantons and witches when they are taken out of prison to be publicly exposed.

The natives of Chiribichi, who live along the coast, fear neither excessive cold or heat; although they are near the equator, they are hardly under the tenth degree of the arctic pole; the continent extends towards the antarctic pole as far as the fifty-fourth degree south of the equator, where the days are the shortest when with us they are the longest, and *vice versa*. The man whom the natives consider the most powerful and the most noble, is he who possesses the most gold and boats dug out of tree-trunks; or whoever has the largest number of relatives and may boast of the brave deeds of his ancestors and of his family. Whoever injures one of his compatriots must look to himself, for they never forgive, and use treachery to revenge themselves. They are boastful beyond measure.

They like to use bows and poisoned arrows. They poison their arrows with the stings of scorpions, the heads of certain ants, poisons which they manufacture, and those little plums I have mentioned, as well also as the juice they distil from certain trees in which they dip their arrows. But everybody is not permitted to make this mixture. There are certain old women skilled in the art, who are shut in at certain times and furnished with the necessary materials; during two days these women watch and distil the ointment. As soon as it is finished the house is opened, and if the women are well and not found lying on the ground half dead from the fumes of the poison, they are severely punished, and the ointment is thrown away as being valueless; for the strength of the poison is such, that the mere odour of it, while compounding almost kills its makers.[1]

Whoever is wounded by one of these poisoned arrows dies, but not instantly, and no Spaniard has yet found a remedy for such wounds. The natives know some, but the remainder of one's life, after being cured, is sufficiently disagreeable; for it is necessary to abstain from many things one likes. First of all, from sexual pleasures for two years, and afterwards, during a lifetime, from liquors, excessive pleasures of the table, and all exertion. Otherwise death quickly follows. Our monks have seen many wounded Indians,—for they live in a state of perpetual war,—but they assisted at the death of only one woman, who was unwilling to undergo the cure; the women fight by their husbands' sides. Nobody has been able to extort from them the secret of this antidote.

From childhood they practise archery with wax or wooden balls instead of arrows. When navigating their boats one of them stands in the prow of the boat singing, the oarsmen following the cadence and keeping time with their oars.

The women are usually sufficiently well-behaved in their youth, but as they grow older they become more inconstant. They follow the common usage of their

[1] Supposed by some to be the fatal poison, curare.

sex in preferring foreigners, and hence they love the
Christians better than their compatriots. They run,
swim, dance, and indulge in all exercises as actively as do
the men. Childbirth is easy, and they show no suffering.
They do not go to bed, nor take any care of themselves.
They press the head of the new-born child between two
cushions, one on the forehead and the other at the back,
squeezing it until the eye emerges from the socket, for they
admire flat faces. When the young girls become marriageable their parents shut them up for two successive years
in dark rooms, during which time they never go into the
open, so as not to tan. During this period they never
cut their hair. Guarded thus jealously, these women are
much sought after as wives, and if they are the first wives
of their husbands they exercise a sort of direction over the
other women, of whom a cacique may have as many as
he chooses. Generally a man is content with one wife;
the young girls of the common people give themselves
to anybody who asks them. Adultery after marriage is
forbidden, and if committed it is not the woman but the
man who is punished. The wife may be repudiated.

All the people in the neighbourhood are invited to the
wedding of young girls of high birth, and the female
guests arrive, carrying provisions of food and drink on
their shoulders. All the men bring bunches of straw
and thatch to build the house of the new couple, which is
constructed with beams set upright in the shape of a tent.
When the house is finished the bride and groom adorn
themselves, according to their means, with the usual jewels
and necklaces and different kinds of stones. Those who
possess none, obtain them from their neighbours. The bride
then sits outside with the young girls, and the bridegroom
is surrounded by the men. A dance is performed around
them, the young girls encircling the bride, and the men
the bridegroom. Then a hair-cutter approaches and cuts
the bridegroom's hair up to the tops of his ears, while a

woman cuts the bride's hair, leaving it in front on a line
with the eyebrow, but not touching it in the back.   When
night falls, the bride's hand is placed in her husband's,
and she is delivered to him.[1]

Both men and women pierce their ears, in which they
hang jewels.   The men eat together, the women never
mixing with them.   The latter are occupied in household
duties, in which they delight.   The husbands pass their
time in hunting, fighting, fishing, and different games.

I have omitted many details concerning the customs
of the natives and their manner of life, because I remember
having described them in the Decade addressed to the
Duke Sforza, when I laid them before our India Council,
and I fear to involve myself in useless repetitions.   I
shall enter my seventieth year on the fourth day of the
nones of February, 1526.[2]   I have so abused my memory
that it is almost destroyed; to such a point that when I
have once finished writing on a subject, I am obliged to
admit, if asked how I have treated it, that I do not know;
especially when it is a question of information which
reached me from different sources, and deals with different
epochs.   There remain, nevertheless, three subjects I
must touch upon; when that is done, I shall have finished
my work,—at least unless new documents reach me.
I wish to state how these half-naked and uncivilised
barbarians understand and practise magic, secondly to
describe their funeral ceremonies, and finally to speak
of their belief in a future life.

There are amongst them professors of the art of magic,
who are called *piaces*.   The people stand when in the
presence of these piaces, and honour them as gods.   They

[1] . . . . . *ut ea utatur ad libitum datur venia.*

[2] This is one of the passages from which the date of Peter Martyr's
birth is deduced: others equally explicit contradict it.   He here admits
that his memory is seriously impaired, but however untrustworthy it may
have been respecting precise dates and incidents in his long and varied
life, he would hardly be in doubt as to the year of his own birth.

choose amongst their children some between the ages of ten and twelve years, whom they believe to be foreordained by nature for this ministry, just as we send our children to the schools of grammarians and rhetoricians.

These children are sent into the mysterious depths of the forests, where their life is more austere than that of the disciples of Pythagoras according to the ancient law. They spend two years in huts and become imbued with the severest precepts. They abstain from all flesh foods, and drink nothing but water, avoiding even all thoughts of love, and living their life isolated from their parents, relatives, and friends. During the daytime they do not see their instructors, who only visit them at night, when they call them before them, dictate their magical incantations, and teach them secrets for healing the sick. After this period of two years, the children return home, bringing with them evidences of the learning they have acquired from their masters, the piaces.

The pupils bring certificates of their knowledge from their piace teachers just as is done at Bologna, Pavia, and Perugia, amongst those who obtain the title of Doctor. Nobody else may venture to practise medicine. Neighbours and friends never have recourse, in case of sickness, to the services of doctors whom they know, but always summon strangers; and especially do the caciques call in strangers. The superstitions practised, vary according to the diversity of the maladies, as does also the remuneration. In the case of a slight illness, the piaces fill their mouths with certain herbs, press their lips to the injured part, licking and sucking energetically and pretending to draw out the humour which causes the illness; after which they leave the house with cheeks puffed out, spitting frequently, and affirming that the sick man will be speedily cured, since they have relieved him of his malady.

In case of a fever or more severe pain, when the patient seems to suffer from a serious malady, the piaces change their method. When they visit the patient, they are careful to bring with them a piece of wood cut from a rare tree, which they know produces vomiting. They dampen this piece of wood by placing it in a dish or basin filled with water. Then, seating themselves beside the patient, they affirm that he is possessed by a demon. Every one present, relatives or servants, believe this, and entreat the piace to supply the remedy. He then approaches the patient, licking his entire body and pronouncing incantations in a low voice. He declares that in this way he drives the demon out of the marrow of the patient, and draws it to himself. Presently he takes the piece of wood, rubs it on the patient's palate, and then forces it down his throat and provokes vomiting; he repeats this operation until the sick man has thrown up everything inside him. During this time the piace pants, trembles, rolls on the ground, howls, and sighs worse than a stuck bull in the circus. He beats his breast and forehead during at least two hours, the sweat falling in drops, like rain on a roof.

The Dominican monks have witnessed this sight and wondered why this agitation did not kill the piace. When asked why they torture themselves in this wise, the piaces answer that these incantations are necessary to drive the demons from the marrow of the patient. They force out the demons and draw them to themselves by suction and friction.

After torturing himself by these wild and frantic movements, the piace, belching disgustingly, throws up a thick mass of slimy matter, in the midst of which is a hard black lump. Carefully removing the black substance from the remainder of this nauseous mess, and leaving the piace half dead in a corner, the people carry it out, shouting the while, and throw the black stuff as far away as possible; the following is the refrain they sing: *Maitonoro quian, maitonoro quian!* which means, Go forth, demon!

When all is over, the patient is asked to pay for his recovery. He is convinced that he will speedily get well, and this opinion is shared by his relatives and neighbours. Therefore the piace is paid, according to the gravity of the disease, with a quantity of maize and provisions. If the patient is a person of consequence and the malady is serious, they give him in addition some of those golden balls they wear on their breasts.

Let it be well remembered that the Dominican monks, whose evidence is above all suspicion, affirm that very few of the sick treated in this manner died. What this mystery may be, and how sick people may be treated in this manner, I leave others to decide; contenting myself with repeating that I have the story from trustworthy witnesses. Let us further note that if there is a relapse, different remedies and extracts from herbs are employed.

They likewise question the devils concerning the future, calling them up by means of incantations they learned in the retreat when they were children. They question them concerning rain, drought, the temperature, illnesses, and touching war and peace; business affairs, journeys, new enterprises, loss and gain; they also ask them what should be thought of the arrival of the Christians, whom they detest because they occupy their lands, impose laws, and force them to adopt new rites and customs, and to abandon their natural tastes.

Questioned concerning the future, the piaces—according to the monks—answered with great precision. Two proofs of this exactitude, chosen amongst many others reported to our council, may be cited. The monks, abandoned in the country of Chiribichi, were anxiously awaiting the arrival of Christians. They asked the piaces if the desired vessels would soon arrive, and the piaces foretold the day of their arrival, the number of their crew, describing the appearance of the sailors, and giving many other particulars. Everything they said was true.

Here is another thing even more incredible. The piaces foretold the eclipses of the moon more than four months in advance; nevertheless they are not learned or scientific. As long as the eclipse lasts, they fast and are bowed with affliction, for they are convinced that this phenomenon foretells some misfortune. Hence they salute the disappearance of the planet with melancholy lamentations and lugubrious chantings; especially the women, who beat one another, while young girls cut their arms with fishbones as sharp as lancets. What food and drink existed in the houses before this time are thrown away into the sea or rivers, and nobody thinks of amusement until the moon emerges safe and sound from the battle in which she is engaged. As soon as the light reappears they laugh, sing, and dance with delight.

Ridiculous as it sounds eclipses of the moon according to the piaces, are fatal to criminals. They say that the moon has been wounded by the angry sun, and when that planet's vexation is past, she resumes her primitive state. Such is the version they repeat, as it was taught them; and nevertheless the true cause of eclipses is well-known to the devil since, being driven from heaven, he took with him his knowledge of the stars.

When, in response to the invitation of a prince or some friend, the piaces want to call up spirits, they enter, at the tenth hour of the night, into a mysterious retreat, taking with them a small number of courageous and daring young men. The magician seats himself upon a little stool, and the young men remain motionless at his feet. He pronounces some senseless words as in ancient times did the sibyl of Cumæ, announcing perfectly simple things in confusing terms. He rings the bells that he carries in his hands, after which, in a piteous voice accenting always the last syllable, he pronounces the following words to call up the demons; *Prororuré, prororuré*. He repeats these words frequently, and if the demon thus called delays his appearance, the sorcerer tortures himself cruelly for these invocations should bring him; if he does not appear, the sorcerer changes his incantations, begins to curse, and appears to give orders in angry tones. In all this, they only conform to the rules the ancients have taught them, when they studied in the mysterious forests. When they understand that the demon is about to come, they shake their bells more quickly, the better to receive him. The demon then takes possession of the piace. Throwing himself upon him with as much violence as a man in the flower of his age might use in attacking a child, he throws the piace to the ground, where he rolls in convulsions, showing all the signs of acute suffering. The bravest of those present approaches the tortured piace, and announces the orders of the cacique or the person for whom the piace has endured this severe trial. The demon answers by the voice of the man lying on the ground. We have stated the usual object of these questions.

When the answer has been received, the piace is asked what he wants for his trouble and whether he thinks the demon will be content with maize or other food. Everything the piace asks is scrupulously given to him. As a shepherd of a flock seeks to drive off a wolf by shouting, so do the natives think that, by shouting and beating of drums when a comet appears, they will drive away the fatal star.

The monks, who have furnished us these particulars and others of the same kind, were aware that we hesitated to accept their word. For that reason the friar Tomaso Ortiz, who knows in the most minute particulars the habits and customs of Chiribichi, has related the following story as a proof of the assertions.

BOOK IX

THE blessed friar, Pedro de Cordova, vice-provincial of our Order of Preachers in Andalusia, is esteemed a saint by all. He was led into the solitudes of the New World solely by his zeal for the propagation of the faith, resolved, by God's help, to discover the secrets of the piaces and to verify for himself whether they really prophesied under demoniac influence and pronounced oracles as did Apollo in Delphi. He learned that it was really true, for he was present during the incantations of a piace and witnesssed the ceremonies. The demons struck the piace unconscious to the ground, like a kite seizing a rabbit. Much astonished the monk put on his stole, and taking holy water in his right hand to sprinkle the piace, he grasped the crucifix in his left and spoke in the following terms: "If thou art a demon who dost overcome this man, in the name of this instrument of salvation whose power thou knowest well (and he exhibited the crucifix) I adjure you not to leave this place without first answering what I shall ask you."

Pedro de Cordova affirms that he asked him several questions, both in Latin and in Spanish, and that the man lying on the ground responded in neither Latin nor Spanish, but in his own tongue, and that his answers always fitted the questions. Amongst other things, the good monk asked him the following: "Now tell me, where do the souls of the natives of Chiribichi go when they leave their corporeal prison?"—"They are taken by us to the eternal flames and fires, that they may be punished with us for their crimes." These things took place in the presence of many of the natives who were present by the friar's orders.

The news of this interview spread throughout the country but failed to convert the people of Chiribichi from their bad habits; and the friar complains that they continued to give themselves up to their passions. The good Pedro de Cordova turned to the piace still lying upon the ground and cried, "Come out from that man's body, thou filthy spirit!" Hardly had he pronounced these words than the piace suddenly sprang to his feet, but he had so far lost his senses that he remained a long time as it were bewildered, and scarcely able to stand. As soon as he could speak again, he hurled maledictions and recriminations at the spirit that had so long held possession of his body.

Garcia de Loaysa, also a friar preacher of the Dominicans, whom Your Holiness has elevated to the highest dignity of the Order by conferring upon him the red hat, and who is now confessor of his imperial Majesty, Bishop of Osma and president of our India Council, confirms that Pedro Cordova is a holy man, and worthy of absolute belief. In my opinion it will not be useless to observe, —since our religion permits it,—that different persons are recognised as having been possessed by devils, and that Christ was several times reputed to have driven out unclean spirits from the bodies of the possessed.

These piaces celebrate festivals, at which they dance together and amuse themselves, for they live separated from other men because of the dignity of their office. They do not understand the sense of their incantations. The same thing often happens amongst us, for although Latin is sufficiently similar to Spanish, it is positive that the majority of those present do not understand what our priests chant. Even worse happens; for, owing to the

culpable negligence of their superiors, many priests venture
to say Mass who merely pronounce the formulas, of which
they fail to grasp the meaning.

You will be interested to hear about their funeral
customs. The dead bodies, especially those of the nobles,
are stretched on mats, woven partly of reeds, and are
gradually dried at a fire of special herbs. When all the
moisture is evaporated, the body is hung inside the house
and treated as a *penate*. This custom is also found in
other parts of the new continent. I have spoken of it in
my first Decades addressed to Pope Leo, uncle of Your
Holiness. The bodies which are not dried are taken out
of the houses and buried, the people weeping and beating
their breasts. When the first year of mourning has
expired, all the friends in the neighbourhood are summoned
and assemble to lament the dead. Each guest arrives
bringing food and drink, or is followed by slaves carrying
provisions. When night falls, the servants go to the tomb
and dig up the skeleton. They cry aloud, tear their
hair, and weep together; after which they sit in a circle,
holding their feet in their hands, bending their heads
between their legs, and giving frantic vent to woeful
cries, extending their legs and raising their heads and arms
towards heaven. They are heedless of the tears that fall
from their eyes and of the mucus from their nostrils, which
only makes them more frightful. The more hideous they
make themselves, the better do they believe they are
fulfilling their duties to the dead. The skeleton is
afterwards burned, all except the skull, which the noblest
of the women takes away to preserve in her house as a
sacred object. The guests then return home.

Let us now consider their beliefs concerning the soul.
They believe the soul to be immortal, and that released
from its corporeal shell it repairs to the forests on the
mountains, where it lives for ever in caverns. They
place food and drink for its sustenance. The voices of

grottos, which the Latins call echoes, are thought by the natives to be souls wandering in those places and answering.

It is known that they venerate the cross, but it is a cross inclined slightly in its shape like an X or resembling another cross formed in this manner: |X|. They place this symbol on the forehead of new-born babes, for they believe it drives away demons. If they have a horrible dream during the night, they seize a cross, believing that it purifies the place. When asked whence they have these beliefs and rites they do not understand, they answer that they have been transmitted from their ancestors to their fathers.

May the people of Chiribichi forgive me if I stop speaking of them as I promised. I had, in fact, promised to close my work with them, unless new informations should be forthcoming. It is fitting to terminate this narrative by an enumeration of the magnificent fleets which traverse the ocean. My hand is weary, and I long to cease writing. In fact, while I was composing my decade addressed to Duke Sforza and the present one dedicated to Your Holiness, much information reached me, of which I have repeated the greater part, reserving the rest for the present occasion. My many occupations do not permit me to devote all my time to writing the history of Indian affairs. Sometimes an entire month passes without my receiving any news, and, therefore, when a leisure moment comes my pen is crowded, and I cannot observe the least order, since the documents reach me without any. Let us now speak of the fleets.

Out of four ships, which sailed last year from Hispaniola, one arrived here. While the council was in session, the sailors reported verbally or described in writing the adventures of Garay, Egidius Gonzales, Cristobal Olid, Pedrarias, and Cortes. It is their narratives we have repeated.

Another fleet sailed from Barrameda at the mouth of the Guadalquivir, the fifth day of the nones of May, 1525. It was composed of twenty-four ships bound first for Hispaniola, where the council for all colonial affairs sits, and was afterwards to scatter to different provinces of the New World. On board one of these vessels embarked my faithful Mendegurra, who was acquainted with the former legates at this court, the Archbishop of Cosenza, and Viansi. He goes to my Elysian island of Jamaica, to take charge of my affairs. He has written me from Gomera, one of the Fortunate Islands, where those about to cross the ocean usually make a stop. He tells me the voyage of ten days was a prosperous one. The faster ships might have accomplished it more quickly, but had to slacken their course to wait for the more heavily laden vessels and prevent them from falling into the hands of French pirates, who had long been lying in wait for them. They were all to put out on the high seas four days later. Each vessel will sail independently, setting its sails as it pleases, for there will be nothing more to fear from pirates. It only remains for us to hope that this journey, begun under favourable auspices, may have a happy termination.

I do not remember whether I have mentioned two other vessels sent by Fernando Cortes from our most distant possession, New Spain, which have landed at the Cassiterides (the Azores) islands under the domination of the Portuguese.

Whether I did or not, I must now tell how these vessels succeeded in escaping the pirates cruising about the archipelago—in fact waiting for them; how they escaped pursuit and what they bring. One of them, unloading its cargo, decided to tempt fortune, and the gods coming to its assistance, it escaped without encountering the brigands. Lupo Samaneca was commissioned by the ships' captains to bring back messages to the Emperor and the India Council. Samaneca has been brought up from his childhood by me, and left three years ago, with my consent for the New World, in company with Albornoz, who was sent to the colonies as royal treasurer.

As soon as this news was received, a fleet of six ships was promptly fitted out; four were of two hundred tons burthen, and the other two were fighting caravels, prepared to engage the pirates if they met them. The King of Portugal added to the squadron four other faster ships, well provided with every kind of artillery. The fleet sailed the seventh day of the ides of June, took on the cargo which had been unloaded, and returned without being molested. It was the end of July that they returned to Seville. We are thus satisfied and give thanks to God, while awaiting the arrival of the captains from one day to another. . . .[1]

There were only two ships sent by Cortes and they were both small. If the number of vessels in these countries is few, it is due somewhat to the resources of the treasury. They only brought seventy thousand gold pesos to the Emperor. I have frequently said that the peso was worth a little more than a quarter more than a Spanish ducat, but I do not think that applies to those pesos, for they are not of pure gold. They also bring an engine of war called a culverin, made of gold, but not of pure gold; at least, according to the report of Lupo Samaneca, now with me, who tried his fortune on the first of the two ships which arrived. This culverin weighs twenty-three quintals, as they are called in Spanish, each quintal weighing four rubi or pounds at six ounces to the pound.

The ships were also loaded with precious stones and

---

[1] At this point of his narrative Peter Martyr digresses, introducing lengthy and wearisome considerations on the subject of ecclesiastical benefices. Devoid of interest in itself and entirely alien to the sequence of his narrative, it has seemed to the translator wiser to omit this page. *Nimis sum evagatus; ad naves vectas redeamus.* With this, the author's admission at the close of his irrelevant digression, his readers must agree.

numerous very rich ornaments. There was on board the
first vessel—that of Lupo Samaneca—an extraordinarily
beautiful tiger, but it has not been brought to us. The
reports concerning Cortes and his extreme ability in the
art of deceiving and corrupting people are contradictory.
It seems to be certain that he possesses such quantities
of gold, pearls, and silver as have never before been heard
of. They are brought to him secretly at night, unknown
to the magistrates, and carried in by a back door of his
immense residence, on the shoulders of the caciques'
slaves. We shall speak later of the towns and their
municipal officers, the numerous and opulent country
houses, the gold and silver mines, the extent of the provinces, as well as many other similar things.

As we are working secretly to devise certain preventive
measures, I am forbidden to talk too much. Nothing
must be said for the moment, until we have completed
the stuff we have begun to weave. Let us, therefore, put
all that to one side, and speak a little about the other
squadron. In my Decade brought to Your Holiness by
my representative the bachelor Antonio Tamarano,
and which began with the word PRIUSQUAM, I spoke
at length concerning the fleet sent to the archipelago of
the Moluccas where the spices grow, and which lies under
or very near to the equatorial line. We said that in our
controversy with the King of Portugal, at Pacencis, vulgarly called Badajoz, the Portuguese lost their case but
refused to abide by the decision.

The armament of the fleet had been suspended, and
after the rupture of negotiations it was first sent to Bilboa
in Biscay, and afterwards to Ferrol, a port of Galicia,
and the safest of all the ports where sea-going vessels
may take refuge. This was about the calends of June
of this year, 1525. The fleet was provided with everything
necessary for a long voyage, and also for battle if forced
into an engagement. It lay at anchor several days

awaiting favourable winds.   It is composed of seven ships,
four of two hundred and twenty tons, and there are also,
to use the vulgar tongue, two caravels, the seventh being
what is called in Spanish a *patache*.   Finally, the necessary parts for building an eighth ship have been loaded
on board, and will be put together as soon as the fleet
arrives at the desired port of the island of Tidor, one of
the Moluccas.   As we have already related in the book
treating of the voyage round the world, addressed to
Pope Adrian, it is in this island that one of the surviving ships remained for some time with fifty of its crew.
As soon as the fleet arrives, two of the lightest vessels
will be used for exploring the archipelago and examining
carefully the countries lying under and on that side of
the equinoctial line.

While this fleet was lying in port, the King of Portugal,
brother-in-law and cousin of the Emperor, incessantly
begged and entreated that he might be spared this great
loss; but as the Emperor was unwilling to offend Castile,
which is as the heart of his empire and kingdoms, he
refused the King's request.   The squadron therefore set
sail with a favourable wind on the feast of Santiago, the
patron of Spain.   As the anchor was raised, trumpets
sounded, drums beat, and cannons were fired in sign of
joy, so that the heavens almost seemed to fall and the
earth shook.   On the eve of the departure, the commander
of the fleet, Garcia Loaysa, Knight of St. John, who four
years before had been sent by the Emperor on an Embassy[1]
to the Grand Turk, swore allegiance before Count Fernando de Andrada, governor of Galicia, who had formerly
defeated the French general, Aubigny, in Calabria.[2]

---

[1] As stated in the Introduction, Peter Martyr was tendered this Embassy
to the Sultan, but prudently declined.   The difficult mission was then
entrusted to Loaysa.

[2] The Maréchal d'Aubigny fought in the Italian campaigns under
Charles VIII., Louis XII., and Francis I.   After the battle of Seminara in
Calabria he retreated, and it is to this check that Peter Martyr here refers.

The other captains took oath before the Admiral, the soldiers and servants before the captains. Loaysa afterwards received from Andrada and the viceroy in great pomp and amidst general applause, the royal standard, which had just been blessed. Profiting by a stern wind, he set sail.[1]

In obedience to the Emperor's orders, the Spaniards have promised to write from the Canaries to our Council, under whose authority they are. Garcia Loaysa is in command of the flag-ship. The commander of the second is Juan Sebastian de Cano, who brought the *Victoria* back to Spain, laden with perfumes, after being obliged to abandon his other ship shattered by storms. The third and fourth ships are commanded by Pedro de Vera, and Roderigo de Acuña, respectively, the latter being a man of illustrious birth, and both having several times commanded squadrons and distinguished themselves by their exploits and great reputation. The fifth ship is commanded by Don Jorge Manrique, brother of the Duke of Najara, who is younger and less experinced than the others; though of better birth, he has consented to accept a less important command, for he not unreasonably thinks that he should give way to more experienced chiefs. The commander of the sixth vessel is a nobleman from Cordova, Hozes; and it is a nobleman who commands the last ship, the little *patache*.

Before taking leave of this fleet, it remains to mention a fact of no small importance, which arouses much interest. What moved the Emperor and us members of the Council, to arm in a Galician port a squadron destined for the spice islands, and this to the serious injury of the great city of Seville, in which Indian business has hitherto been transacted? This port of Galicia offers safety and is, moreover, situated at the extremity of Spain, nearest

[1] For particulars of Garcia Loaysa's voyage to the Moluccas, consult Navarrete, tom v.

Great Britain, bordering on the frontiers of France, and
very convenient for merchants from the north looking for
spices. Mention of two formidable dangers, which our
sailors escape in this port must not be omitted; the stretch
of ocean separating it from the mouth of the Guadalquivir,
which is navigable as far as Seville is so swept by tempests that the lightest winds off the promontory of Sagres
and its neighbourhood drive ships on the rocks and
shatter them more mercilessly than if they were thrown
upon the reefs of Scylla or into the whirlpool of Charybdis.

Pirates constitute another danger. They prowl along
these coasts shut in between stern mountains and deserted
valleys, which are uninhabited, owing to their sterility.
The valleys serve the pirates as hiding-places. Informed by their watchers placed high up on the mountains,
they attack passing ships. This is the reason why it was
decided to equip the fleet in this port.

The course to be taken by the squadron will be that
followed by the Portuguese Magellan, when he made the
journey round the world, following what philosophers call
the torrid zone and advancing in the antarctic hemisphere
beyond the Tropic of Capricorn.

Another squadron commanded by the Italian, Sebastian
Cabot, will also take that same direction. I have mentioned him and Magellan in the book on the journey
round the world dedicated to Pope Adrian, and the
second preceding book addressed to the Duke of Sforza.
Both these fleets are being fitted out in the Guadalquivir;
they will first go to Hispaniola and the other islands,
San Juan, Cuba,—otherwise called Fernandina,—and
Jamaica, where I hold my benefice, and which has been
renamed Santiago. After that they will divide and sail
for the new continent and New Spain conquered by
Fernando Cortes. I have promised some day to speak
of the grandeur and the resources of this last possession.
For the moment, however, there are as many fleets

ploughing the ocean waves, and as many vessels coming
and going from the New World, as there are merchants
coming from Italy to fairs at Lyons, or from France and
Germany to the fairs at Antwerp in Belgium.

Gladly, Most Holy Father, would I penetrate by some
opening into the interior of your apartments and witness
the joy of your heart manifest itself in your face when you
first learn of these discoveries, and when these most
curious particulars of heretofore unknown countries
are told you, and you learn that they have been spirit-
ually given as wedding gifts to the Church, Christ's
spouse, and that nature is inexhaustible in her gifts,
according to her royal bounty. And if there still remain
unknown countries to be discovered, they are preparing
to later obey you and the Emperor. May Your Holiness
be content with this new effort, as the beginning of a
feast. I wish you a happy life.

From the town of Toledo in Carpentana, and the
Imperial Court.

The thirteenth day of the calends of November in
the year 1525.

BOOK X

FROM one hour to another our ocean brings forth new prodigies. When the illustrious nunzio of Your Holiness, Balthasar Castiglione,[1] a man gifted with every sort of virtue and grace, saw the two Decades dedicated to the Pope and the Duke of Milan bound together, he begged permission to offer them himself to Your Holiness. I acceded to his desire; but he has fallen seriously ill, and has been unable to busy himself with his affairs as he would have wished, although they are not numerous. During his illness he has sent no trustworthy secretary to carry despatches—and at the same time my writings—to Your Holiness, and this delay has enabled me to add some particulars as an appendix.

Three vessels have arrived from the New World, coming from New Spain, now under the government of Fernando Cortes, whom I have frequently mentioned. One of these ships is a caravel and the news it brings is deplorable. But to render more intelligible the course of events I must begin by speaking of the letters brought by the other two ships above mentioned. Amongst these letters we must distinguish those which are of a general character and those which are private.

[1] Balthasar Castiglione enjoyed the friendship of Leo X. and Clement VII. He was born near Mantua in December, 1478. His best known work is *Il Cortegiano*. Upon hearing the news of his death at Toledo in 1529, Charles V. exclaimed: "*Yo vos digo que es muerto uno de los mejores caballeros del mundo.*" Castiglione's life was written in 1780 by Serassi, *Vita del Castiglione*.

First of all, there is a long report of general interest drawn
by Cortes and his officers—his intendant, treasurer, and
factor. It contains a great deal about the nature of the
soil, the presents sent to the Emperor, the small number
of vessels encountered in those parts, this last fact being
stated to excuse the small quantity of precious stones
and gold sent to Spain. Cortes insists on his enormous
expenses, complaining of his poverty and the debts he
has contracted. He reminds us of the ships he has built,
with which he hoped to reach the equinoctial line, which
is not more than twelve degrees distant; because the
people along that coast told him that near by there were
islands producing gold, spices, and precious stones. He
has dwelt at length upon these different points and has
not spared his complaints about the ships that were
burned with all their stores, and the jealousy of his enemies
which had hindered him in carrying out the enterprise
he had undertaken. Moreover, Cortes pledges himself
to make good the losses if the meddlers leave him alone.
He enumerates the recently discovered gold and silver
mines, which are numerous and various; the difficulties
demanding new remedies; the contribution of sixty-three
thousand gold pesos he had been forced to make, despite
the advice of the magistrates, under pretext of raising a
new army; the generals he has named to conquer other
neighbouring and new provinces, and many other similar
things.

The private letters and secret reports have been drawn
up by the accountant and secretary Albornoz, in unknown
characters, vulgarly called cipher. It was confided to
Albornoz when he left, for at that time suspicions existed
concerning the intentions of Cortes. These letters are
full of attacks on the craftiness of Cortes, his consuming
avarice, and his partially revealed tyranny. Whether
they are warranted or, more likely, whether they were
drawn up to please certain people, as usually happens,

time alone will show us. Serious men have already been chosen to go thither and open an enquiry. When all these mysteries are disclosed, I shall inform Your Holiness. But let us return to Cortes.

The disobedience of Cristobal Olid, of which I have spoken at length in my preceding books, so infuriated Cortes, that he desired to live no longer if that rebel went unpunished. His nostrils and throat swelled with rage.[1] On several occasions he showed signs of madness and indulged in unrestrained language. According to the general evidence, Olid was then more than five hundred leagues distant east from the salt lake of Temistitan. To overtake him it would be necessary to march over almost inaccessible roads. He had established himself on a gulf discovered a long time ago and named the Gulf of Figueras. He hoped to discover the strait that has been sought with such persistency. It was due to this fact that three captains, who had landed in the country, killed one another; I shall later speak of these deplorable combats; but for the present I do not wish to leave Cortes.

When the news spread that Cortes had raised an army, the royal officials gently remonstrated with him in the beginning, cautioning him not to adopt a course which promised so many undesirable results; for it was a question of a war between Spaniards. They begged him not to provoke so great a calamity among the Christians, and not to risk his position by exposing himself to such danger. For they felt certain at the time that everything would be lost if Cortes abandoned the capital of the empire without leaving soldiers in the province of Temistitan, which had been only recently conquered and which still lamented the massacre of its ancient rulers and the loss of its tutelary deities, friends, and neighbours. If Cortes, whose name inspired all those nations with a sort of terror, were to

---

[1] Cortes rarely gave vent to his passions, but despite his self-control, his anger was betrayed by the swelling of the veins of his neck.

leave, was it not to be feared that some misfortune would follow, and that all would be lost? Which God forbid. The Emperor would take upon himself to punish Olid, who would no doubt be chastised for his treachery. Such were the arguments the officials repeated, but in vain. In their own name and in that of the Emperor, they again prayed and enjoined Cortes to renounce his undertaking. He promised and even swore not to march in person against Olid, but against some rebellious caciques not far distant.

He did not, however, keep his promise, and by forced marches pushed towards the east, still burning with fury against Olid. In the course of his march Cortes came upon vast lagoons along the seacoast, swamps in the valleys, and elsewhere steep mountains. Everywhere he commanded the natives to build bridges, dry up swamps, level mountains, and nobody dared refuse. With fire and sword he ravaged the territory of those who did not share his views; cutting his way through everything that opposed his march.

He had inspired the natives with such terror, by his defeat of so powerful a sovereign as Muteczuma and the conquest of his vast empire, that they believed him able to destroy the heavens if his fancy so prompted him. He took with him much baggage and many horses, a method of campaigning which was unknown to these nations. He collected his auxiliaries from the neighbours of those whose territories and kingdoms he traversed, and who had formerly been their enemies. On the other hand, he sent ahead overland two captains, one Pedro Alvarado, starting from the south coast, and the other a certain Godoy, starting from the north coast. These captains have sent reports to Cortes which are now, in our hands, describing these new, vast countries, and the warlike tribes inhabiting them; the cities built in lakes, upon mountain tops, and on the plains. The father of

Cortes, who is now here, has received a volume on this subject from his son, and has had it printed in Spanish; it is now exhibited for sale in the public bookstalls.

His sea force consists of three large ships and many high-born officers, under command of captain Francisco de las Casas. I have already spoken, and I shall again later on, about this. But let us return to past events which the order of my narrative demands. Cortes had instructed the commander of his sea force to capture Olid, if possible; and this he did, as I shall relate at the proper moment.

Such was the state of things when the two vessels recently arrived in Spain, bringing seventy thousand pesos of gold and two tigers, sailed from the country of Temistitan. One of these animals died at Seville from sea-sickness and fatigue; the other, which is a female and has been tamed, is still here. The culverin, of which there has been so much talk, is still to be seen. It is not in reality made entirely of gold, as has been reported, but it is very curious to examine. The ornaments, the weapons covered with gold and precious stones, the artistically wrought jewels, sent either by Cortes or by other conquerors of the country, have been seen by everybody. Persons who have come here in company with the most reverend legate of Your Holiness will one day verbally describe them to you. But enough said about these two ships. Let us now speak of the one caravel out of all seven ships, which succeeded in leaving the port of Medellin, the naval port of New Spain.

In the first place, why did Cortes decide to thus name this port? We shall explain. Medellin is a very well known town in Castile, and it was there Cortes was born. He therefore wished that the place destined to serve as the port for all these countries should bear the name of Medellin, in honour of his birthplace; and his desire has been gratified. It is likewise he who gave to the entire country the name of New Spain, and asked the Emperor to confirm his appellation.

There were seven merchant vessels lying in the port of Medellin, ready to return to Spain with full cargoes, when dissensions broke out among the royal officials. Some wished to send the gold and precious stones that had been collected by those ships to the Emperor who by the by, needs money badly because of the wars he is carrying on. They alleged that they should take advantage of the presence of those ships, since such an opportunity rarely occurred. Another reason was because two hundred thousand pesos of gold had been promised to the Emperor through the intermediary of Juan Ribera, secretary of Cortes, on condition that ships should immediately be sent over to carry back that amount. Their colleagues were of an opposite opinion, declaring that they should await the return of the governor, Cortes, and make no change in the established usage during his absence. They ended by taking up arms. By a mere chance Francisco de las Casas, commander of the maritime forces of Cortes, arrived, quite proud of having strangled Olid. He sided with the partisans of Cortes against those of the King, and it appears that the treasurer, Albornoz, had his horse wounded under him and was himself wounded and thrown into prison. The victors rushed to the shore, seized the captains of the seven ships, and, to prevent their departure, unloaded the vessels and carried off the tillers and rudders.

The commander of the caravel which succeeded in reaching Spain, furious at this disaster, awaited a favourable opportunity and returned to his ship. Although without sails and deprived of all his nautical instruments, he attempted a praiseworthy feat of navigation. He had cast aside as worn out and useless some old torn sails; with these rags, full of holes, and one large new canvas, he improvised a sail. Without saying a word to those who used violence against him, he raised his anchor and set sail. Aided by a favourable west wind, he reached Spain after the quickest passage that has ever been made by a ship returning from the extremity of the ocean.

The captain of this ship had no letters or instructions from any of the colonists, but the stories told by his sailors were in such agreement that they were believed. They claimed that they believed Cortes and all his followers had been killed by the natives whose territories he sought to cross in order to gratify his rage. He had left behind him the greater part of his lieutenants, having given them instructions to make ready to follow him; but when they set out they found the bridges broken and all communications cut off behind him. News was even circulated that skeletons of men and horses covered with sea-weed, which had been washed up by the tides and tempests and had taken root amongst the undergrowth, had been found in certain marshes. Such are the particulars concerning Cortes and the royal functionaries occupied in quarrelling with one another, which were brought by the caravel that succeeded in escaping.

Concerning the four captains who fairly pant with desire to discover the strait, the sailors give the following information; but one must take up this story a little farther on.

If Your Holiness remembers well, Most Holy Father, a venerable jurisconsult, Antonio Tamarano, presented you in my name after the death of Pope Adrian, with the Decade beginning *PRIUSQUAM*, and he reported to me that you had accepted the dedication. In the course of that book I had spoken of the noble, Egidius Gonzales d'Avila, commonly called Gil Gonzales. I explained how he discovered such a stretch of fresh water that he called this lake a fresh-water sea. The populous shores of this lake, the abundant rainfall, the ceremonies, customs, and religious rites of these nations the gold mines, the preliminaries of peace and treaties, war, and the fierce battles against the sovereigns of Nicoragua and Diriangen, and the return of Gil Gonzales to Hispaniola, where he raised a troop of soldiers and horsemen whom he conducted to the gulf called Figueras which separates the shores of the continent into two parts just as the Adriatic appears to separate Italy from Illyria and the remainder of Greece,—all these things I have related. It is known that he believed a navigable river discharged this mass of water into the gulf, just as the Ticino serves as an outlet of Lake Maggiore or the Mincio for the Lake of Garda. I have written at length on this subject and this question.

I must not forget to explain the reason of the name of this gulf, so much talked about at the present time. The first discoverers called it the Gulf of Figueras because, on their voyage of exploration they found there trees whose leaves resembled those of the fig, though their trunks were different. The trunk is in fact solid, while that of the fig-tree is porous. Since the fig-trees are called *figueras* in Spanish, they bestowed the name of Figueras on these trees. The natives use the trunks and large branches of fig-trees for making vases, which look as though they had been turned, and are used to ornament sideboards and other table service. There are long platters, bowls, cups, plates, and other similar utensils of common use, all artistically fashioned.

Egidius Gonzales, or, if preferred, Gil Gonzales, marched overland to the lake he had discovered, but did not find the outlet he sought. In the kingdom of the cacique Nicoragua, from whom he had parted on the best of terms, he encountered a lieutenant of Pedro Arias, governor of Castilla del Oro, called Francisco Fernandez. The latter had taken possession of the country and founded a colony there. In a few words, the following happened. Gil Gonzales complained that he was attacked and that his discovery was interfered with. The above-mentioned sailors state that three engagements took place, in which eight soldiers were killed, many wounded, and thirty horses killed. It is in this manner that the Spaniards, who cannot bear to work together, kill one another as soon as they meet.

It seems, according to the sailors' story, that Gil Gonzales had plundered Francisco Fernandez of two hundred thousand gold pesos, though the gold was not pure. According to Pedro Arias, the governor, who has sent us a heavy batch of despatches from the continent, Gil Gonzales only took from his lieutenant one hundred and thirty thousand pesos, though in other respects he complains bitterly of his attack. This sum had been collected from the neighbouring caciques, whether by force or in exchange for Spanish merchandise we need not here discuss; it is also of little consequence, as there are more important interests to consider.

Such were the dissensions among the Spaniards when Egidius Gonzales encountered Cristobal Olid, sent by Cortes, who had also founded a colony which he called Santa Cruz not far from that spot. Olid captured Gonzales. He gave this name to this new colony because, after many shipwrecks which he has lengthily described, he had escaped violent storms and had landed on the same day the Roman Church celebrates the victory won by the Emperor Herodius[1] against the Persians.

Hear now what a strange trick fortune played. The fourth captain, Francisco de las Casas, arrived on the scene, sent by Cortes against Olid. The latter went to meet his former companion in the army of Cortes. A naval battle followed; Francisco fired upon and sunk one of Olid's ships with all its crew, but he was obliged to put out to sea, while Olid returned to land. Now this gulf is exposed to violent northers and swept by frequent

[1] Meaning presumably the Byzantine Emperor Heraclius, since it was he who was victorious over the Persians in 622–25 A.D.

storms; moreover it extends amongst lofty mountains. It happened that several days later, Las Casas, after being tossed by winds and having lost most of his men, horses, and ships, fell into the hands of his bitter enemy Olid, who took him prisoner. Olid thus found himself in possession of two prisoners, both more important leaders than himself. He imprisoned his involuntary guests, considering them as a part of his plunder; but it was plunder destined to ruin him.

Las Casas and Gil Gonzales plotted to kill Olid. They corrupted his servants, inducing them to promise not to come to the aid of the traitor whom they wished to attack, and who had involved so many innocent men in the crime of high treason. One night when they were sitting together on the pretext of supping, they seized the knives from the table and threw themselves upon their detested host. After serving the repast of their master, the servants were busy eating. Olid was repeatedly stabbed but not killed. He succeeded in escaping and took refuge in one of the native huts with which he was acquainted. It was announced by the public crier that whoever gave shelter to the traitor Olid, or failed to denounce his hiding-place, if he knew it, would be punished with death; while a reward would be paid to whomever gave him up. He was eventually betrayed by his own men. An accusation of treason was drawn up against him and published by the herald; after which he was strangled. Such was the end of Olid, and such is, unless I am mistaken, the fate which will shortly overtake his companions.

Let Your Holiness now give ear to the account of another crime, or rather an eccentric vagary of fortune. Francisco de las Casas, one of the two generals commanding the fleet, after strangling Olid, is said to have forcibly brought his companion, Gil Gonzales, to the town of Temistitan, the latter confiding in him, but not having as powerful a force at his disposition. We therefore have

generals who, by their folly, have garnered sufficiently
bitter fruits along the gulf of Figueras; and by their
cupidity and ambition have ruined not only themselves,
but many provinces living in peaceful submission to the
Emperor. It is said that Gil Gonzales was seen in the
hands of Francisco de las Casas in Temistitan; it is likewise true that the contrary is asserted. Such are the
contradictory reports circulated concerning Gil Gonzales.

I had finished the book containing two Decades when
we received from the Council of Hispaniola news of the
arrival of two fleets of ships, the first numbering four
and the second seven vessels. From New Spain nothing
but that one vessel which escaped has arrived. Finally
we have read in council a considerable number of despatches from Pedro Arias, governor of Castilla del Oro.
He deals lengthily with his deeds and adventures, the
difficulties attending the enterprises undertaken by himself
and his companions, the approaching departure of the
treasurer of those dominions, who will bring a sum of gold,
the amount of which he does not state, the road he has
begun, which will establish easy communication between
the two oceans, and render information concerning the
islands under the equator accessible. Hardly more than
sixteen leagues separate the port called Nombre de Dios
from the gulf of Panama, admirable for the excellence of
its port, and which is distant six degrees and a half from
the equinoctial line, where during the entire year the days
and nights are of equal length. In my preceding Decades
I have spoken sufficiently of the beginnings of all these
enterprises.

In another chapter, Pedro Arias complains of the
violence used by Gil Gonzales toward his lieutenant, Francisco Fernandez, whose modesty and disinterestedness,
he commends an opinion far from being shared by other
people. We shall some day hear the accusations of the
opposite party, and then know how to decide. Pedro Arias

gives lengthy details and explanations about a number of
other particular facts, which I cannot and will not repeat;
they would afford no interest to Your Holiness; he most
humbly beseeches the Emperor to let him return to his
wife and children, [in Spain] for he is overcome by age
and infirmities.

His request has been granted; he has been recalled, and
in his place a noble knight of Cordova, called Pedro Rios,
has been appointed. The latter is here at the present
time, preparing to start.

When I recounted in the preceding chapters the history
of Francisco Garay's misfortunes, Olid's arrival at Cuba
where he prepared his expedition to Figueras, the preparations of Egidius Gonzales to start for the same place,
and finally the plans of Pedro Arias, I said at the same
time that our council had been unable to adopt other
preventive measures than the granting of full powers to
the council of Hispaniola and ordering that the neighbours
should exercise their best efforts to prevent the rivalry
of these captains from provoking a general and much
dreaded catastrophe. Upon receipt of our instructions
and those of the Emperor, the council of Hispaniola appointed as commissioner one of their own number; they
chose an honest man holding the post of revenue collector
in the colony, the bachelor Moreno.

His departure was delayed until everything was over.
The greatest confusion prevailed when he arrived, and his
report does not differ save in a few details from what we
have related. These civil discords have at least taught us
several curious things. Thus it is that in his conversations
with Moreno, Francisco Fernandez told him that in the
neighbourhood of that lake he had found a waterfall of
fresh water which flowed into the gulf. We know that the
Nile flows in the same manner from the lofty mountains
of Ethiopia, and after irrigating Egypt, empties into the
Mediterranean. If the fact be true—though it is not yet

proven—it will be useless to search for the large, navigable river carrying off the water of the lake, which Egidius Gonzales has for such a long time wished to discover.

Upon his return, Moreno reported that in the countries he had visited he heard nothing said about the defeat and pretended massacre of Cortes and his companions. That region, however, is more than five hundred leagues from the province of Temistitan. But while he was anchored at Havana, the port of Cuba, Diego Ordaz, one of the lieutenants of Cortes and by no means the most insignificant, came to see him. He reported that he had just been enquiring if anything had been heard of Cortes, for at Temistitan, the capital, nobody knew whether he was alive or dead. Nor do we yet know.

To correct such great misfortunes, a nobleman, the jurisconsult, Luis Ponce de Leon has been chosen as delegate; he was for a long time a magistrate in the province of Carpentana, whose capital is Toledo, where we all reside at the present time with the Emperor. Ponce was chosen because of his great integrity and the prudence he had shown in the exercise of his functions. He is a modest man, and remarkably intelligent, so we hope that, thanks to his foresight, the storm-tossed imperial vessel, may come tranquilly into port under happy auspices.

His instructions direct that, should he find Cortes still alive, he must overwhelm him with flattery and inspire him with truly loyal sentiments. For Cortes has never openly defected, and the Emperor's name is always pronounced with respect in his speeches and letters. But, as I have already said, vague suspicions are entertained concerning his real intentions and conduct, in consequence of conjectures and accusations launched against him. He is a proud-hearted man, always ambitious of new dignities. He has already for a long time enjoyed the titles of governor and adelantado of the immense regions embraced under the name of New Spain. He recently asked the investiture as knight of St. Iago. Ponce, whose departure is at hand, takes with him the insignia to confer upon him. He has already taken leave of the Emperor and sails with a fleet of twenty-two ships. If, on the contrary, Ponce finds upon his arrival, that Cortes has already joined his ancestors, he must adopt another policy. Certainly no other captain will dare to raise his head, and if the natives do not revolt, everything will go well and the whole will be laid at the feet of Your Holiness.

In this great town of the lakes, which begins to take on the appearance of a city, fifty thousand houses have been built, and thirty-seven churches, in which the natives, mixed with the Spaniards, most piously attend the Christian ceremonies; for they have abandoned their ancient rites and odious human sacrifices, which they now even regard with horror. This blessed harvest will be astonishingly increased by the apostolic fervour of the Franciscan friars who have undertaken to instruct the natives, that is, if our internal dissensions do not create obstacles to such progress. Enough, however, of this subject.

Let us return to Esteven Gomez, of whom I have spoken at the close of the book beginning with the word *PRIUSQUAM*. I have said that he had been sent with a caravel to seek for a strait which may exist between Florida and the country called Baccalaos. Gomez, who returned ten months after his departure, found neither the strait nor Cathay, as he had promised to do. I had always thought this good man's ideas were groundless, and I openly told him so. He is not without supporters. He nevertheless discovered agreeable and useful countries, corresponding exactly with our latitude and polar degrees. The licenciate Ayllon, a member of the council of Hispaniola, accompanied by his friends and servants, has explored

the same countries with two ships. These countries
are north of Hispaniola, Cuba, and the Lucayan islands,
and not distant from the Baccalaos, Chicora, and Duraba,
of which I have above spoken at length.

After having described the manners and customs of these
nations, after having enumerated the excellent ports and
immense rivers, the Spaniards say they found plains overgrown with ilex, oaks, and olives, where wild grape vines
rioted over the forest trees, and all other trees common in
Europe. They give these particulars, not in an ordinary
summary, but in a voluminous heap of letters. But what
need have we of what is found everywhere in Europe?
It is towards the south, not towards the frozen north,[1]
that those who seek fortune should bend their way; for
everything at the equator is rich.

Your Holiness will learn a laughable fact and a singular
rumour concerning this voyage, which rapidly exploded.
Esteven Gomez found nothing he expected to discover,
but rather than return with empty hands, he violated our
instructions which forbade him to use violence against
any natives and filled his ship with people of both sexes,
all innocent and half naked, who had lived contentedly
in huts. Hardly had he reached the port whence he had
sailed, than an individual, hearing of the ship's arrival
with a cargo of slaves, mounted his horse and without
waiting for further information galloped to us, and
quite out of breath exclaimed: "Esteven Gomez has
returned with a ship-load of cloves and precious stones."
He hoped to be well rewarded, and, without comprehending
the stupidity of this man, the partisans of Gomez went
about the court with exclamations of joy. They loudly
proclaimed that Gomez had brought not slaves (*esclavos*)

---

[1] How erroneous was this forecast, the development of the earth's
resources in Canada, the Klondike and Alaska, to say nothing of the vast
wealth produced by the grain and lumber industries of the North and West
overwhelmingly proves.

but cloves (*clavos*), cutting off the first half of the word. In the Spanish tongue serfs are called *esclavos*, while the stems of cloves are *clavos*. When this transformation of *esclavos* into *clavos* was later discovered, everybody derided the partisans of Gomez and their gleeful exultation. Had they only stopped to consider that the celestial exhalations transferred to terrestrial substances adapted to receive them only produce aromatic odours in the countries lying beneath or near to the equator, they would have remembered that Gomez could have found no cloves during the ten months of his voyage.

I was writing this appendix when the wheel of fortune—as is usual—gave a turn; so true is it that she never concedes an ounce of honey, to which she does not add as much, or more, gall. The streets of the illustrious city of Toledo echoed with trumpet blasts, the roll of drums, and the piping of flutes in honour of the renewed alliance with the King of Portugal, already brother-in-law and cousin of the Emperor. This is the result of the Emperor's betrothal to the King's sister, after refusing alliance with the young English princess—a thing esteemed by all Castile to be important. In the midst of the festivities, serious and deplorable news, filling the Emperor's heart and those of the Castilians with disgust, was heard.

In my book describing the voyage around the world, dedicated to Pope Adrian, I said that the ship called *La Trinidad*, which accompanied the *Victoria*, was damaged and had remained behind at the island of Tidor, one of the Moluccas which produces spices; there were seventy men on board that ship besides their officers. I knew all their names, from our account books. The *Trinidad* had been repaired, loaded with cloves and precious stones, and was on her way to Europe, when she encountered a Portuguese fleet. The captain of this fleet, Jorge de Brito, surprised and conquered it, and took it to Malacca, a place supposed to be the Golden Chersonesus. He was careful to strip the vessel of everything it carried, but the saddest of all to recount is the melancholy fate of the sailors. They encountered such terrific seas that, buffeted by incessant storms, almost all of them perished of hunger and exhaustion. It is said that Jorge de Brito, after the capture of the *Trinidad*, went to the Moluccas and took possession of our islands, which are seven in number, building a fortress on one of them. He likewise seized everything that had been left on the island for the needs of trade. The produce of those two robberies exceeds in value two hundred thousand ducats. Such at least is the report of the sailors and officers who survived and returned with the *Victoria*.

Cristobal de Haro was the director general of this enterprise for buying spices. He is a man in whom our council had great confidence. He has given me the names of the five ships which accompanied the *Victoria*, and those of all our sailors down to the humblest members of the crew. He demonstrated to our council, which assembled to hear him, his reasons for estimating our losses at that value, indicating in detail the quantity of spices on board the *Victoria*, the amount of merchandise they left for buying, either at Maquiana, King Zabazulla's country, which is one of the seven where spices grow, or at Tidor, belonging to another native king and his son, and which is controlled by the administrators and principal lords of both sovereigns. This merchandise had been left in the charge of Juan de Campo, who remained in the archi-pelago. But Haro made an inventory of the steel and copper blades, the different kinds of hempen and flaxen cloth, pitch, quicksilver, mineral oil, Turkish candles, artists' colours, coral, red umbrellas, hats, mirrors, glass beads, little bells, spoons, and chairs worthy of royalty, not to mention the firearms with their necessary ammunition, which the royal officials in the archipelago, such as the auditor and the treasurer, exchanged for spices to load our vessels. What the Emperor's decision will be is not yet known.[1] I think he will hardly disclose it for a few days, because of the renewed alliance with Portugal. Even had twins been born, it would be sufficiently unpleasant to allow such an insult to remain unpunished. I think the affair will be treated first by diplomatic negotiations; but I also hear a piece of news that will not please the King of Portugal.

In spite of his good intentions, the Emperor will be unable to conceal his opinion when the owners of the cargoes petition him for satisfaction. To refuse justice to his enemies would be dishonourable. How then can he refuse it to his own subjects? It is said the elder Portuguese do not conceal their fear of seeing the kingdom destroyed by these audacious attacks. They are also excessively arrogant towards the Castilians, without whose products they would perish of hunger, for that kingdom originally began as a small county of Castile. The Castilians therefore foam with rage. They want the Emperor to bring Portugal again under the domination of Castile, as his father, King Philip, once openly declared was his intention. Time will decide what verdict is to be given. Meanwhile, I wish Your Holiness good health, and humbly kiss your feet.

[1] The agreement between the Spanish and Portuguese signed in Zaragoza by which Charles V. ceded and sold to the King of Portugal the Spanish possessions in the Moluccas may be found in Navarrete, *op. cit.*, tom. iv., p. 389.

INDEX

A

Abdullah, known as El Zagal, defender of Baza, I, 15

Abenamcheios, a cacique, attacks Spaniards, I, 228; capture of, 228; in plot to massacre Spaniards, 233

Abibaiba, a cacique, living in the trees, I, 229*ff;* and Abraibes attack Rio Negro, 232; in plot to massacre Spaniards, 233

Abraibes, kills Raia, I, 231; and Abibaiba attacks Rio Negro, 232; in plot to massacre Spaniards, 233

Aburema, the river, I, 273

Aburema, discovery of, I, 323

Acateba, Columbus discovers, I, 324

Accursi, Giovanni, of Florence, I, 189, 250

Acla, II, 179; founded by Spaniards, 213

Acosta, cited, note, II, 42, 107

Acuna, auditor of Royal Council, II, 240

Acuña, Roderigo de, commander of one of the fleet, II, 402

Adda, referred to, II, 283

Adelantado, the, *see* Columbus, Bartholomew

Adrian of Utrecht, counsellor to King Charles, I, 40; made Bishop of Tortosa, 41; elected Pope, 41; note, II, 57; urges martyr to continue works, 246

Æneas, I, 79

Aganeo, or Boinca, I, 274

Agathyrses, war-paint of, I, 143; referred to, II, 316

Aguanil, Spaniards in, II, 10

Aguilar, Geronimo de, story told by, II, 29*ff;* later life of, note, 31; acts as interpreter, 32, 61

Ahuitzotl, son of Muteczuma, note, II, 115

Aiguitin, the river, I, 324

Airovistus, conquering of, cited, II, 60

Alaman, cited, note, II, 36, 61, 107

Alaminos, Anton, a pilot, II, 6, 27; pilots squadron, 12; directs Spaniards to Tabasco River, 32; sent to explore West, 36

Alarado, commander of Badajoz, II, 26

Albornoz, II, 406

Alcocer, Pedro de, cited, note, I, 36

Alexander VI., on the papal throne, I, 22, 91; Pope, draws a bull, 257

Alexandria, fruits in, II, 308

Alguri, Cansu, reigns in Cairo, I, 26

Almazen, Perez, letter to Peter Martyr, from, I, 33

Almeria, in possession of enemies, I, 15; Cortes founds, II, 64

Alpha, discovery of, I, 92; harbour discovered near, 94

Alpheus, I, 388

Alta Vela, an island, I, 391

Alvarado, Pedro de, II, 12; Cortes leaves command to, note, 129; in command of camp, 174; captured in Naciapala, 341; discoveries made by, 359 *et seq.;* cacique welcomes, 362; Cortes sends ahead, 408

Amaiauna, I, 168

Amaquei, a district in Bainoa, I, 368

Amaquemeca, capital of Chalco, II, 88

Amecameca, note, II, 88

America, first landing of Spaniards in, note, I, 135

Anacaona, sister of Beuchios Anacauchoa, I, 123; persuades and helps brother to entertain Spaniards, 125*ff.*

423

W

X

Y

Z